CULTURE AND PERSONALITY

CULTURE AND PERSONALITY

by

JOHN J. HONIGMANN

ASSOCIATE PROFESSOR OF ANTHROPOLOGY
University of North Carolina

GREENWOOD PRESS, PUBLISHERS
WESTPORT, CONNECTICUT

The Library of Congress has catalogued this publication as follows:

Library of Congress Cataloging in Publication Data

Honigmann, John Joseph.
   Culture and personality.

   Reprint of the 1954 ed.
    1. Personality and culture.
BF698.9.C8H59 1973   155.9'2   72-10981
ISBN 0-8371-6641-1

Originally published in 1954
by Harper & Row, New York

Reprinted with the permission
of Harper & Row, Publishers, Inc.

First Greenwood Reprinting 1973

Library of Congress Catalogue Card Number 72-10981

ISBN 0-8371-6641-1

Printed in the United States of America

To Cornelius Osgood

CONTENTS

Contents

PART SIX.   CONCLUSION

PREFACE

In a young, rapidly expanding field of study the sum and organization of knowledge barely remains unchanged from one issue of a technical journal to the next. Culture and personality is such a field. There is every reason to expect that many things which are said in this book will have to be modified within a relatively short time. Accumulating data may recommend changing certain definitions. Perhaps even the definition of culture and personality, if current approaches expand, will be changed. A few more years of activity as intensive as that which marked the past two or three decades should also provide substantial support for some of the hypotheses which anthropologists entertain today and which are liberally scattered through the following pages. When valid answers to existing questions begin to appear they will not be made solely by anthropologists. Culture and personality is, as the name suggests, a synthetic or a cross-discipline and not an insulated department of social science. In the same way that present knowledge in the field reflects the work of psychologists, psychiatrists, sociologists, and anthropologists, so future results will emerge from the continued integration of ideas from these and other specialists.

It seems reasonable to try to acknowledge some of the sources from which we have drawn in preparing this volume. Among anthropologists whose ideas the already sophisticated reader will recognize are Ralph Linton, Margaret Mead, Ruth Benedict, John Gillin, Gregory Bateson, Esther Goldfrank, Clyde Kluckhohn, and Douglas Haring. Many other anthropologists, who have not primarily specialized in matters acknowledged to pertain to culture and personality, have influenced the writer's point of view. They include Cornelius Osgood (to whom this book is dedicated), George Peter Murdock, Wendell C. Bennett, Irving J. Rouse, Clellan S. Ford, Godfrey and Monica Wilson, Eliot Chapple, and Carleton Coon. Psychologists who have directly or indirectly contributed to the author's thinking about human behavior include A. H. Maslow, Otto Klineberg, and Gardner Murphy. A great debt is owed to psychiatrists whose influence has been effective mainly through their published writings, like Abram Kardiner, Jules Massermann, Karen Horney, Erich Fromm, Géza Róheim, and David Levy.

Despite the variety of sources mirrored in the ideas which follow, an attempt has been made to limit discussion of sociological, psychological, and psychiatric topics more ably handled by specialists in the special fields. Subjects like learning, group interaction, and motivation are approached principally from the perspective of cultural anthropology. For fuller treatment end-of-chapter suggestions refer students to appropriate sources. It is expected that most readers coming to culture and personality will have had some elementary training in anthropology, sociology, and psychology. Indeed, it is a common college requirement that students who wish to be admitted to courses in this subject have prerequisite work in psychology and either in cultural anthropology or sociology. With such cross-disciplinary familiarity the following pages should present no undue difficulty.

For aid in completing the present manuscript acknowledgment is due to the Institute for Research in Social Science, University of North Carolina, and especially to Gordon W. Blackwell, Director.

JOHN J. HONIGMANN

December, 1953

PART ONE

CONTENT AND SCOPE OF THE FIELD

. . . the most illuminating material for a discussion of cultural forms and processes is that of societies historically as little related as possible to our own and to one another. . . . They are a laboratory in which we may study the diversity of human institutions.

RUTH BENEDICT

Chapter 1

A COMPARATIVE APPROACH

The student of culture and personality studies what happens to personality by virtue of an individual's membership in enduring groups whose members follow socially standardized ways of acting, thinking, and feeling. Since the subject matter includes groups as well as their behavior, it is not surprising that coöperation in this field has been forthcoming from both sociologists and anthropologists. In the main, however, culture and personality remains largely a pursuit of cultural anthropologists who are familiar with psychological methods and principles. The anthropologists seek from psychology illumination regarding the needs, wishes, drives, and impulses of man and the behavior necessary for man if he is to obtain satisfaction from the outer world (Kardiner, 1939:2).

To provide an introduction to the chapters that follow and to furnish concrete data in which the reader may anchor his thinking, the bulk of this chapter is given over to two "case studies." The first introduces the Kaska Indians of southern Yukon Territory and northern British Columbia. In the second we will learn about the Samoans as reported on by Margaret Mead (1950a). Through such a comparative approach the student will come to see how individual behavior, both in its observable and unobservable dimensions, varies with membership in different communities. How these variations

3

arise and are sustained will occupy us through many more of the ensuing pages.

Overlapping the border of Yukon Territory and British Columbia are the Athapaskan-speaking Kaska Indians (Honigmann, *1949a*). Their territory bisected by the Alaska Highway in 1941, the two hundred people constituting the tribe follow a commercial fur trapping economy that has largely replaced an earlier pattern of living based on hunting and fishing.

In winter the Indians live in a series of settlements located along river pathways. Each such settlement shelters a nucleus of kin—typically a woman, her husband, unmarried sons and daughters, and married daughters with their spouses and children. More distant relatives may attach themselves to such an extended family. Sometimes they receive only a cool welcome but usually they may exploit the fur resources of the host's trapping territory. The men of the settlement travel up to fifty miles from their homes to set traps for mink, marten, lynx, and fox. Always they keep a lookout for edible game like spruce hens, grouse, moose, or bush caribou. When the ground is covered with snow the transportation of guns, bedding, food, and fur is aided by dogs, the animals drawing simple hand-hewn toboggans. Adults do not ride on such trips; the dogs are neither numerous nor strong enough to draw passengers heavier than young children. In hilly country the dog drivers are forced to help the animals draw the loaded vehicle up steep inclines. Travelers in winter keep their feet covered with large moccasins that are packed with socks and other duffel. Snowshoes aid mobility. While men visit their traps in the forest, women remain in the log cabins of the settlement or trap small game and shoot rabbits in the immediate vicinity of the residences.

Within a settlement there exists no clear-cut pattern of leadership nor are there any tribal chiefs or councils among the Kaska Indians. This does not mean that every man is a law unto himself but government as we recognize it has not been developed by these people. A dichotomous moiety system divides the population into two ideally exogamous groups named the Wolves and Crows.

In the spring the settlements become deserted as the inhabitants make their way by boat to Lower Post, site of a church, several stores, and a few other dwellings. Here most of the Indians pass the summer living in tents and subsisting from the proceeds of their fur catch sold to two or three rival white traders. Imported eggs, flour, sugar, tea, coffee, bacon, tinned meats, sweet biscuits, and cereals are purchased in exchange for the winter's earnings, as well as clothing, guns, and bootleg whisky. (Canadian Indians were legally forbidden to drink alcoholic beverages when this study was made. The law did not stop them from securing whisky or brewing illicit beer and wine in all seasons.) Food purchases increase in the fall when half a ton of supplies may be secured to be taken into the bush for winter consumption in the settlement. People look forward to summer as a time for recreational dances and gambling; the old gambling games accompanied by pounding drums remain very popular. Couples dance in white man's fashion to the strains of mountain music played on violin and guitar. White trappers operating in the area often attend these dances. Also in summer the moieties sometimes tender feasts to one another, such an occasion being called a potlatch.

Despite the fact that some Kaska women try to avoid pregnancy, frequent childbearing is the rule. Children are born without professional medical attention and only an old woman skilled in techniques of parturition normally attends. She washes a newborn baby in warm water, lays it straight with the hands at its sides, and swaddles it in blankets that are then laced into a velvet or moose skin pack. In such an envelope a baby may easily be carried across the mother's shoulders, facing the latter's back, supported by a large woolen shawl. No food is offered the infant on its first day of life but thereafter it regularly receives the breast plus a supplementary bottle. Suckling is a very casual process, the baby lying in the mother's lap or else reclining on a bed with the bottle of warmed milk propped against a pillow. Whenever and wherever the infant cries it will be offered the breast. On the other hand we did not observe any fondling of the nursing infant. People are relatively infant-centered in the sense that attention is readily available to babies; small children remain in the mother's care without being relegated to the care of older siblings or nursemaids.

A few months after birth, if the weather is warm, the child's hands are freed from the swaddling cloths. By the age of six months a mother will discontinue the pack in favor of a shawl or blanket in which the baby sits astride the carrier's back. Thick diapers continue to be used until walking commences. Then slit trousers are put on a child through which he can urinate and defecate freely. Still the youngster is never left alone in the house and remains the recipient of considerable attention from parents, aunts, and siblings. These relatives may bounce him on the knees, praise him with kin terms, and cuddle his face with their lips and mouths. However, adults manifest only casual interest in promoting the child's development. Rarely did we see a toddler held upright to walk. On the other hand, people are responsive should any expected sequence of maturation fail to appear. Finger sucking is neither discouraged nor is it common. Weaning from the breast usually comes before the age of two (sometimes suckling continues until three) and is gradually achieved as solid foods assume an increasingly important place in the diet or the bottle takes the place of the breast. Weaning from the bottle comes even more casually and slowly. The birth of a sibling usually occurs soon after the child is two years old.

With the accomplishment of weaning from the breast and the birth of a sibling, societal demands on the child multiply. Sphincter training begins through verbal encouragement although it is not seriously expected to take hold until three or four years of age. Parents take no serious notice of wetting before three years but from then on scolding increases ("you dirty boy!") and there may even be spanking. Three marks a crucial age for the Kaska child, for then a significant change enters its relations with the mother. This phenomenon, which we have called "emotional rejection" (not to be confused with outright rejection), consists of an emotional withdrawal of the mother who, until now, has been a primary source of affective stimulation. She becomes less responsive to the child's demands, less eager in her attention, more remote and disinterested in her appreciation. Crying is no longer sympathetically responded to, except with a sharp "Don't cry for nothing!" Fretting for attention soon disappears in the child, who continues to be carefully clothed and provided with sufficient food. A frightened youngster of three or four continues to run to the mother but soon learns how little gratification such appeals bring. Sometimes a four-year-old goes off by himself to mouth his fingers until the crisis passes. The father, who has never been as demonstrative as the mother, retains some of his moderate warmth and does not hesitate to pick up a crying child. Attachments to the father appear in both sexes during this period. It is now that a child shows an eager exhibitionism should a stranger enter the family. He also warmly appreciates the bouncing and other play which he continues to receive from adolescent male relatives.

Through training the child is explicitly guided away from aggression, shouting, and unruly behavior. Disobedience wins punishment by scolding and physical chastisement, although people ideally disapprove of the latter form of discipline. Actually most parents go no further than shaking an unruly child or pummeling it with a clenched fist. Threats instill fear that is in turn counted upon to keep a youngster from wandering away from camp. Horses, dogs, wolves, the bush, and night are presented as dangers. Discipline is exercised mainly by parents and rarely by other relatives. Until adolescence a boy receives little training in how to make a living but then he begins to accompany a brother or maternal uncle on the trap line. The girl's induction to work starts when she is only six or seven, an age when she starts to fetch water from the river in a diminutive kettle. Education is mostly unformalized and unplanned. Not only does the child learn by emulating the behavior of an older person but no explanation of a task is given. In this community, where leadership is very slightly elaborated, a small girl is told to "make tea" and nobody attends as she steeps the leaves in cold water. In the same casual manner she tries to make fire by putting the kindling on top of billets of wood.

Errors are discovered and rectified over several trials and some advice is also given. Inculcation of modesty begins early and sharply in both sexes, the topic of sex coming to be surrounded by special restrictions and reprimands. Sexual play in childhood is avoided partly by the fact that children associate in unisexual playgroups. Segregation, however, does not prevent seven- or eight-year-olds making a nuisance of themselves through teasing small aunts or nieces. With the exception of occasions like dances and drinking parties, the public separation of boys and girls continues through adolescence (and, in considerable degree, throughout life). Yet at night adolescent boys and girls contrive to meet for purposes that include sexual intercourse. Some pre-marital sexual experience is expected and parents object strongly only if their daughter becomes promiscuous.

A girl's economic status changes little at puberty except that rabbit snaring may become added to her duties and a small rifle becomes her property to use in small game hunting. The fact of menarche is carefully concealed. The initial sexual advances of boys provoke in the girl intense confusion that she can poorly manage. Should she become promiscuous, however, then she will learn to joke with boys and to accept their approaches with greater equanimity. Adolescent boys assume economic responsibilities like providing small game and heavy wood for the family. With his initially small earnings from fur the youth buys clothes for himself plus additional food for the family. Laziness at this period is unmercifully plagued and criticized. Each sex wins praise for its contribution. The boy, like the girl, experiences much difficulty in interacting easily with the opposite sex. Such interaction begins with adolescence when he also makes his first shy appearances on the dance floor and has beer offered to him seriously at drinking parties.

Neither sex appears in a hurry to grow up. Sooner or later, however, close association between a couple becomes noised about and then marriage may be mentioned by the parents. Catholic Church marriages are increasing in frequency but many people distrust them because of the difficulties put in the way of divorce. In the bride's winter settlement the new husband works for his wife's household while occupying a separate tent or log cabin with his spouse. As the marriage endures and produces children the relations of the spouses increase in warmth, reaching their maximum of emotional intensity in old age. No courtesies are developed toward the old but a government ration helps them maintain a show of self-support. Ideally age is regarded as a period of wisdom derived from abundant experience. Actually the old, particularly the men, have cause to be anxious about their declining ability for which no cultural compensations—like leadership or awe—are offered.

What kind of people are the Kaska? How does the anthropologist sum up their personality after he has lived with them closely under a variety of conditions?

1. One impressive feature about these people is their independence. The Kaska Indian is unaccustomed and unwilling to respond to any leader and nobody has authority over anybody else except over his own child. At the same time the person feels within himself a profound sense of responsibility for his own acts and for his personal success or failure.

2. Although they remain without any indigenous police or leadership system, the Indians regard aggressive acts and interpersonal hostility with extreme distaste. Bound up with the dislike for hostile action is the Indian's keen fear of being disliked. The individual tries to avoid arousing anger and tries to treat his associates in a deferent manner. This, of course, means that one person has regard for the other's desire for independence. Friction is not completely lacking in the community and explosions of alcoholic rage leave no doubt about the fund of latent hostility that the people rather successfully control in their day-to-day relations.

3. The Kaska Indian is flexible rather than rigid in his behavior. He lacks consistent orderliness and nobody who knows him would say he is compulsive with respect to time, the carrying out of routines, or the training of his children. It is difficult to phrase positively the quality of behavior which we are pointing out. The word *flexible* best suggests what we are trying to say, namely, that the Kaska individual is endowed with a highly tolerant and somewhat indecisive attitude

toward life. These qualities, it will be admitted, are not characteristic of most Americans. Procrastination, a very outstanding feature of Kaska behavior, fits well into such a setting.

4. Another quality that strikes the observer forcefully is the Indian's tendency to suppress in his behavior all strong emotion. Only thin affective bonds relate parents and children or husband and wife. The sexual relations of unmarried boys and girls are accompanied by considerable ambivalence and horseplay which appear to be related to the pattern of emotional suppression. It is as though the young people were striving to shut out tender emotions in their relationships. Our interviews indicate that this is precisely the case. We might characterize the Kaska as emotionally isolated and cannot fail to note that such a quality seems quite congruent with their political and interpersonal independence or atomism.

5. Finally, the Indians are intensely practical and concrete. Speculative thought, abstract reasoning, and planning for the future have little place in their lives. Reasoning tends to be by analogy and the greatest concern is invested in immediate problems. Immediate difficulties make the greatest sense to, and arouse the strongest response in, these people. Ornament and decoration also tend to be neglected by the Kaska and this might be taken as another facet of the concreteness that marks their behavior and thinking.

From the cold forest of northern Canada we turn next to the warm Pacific island world for a look at the Samoans.

CULTURE AND PERSONALITY IN SAMOA

Before completing this review of Samoan life the reader may feel that the Samoans differ from the Kaska more sharply in details of technology and social organization than in certain aspects of personality.

In their equatorial environment the islanders live from coconut, banana, and breadfruit trees, yam and taro plants, poultry, and pigs —all of which are domesticated (Mead, *1950a;* Mead, *1949f:*115–120). Hunting is of negligible importance as a source of food but fishing in waters that teem with fish is of considerable significance.

In contrast to the Kaska, whose technology is based on commercial fur trapping with food gathering as an auxiliary technique, the Samoans are food producers. Ocean fishing contributes further to a dependable abundance of food. Living in villages of two hundred or more kinsmen, in houses of thatch without walls and doors, the Samoan family lacks the privacy of its Kaska counterpart just as it lacks the need to insulate itself from a rigorous climate. During inclement weather, screens shelter the inmates of the dwelling. In these buildings the women prepare food, kava (a nonalcoholic stimulant served ritually), bark cloth, and mats, while the men busy themselves in gardens and on the sea. Women prepare food but men cook it.

In distinction to the egalitarianism of the Kaska community, the Samoans live in a world of rank. The population is stratified into two broad classes—the titled nobility and the untitled commoners. Among the nobility exist many finer distinctions in rank, depending on the title possessed. With each gradation go specific privileges and duties. Titles are not derived automatically by birth but must be acquired through a kind of inheritance, the successor to such a status being chosen by a group of relatives. Each family and village recognizes a leader, the *matai,* a man who is treated with great respect. Normally the villagers cluster in loosely organized districts headed by overlords. The village chiefs form a district council just as the household heads form a village council. Wars between villages and between districts used to be chronic.

As soon as a child is born in Samoa a small ritual is performed to guarantee that he will develop those qualities appropriate to his sex. If the baby is a girl, the umbilical cord is buried under a paper mulberry tree, the plant from which women make bark cloth. If the infant is a boy, the cord is thrown into the sea or placed under a taro plant in order to insure a good fisherman or an industrious farmer. These rituals are not better suited than is most other magic to bring about desired consequences. They do, however, indicate the conscious foresight of adults with respect to children.

After a day or so the baby begins to receive breast milk and soon thereafter coconut milk and sugar cane juice as well. Breast feeding by a mother or wet nurse takes place whenever the child cries, and this pattern of "generous" or "demand" feeding continues for fifteen or twenty months (unless another pregnancy intervenes). Nursing the baby, however, is not an intense emotional business for the mother. Children are fed solid premasticated food from the age of one month. The newborn's contacts with his social environment do not take place only through the mouth, however important that zone may be. Tiny children are held in the arms and, as soon as they are capable of holding up their heads, will be carried astride the left hip. Further tactual impressions from the world result when the still nursing baby sleeps alongside its mother. After weaning, however, the night is passed alongside a woman other than the mother or possibly the child sleeps with an elder sister. Weaning ushers in other new experiences. Now the child comes to be entrusted to an older sibling, usually a sister, during the daytime. The little nursemaid carries the baby on her hip or astride her back. It is probably significant that no encouragement to walking is given to the Samoan baby, that its birthday is not remembered, and that the first steps or the first words are not greeted with exuberance or ceremony (as, for example, among the Eskimo). The baby is really of little interest to the group after its birth. Lack of intensity also marks the toilet training of small children. In a word, the socialization of the Samoan child is consistently without intensity. Although birthdays may be lost, the *relative* age of the child is very well remembered and continues to be stressed throughout life. Later rank enters the picture to upset the importance of age in Samoan social relations. All in all youngsters do not comprise a class apart. They must not be spared from spectacles like birth and death. A noisy group of rascals may be driven away from a place where some woman is giving birth but without any idea that such situations are improper for children. In olden days children were probably even able to witness the public defloration of the *taupo*, or village princess. It is to be expected that since children sleep in the same room as adults they will also witness sexual intercourse between the parents.

The casualness with which children are treated is more strongly developed in some situations than in others. Parents or guardians do not ignore children to the point where the latter's lives may be endangered nor do they give children freedom to complicate the problems of living. Children are taught to be afraid of fire and warned not to tangle the strands of the weavers. They receive instruction to stay out of the sun, avoid sharp objects, and maintain modesty by keeping the loincloth in place. Disciplining comes from the guardian, usually an older child, who is responsible for the youngster's conduct, although any older person may command a child's behavior. A young nursemaid, however, is easily bullied by her younger charge who, if she creates a scene, may attract the sharp attention of elders. The techniques of disciplining include shouting, "talking to" the child, and physical punishment. Just when the child becomes old enough to revolt against the guardian, the former in turn becomes a monitor, saddled with the responsibility to which he or she has just been subject.

There is one occasion in which children are far from ignored. At dances even young babies receive an opportunity to perform in public and find their efforts treated with applause. "The attitude of the elders toward precocity in singing, leading the dancing or dancing, is in striking contrast to their attitude toward every other form of precocity. . . . Little boys who would be rebuked and possibly whipped for such behavior on other occasions are allowed to preen themselves, to swagger and bluster and take the limelight without a word of reproach" (Mead, *1950a:*116). Yet even dancing preserves the atmosphere of casualness in which the child matures without hurry and without fear of being left behind.

By about age seven, play groups in Samoa divide on sex lines with considerable antagonism appearing between boys and girls. This does not mean that sex differences were not previously understood but now the distinction between boys and girls becomes emphasized. Also time for play becomes limited to after supper because during the day children must contribute their activities to the household tasks. By

the age of nine, however, boys are freed of baby care and may wander
far afield. Girls, whose development in particular Margaret Mead
has traced, remain more restricted.

Neither sex is limited to living with his own parents. The girl receives a welcome in the household of any relative in the village and
she moves from one to the other in accordance with the work demanded, the degree of scolding, the quality of food, or the number of
babies to be cared for. Reciprocally, fear of losing a worker mitigates
a family's discipline, giving the girl more control over her social relationships than appears at first glance.

At age fifteen or sixteen years the community intensifies attention
to young people. Then children of both sexes join appropriate associations. A boy enters a fraternity of untitled men while a girl assumes
membership in the *aualuma*, a group whose membership includes
nearly all the women of the village. In this company the adolescent
learns to coöperate with others. Busy years follow when bark cloth
making and weaving occupy much of a girl's time. Should a young
woman acquire a reputation for laziness or ineptitude now, her opportunities in marriage will dwindle. Yet custom dictates that she
must not try *too* hard. She must avoid any reputation for virtuosity
that might indicate presumption beyond the behavior expected of
her age and status.

Direct experience with sex has begun for the girl. Children of both
sexes begin to masturbate at the age of six or seven, the boys in a
group and girls individually. Masturbation continues until adolescence when the separation of the sexes is somewhat relieved and they
are once more permitted to associate without fear of criticism. The
girls are shy at this time; they giggle and blush. The boys too act ill
at ease and prefer to associate with girls at night. In this setting there
occur initial attempts at sexual intercourse. Frequently a youth is
initiated into sex by an older woman, a girl by a divorced man or wid-
ower. But between fifteen and seventeen girls are clandestinely
courted by lovers of their own age and the community remains tolerant as long as the affair remains unpublicized. A girl must not receive many lovers, or she will acquire a reputation for promiscuity.

Between individuals who have had sexual relations there is shyness that intereferes with any public demonstration of affection. Jealousy or passionate attachments between lovers are discouraged yet evidence indicates that jealousy does arise. Between eighteen and twenty-two a marriage may be arranged or grow out of a clandestine affair. The girl hangs back, perhaps claiming that she does not wish to be tied down with family responsibilities. Sometimes she does not care for a particular suitor. If she agrees to a boy's proposal a complicated series of gift exchanges begins between the families of the bride and bridegroom at the conclusion of which the couple take up resident with either the wife's or husband's people. It will be several years before they set up an independent household. Children do not alter the couple's status unless the man is a chief or the son of a chief. Then he has control over his children as well as over other children in the household. Many men acquire titles, great or small, and then quit the organization of untitled men to join the titled men's fraternity, a promotion in which his wife shares honors.

As age creeps upon the individual, the community's preference for the most able may lead to the loss of a great title which will be conferred on a younger, stronger heir. Fathers are not pleased when their titles must be surrendered to sons although the old man receives a minor title instead. Old men watch children and offer advice. As for women, they continue to work much longer than men and when plantation tasks finally become too heavy they contribute to the household by making bark cloth, weaving, or teaching girls. Women grow old more gently than men in Samoa.

Even as brief a summary as this furnishes some understanding of how a human being is helped to become a social personality through responding to the expectations of his community. What are some of the distinctive marks of Samoan personality that emerge from the experiences which Margaret Mead describes?[1]

1. If we are surprised at the small provision for privacy in the Samoan village, the Samoan's attitude toward privacy holds equal in-

---

[1] For greater detailing of some of these generalizations see Mead, 1953b.

terest for a Western reader. Individual activity is regarded with suspicion, perhaps even as a little wrong. Not only does the community make small provision for solitude but people are trained not to seek it. Of course, Samoans, although sometimes desirous of privacy, do not have the same need for it that Americans have. As children they have been brought up "in public," as it were, and have not been led to expect privacy nor its desirability.

2. Another distinctive attribute about the Samoan is his attitude that procodity above one's age and rank is a very great wrong. "Do not presume" is a stringent commandment in Samoa. People do not push themselves forward. Notice, the child is not made much of, except on the dance floor. His first steps and other early achievements do not bring applause. People who bring up the child effectively discourage the development of strong self-assertion and exhibitionism in the individual. All the individualistic virtues which Americans admire thus become relatively useless in Samoan life. We would feel quite unhappy about somebody in our midst who showed as little initiative as the typical Samoan. He in turn would be distressed by an aggressive go-getter. In association with such values it is not surprising that innovation in Samoan life comes to be restricted to craftsmanship and dancing. An invention brings the innovator no lasting prestige. Furthermore, with prestige lacking as an incentive to social change, social change tends to be slower in these islands than in America.

3. The Samoan individual remains detached from strongly emotional interpersonal relationships. His sexual affairs tend to be ephemeral and transitory although jealousy sometimes occurs (but is not supposed to). People think an intense infatuation is as disgraceful as promiscuity. Children also grow up in an "atmosphere" of slight emotional intensity. They are not made dependent upon the affection of only two parents in a household that includes grandparents. There are always the households of other relatives where the child will be received, fed, and made use of without becoming involved in strong emotional ties. The very unintense behavior of Samoans toward each other provides a social climate in which the child matures and learns to behave with emotional detachment in his own right.

4. Another characteristic of Samoans is their distinctive attitude toward defaulting. Whereas American children learn to behave properly through feelings of guilt or pangs of conscience, in Samoa "there is no room for guilt. Transgression and non-transgression are matters of expediency" (Mead, 1953b:655b). Samoans respond to flushes of shame where in America guilt feelings punish nonconformity. Later we will examine the kind of social environment that anthropologists believe may be responsible for the induction of sensitivity to shame rather than guilt in personality.[2]

SOME COMPARISONS

It is quite apparent that the Kaska Indians do not behave precisely like Samoans. Given enough knowledge about each group the reader would find it not impossible to make certain predictions about how persons occupying particular positions (say a child, a man in his prime, or an old man) would act and even feel under particular circumstances. The statements anthropologists make about human behavior are of two basic types—with many sentences in many field reports falling between the two extremes.

For example, one can describe an individual Kaska Indian's anxieties and motor behavior when he goes hunting and dwell on the pleasure he receives from slapping down his bundle of furs on the white storekeeper's counter. The anthropologist may identify the Samoans as sharing a high degree of sensitivity concerning rank and status. He can hold up the Kaska Indian as sensitive about arousing anger or hostility in interpersonal relations. When we make such statements, in which the focus is on the behavior of the individual, whether standing alone or in a group, we are describing personality. Such generalizations specify and even predict how persons in a given social environment act, think, and feel. Statements of this sort constitute the heart of culture and personality.

However, it is possible to speak of the Samoan or Kaska community from a somewhat different perspective. One may point out that Kaska economy is based on hunting and commercial trapping

---

[2] See below, pp. 291–294.

from which relatively small surpluses are forthcoming. The Samoans, we may write, practice food production and with the aid of ocean fishing produce relatively large surpluses of food. Such descriptions, relatively unconcerned with the behaving individuals who make up a community, refer to culture. Descriptions of culture specify more abstractly the activities taking place in a particular social environment. Cultural generalizations differ only in degree from personality descriptions but some anthropologists propose to separate them very sharply (White, *1949*). Actually many students of human behavior work back and forth between the two levels. The distinctive feature of culture and personality, however, is a very conscious and intense interest in the fate of individuals in a given social environment. Margaret Mead would add that the presence of some psychological theory, no matter how implicit or tentative, also differentiates the culture and personality approach. She points out what we have already said, namely (Mead, *1953a*:643):

The tendency to characterize some anthropological works as involving "culture and personality" and others as not is really an attempt to draw an artificial dividing line at some point in the formulation of the problem. Actually, there is a continuum, at one end of which formal ethnographic work—like most social history—dodges the issue with statements like "Murder was much more frequent among the coastal tribes" or "During the next century the times became much more unsettled, and robbery and murder were rife," without posing the problem of what correlates of the changed incidence of violence there were in the intrapsychic organization of individuals.

In other words, the culture and personality approach lifts the lid of social behavior and enables us to see culture as it is carried out on the level of individual thinking, feeling, and doing.

Culture and personality pays considerable attention to the process of growing up in particular communities. For example, the Kaska and Samoan accounts just presented described the children in both communities as maturing in an emotionally relatively diffuse and unintense social climate marked by low affective pressure. Use of the comparative method indicates that Samoan and Kaska children also grow up to be relatively unintense individuals. We should like to know more precisely the psychological consequences of growing up in a diffuse and unintense social climate. The comparative approach enables us to study ways of rearing children in the light of contrasting patterns. Among the Kaska and Samoans children above the age of two or three are treated as not essentially different from adults. This contrasts with our belief that the child is very fragile, easily injured, extremely susceptible to illness, and incapable of responsibility. What are the consequences of such diverse ways of regarding children? Are American adults different from Kaska Indians or Samoans by virtue of having been treated differently as children? Anthropologists believe that an affirmative answer must be given to this latter question.

The comparative interest in culture and personality does not focus only on the process of growing up. Salient differences in behavior between two groups may also be singled out—the reluctance to presume in Samoa or American self-assertive competitiveness, for example. The question asked is how these tendencies relate to other aspects of group and behavior. Thus the nonpresumption of Samoans is related to the slow rate of change in island life just as rapid social change in America is related to our restless drive for success.

Suggestions for Further Reading

The reader may care to try an experiment that should illuminate the degree to which the standard anthropological approach to behavior differs from or overlaps the viewpoint of culture and personality. To do so let him read accounts of the Kaska Indian or Samoan *culture* and compare the emphasis in these to the emphasis given in this chapter or in Margaret Mead's *Coming of Age in Samoa* (1950a). The latter book does contain cultural data but contrast it with Murdock's summary of Samoa in *Our Primitive Contemporaries* (1934). For the Kaska, pages 50–248 of the author's *Culture and Ethos of Kaska Society* (1949a) present an essentially cultural treatment.

For a few students, who are beginning to study culture and personality, time may be taken to review the general theory of anthropology and personality psychology. Recommended reading in this connection includes *The Cultural Background of Personality* by Ralph Linton (*1945*) and at least the first eight chapters of Clyde Kluckhohn's very readable *Mirror for Man* (*1949a*). For somebody who has never read *Patterns of Culture* this classic work by Ruth Benedict (*1946b*) is available in a popular-priced edition and is practically compulsory.

Chapter 2

CONCEPTS

A keen observer of historical developments in science has written that only through broad, new ideas does science advance. Newton's laws, the notion that the earth is surrounded by a sea of air, that matter is composed of atoms uniting in definite proportions—all these were adventurous and original conceptualizations that set off a spurt of scientific growth (Conant, 1952:26). The crude notion of personality existing in an either-or state distinct from culture has turned out to be a similar stimulant to the growth of social science. The name of the field—"culture *and* personality"—betrays the notion of culture as a process or realm distinct from personality. Such an either-or conceptualization has few adherents at the present time. Nevertheless, although inadequate today, the theoretical formulation of some kind of interaction between them led to the accumulation of much useful knewledge.[1] A vigorous interdisciplinary movement developed around that fruitful but illogical notion which today is sometimes rephrased as "personality *in* culture."

The object of this chapter is to clarify the meaning with which certain technical terms—like culture, personality, and character struc-

---

[1] A recent article commenting on the steps that led Dalton "to the epochal concepts of the chemical atom, atomic weight, the law of multiple proportions, and so forth" concludes, "each and every one of his steps as just given was factually wrong or logically inconsistent" (Holton, 1953: 91).

ture—are used throughout this volume. The student is urged to remember that although he may have encountered different definitions for some of these concepts, those meanings may not be entirely suitable for present purposes. To be sure that we will all be speaking the same language agreement will have to come on a common use of certain essential words.

CULTURE

In its technical sense "culture" is a short way of saying many things. The word points to two classes of phenomena, namely (1) to the socially standardized behavior—actions, thoughts, feelings—of some enduring group and (2) the material products of, or aids to, the behaviors of that group. Furthermore, the term means to designate that these referents are bound together in some kind of a system or whole.

As used in this volume the term *culture* suggests several levels of phenomena. It includes observable actions and material things. This initial level may be called "overt culture." Sometimes, however, material products of behavior and tools accompanying production are classed separately and designated by the phrase "material culture." It is fair to point out that not all anthropologists include material objects in their definition of culture. Their explanation for omitting this class of referents is logical. The definition they follow remains suited to their special interests, for example, the manner in which a community's behavior comes to be socially standardized or learned.[2] Logically distinct from overt culture is "covert culture," meaning ideas and feelings—phenomena which cannot be directly observed. Covert culture becomes known from activities like speech or through analysis of material products of action (movies, books, etc.). The problem of verifying our ideas about a group's covert culture will be dealt with later.

Note that we have so far avoided saying that overt culture *is* the actions and artifacts of a group. We prefer not to say that covert culture *consists* of ideas and feelings. Equalizing these terms and their referents too easily promotes confusion to the beginning student. The abstract nature of terms like *culture* and *personality* should be em-

---

[2] See, for example, Gillin, *1948b*:187.

phasized (Spiro, *1951*:23–24). Each stands for a varied mass of data rather than for any substantive entity. Culture is incapable of motion, decline, death, growth, or determinacy unless one speaks figuratively. Most important of all, culture cannot command people to do things. People endowed with particular expectations prod other people. Culture remains an abstraction based on observed facts as well as on the inferences made from those facts.

With the understanding that culture is an abstraction based on behavior it is nevertheless possible to use expressions like "changing culture" or "the culture grows more complex." Such usages are quite figurative. Every once in the while it is well to stop and realize precisely *what* is changing or *what* is growing. By keeping the referents of a term firmly in mind the scientist also remains aware that activities, thoughts, feelings, and material end products must be manipulated in order to direct cultural change or restrict cultural complexity.

In its technical sense the term *culture* has very embracive meaning. The word includes the lullabies of an Eskimo mother chanted to the baby in her arms, the tendency of the Kaska mother to withdraw emotionally from her child, as well as the burial of a newborn Samoan girl's umbilical cord together with all the ideas associated with such a rite. The word designates the fear felt by a Dobuan husband when he is living in his wife's village and the giving-with-intent-to-shame characteristic of a Kwakiutl nobleman. Of course, culture also refers to the traps, radios, and symbolic objects (flags, signs, traffic lights) used in everyday living. The anthropologist attends to a wide range of phenomena when he engages in ethnography or field work.

As indicated above, we mean by culture an interrelated system of parts. The treatment of a child in the family bears a discoverable relationship to the aspirations and striving of future adults. Tracing connections between the various items in a community's repertory of behavior represents one of the chief tasks of anthropology.

Culture Patterns

We can think of culture as encompassing artifacts plus patterns. An artifact is an aspect of material culture, something man-made and tangible, like a book, hammer, hammock, or house. A plowed field must probably also be regarded as an artifact but in distinction to the artifacts that end up in museums it is less easily manipulated by the anthropologist. Students of culture and personality do not wholly ignore artifacts. It is sometimes possible to gain information concerning relatively deep areas of the personality from material culture. By and large, however, in this book we will be more concerned with culture patterns than with artifacts.

The term *pattern* may be defined as Kardiner (1939:7) has defined the word *institution*, namely, as a relatively fixed mode of activity, thought, or feeling. Pattern denotes regularity.[3] The word signifies that some activity, thought, or feeling state is recurrent, socially guided or regulated, and marked by a delimitable range of variation (Herskovits, 1948:201–213). Thus a Punjab village reveals patterns of the eldest male in the household serving as the head of the extended family and Muslim spouses avoiding mention of each other's names. Cock fighting is also a pattern and speaking of the country as a whole we can say that fervent identification with the nation is a pattern generally shared by Pakistani people—even children.

Any particular pattern of culture may be restricted to a section of a community or it may be relatively common to the group as a whole. In other words a pattern may be universal or it may as a specialty be reserved for certain classes, occupational groups, or categories like men or women (Linton, 1936:272–275). Formation flying is a specialty pattern restricted to the air force; cock fighting in the Punjab is a specialty restricted to men. Eating with knife and fork, however, is a universal pattern found throughout our society. There are also alternative patterns, as Linton points out. Alternatives represent different behavioral modes available for use in the same situation or for achieving the same ends. The number of alternative patterns may vary between communities. "The cultures of small societies

---

[3] Our use of the term *pattern* resembles the way in which Levy (1952:57, 102) uses the word *structure*—for "an observable uniformity of action or operation." In his theory the term *institution* is made to refer to a socially vital, normative pattern.

living under primitive conditions usually include only a moderate number of such alternatives, while in such a culture as our own they are very plentiful. Examples of such alternatives for ourselves would be such things as the use of horses, bicycles, railroads, automobiles, and airplanes for the single purpose of transportation overland; our variety of teaching techniques; or our wide range of beliefs and attitudes toward the supernatural."

Manifest and Ideal Culture Patterns

Patterns of culture may be manifest or ideal. A manifest (or real) pattern of action, thought, or feeling actually occurs in distinction to the ideal pattern which people hold as desirable but by which they do not always live. One cannot accurately predict manifest behavior from the ideal norms expressed by a group of people. Hence the careful distinction between ideal and manifest patterns is very important. Kaska Indians are ideally generous and nonaggressive but manifestly the anthropologist discovered limits to their generosity and in time learned to predict situations when interpersonal aggressiveness would appear. Many New Yorkers hold that (ideally) no man should sit while a woman remains standing but few New Yorkers rise when a woman enters the subway car in which they are riding. The belief and ritual system known as Islam contains many ideals by which Muslims do not order their lives but of which they proudly speak. Of course, often much correspondence exists between the ideal and manifest patterns in a culture. Such correspondence, however, must be verified and not taken for granted if we want to remain in a position for the most accurate prediction of behavior. On the other hand knowledge only of the ideals of a culture does allow some prediction. Such awareness may, for example, predict the range of variation that accompanies certain actions—viz., aggression in Kaska culture or food habits in Pakistan.

In an illuminating paper John Bennett (*1946*) shows how divergent interpretations of Pueblo culture (Hopi and Zuni) are partly related to the fact that some anthropologists working in the Pueblo area emphasized ideal and others manifest behavior patterns. His paper shows how the presuppositions and values of field workers led them to emphasize one level of culture rather than another. Those scientists attracted by the idea of the rural folk community dwelt on the ideal Pueblo patterns which corresponded to the idealistic folk culture while anthropologists with an urban bias tended to emphasize the restrictive, theocratic aspects of the manifest culture.

Community and Society

The words *community* and *society* have been used several times but have not been distinguished in any precise manner. Loosely speaking the term *community* may be applied to any group which holds together long enough to develop a culture. The term refers to an area of relatively intense common life (Wilson and Wilson, 1945:30–31). This definition indicates that the social scientist has delimited a temporal-spatial segment of life—like a region in the United States, a tribe of Indians, a village in Pakistan, a squadron of some two hundred men within the United States Air Force, or a historical era like the Victorian Age.[4] This segment constitutes the focus of the anthropologist's attention. As the Wilsons point out, "The boundaries of community, like those of society, vary with the point of reference, and the exact line of demarcation is not always clear, but in cases in which the relevant facts are known it can be defined as falling within certain narrow limits." Any community may be ethnographically described. True, many of the artifacts and patterns will be shared with other communities. Nevertheless we assume that every community possesses an analyzable culture.

In distinction to community, the term *society* will be used in this book to refer to the spatial and temporal range of social relationships consciously realized by the members of a particular community (Wil-

---

[4] For a regional study see Hutton, *1946*; tribal studies have been the main occupation of anthropologists; for town-village studies see West, *1945*; Young, *1941*; Honigmann, *1952a*; or Hollingshead, *1949*. Squadron studies have occupied the author and material from his experience will several times be alluded to in the following pages. The historian's approach to community analysis will be found in Plumb, *1950*; or Allen, *1931*.

son and Wilson, *1945*:24–25). Although the manufactured products of a group may travel from one corner of a continent to the other, if the group is not aware of the ultimate recipients of their product its society does not encompass the whole continent. The range of the conscious relations of communities may be expected to vary and a society must always be defined with reference to a particular community. Kaska society denotes all of the contemporary and historical relations consciously realized by the Kaska Indians.

Of the two terms, *society* and *community,* the latter is undoubtedly of greatest importance as far as readers of this book are concerned. We will see that personality is closely related to membership in a particular community and that the members of a community tend to possess in common certain aspects of personality.

The Ends of Culture

The patterns which constitute a culture serve the ends of human survival and adjustment. By survival is meant the adaptation of the organism in a particular environment. Culture assists the human organism to overcome the variety of lethal threats (hunger, exposure, danger from enemies) by which it may be confronted and to which it is by nature subject. Although communities sometimes sacrifice an individual in order to promote the welfare of the group, such a pattern does not deny the assumption that biological survival is one of the ends served by culture.

Adjustment refers to the satisfaction of human needs or tensions that are not directly tied up with survival. The failure to satisfy such demands does not directly threaten the existence of the organism although persistent nongratification may seriously complicate survival. It should be clear that any particular culture pattern may be adjustive but not adaptive. Murray and Kluckhohn (*1953*:36) cite the example of suicide. Suicide is a means of overcoming perplexing problems and anxieties. It reduces a variety of tensions but in doing so it also kills the person.

The goals of adaptation and adjustment underlie many human relationships. Culture is both positively and negatively related to these goals. That is to say, certain behavior patterns may promote survival and tension reduction while others promote tension and stress.

PERSONALITY

In its present technical sense the word *personality* refers to the actions, thoughts, and feelings characteristic of an individual. We may also speak of personality patterns in the sense that people evidence regularities of behavior which, however, are usually situationally expressed. So, for example, among the Kaska Indians we identified Dorothy Plover, a young woman of twenty-two, as proud of her foreign Indian heritage, self-assertive, strongly attached to her father, morbidly afraid of the grizzly bear, promiscuous, and tending to use people to further her personal ends (Honigmann, *1949a*:348–349). Naturally all of these patterns never appeared simultaneously. The word *personality* also denotes that the patterns of behavior tend to be systematically interconnected. Dorothy's attitude to her children bore a relationship to the identification she felt with her father and this entered into the way she responded to a set of Rorschach's Ink Blots. In the same way a man's office behavior relates to his style of action, thought, and feeling at home. Because personality comprises recurrent behavior it follows that knowledge of personality furnishes a basis for predicting individual behavior.

By this time the reader probably recognizes the extent to which personality patterns also constitute part of the socially standardized behavior patterns of an enduring group. The personality concept overlaps the culture concept. In part at least personality means culture reflected in individual behavior (Murphy, *1949*). If Samoan culture includes a standardized indifference to young children, then the Samoan parent who tolerates with indifference the presence of young offspring is executing a culture pattern that, because we speak of an individual, may better be thought of as a pattern of personality. As a matter of fact, it is from concrete regularities of individual behavior that the anthropologist derives the culture patterns of the community which he studies.

We want to be clear about the range of phenomena designated by the term *personality*. Lewis (1951:421–422) has distinguished between relatively inclusive and exclusive definitions of personality. The former include actual behavior in their environmental orbit while the latter refer only to so-called mental or psychic states. The former stand resolves many of the problems encountered in trying to relate the concepts of culture and personality. It is one we follow in this book. On the other hand, the concept of personality means more than observed behavior. It includes also the thoughts and emotions of the individual, for example, the fear which restrains him from acting. Socially disapproved acts occur everywhere. When they are followed by guilt or shame such realizations of wrongdoing must also be understood as included in the notion of personality. The term *behavior* is used for both these levels—the observable one of action and the unobservable one of thought and feeling.

Theoretically at least, an individual personality is analyzable into unlearned and socially standardized (or learned) aspects. Actually there is relatively little in an individual's behavioral repertory, apart from a few reflexes, not in some degree standardized by the groups with which he has been affiliated. The anthropologist, however, is not much concerned with the unique learning of individuals. Rather he is attentive to the learned facets of personality that are shared between individuals.[5] These distinctions may be conveniently summarized in the following paradigm:

An individual personality theoretically contains the following classes of behavioral elements:
1. Unlearned elements (e.g., *blinking of the eyes*).
2. Learned elements ranging from unique to universally shared:
   a. Unique learned elements are learned by the person by virtue of personal experience in a social group (e.g., *a specific individual's personal attitude toward authority*).

---

[5] Here lies the distinction between culture and personality, and psychology. As Sargent (1950:15) points out, "Most sociologists and cultural anthropologists are impressed with the uniformities or similarities of human social behavior found within a group. . . . The psychologist is interested in uniformities but is also impressed with individual differences in personality and social behavior."

b. Shared learned elements are those acquired in some degree by a proportion of the members of a social group (e.g., *in Samoa, the attitude that precocity is a great wrong*).

Modal Personality

Shared and learned patterns of activity, thought, and feeling are the focus of interest in culture and personality. Various names have been coined for those elements of personality that are relatively frequent in a social group but here the term "modal personality" will be adopted despite its misleading suggestion of statistical accuracy.[6]

Modal personality, we shall see, is largely socially derived. It presents a product of the interplay of the human biological heritage—man's organic capacities—and the experiences of individuals in groups that direct and shape the expression of those organic capacities (DuBois, 1944:2). The shared elements of personality range from activities like eating, smoking, and games to highly generalized views of life. As Linton points out, different modes of behavior have long been recognized qualitatively by travelers abroad. However, the average man tends to exaggerate the differences that he sees between, say, nations. He tends to impute greater or lesser worth to particular modes of behavior. As a scientific discipline culture and personality is dedicated to seeing the facts without distortion and with impartial objectivity.

Early professional attempts to formulate descriptions of modal personality often differed little from the irresponsible stereotypes advanced to further national welfare. A German psychoanalyst, Maeder,

---

[6] Approximate synonyms include "communal personality," "societal personality," and "basic personality." The latter term was coined by Kardiner (1939:132), for whom it denotes techniques of thinking, the security system (i.e., style of life through which persons insure protection, esteem, support, approval), the feelings that motivate conformity (i.e., shame or guilt), and attitudes toward supernatural beings. Linton (1945:128–129) does not follow this usage when he employs "basic personality" to include socially shared elements "of any degree of specificity, ranging from simple overt responses of the sort involved in 'table manners' to highly generalized attitudes" that "may underlie a wide range of more specific responses in the individual." Our concept of modal personality is nearly identical with Linton's phrasing of basic personality.

however, in 1912 saw the English imbued with an ideal of slimness for feminine beauty. This ideal he related to sexual repression, a covert state of British modal personality, that also expresses itself in prudery, excessive etiquette, the suppression of feeling, and the love of animals and pets. Some years later Seligman sought to describe Japanese "temperament" with the aid of the extraversion-introversion theory of Jung. He regarded the Japanese as extravert, practical, and concrete. They form conclusions quickly, are little given to abstruse meditation or abstract reasoning, and remain relatively devoid of a sense of sin. "Morality," he said, offering a generalization that would be supported in later years by Ruth Benedict (1946a:223), "is predominantly of the group . . ." The people are governed less by guilt than by a strong sense of "decorum." Still another early illustration of modal personality description is Morley's characterization of the modern Maya Indians of Yucatan.[7]

They are industrious and hard-working even on a poor diet; cleanly in their persons but untidy with their belongings; seemingly insensitive to suffering, fatalistic, and unafraid of death. They are conservative, but individualistically independent, though not at all competitive. They are talkative, sociable, cheerful, fond of practical jokes; are not highly sexed, but inclined to promiscuity; are strong on family ties, but not given to showing their affection. They have respect for law and a sense of justice; are honest, averse to thieving and begging; are not quarrelsome but do harbor revenge. And they are not religious, but strongly "superstitious" —which probably means that they do not bring much piety or feeling to their religion except the emotion of fear.

One other brief and recent illustration of a word picture of modal personality involves the Papago Indians of the American southwest. "In sum, the Papago personality which emerges from the present research is one of a simple, spontaneous people with a predominantly affective and esthetic, rather than a conceptual systematized perception pattern and approach to life. . . . At the same time they have demonstrated their ability to cope adequately with the practical prob-

---

[7] From Kroeber, 1948:587.

lems of daily living and to cooperate effectively in thinking through and seeking practical solutions to the paradoxes and enigmas which have beset the tribe" (Thompson, *1951b*:114).

Recent years have seen the burgeoning of investigations into modal personality, especially with reference to modern nations. Such preoccupations with what is often called national character is in part a product of a world shrunken by radio and modern forms of transportation. As our neighbors, enemy and allies, have come closer the need of understanding them as people increased. Then, too, psychological warfare depends for its success on a firm knowledge of modal personality (Farber, *1950*:307). At the same time anthropology, having turned to the study of modern national communities, perhaps found the cultures of these groups too complex to describe in the traditional ethnographic fashion. Condensing the magnitude of these cultures into relatively few personality trends has proven to be an efficient way to study some aspects of modern nations (Mead, *1951c*).

Sharp objections have been leveled against the manner in which modal personality research has been conducted. The qualitative nature of such studies has aroused objection, critics expressing dissatisfaction with the fact that field workers give no idea of the frequency of a mode or the extent of deviation. Rebuttal of this charge is difficult without anticipating what we have to say about the conceptualization of personality into a relatively peripheral, simple region and a more comprehensive region of nuclear values and generalized attitudes. The latter region includes what Margaret Mead and other anthropologists call character structure. Mead (*1953a*:648) has pointed out that character structure is not subject to variation like peripheral patterns of behavior. Patterns of character structure, she maintains, which are widely shared are generalized "in such a way that the addition of another class of informants previously unrepresented will not change the nature of the statement *in a way which has not been allowed for in the original statement*" (author's italics). To reply to this defense we must point out that at present we have only the field worker's word concerning the frequency of the pattern and the adequacy of sampling. Demonstration of the method to the extent of at least a few quantitative patterns would be welcome and might allay doubt.

It is also pointed out that when large, modern nations are dealt with by workers in modal personality and those nations are not homogeneous but stratified and otherwise differentiated, we receive no clear idea of the extent to which shared elements of behavior are associated with urban or rural areas, social classes, or other subdivisions of the area (Farber, 1950). Techniques to satisfy these objections would probably demand an enormous increase in the time devoted to field work in communities with complex social organization. However, the importance of specifying the social subdivision to which data pertain is indicated by the difficulty of defining the modal personality of American Jews without reference to the diverse national backgrounds, social class position, or degree of assimilation to American values found among Jews in this country (Orlansky, 1946). There has been a tendency to ascribe to Jews inferiority and self-abasement feelings, presumably related to their status as a discriminated against category. A New York City College test found no significant differences in this respect between Jews and non-Jews. A Minnesota test found Jewish freshmen with higher inferiority scores than non-Jewish freshmen. But a Columbia-Barnard study found Jews showing higher social dominance than Protestants and Catholics. Such slight agreement probably derives from the fact that American Jews do not form a homogeneous group but vary with social class, occupation, and national origin.

Caudill (1952:73–78) has taken special pains to avoid implying a uniform modal personality to his sample of Japanese Americans. He speaks of modes of adjustment and distinguishes two such for the Issei. The first is one of successful self-assertion and labile emotional control; the second involves passive self-submergence with the individual highly dependent upon others for the satisfaction of his needs. He similarly finds several modes operating among the Nisei and in comparing the two categories finds, for example, that unlike the Issei the Nisei have a high percentage of masochistic adjustment. Caudill's refined methodology for studying modal personality should greatly sharpen the perceptions of other workers in large and heterogeneous modern communities.

Students who first encounter the concept are often concerned about the relationship of modal personality to group stereotypes. If a stereotype means thinking about groups ethnocentrically and in value loaded terms, then the modal personality picture is distinguished from the stereotype in its objectivity. Anthropological analysis tries to remain unaffected by ethnocentrism and avoids making judgments of good or bad about the phenomena studied. Stereotypes, too, are often distinguishable as deliberately exaggerated pictures of modal behavior tendencies. Like propaganda, stereotypes stack the cards instead of being concerned with a balanced description and interpretation. Stereotypes, when they conform to truth, give a one-sided and falsely consistent picture of the modal personality. The fact that people may have relatively contradictory tendencies in their make-up has also escaped the notice of some social scientists. Modal personalities basically differ from stereotypes in that they are derived through study or research and not uncritically accepted because they satisfy emotional needs.

Acceptance of the notion of shared elements of personality does not require us to reject the common sense observation that in any community there exist differences in individual personality. A division of labor has been established in social science. The anthropologist in distinction to the psychologist perfers to study personality without attending primarily to individual differences. He directs himself toward abstracting frequent elements of action, thought, and feeling in a particular community. He does not maintain that all the members of that community have uniform personalities.

Overt and Covert Personality

Personality, either individual or modal, has both covert and overt aspects. The overt elements are represented by motor habits, including speech, and constitute the evidence upon which are based all the constructs designating the unseen elements.

Covert personality refers to behaviors like memory, dreaming, valuing, feeling. One of the most significant things about this unseen "area" is that it logically includes the socially standardized motives or life goals that impel the overt actions of the individual. Personality formation, with which culture and personality is very much concerned, has been described as "the process of developing motives in the service of which the individual uses any and all capacities which he has" (Newcomb, 1950:391). Much attention will be paid to human motives throughout this book.

A motive may be defined as a condition *within* the organism that impels behavior toward personally desirable goals. Illustrative of a learned and socially shared motive is the Kaska Indian's dependency or longing for care and affection (Honigmann, 1949a:280). The eagerness of the Plains Indian to accumulate war honors, the intention of a Kwakiutl chief to overcome his rivals in gift giving and gift destruction, the desire of a Samoan girl to win approval through nonpresumption all depend on the operation of socially standardized life goals. The insecurity of the Dakota Indian child who conceives of the world as a dangerous or hostile place and feels deprived and unsatisfied is also motivating. He responds to his environment in terms of these covert world and self-views (Macgregor, 1946:205–206).

Motives change. People of the Western world used to be impelled to strive for "salvation"—a state of bliss to be enjoyed after death. This goal has largely disappeared from the life of the middle-class citizen to be replaced, says Kardiner, by the goals of success as measured in the esteem of others.

Status Personality

In every enduring group certain standardized activities, thoughts, and feelings come to be associated with, and expected from, the persons who occupy particular positions in the community's social structure. Although the positions are repeatedly vacated and filled by different individuals, the appropriate behaviors assumed by each occupant of the status change more slowly. To those aspects of personality associated with particular status points of a social structure, the name "status personality" is given (Linton, 1945:129–131).

The behavior that comes to be expected from the occupant of a particular social position makes up part of the social role of the person. Thus, for example, the socially standardized role of the mother in the Kaska community includes the cherishment and nurturance of the young baby. Later she changes her role when she becomes relatively remote and affectionally aloof with respect to the three-year-old child. Similarly the peacetime role of an unwilling reserve officer who has forsaken a private business upon reëntering the air force includes bitter griping about inefficiency and mismanagement that he perceives in that organization.

Every individual, of course, occupies many statuses in a particular community and plays many roles in the course of his life. Anthropology has studied some highly interesting statuses in the vast fabric of human culture. The monographs describe roles ranging from those of powerful kings in East or West Africa to petty chieftains in the desert society of the Middle East. Our accounts are rich concerning fabulously peaceable and restrained Plains Indian chiefs, the malicious intent associated with the American Indian sorcerer, the hip-swinging provocativeness demonstrated by the women in some tribes, the shy retiringness of veiled women in a Pathan village of North West Frontier Province, and the idealization of the past characteristic of an upper-upper class New Englander. Some of these roles are sex-linked, others are limited to a single person in the community at a particular time, while others are restricted to the members of specific social classes.

Ideal and Manifest Personality

Ideal and manifest (or real) aspects may further be distinguished in personality. The ideal patterns of action represent to the person how he *should* act, for example, in order to find favor in the eyes of his community or to remain at peace with himself. Ideal standards may sometimes appear in interviews that are designed to discover how an individual *would* act in given circumstances. Manifest personality means the *real* behaviors experienced or revealed by an actor. Students should remain sensitive to the distinction between ideal and manifest orders of behavior. Perfect correspondence between these aspects of personality need not be expected.

Margaret Mead (*1951c*) has made much use of official Soviet sources in order to infer the ideal modal personality of the Great Russian. She did this under conditions where it was not possible to observe very much of the real behavior of Russians in their customary milieu. Apart from opening a new corridor of research into official ideologies, Mead's work demonstrates how knowledge of the ideal aspects of personality makes more lucid the public behavior of nations as reported in the daily newspapers.

CHARACTER STRUCTURE

For centuries men have sought to gauge the shared but covert elements of groups. Often the attempts have been unsystematic and suffered from being prejudiced in favor of, or against, the group under analysis. Meyer's nineteenth-century attempt to define German character structure illustrates these weaknesses. Meyer (*1892–93*) begins by pointing out that the German language often fixes the accent of a word on the root or stem. This fixed accent, in place of the variable accent found in English, he regards an expression of the German's "logical impulse." He then examines German poetry assuming that it reflects the "national soul." German poetry is seen to reflect "the struggle for truth" between the extremes of individualism and subordination. Germans emerge showing a "love of organization, ominous in its strength . . . they are conscientious, thorough, reliable." Sometimes they overuse these qualities at the expense of kindness and sympathy. For this reason they are seldom loved as conquerors or administrators.

One of the landmarks in studies of this kind came with publication of "Culture, Genuine and Spurious" (Sapir, *1922*). The purpose of the essay was to infer from behavior the "spirit" or "national genius" of a people. Genius means the "general attitudes, views of life and specific manifestations of civilization that give a particular people its distinctive place in the world." Genius finds expression in the modes of thought as well as in concrete behavior.

Sapir found French behavior characterized by "qualities of clarity, lucid systematization, balance, care in choice of means, good taste." Russian culture reveals a tendency to regard people not as types but as "stark human beings existing primarily in and for themselves." It is noteworthy that in comparing these two European groups, Sapir resists the tendency of trying to measure the degree to which they differ in a common characteristic, say in "lucid systematization." Rather he lets each nation speak for itself, singling out the element that he finds distinctive of that group. "The very same element of civilization may be a vital strand in the culture of one people, a well-nigh negligible factor in the culture of another." He focuses on the "vital" strands of what we would call French and Russian character structure.

Covert personality includes the socially acquired, unconscious central motives and values by which the individual interprets the world around him and in terms of whose dictates he is impelled to act in a wide series of specific behaviors. This organized, nuclear, and generalized "area" of the personality we call character structure. Put more simply, character structure refers to the nuclear motivating core of the personality.[8] A broad range of expressive acts, thoughts true or false, and feelings of well being or ill feeling may be motivated by these central needs and interests. Fromm (*1941*) maintains that ideas which are not rooted in the character structure are of little significance in the life of the person, being superficial responses to conventional pressure. He identifies the character structure of modern industrial man as valuing orderliness, discipline, and punctuality; as imbued with an idea of the necessity of work. These values he points out are useful in an industrial nation like our own (Fromm, *1949*:5).

David Rodnick (*1948*:4–8) shows for postwar Germans how intense psychological insecurity may characterize the character structure of a national community. The German, Rodnick says, customarily feels that the situation around him is hopeless. The cards look as though they were stacked against him and his world is piled full of insurmountable difficulties. He feels lonely even among Germans but is eager to identify with other persons and to win friend-

---

[8] For discussion of peripheral and nuclear areas in personality see Stagner, *1948*:68–69, 148–150; Kluckhohn, *1949a*:208.

ship and approval. Yet he believes that to show softness in interpersonal relations invites only hostility and the danger of being taken advantage of. He fears authority because it is hurtful unless it reflects the German's own wishes. Authority that runs counter to the wishes of Germans will be passively resisted, Rodnick predicts. Resignation with a vague hope that things will improve are typical attitudes with which the German responds to his environment. To impose some kind of orderliness on the world produces partial reassurance against his pervasive insecurity.

Compare the German character structure with the nuclear motivations revealed by Pathan and Punjabi men in Western Pakistan. In these areas men harbor strong needs to remain capable and successful masters of an external situation. Tremendous importance is placed on maintaining the feeling of ego invulnerability and control and a strong series of defences exist to prevent recognition of ego weakness. Unfamiliar situations, which threaten seriously the achievement of successful control over an external problem, reveal this motivational complex in action. We observed in Punjabis a pronounced fear of failure in interviews where we asked them about what they had seen in cinema films or in Rorschach cards. Men sometimes refused the latter test, fearing that they could not carry it through. Sometimes a man seeks to preserve security by manifesting a cavalier approach to an unfamiliar situation that tests his capacities. He becomes pretentious or exhibitory, trying to promote a favorable impression in his audience not by solving the problem but by pretending to be a highly adept, dashing, and fearless individual. All these behaviors are motivated by a strong, unconscious characterological fear of failure.

SELF-REGULATION AND PERSONALITY

Erich Fromm (1953:517) has made the point that a particular character structure is one of the ways in which a community insures the perpetuation of its culture and brings about conformity of its members. "In order that any society may function well, its members must acquire the kind of character which makes them *want* to act in the way they *have* to act as members of the society or of a special class within it. They have to *desire* what objectively is *necessary* for them to do. *Outer force* is to be replaced by *inner compulsion,* and by a particular kind of human energy which is channeled into character traits." Riesman (*1950*:6) adds that, like social structure, character structure limits choice and channelizes "action by foreclosing some of the otherwise limitless behavior choices of human beings."

How does character structure regulate and limit behavior? Character structure may be conceived of as a self-regulatory device "built into" personality. It provides personality with a selector mechanism

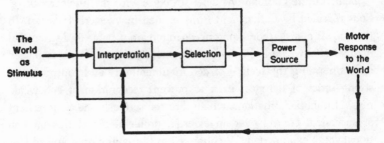

FIGURE 1. Personality as a Feedback (Self-Regulatory) System. (Adapted from L. K. Frank [*1948*])

to choose responses to an external situation. Character structure, however, constitutes not only the center where responses are selected but also the screen that reflects the subjectively perceived external situation. This perceptual function of character structure is carried out by virtue of the acquired world and self-views. In terms of these the individual interprets reality and himself (Frank, *1948*; Barrett and Post, *1950*).

The diagram in Fig. 1 is intended to demonstrate how the interpretation of the external world by character structure leads to the selection of an appropriate response that is fired by the biochemical processes of the organism. The response, which is both a kinesthetic and emotional experience, constitutes a further signal to the organism and takes its place alongside the stimulus signals contributing further to the subjective interpretation of that stimulus (Newcomb, *1950*:88–96).

Perceptual activity is of crucial importance in these operations of character structure. Such activity, as Abt and Bellak (*1950*:52) point out, has roots in the individual's past experiences and extends forward to fashion his orientation to the future. "There is evidence to suggest that as a result of his past perceptual activity the individual tends to build up or acquire a sense of certainty with respect to the consequences of his present perceptual experiences. Precepts that in the past have been validated by his subsequent experiences evidently tend to become fixated as perceptual response tendencies and tend to lead to a feeling of comfort and security."

There is another sense in which a feedback process emanating from character structure may be demonstrated in social interaction. Probably few readers have escaped the experience of being confronted by a situation which they interpreted as a threat. In turn they responded to the situation as though it did constitute a threat thereby precipitating a real threat—perhaps a punch in the nose. Such a sequence may continue until one of the parties breaks loose, perhaps exclaiming: "You got me wrong; I didn't come around to pick a fight!" What happened in this sequence is that the initial hostile response determined a defensive hostile reaction in the other person. Such a reaction, of course, confirmed the view of the situation from which the first blow had proceeded. The world-view literally created trouble for the person. In the same manner Dakota Indian children interpret the world as a dangerous place. In psychological tests, when asked to make up a story about pictures, they see these neutral pictures as containing characters like themselves, uncertain, with little to eat, and little to make life comfortable (Macgregor, *1946*:205–206). Character structures carry their fate with them, responding to the world as they have learned to interpret it subjectively and thereby forcing from the world the very reaction they anticipate.

Bateson (*1949a*:36) distinguishes between regenerative and degenerative feedback processes in human behavior. In the regenerative type, increase in A sets up increase in B, and so on, the steps finally culminating in a further increase in A. For example, Samoan personality contains a self-minimization tendency manifested in non-presumptive behavior. Such behavior encourages similar behavior in other persons (at least it does not stimulate ego enhancing behavior). Self-minimization behavior in others presumably serves as an encouragement for the individual to continue following approved behavior patterns; that is, there is a further increase in self-minimization. Such cycles continue until a factor outside the circle (like a failure in energy, drive, or food supply) stops the process. Or else there may be a "climax" in the sequence, following which the circle stops or slows down, apparently because reinforcement is currently insufficient to keep the process in action.

Degenerative (also called self-corrective) circles contain one step which instead of producing further increase in the original impulse promotes a decrease in the process. Degenerative circular processes play an important role in maintaining conformity to cultural norms. For example, if to attract followers a high-ranking leader associates with persons of lower rank, he may himself lose his rank so that his chance of attracting followers is reduced. Up to a certain point the "fraternization" passes unnoticed, but there comes a point when increase in the number of such associations produces a decrease in rank and leadership (Homans, 1950:184). Kaska Indians value being able to survive through what they believe to be their own efforts. Consciousness of being dependent on others is, therefore, threatening. On the other hand there is a simultaneous trend toward passivity in the Kaska character structure. Up to a certain point receiving help gratifies the feeling of being in command of one's life. The Indian manages to survive through his efforts of getting another to help him. When a certain limit is passed, increase in aid produces a *decrease* in the feeling of self-sufficiency. Now a degenerative circle is brought into operation with anxiety as one of the constituent links. To reduce anxiety the individual may wrench himself out of his dependency situation and strive for greater independence.

ETHOS

One final basic concept remains to be introduced, a notion long current in social science. "Ethos" refers to the emotional quality of socially patterned behavior. This quality reflects the motivational state of the actor. By an emotion we mean a disturbance of the organism accompanied by pleasant or unpleasant feelings. In ethos we study behavior (as well as material products of behavior) for the emotions that can be revealed.

Emotions, as Asch (1952:110–111) points out, reflect the fate of human motives and are products of situational understanding. "One may say that emotions mirror the course of motivational events. They arise in direct response to the realization of our dependence on the surroundings and of the constant necessity of choosing and deciding. . . . Emotions express in the most vivid way our apprehension of the relation between given conditions and ourselves." The important factor in determining emotional behavior is the relationship which we perceive, consciously or unconsciously, between an external event and inner goals or motives. This cognitive theory of emotion helps explain the relationship of emotions to the comprehensive world and self-views that make up character structure. Emotion reflects how the motivating core of the personality interprets situations which the individual encounters. Through understanding the emotional quality of behavior we are led to comprehend the nature of human motivations and basic characterological values.

Ethological descriptions of culture must be distinguished from cultural descriptions. The latter involve an observer who specifies merely the formal aspects of a situation. For example, an American's morning behavior may be set down as follows: "Every morning after Americans have arisen they clean their teeth with a toothbrush spread with dentifrice. With the teeth tightly clamped, the brush is inserted between cheek and teeth in such a way that the bristles are at right angles to the surface of the teeth. Then the brush is vigorously propelled in and out of the mouth.[9] Behind this activity is the idea that dental decay will be reduced by following such a daily routine."

In this example the form of the behavior is given in a fashion

---

[9] These are not directions that a dentist would recommend for cleaning the teeth. They pretty well describe prebreakfast behavior that any reader will observe when he enters a Pullman washroom.

analogous to the way in which an architect's drawing reveals the form of a building. In contrast, what we are about to attempt resembles the manner in which an art critic or art historian might approach the building.

The emotional quality of the morning tooth cleaning may be set down like this: "With careful regularity, every morning, Americans, filled with a dread of tooth decay, vigorously clean their teeth. Behind this activity is the fervent expectation that brushing the teeth will spare them the pain of toothache and the agony of a dentist's chair." The words *careful regularity, dread, vigorously, spare,* and the whole tone of the paragraph serve to communicate the emotional quality bound up with tooth cleaning in the United States. Here follows another description of emotional attributes of customary behavior, this time about Soviet Russian culture: "Ruggedness—that's a Soviet athlete's most prized quality. That's why about 10 million men and women go in for cross-country running. Why millions, despite shortages in equipment, compete in cross-country ski races. Why mountain climbing and swimming under a full pack, and rifle markmanship contests are major Soviet sports. Baseball? Golf? They're for jelly-fish capitalists—not for Soviet workers" (Goodfriend, *1950:19*). This statement, obviously intended for a popular rather than a professional audience, attempts to reveal the emotional intensity with which Russians respond to outdoor activities. It offers the "flavor" of Russian sport more than it describes formal behavior with guns, skis, or when climbing mountains.

It may be possible to characterize large areas or a nearly complete culture in emotional terms. This is what Ruth Benedict (*1946b:72*) does when she speaks of the Pueblo way of life as Apollonian and Plains Indian culture as Dionysian.

The desire of the Dionysian, in personal experience or in ritual, is to press through it toward a certain psychological state, to achieve excess. The closest analogy to the emotions he seeks is drunkenness, and he values the illuminations of frenzy. With Blake, he believes "the path of excess leads to the palace of wisdom." The Apollonian distrusts all this, and has often little idea of the nature of such experiences. He finds means to outlaw them from his conscious life. He "knows but one law, measure in the Hellenic sense." He keeps the middle of the road, stays within the known map, does not meddle with disruptive psychological states. In Nietzsche's fine phrase, even in the exaltation of the dance he "remains what he is, and retains his civic name."

Two approaches to ethos may be distinguished in American anthropology. The first describes the predominant emotional qualities of culture without reference to covert needs, aspirations, or values which emotional expression reflects. The second approach aims at the description of the ethos while at the same time referring the emotional attributes to appropriate motivational states of the actors. In the following quotation (Honigmann, 1949a:305–306) the emotional qualities of a wide range of Kaska culture are referred to the way in which the Kaska individual conceives of himself and the universe.

The Kaska view of the world wavers between an idea that experience is manageable and an awareness that life is threatening and difficult. These opposite attitudes lead to two principal means of responding to adaptive and adjustive problems. For many of the hazards of existence, there are tested problem solutions with the aid of which one can efficiently overcome a harsh and rigorous environment. In these situations it is possible to be resourceful, capable, and masterful. Unfortunately the context of life offering security is extremely limited. To stay within the area of safety requires constant watchfulness and caution. As soon as experiential boundaries widen, catastrophe may be expected. The uncertainties of life must be avoided lest by testing resourcefulness too sharply they promote failure. Society like the physical environment, also holds dangers. Here safety lies in avoiding interpersonal relations which promise to stir up intense emotions or invite excessive effort against which there are no effective safeguards and which tax the resources of the ego.

Gregory Bateson (1936) was one of the earliest anthropologists to actually use the concept of ethos in the analysis of field data. He describes his book, *Naven*, as an attempt to discuss certain ceremonies of the Iatmul tribe from two closely related aspects, the affective and ethological. By the former he refers to the relationship of a cultural pattern to the emotional needs of individuals while the latter aspect denotes the relationship between the emotional (affective) aspects of a culture pattern and the emotional emphases of the culture as a whole—the ethos. Thus he distinguishes between an overall cultural ethos and one limited to a particular situation. There may also be distinct ethoses applying to the behavior of each sex. Bateson makes clear that behavior is not the primary focus in studying a culture for its ethos. The anthropologist looks behind the formal behavior for a pattern that can be abstracted. It is the "tone of behavior" which the investigator abstracts from behavior and which he describes in a journalistic or artistic style. An ethos is often transitory, hence the term *Zeitgeist,* used synonymously with the former concept. Methodologically Bateson makes an important point when he says that ethos abstracted by anthropologists need not correspond to the community's ideas and values because it is the people who think and feel, not the culture. The subjective nature of ethological interpretation is brought out when Bateson says that persons reared in one ethos may feel distaste for a foreign ethos. Anthropologists must remain aware of such bias.

From the ceremonial behavior associated with initiation among the Iatmul, Bateson abstracts two ethoses. The male picture reveals individualistic pride and violence in accomplishment expressed through assertive, boastful, swaggering behavior. He speaks of the tone of the men's behavior as "expressive of harshness and irresponsibility." The whole situation reveals a picture of harshness marked by histrionic dramatization and overcompensation. The female ethos stems from a tendency to submission and "negative self-feeling" and is expressed in nonviolent, nonassertive behavior marked by a lack of ostentation.

Suggestions for Further Reading

A somewhat historical introduction to the growth of culture and personality research has been written by Hallowell in "Culture, Personality, and Society" (*1953*). A real history of this and other twentieth-century anthropological developments remains to be written. For further understanding of the culture and personality concepts the reader is referred to texts in anthropology and personality psychology. Should he examine several works in those fields he may discover for himself that these and other terms enjoy no single standardized usage in contemporary social science. Almost every worker uses them in a fashion congruent with his interest and problem. This is less true of the concept "national character," by which most anthropologists mean the character structure of a modern nation. See Gorer's "The Concept of National Character" (*1950*) and Mead's "The Study of National Character" (*1951d*) as well as her article, "National Character" (*1953a*). For more conventional material, including sketches of the Maori, Sioux, and Lepcha, there is Beaglehole's "Character Structure, Its Role in the Analysis of Interpersonal Relations" (*1944*) and Klineberg's "Recent Studies of National Character" (*1949*).

Motivation in its several aspects is well treated in Maslow's "Dynamics of Personality Organization" (*1943a*). The same author's "The Dynamics of Psychological Security-Insecurity" (*1942*) and "Preface to Motivation Theory" (*1943b*) are also highly useful. Every student should be acquainted with the basic personality concept connected with Kardiner (*1949a*). Burrows' "From Value to Ethos on Ifaluk Atoll" (*1952*) and Gillin's "Ethos and Cultural Aspects of Personality" (*1952*) demonstrate the utility of the ethos concept. Another approach to ethos is represented in F. Kluckhohn's "Dominant and Substitute Profiles of Cultural Orientation" (*1950*).

Chapter 3

APPROACHES

Different emphases may be distinguished within the field of culture and personality that distinguish the work of various investigators. This chapter proposes to examine the genetic, descriptive, structural, and phylogenetic approaches to the field. Each of these emphases will be discussed as though it were independent, although in actuality overlap between them may be expected. Individual scientists maintain a single interest and sometimes pursue several emphases in a single piece of work.

THE GENETIC APPROACH

Genetic studies in culture and personality concern themselves with how the modal personality develops or with the relationship of ethos to the learning period of childhood (Werner, *1951*). The basic postulate guiding workers who follow this approach holds that the socially standardized experiences of children in a particular social environment provide the learning of numerous personality patterns and large areas of character structure. On the other hand, the assumption need not be made that all of the personality has its genesis in childhood.

As an example of a piece of research oriented genetically we may examine Erikson's work (*1939; 1948*:180–183; *1950*, chap. 3) with Siouan personality. Erikson studied intensively a group of Midwestern Plains Indians who in the space of a few decades exchanged a culture that featured warfare and buffalo hunting for one based on commercial stock raising and farming. Nevertheless the Sioux have not fully assimilated white values; for example, the Indians do not attempt to accumulate wealth but distribute much of what they earn through giveaways resembling aboriginal models. An explanation for the apparent "resistance" to certain white personality patterns is seen in the fact that the Sioux have also not altered many former patterns of child rearing. To these Erikson directs his attention.

A note of indulgence toward the Sioux baby was apparent even before the newcomer came into the world. Kin of the mother prepared a "bottle" from berry juices mixed with herbs to feed the infant while a woman stimulated the mother's breast flow of milk by sucking. This made it easy for the baby who did not have to work hard to obtain its first nourishment. Feeding came whenever the baby whimpered and nursing lasted from three to five years, unless interrupted by an intervening pregnancy. Prolonged nursing especially marked the career of a boy although it carried one potential conflict: the prolongation led nursing to coincide with teething. Hence it happened that small boys bit their mothers' breasts. When that happened a woman thumped her youngster on the head and likely set off a temper tantrum. Siouan adults remained more than tolerant of such explosions. Temper outbursts, they assumed, made the child strong. With the youngster's limbs encased in the pouch of a cradle board it remains unlikely that any considerable amount of induced rage could have been abreacted by muscular movements. From this may have arisen a backlog of unreleased rage that contributed to the readiness for anger and cruelty in adult Sioux character. The mother's frustration of her child's biting tendencies may relate to the adult habit of clicking the teeth with the fingernail, hitting something against the teeth, or, today, snapping chewing gum. These are not the only attributes of the adult Siouan personality that Erikson traces to childhood. He views the early handling of the child as encouraging attitudes "of undiminished self-esteem and trust in the availability of the food supply" and in the dependability of the tribe's generosity. The pattern of adult generosity depended on high self-esteem and continued the earlier generosity of the mother with her food, as well as the extreme generosity which parents showed in other contexts of childhood. The aggression of the warriors, already alluded to as deriving in part from inhibited rage, in turn underlay the self-torture that was a regular part of the Sun Dance. Then men harnessed themselves by the chest muscles to thongs connected with a pole and pulled back on these thongs until the flesh of the chest tore through. Such self-torture represents aggression ritually turned toward the self—"a sacred and collective turning against the self of the 'original sin' of biting temper which had compromised the paradise of babyhood."

Some of the connections advanced by Erikson to obtain between childhood and adult life have met a sharp challenge. That enforced immobility on the cradle board frustrates a young child and the connection of a widespread trait of ritual self-torture as a reaction to early frustration are two statements in this category. Critics, on the other hand, have failed to recognize Erikson's interpretations as merely hypotheses offered in the spirit of science. Some critics react as though he were asserting dogma. Erikson further recognizes that infantile disciplines do not operate by themselves. As he puts it, certain goals of group life are energized by certain forms of treatment in babyhood. The goals persist, however, "because public opinion continues to consider them 'natural' and does not admit of alternatives" and also because they "work" in a particular community (Erikson, 1950:121).

Geoffrey Gorer (*1949a;* Gorer and Rickman, *1950*) has recently aroused a storm of opposition in academic circles for his work with some aspects of Great Russian modal personality. Working in the United States using Russian informants, literature, films, and folklore, Gorer sought not to explain all of Russian culture by reference to childhood patterns but rather to relate logically one or more childhood patterns to certain features of standardized adult behavior. His study concerns mainly the behavior of peasants, whether in rural areas or in cities to which they may have migrated.

Among the peasants of the Soviet Great Russian Republic a child is not welcomed with particular enthusiasm. Once born, however, it is protected as carefully as possible from painful experiences like hunger and cold. The mother feeds her infant generously and frequently, the breast being offered for as long as two years. In the absence of the mother a substitute for the breast is provided in the form of a comforter made of chewed and sweetened bread tied in a piece of cloth. From birth until nine months of age infants are swaddled in long strips of cloth which bind the legs straight and keep the arms extended at the sides of the body. People claim that the baby has sufficient strength to maim or destroy itself, hence its potential ferocity must be controlled. Nursing and bathing constitute two situations in which the swaddling clothes are removed to allow free movement. The relation of the child to parents is somewhat capricious. Punishment follows quickly should the child's behavior annoy a parent and also commonly comes from a father when he is drunk. Such punishment lacks intensity. In fact, the whole relationship "between parents and children is usually without intensity."

Occidental versions of child training have been assimilated by the intelligentsia and elite in Great Russia, who have also abandoned swaddling. Intellectuals nurse children on schedule and practice early disciplining for cleanliness. But among the peasants, with whom Gorer is particularly concerned, child training cannot be characterized as wholly lenient. He reasons that the constriction of movement imposed by swaddling is extremely frustrating and reacted to with intense, destructive rage which finds little possibility of physical expression. Such rage becomes directed "at the constraining, rather than at the personalized constrainers," apparently because of the low intensity marking relations between adults and children. Judging from the characters in folklore, who are apt to be creatures with iron teeth, the rage felt toward swaddling is reflected in fantasies of biting and destroying via devouring. Yet, at the same time, the child fears that if he were to gratify these destructive wishes he would be destroyed in the same way. In this way constraint becomes essential for its own safety.

How are these patterns of early childhood experience related to adult Great Russian personality? Gorer sees a sense of very pervasive and unfocused guilt characteristic of the Great Russian. This, he suggests, is continuous with the early rage and the vaguely focused but evil hostile impulses of childhood. The Russian tends to burden himself with the sins and miseries of the whole world. Relief from the sense of oppression comes from the Orthodox rite of confession as well as through orgiastic feasts, drinking bouts, and repeated copulatory episodes. These outlets overcome guilt and are emotionally equivalent to the release obtained by the baby whose swaddling is loosened. Great Russian character further exhibits a profound optimism, even under the most adverse conditions. Failure to gratify personal desires does not promote anxiety. Apparently such bounteous optimism is related to the frequent indulgence through eating enjoyed by the infant. The irregular feeding schedule of peasants Gorer relates to the marked absence of compulsive characteristics: un-Sovietized Great Russians are flexible in that they pay little attention to order and time. Finally, there is the Russian's particular attitude to authority, marked by the feeling of a great gap between leader and followers. This lack of a close identification between authority and citizen continues the unintense identification that existed between parent and child. Gorer says it a little differently: "There would seem to be a connection between this attitude and the fact that the earliest constraint—the swaddling—is not part of the self, and not personified."

It should be clear that the genetic approach does not try to give the historical origin of any aspect of culture. It remains concerned with how a new member of the community learns his culture, or receives his social heritage, and how the learning process itself affects him. The historical development of culture is quite a different type of problem handled with very different anthropological methods. The distinction between the two approaches must carefully be kept in mind if confusion is to be avoided.

Genetic research has proven very little about the relationship of childhood experience to adult personality. As a consequence, nearly all statements in this field must be understood as tentative, a common feature encountered in young sciences. No student of the history of science who recognizes how important the creative impulse has been in furthering knowledge would suggest that there is anything wrong in suggesting tentative, original, and theoretically logical connections between facts as long as there remains a willingness to discard such hypotheses if demonstrated to be untrue. It is also wise to remember that when one fact is related to another, it does not follow that other additional antecedents or correlations cannot also be discovered. Because this latter caution has been overlooked, Geoffrey Gorer (*1949a*) is forced to write: "I should like to stress as forcibly as possible that I consider the hypothesized derivatives from the swaddling situation only one of the presumably larger number of antecedents to the development of Russian character. The vulgarizations and misinterpretations of my paper 'Themes in Japanese Culture' have falsely imputed to me a belief in a monistic antecedent to Japanese adult character—in that case the imposition of early toilet training."

Resistances to Genetic Theory

Gorer's sharp tone in this passage indicates that there exists a marked resistance in professional circles to genetic interpretations of modal personality. A number of factors appear to determine such distrust:

1. Foremost, perhaps, is a long-established tendency to account for national behavior in terms of the political history or the geographic and economic situation of the people. Geographical interpretation has somewhat declined in popularity but the derivation of aggressive tendencies, for example, from a combination of factors like dictatorship, scarcity of raw materials, and the threat of powerful neighbors is familiar enough in social science analysis, starting with high-school history textbooks. Anthropology, naturally, does not rule out the role of the individual or great man but by definition claims for itself the privilege of examining not only single but the multiple factors that correlate with social events. Culture and personality, a branch of anthropology, has adopted specialized psychological interests, namely, concerning how the standardized modes of child rearing are related

to adult behavior. This does not deny the influence of other factors. No worker in the field of culture and personality believes that genetic explanations of national character rule out the simultaneous operation of other forces. Most of us feel that by working in a new frame of reference we are assisting in throwing light on a significant new determinant in an already complex sea of forces (Hartman, *1951*).

2. The type of methodology supporting much work in culture and personality helps to alienate the field from scientific workers (Farber, *1950*). In the first place, as Farber says, "Investigators trained in a rigorously empirical, experimental tradition are apt to find themselves ill-at-ease and inhibited in confronting the problem of national character." Particularly distressing is the lack of a systematic methodology guiding observation on this problem. In company with non-scientific writers, some workers in culture and personality have been too ready to forget caution and remain content with sweeping, impressionistic generalizations. This is to suggest that to a degree our work is unscientific, at least in spirit. Of course, science is cumulative and no science is born full grown. The rigorous procedures of one science, say psychology, do not necessarily suit some other research field and workers must be allowed to work out their own useful techniques guided only by logical thinking, the test of prediction, and the degree of refinement of their data.

3. The associations aroused by references to infancy and childhood probably have some relationship to the resistance encountered by the genetic approach in culture and personality. American academic circles appear to find something humorous in attempts to relate, say Japanese adult compulsiveness to the toilet training of the Japanese child. Nobody is amused by statements which reduce complex forms of matter to unseen atoms or to yet smaller particles. But critics refuse to entertain seriously hypotheses attempting to deal on a national scale with phenomena like breast feeding or toilet training.

4. The genetic approach has been widely applied to groups ranging in size from small New Guinea tribes to large European nations, like Germany and Soviet Great Russia. It is obvious that many substantial differences exist between these types of communities. That

is another reason why critics have remained dubious about the validity of an approach which fails to take adequate account of the differences between the types of groups concerned. As already pointed out, many studies in modal personality ignore investigation into possible variations between, say, rural and urban divisions in a nation or between social classes. The tribal communities familiar to anthropology frequently lack these patterns of organization. Reasons will appear below for affirming that socially standardized childhood situations differ between the divisions comprising a large complex nation. Many workers do not attend to these variations systematically. In other cases, however, the national subdivision is explicitly identified. Thus Gorer specifies that he will talk mainly of Great Russian peasants and not of all the Soviet Union.

5. Another objection made to the genetic approach holds that the techniques being utilized here are inadequate for the task. One reason for inadequacy has already been stated; the approach fails to take systematic account of class and regional differences, for example through rigorous sampling. Goldman (*1950*) suggests that use of the interview method itself remains questionable when relied upon for data about overt and covert behavior. He is particularly concerned with the fact that a number of investigations into Russian, Japanese, and other modal personalities of modern nations have been undertaken in the United States using as subjects former citizens of those countries. Distortions of memory and bias by emigrés are only two of the dangers invited when interviewing remains unchecked by observation. In Goldman's words, such investigations have scarcely been "commensurate with the magnitude of the research objectives."

6. Also standing in the way of wider acceptance of genetic studies is the relatively narrow learning period implicitly assumed by some followers of the genetic approach. That is to say, concentration on the experiences of early childhood often gives the impression of overlooking the fact that learning occurs after five, six, or seven years. Such later learning appears to be relevant for an understanding of modal personality formation, including the formation of character structure. An early childhood emphasis is doubly dismaying when,

using such a relatively narrow segment of time, large areas of adult personality are confidently explained.

7. Further limitation on the acceptance of genetic studies in social science results from the misconception of what such studies try to accomplish. We have already indicated that few anthropologists believe that child training is the sufficient explanation for patterns of cultural behavior. Genetic studies focus on the individuals whose behavior makes up culture but do not claim an exclusive role for early experience as far as the dynamics of that behavior are concerned. Margaret Mead rejects firmly and explicitly the "frequently repeated assertions that workers in the field of contemporary culture have claimed that some early discipline, swaddling, strict toilet training, *caused* the Russian or the Japanese personality, rather than recognizing that what is being studied is the way in which human infants, able to take on any culture, learn to be members of their own historical culture, through a series of culturally regular experiences" (Mead, *1951a*:427–428). She notes that attack on genetic studies which carry a connotation of cultural persistence and gradual change is explicable "in a world in which revolutionary breaks with the past occupy such a large proportion of world population . . ."

The sometimes very sharp opposition voiced with reference to genetic explanations in culture and personality have not been without effect. Noticeably greater care has entered into the formulation of genetic hypotheses. Earlier notions of simple one-to-one causality have been abandoned in favor, sometimes, of equally unsatisfactory talk of childhood patterns being *clues* to adult personality. Geoffrey Gorer in his book on the Great Russians speaks of how recognition of the swaddling pattern "illuminated" for him areas of Great Russian personality. Does this mean that sequences of child training are to be regarded somewhat like the Rorschach test as giving hints of possible covert personality patterns? That is, from a situation like swaddling is one merely aided in constructing adult personality? The student armed with a knowledge of the swaddling pattern then assumes possible diffuse rage, guilt, and a sense of isolation as components of Great Russian character structure without however relating them dynamically to swaddling. He may see, as by analogy, in the unswaddled abandon of the Russian infant the orgiastic pleasure associated with large-scale feasting, drinking, and copulation. Such diagnostic use of childhood patterns removes the manifest difficulty of swaddling being related to passivity in Pueblo culture and rage in Sioux or Russian culture (Goldman, 1950:157). It suggests that common child rearing patterns (like swaddling, cradleboarding, and others) may in different communities be associated with quite diverse adult personality features. Hence they cannot be related predictably to any one such feature. It should be noted that this theory of the merely diagnostic relevance of childhood experience to adult personality, if seriously adopted, rules out the possibility of a genetic science of personality development. By adopting this impressionistic approach we will cease to look for predictable linkages between childhood and adulthood situations and, of course, give up efforts to control one set by modifying the other. No strong tendency toward the "clue-centered" approach exists. Its appearance in some writing appears to reflect the momentary confusion produced by the objections of hostile critics whose logic was impressive enough to suggest that existing theories need some reformulation. Such theories have often been too simply based on outworn models of mechanical causality (Frisch, 1953). Before abandoning a genuine scientific approach to genetic studies it is well to recall that the genetic approach has contributed immensely in psychiatry and psychology toward the understanding of individual human development in Western society. The success in those fields offers justification for following a similar approach in making comparative investigations into modal personality.

THE DESCRIPTIVE APPROACH

Description in culture and personality means the exposition in written or some other graphic form of ethos, modal personality, or character structure. Description may be limited to one particular time and place or may comprise a number of chronologically arranged pictures showing change through in time, without, however, attending to the processes associated with change. In any event, scientific description must be relatively objective and subject to verification.

Descriptive studies of personality paint a picture of what people are like, without specifying the childhood or other facts which may be functionally connected with their behavior. The emphasis is purely on rendering material explicit much as the cultural anthropologist tries to do when he reports in detail on culture. People as far back as the Greeks and Romans sought to describe systematically the modal personality of their neighbors (without, however, using concepts like "modal" or "personality"). Nonprofessional travelers continue this approach when they write about their experiences with foreign folk. Kant's description of the Germans, paraphrased by Kroeber (1948:586), illustrates an acute observer's synthesis of a vast amount of behavioral data. "The German is home-loving; solid but not brilliant; industrious, thrifty, cleanly, without much flash of genius; phlegmatic, tough in endurance, persistent in reasoning; intelligent, capable, but lacking in wit or taste; modest, without confidence in his own originality, therefore imitative; overmethodical, pedantic; without impulse toward equality, but addicted to a painstaking hierarchical grading of society that sets title and rank above natural talent; docile under government, accepting despotism rather than resisting or altering the established order of authority."

What we call the descriptive approach is what Goldman (1950:154) refers to as the method of studying national character which "focuses upon an investigation of fundamental attitudes and values—characteristic of homogeneous society, or within a heterogeneous society of occupational, social class, regional and ideological groups."

The following breathless paragraph by the anthropologist, Weston LaBarre (1949b:215), illustrates how the descriptive approach may be utilized comparatively to impress students with the diversity of human interests and values:

The Alaskan Eskimos take to machinery like a duck to water and are in demand as sailors on coastal steam vessels. On the other hand, it seems impossible to teach a Bengali Indian even a simple thing like driving a truck: he loses what little integration he may have had and deliquesces into disorganized panic in the face of that mystery, a machine. The Yaqui Indians of Mexico have a singular gift for machinery and are preferred as laborers by American engineers; yet mechanical ability is by no means characteristic of Mexican Indians in general. The Chinese are hopeless incompetents in the care and management of powered industrial machinery; yet their next door neighbors, the Japanese, took over a machine civilization fairly completely in about fifty years. In the Southwest Pacific, the Papuan is given to a very easily aroused hilarity, while his neighbor in New Guinea is morose and taciturn—so much so that one can actually draw a line on a map of Oceania separating "Papuan hilarity" as a culture trait from "Melanesian moroseness.". . .

The historian, Henry Steele Commager (*1949*), has been consistently interested in American personality. He approaches his subject matter descriptively and with little psychological terminology when he pictures Americans as so optimistic, self-confident, and self-satisfied that until recently they have been little interested in planning for the future. Commager believes that rather than plan the American trusts in his own ability and in the inexhaustibility of natural resources. He notes the readiness with which quantitative standards of evaluation are used by Americans. Even right and wrong becomes a matter of majority decision. Judgment is closely governed by a desire for concreteness and practicality; speculation and abstraction have little appeal for the American. Ingenious and inventive, the citizen of the United States opposes social inventions; hence he is predominantly conservative and a conformist—although he extolls the virtue of tolerance. Such attachment to the traditional, however, does not interfere with a certain carelessness or uncompulsiveness that leads Americans to disregard many rules and regulations and to be chary of too chary discipline. American behavior manifests equalitarianism and a dislike for authoritarian restrictions on conduct. Individualistic behavior has probably declined during the last century, Commager feels, but the value on individualism persists as part of American character structure.

Weston LaBarre's description (*1945*) of Japanese personality illustrates how overt behavioral characteristics may be related to covert aims. He also shows how several overt traits may be synthesized in fewer covert states of character structure. LaBarre obtained his data from first-generation Japanese aliens in the United States and from American-born descendants of Japanese who had received part of this education in Japan. Both groups were studied in War Relocation Authority camps during 1943. Commenting first on the extreme politeness and ceremoniousness of the Japanese, the author points out that these traits are utilized to mask feelings, especially aggressive feelings.[1] The character structure of the Japanese, says LaBarre, includes a pervasive compulsiveness which underlies the perfectionism, neatness, perseveration, persistency, and conscientiousness shown in Japanese behavior. Endowed with a very tyrannical conscience or superego, the individual presents himself as very self-righteous. At the same time he seeks to throw off impulses that are not congenial to his conscience; thus the familiar mechanism of projection comes into play. In other words, the Japanese tends to project his unsanctioned impulses onto somebody else. Fanaticism, arrogance, and touchiness are other aspects of Japanese personality, the latter trait reflecting what might be called a sense of low self-esteem or self-devaluation. Ritualistic suicide (hara-kiri) can be understood against a background of easily affronted pride. Japanese suicide is based on "the desire for a spectacular revenge against a sense of outraged face. The sense of the dignity of the ego is thus theoretically preserved by a destruction of the self." LaBarre suggests that the aggression which the Japanese spend so much energy controlling occasionally escapes into masochistic impulses and hypochondriasis. Hence the people are ready to respond to any advertisements, no matter how extravagant they may be, that promise to remedy or strengthen bodily disorders or

---

[1] Whether the individual also masks or denies his feelings to himself, in the manner of the Kaska Indian, is not clear. We are beginning to learn, however, that while all people sometimes suppress emotions, communities differ in the intensity with which they institute such control, the importance they attach to it, and the kinds of feeling they are most intent on controlling. Some Germans are also emotional suppressors but they are particularly careful to withhold the expression of the tender emotions.

functions. Jealous and invidious, the Japanese is also sentimental, a quality expressed in a number of ceremonial observances, such as the cherry blossom festival.

For an example of ethological description we turn to the Yurok Indians living on the Pacific coast of California. E. H. Erikson (1950, chap. 4) points out the restricted radius of this community's existence, their extreme sense of localization within that radius, and the acquisition and retention of possessions that is the center of each individual Yurok's existence. These three aspects of culture add up to a quality of "centripetality" in the Yurok behavior. A second dominant note in Yurok ethos is a kind of "puritanism." Children learn that physical gratification is incompatible with economic success and the Indians phrase a number of possible offenses in terms of their economic consequences. To sin, i.e., to gratify physical appetites, interferes with the acquisition of possessions. Notice how Erikson in his description of Yurok ethos grasps in a few abstractions (like centripetality and puritanism) the outstanding qualities of Yurok existence.

Descriptive studies have encountered little strong objection apart from the charge that particular writers sometimes allow their personal or national biases to color their accounts. Otto Klineberg (1944:148–149) warns of the temptation to present a picture of people that is born out of the prejudices of the observer's group. Subsequent writers dealing with the same people have sometimes been accused of standardizing error by perpetuating both favorable and unfavorable stereotypes. Anthropologists are trained to avoid the danger of approaching facts with culture-bound perceptions and values. Field training for students is designed to teach such objectivity.

THE FUNCTIONAL APPROACH

Description refers to the reporting of personality or ethos either at one moment in time (the Japanese of the fourth decade of the twentieth century) or through time (for example, the changes in Western man's character structure during the past five hundred years). The emphasis is on presenting data rather than on interrelating factual data. The functional approach in culture and personality has for its object to relate facts of modal personality either to each other, to facts of technology, to social structure, or to some other class of data. The genetic approach, of course, constitutes a special type of functional interest. We have singled it out because of its important place in contemporary research. Where the genetic approach relates events of childhood with data of adult personality the functional approach often investigates the relationship of facts at one point in time. Thus we may relate the socially standardized attitudes and behaviors toward American elder brothers to the socially standardized behaviors of representatives to senators in our House of Representatives, a hypothesis brought forward by Geoffrey Gorer (*1948a*).

The functional approach in culture and personality is part of the movement in anthropology which maintains that the biologically given characteristics of the human organism and the social-cultural phenomena in a given community are functionally interrelated and that tracing these interrelations is one of the tasks of anthropologists (Chapple and Coon, *1942*:vi, 4; Piddington, *1950*:14–15).

Margaret Mead (*1949b*) lists some of the areas and problems to which attention is paid in studying the functional relationships of personality. One may study the relationship between conceptions of family structure and conceptions of political structure. Or we may relate attitudes toward family and political authorities to the conception of the supernatural. In unpublished material Conrad Arensberg has urged looking for the congruence between personality patterns and social structure. The surface amiability and suppression of aggression of the Kaska and other northern forest Indians, he would say, is structurally congruent with the necessity of maintaining a minimal degree of coöperation between neighboring bands so that mutual assistance may be rendered if the game supply fails.

For a more detailed illustration of the functional point of view we may examine how the restrictive attitude toward children's sex behavior, found in some segments of American society, relates to other aspects of the culture of these same Americans. Jules Henry

(1949:92–93) maintains that such inhibition is one of the ways in which middle-class Americans emphasize the enormous difference between adult and children's roles. The limitation on sexual activity can be further understood as only one of the demands that the middle-class parent imposes on his child and takes its place alongside the family's demands for early participation in household chores, that the child be home earlier at night than a lower-class child, that he prepare for a profession, and so on. This body of responsibilities and restrictions imposed on middle-class children becomes associated with a disciplined middle-class personality.[2] Note that Henry does not say that sex restrictions *cause* a compulsive or disciplined character. He sees limitations on sex behavior to be part of a greater body of middle-class parental restrictions *all* of which are needed for the predicted end product to appear.

Dinko Tomasic (1948) offers another example of the functional interpretation of culture and personality data. Describing certain features of the modal personality of nineteenth-century Dinaric pastoralists, he connects the hostility and violence characteristic of that personality to the individualistic character of Dinaric social structure. The thoroughgoing individualism of the community, he points out, prevents the organization of a centralized political authority capable of curbing aggressive conduct. The absence of any superordinate body, in turn, demands that every man be ready to rely on physical force to maintain his rights. The Dinaric personality, one might say, is congruent with, and has survival value in, the atomistic community of which these people were a part. Other data are available to cast doubt on the expectation that political individualism will predictably be associated with hostility and violence. The Kaska Indians also comprise an atomistic community. But Kaska personality includes a profound antipathy to aggression or violence. Unlike the

---

[2] Compare this to Fromm's characterization of Western man as relatively well disciplined (above, p. 38). Note, however, that Commager sees Americans as uncompulsive and restive under too many rules. Both Commager and Henry appear to be equally reliable observers but while the latter, with a strong interest in psychiatry, talks about covert states, the former looks more on overt behavior.

Dinaric pastoralists, the Indian strongly espouses deference as a goal in human relations. Among the Yukon people individualism is accompanied by relatively little violence in day to day relations (Honigmann, *1949a*:264–271). The Eskimos, on the other hand, are said to reveal almost the same patterns as the Dinaric pastoralists. Here, too, one witnesses the association of political atomism with rewards accruing to the person who is renowned for his violence.

When instead of limiting functional connections to a particular community the anthropologist counts how many times a specific relationship of facts obtains in a series of different, scattered communities, then he is working to discover a scientific principle or law. To this topic we shall return.

THE PHYLOGENETIC APPROACH

A relatively few workers in the area of culture and personality pursue an approach which, because of its unique assumptions, is best not classified with either of the foregoing emphases. In general the phylogenetic point of departure has been used most energetically by some (but not all) psychoanalysts. The basic postulate is that culture, or at least parts of culture, are derived from innate tendencies that man has inherited out of the distant past. There is no belief that each generation reconstructs its culture afresh but rather that we grow up among cultural forms through which basic human instincts can be channeled. Kardiner (*1939*:16) defines the phylogenetic point of view saying that it takes the position that

. . . man is phylogenetically endowed with certain drives or "instincts" which press for satisfaction through objects in the outer world; that these "instincts," in the course of their ontogenesis, go through certain phylogentically predetermined and regularly repeated phases of development, at each of which an arrest of development may take place; and that, in some way as yet unknown, institutional systems [i.e., culture patterns] are derived from these "instincts." . . . The institutions [i.e., patterns] of a culture, from this point of view, are adventitious excrescences consequent upon certain drives seeking for expression, and hence quite meaningless as influences upon human nature.

The contrast is clear between this and the genetic point of view, which sees culture patterns as molding individual responses. The phylogenetic approach sees the pattern as "a by-product of biological force."

We may illustrate the phylogenetic viewpoint with incest rules, ideal patterns found in all communities, and corresponding rules of exogamy, which require an individual to marry outside of some group like the clan or sib. These rules, writers like Money-Kyrle (1939:49–56) maintain, are derived from incestuous impulses such as every child invariably experiences toward the oppositely sexed parent. The impulses are socially disallowed, punished, and repressed into unconsciousness. The repression may be more or less deep. Unlike the modern civilized adult, the "savage" can repress the impulse to only a slight degree. Troubled by the threatening breaking through of the disallowed and punishable wishes he goes around with an exaggerated horror of incest. The "large group of prohibited relatives" whom the "savage" is forbidden to marry (i.e., his sibmates) represent an overdevelopment of the incest rules, which, however, are to be found in some degree in all communities. Like the neurotic, says Money-Kyrle, the "savage" overcompensates for the temptation that he cannot overcome or repress deeply enough by avoiding all the women who symbolize mother or sister.

Several objections may be raised to this theory. The existence of any such innate instinctual impulses remains an unproven assumption. The notion that all people outside the orbits of civilization have widely ramifying incest taboos just is unwarranted. The allegation that people outside of civilized communities are unable to institute effective control over disallowed unconscious impulses—no matter whether innate or acquired—is gratuitous and not supported by facts.

The myths and folktales of a culture have also been freely derived from incestuous impulses, like the Oedipus complex which directs a boy toward his mother with consequent hatred and jealousy of the father. Again arguing that every person by virtue of being socialized represses these unpleasant childhood wishes, Money-Kyrle (26–44) points out that the unconscious material can be detected readily in dreams and in myths. Generally when the wishes appear in these productions they are disguised in order to make them palatable to conscious standards. Myths may allow the members of a community to project "the child's family romance . . . upon the gods of sky and earth." Every child who hates his father, the psychoanalyst reasons, probably also feels guilty for this sentiment. Unconsciously he entertains reparations fantasies and fears punishment, often through castration. These fantasies also appear in myths where crimes of parricide are punished, thus allowing the unconscious guilt feeling of the individual to be vicariously undone. Stories of Oedipus and Electra are cited by psychoanalysts to buttress their argument. Such "few examples are enough to prove that in general myths . . . are thinly disguised representations of certain fundamental types of unconscious fantasy well known to psycho-analysis." Most anthropologists remain unconvinced by such proof, especially where the original impulse is verified by nothing more than the myth which it is said to express. When myths do not clearly reveal incestuous wishes along with hostile sentiments directed toward the like-sexed parent, then these elements are sometimes forced into the tale by the phylogenetically minded psychoanalyst.

Is there independent evidence for a universal Oedipus complex—that is, of sexual wishes toward the oppositely-sexed parent with associated fear and hostility toward the like-sexed one? Kardiner (1939:481) says, the answer "must come from clincal evidence, and not from guessing." He believes that the literature contains records of modal personalities showing no evidence of incestuous leanings. The Trobriand Islanders are in this category. He associates the absence of the Oedipus complex to the many opportunities afforded the child to gratify sexual impulses. Malinowski, however, himself reported the Oedipus complex for the Trobriand people, a position amplified by psychoanalysts who read his reports. Dorothy Eggan (1953:286) supports Kardiner's position by maintaining that nothing in the facts suggests an Oedipus complex in Hopi personality. The sharing of many relatives in common, she maintains, contributes to a wide diffusion of affection; hence there is no intense concern with the parent of opposite sex. Others, reading the same evidence, do not agree with her conclusion. Obviously, then, much disagreement exists concerning the universality of the Oedipus complex, the resultant confusion being intensified when we find that different definitions of the phenomena are in use. Stagner (1937:269) defines the process like Eggan and, to some extent, Kardiner as a "focussing of the child's affections upon the opposite-sexed parent with a consequent increase in the rivalry toward the like-sexed parent for a monopoly on the affection of the favored one." One expects such behavior of a five- or six-year-old middle-class American child. If the Oedipus complex as defined is a socially engendered phenomenon then one can understand why Kardiner and Eggan might fail to discover what some psychoanalysts call an innate, instinctual tendency. Viewing the Oedipus complex as an innate, incestuous impulse, of course, demands its universality.[3]

Most workers in the field of culture and personality reject the phylogenetic approach. In the case of the Oedipus complex they believe that hostility toward the father may well show up in some groups and may indeed be accompanied by rivalry for the affection and attention of the mother. Such behavior they expect is derived from social conditions, for example, in the small family where a child's affectional satisfactions are tightly dependent on only two adults. These adults become very precious. Lack of attention from one arouses ready jealousy. Hostility is more likely to attach to the father because dependence, for a variety of reasons, is more intense on the mother. It is in her that the child sees his security and safety bound up. To this argument Róheim retorts that analysts like Kardiner use their theory in order to defend against recognition of the Oedipus complex in their own lives. They are blind to this force in themselves as well as in others, namely the people whom they

---

[3] From this argument we see why Róheim (1950:167, 191) assumes the primacy of the individual in culture while Kardiner and most other workers in culture and personality deny such primacy in favor of a more complex theory of interdependence between organism and environment.

study. They repress their Oedipus complex. Such a retort appears to be gratuitous. If intellectual differences are to be settled by psychoanalyzing one's opponents, then there is real danger that psychoanalytic terms will become labels for name calling. Name calling, of course, is no substitute for scientific and rigorous logic.

Suggestions for Further Reading

An overall view of culture and personality with a critical assessment of its position to date can be found in Klineberg's *Tensions Affecting International Understanding* (*1950*). Chapter 15 of Kroeber's *Anthropology* (*1948*) also is unusually comprehensive in this regard. A rather technical discussion of psychoanalytic influences in culture and personality is Hartmann, Kris, and Loewenstein, "Some Psychoanlytic Comments on 'Culture and Personality'" (*1951*). Kluckhohn has prepared a far more thorough examination of the relations between psychiatry and culture and personality study in "The Influence of Psychiatry on Anthropology in America During the Past One Hundred Years" (*1944a*).

The student might utilize existing sourcebooks of culture and personality to read some contrasting emphases in the field. In Haring (*1949*) compare Erikson's genetic account of "Childhood and Tradition in Two American Indian Tribes" to Belo's descriptive picture of "The Balinese Temper." Hallowell's paper on "The Social Functions of Anxiety in a Primitive Society" in the same source investigates the functional relationship of anxiety to social structure while Róheim, leading exponent of phylogenetic theory, states that position in "Psychoanalysis and Anthropology." Kluckhohn and Murray (*1953*), another sourcebook, contains Horton's carefully designed research into "The Functions of Alcohol in Primitive Societies."

Goldfrank, in "'Old Man' and the Father Image in Blood (Blackfoot) Society" (*1951*), interestingly attempts to relate changing mythological conceptions of the Old Man in an American Indian community to altered circumstances of cultural life and family relations. For further insight into the phylogenetic theory study Róheim's defensive "The Anthropological Evidence and the Oedipus Complex" (*1952*).

Lindesmith and Strauss have written one of the most perceptive, if largely negative, appraisals of the field in "Critique of Culture-Personality Writings" (*1950*).

Chapter 4

PURPOSES

Science means the pursuit of verifiable knowledge. The general purpose underlying research in culture and personality is to learn how group life affects individual behavior. Knowledge, however, seldom remains an end in itself. As the history of science makes clear, understanding furnishes the means of controlling those facts whose relationship we comprehend. A second purpose in pursuing the study of culture and personality is to apply our understanding in order to control the phenomena studied.

CULTURE AND PERSONALITY AS BASIC RESEARCH

We may distinguish between basic research, undertaken with the conscious goal of solving a scientifically defined problem irrespective of pragmatic concerns and applied research which aims to supply knowledge needed for the control of a practical problem. Scientists working in any field of discovery may be found specializing in either of these purposes.

The nature of scientific methods in culture and personality research will be developed in the following chapter. At this juncture we require some general notion of how science proceeds to gain knowledge. Our definition of the scientific process will suit the situation in which anthropologists generally find themselves when they study human behavior—unable to employ deliberate experimentation. In this respect most of the social sciences differ from disciplines like chemistry or physics but bear a close resemblance to the sciences of astronomy and geology. Our definition of science can actually cover procedures in any of these disciplines.

Science, Hypothesis, and Theory

Science consists essentially in searching for verifiable (or predictable) connections between facts. Each science, naturally, pays attention to certain classes of facts—anthropology to facts of socially standardized human behavior and the material products resulting from that behavior. The connections which anthropology makes between facts may be limited to a particular community, like the Kaska Indians. Thus we look for a relationship between the fact that Kaska mothers feed their infants generously and the fact that Kaska trappers and hunters tend to be basically optimistic.[1] A statement in its unproven form which joins two or more facts we term a hypothesis. Scientists aspire to universal connections that will hold most of the time in many communities. Only by ascertaining whether two facts, say a and b, tend to occur together in Kaska, Eskimo, Samoa, and other communities is it possible to predict that the occurrence a tends to be associated with the presence of b. Science cannot be satisfied with hypotheses limited to particular communities. The aim must be to discover statements that link facts which occur together in a number of communities. Once such statements are contrived proof is needed that these facts are really dependably related. Verification of a hypothesis lies in determining the degree of probability with which it can be predicted that given a, then b will also be encountered. This does not mean an inevitable coincidence between a and b but a likely concurrence between the phenomena in question. The laws of all science represent tendencies of association. Science never implies that conditions in the universe may not alter so as to upset the principles previously obtained. While particular connections made in

---

[1] At this point we choose not to emphasize that these two "facts" really constitute generalizations built up from many particular observations of human activity. Each such activity constitutes a primary fact.

a single community are a necessary foundation for the realization of universal principles, they cannot in themselves satisfy the aims of science.

In this book hypothesis denotes a tentative connection between two or more facts, a connection that has not yet been clearly verified but which is susceptible for verification. The term *principle* or *law* refers to a quite firmly established hypothesis, one that at the time of writing has been proven as true, i.e., very probable. The term *connection* will be used somewhat loosely to cover the meaning of both hypothesis and principle. *Theory* refers to particular laws and hypotheses as well as the accompanying body of logically ordered assumptions and concepts with which the scientist proceeds to do research. A theory, in other words, is the deductive apparatus with which we attend to facts of the material world. The theory underlying research in culture and personality comes from several realms of knowledge but particularly from psychology and psychiatry. Kardiner (1945:xvii) means this when he says that "an expert knowledge of psychodynamics" is necessary for anyone who would make contributions to the study of culture and personality. To deal with facts of personality in group situations the student must be familiar with already discovered laws, hypotheses, concepts, and assumptions concerning human behavior. For example, it is scarcely possible to understand current discussions of the influence of group membership on the individual without being aware of unconscious dynamics of action; nor can one comprehend the derivation of socially patterned behavior without knowledge of such processes as learning, conditioning, anxiety, and security. A considerable portion of the language with which we discuss facts of personality and culture comes from the psychological sciences—words like *personality, need,* and *defense mechanism.* Theories of group life and culture also support research in culture and personality and so the student who enters this peripheral field will also have to assimilate some of the ideas and concepts of sociologists, social psychologists, and anthropologists.

Neither all understanding nor all truth is scientific. Danger lies in unduly emphasizing the scientific understanding of human behavior if it overlooks the contribution of another kind of knowledge which may be called humanistic. The wide public appeal of such books as Mead's *Coming of Age in Samoa,* Fromm's *Escape from Freedom,* and Benedict's *Patterns of Culture* stems from a desire of many people to know, more or less inductively, something about the range and variety of human behavior. The literature of anthropology in general and of culture and personality in particular offers an opportunity to satisfy our curiosity and interest in man, his works, his malleability, and his talents. Anthropology has one foot planted in science and another in the humanities. In the one knowledge means the application of theory to derive testable hypotheses on a universal scale whose verification then remains in order. A student of the humanities, however, will be satisfied with the particularistic interpretations of Swazi, Naskapi, or Welsh village life. Ethnographic pictures of community action, thought, and feeling equal a kind of truth whose verification in the scientific sense is not essential. The humanities enrich the understanding of ourselves and nurture a respect for fellow men. There exists some danger that an increasingly scientific anthropology will neglect the continued cultivation of these values (Kroeber, *1935*).

CULTURE AND PERSONALITY AS APPLIED RESEARCH

Before talking about some of the prospects of an applied science of personality it may be well to recall what Conant (*1952:58*) thinks about the scientist's motivations. "For most scientists," he writes, "I think the justification of their work is to be found in the pure joy of its creativeness; the spirit which moves them is closely akin to the imaginative vision which inspires the artist." The scientist does not usually measure his success by material standards or the conquest of human problems. The present author has learned from his classes that this picture of scientific motivation distresses some students who are drawn into social science by the inspiration of helping to solve pressing social problems. Conant is, of course, talking primarily of physical scientists but quite possibly there are many workers engaged in social science whose values remain equally unconcerned with any eventual application of their discoveries.

Many social scientists explicitly state that they do not wish merely to pursue laws of social behavior. They prefer to find ways of applying those laws in order to realize particular social conditions. The goals to which knowledge of human behavior may be put vary from fighting a quicker or more efficient war, or creating a less hostile personality type, to furthering intercultural understanding. We shall examine some of the uses to which the growing knowledge of human behavior has already been put. First, however, it should be understood that scientific control cannot extend far beyond sound knowledge. Before human phenomena can be managed it is necessary to understand the facts and conditions that are responsible for those phenomena. Without a sound, basic understanding, attempts to control are wasteful and constitute tinkering which is as potentially dangerous as the surgery of an untrained medical aid. Our values as a democratic nation do not allow irresponsible tinkering with human lives. Hence social engineers must know what they are doing. They must be in the position to predict the relevant consequences of their attempts to interfere with the course of human behavior.

Anthropology in the Service of the Military

The Second World War saw a sudden burgeoning in the application of social science to human problems. Anthropologists and psychologists left academic halls to join government agencies where they received an opportunity to apply their skills to perfecting the great American military machine.[2] Some of the work which these scientists performed is in the field of culture and personality.

---

[2] After the war the movement led away from Washington and back to the campus. As somebody has written:
> Professors back from secret missions
> Resume their proper eruditions.
>   Though some regret it;
> They met some big wheels, and do not
> Let you forget it.

The development of that new military technique, psychological warfare, or "sykewar," is a case in point (Linebarger, *1948*; Lerner, *1949*). During World War II the problem of predicting how the enemy would react under given conditions suggested the wisdom of securing a firm knowledge of the enemy's character structure and established behavior patterns. Obtaining such knowledge in the traditional manner of anthropological field work—through firsthand contact—is more than difficult when war is in process. To meet this problem anthropologists developed methods of interviewing enemy nationals in the United States while at the same time studying novels; historical, economic, and political literature; and folklore for the insights these sources could provide into modal personality.[3] Clyde Kluckhohn (*1949a*:174–175) suggests that "the greatest services of the anthropologist were in preventing his colleagues from casting both enemies and allies in the American image, and in forever reminding intellectuals of the significance of the nonrational."

Kluckhohn illustrates the military role of anthropologists in the controversy that raged in Washington over the kind of propaganda treatment to be accorded the Japanese emperor. One official opinion urged that the United States attack the imperial pattern as the prop of a fascist state. The group urged that there be no silence on our part which might suggest tolerance of the monarchy after allied victory over Japan. Anthropologists in government service opposed this policy and urged another, the keystone of which held that "the solution of conflicts between the United States and other peoples can never rest on cultural imperialism that insists upon the substitution of our institutions for theirs." Anthropologists backed up their opinion by pointing out to policy makers that the emperor "was the nucleus of the Japanese sentiment system" and hence to attack that institution would be to intensify and to prolong the resistance of the enemy. This insight depended on a knowledge of Japanese modal personality whose acquisition led to the development of several new techniques of data collection.

---

[3] See for example Ruth Benedict, *1943a*, *1943b*.

Assessment of the value of sykewar to our military operations demands more research than has yet appeared. In a critical review Renzo Sereno (*1950*) points out that "this kind of warfare depends on the skill and ability of the syke warrior to understand the problems of the enemy or target people and their patterns of thought and action, and to affect them with all the means at his disposal. In other terms, it depends on detachment. . . . Other people's emotions become tools in their hands . . ." Sereno feels that few if any scientists can operate with so great a degree of detachment. He asserts that no analysis has ever been made to estimate the success of psychological warfare and suggests that sykewar helps political leaders to camouflage reality and to dodge responsibility: ". . . psychological warfare appears once more as a large-scale enterprise the purpose of which is to reassure those who sponsor and practice it."

Tailoring Human Nature

Any attempt to tailor modal personality in order to realize a particular personality type must admit the subjective nature of values. In other words, decision must first answer the question of what patterns of personality are desirable. A serious difficulty arising out of the subjectivity of values lies in the fact that some values are hard to demonstrate rationally to others.

Gillin (*1948a*), among other writers, has characterized Western man as insecure (Edman, *1951*). This insecurity derives from the fact that in the West three former props of self-confidence have been pulled out from under modern man. These are, first, a surrounding of kin whose behavior can be predicted and in whose circle the individual can expect succor if he is in trouble. Second, the prop of material wealth and symbols of wealth has lost its assurance. The depression taught men that there was no reliable security in material possessions. Religion furnished the third prop. "If one's relatives show no interest in one and if one's God has been exploded by indifference and skepticism, what does one have left?" Now, throughout his paper Gillin assumes that security is desirable in place of insecurity. On the basis of his assumption he suggests that psychological security can be reinstituted more firmly than ever by substituting "inner resources" for the displaced external props. This leads to the practical question of how may we train our children so that they will attain these internal resources? The question cannot be answered without a fuller knowledge of how personality is formed. Particularly needed are data from communities comprised of people whose emotional life is secure by virtue of the fact that they possess inner resources enabling them to remain at peace despite the ordinary vicissitudes of life. Anthropologists will have to study such communities to investigate how these inner resources are inculcated during the formative years of childhood. Gillin's program illustrates an answer to one kind of demand that the applied anthropologist is having thrust upon him. It does not answer whether psychological security attained by *any* mode of child training can withstand stresses of modern living like war, atomic bombs, and rapid culture change.

Weston LaBarre (*1949a*) also is much concerned with tailoring human nature. He specifies the psychological needs of modern man very explicitly. The world requires people who can accept and be tolerant of differences among human beings; who are not chronically frustrated and hence not vicious; who can question their beliefs; who can deal with reality confidently; and who are not committed to the blind emotional defense of fixed positions. It will readily be granted that the science of culture and personality is as far from able to fill LaBarre's prescription as it lacks the kind of knowledge that Gillin requires.

Does anthropology claim too much when writers discuss pressing contemporary problems? Perhaps we are a little rash in advertising the potentialities of a science that is still very young and undeveloped. Robert Endelman (*1949*) not too gently takes anthropologists to task for claiming more than their discipline can yet deliver. He accuses them of the perhaps easily pardonable sin of selling anthropology too fervently. It is fortifying, however, to hope that because of its comparative point of view, "Social anthropology is the science that is perhaps best calculated to disclose the qualities of the human material which we subject to the stresses and strains of our social engineering, to show the limits within which men can be moulded and to discover ways of life that permit the individual the fullest self-expression and cause him the least frustrations" (Krige, 1948:19).

The most overwhelming difficulty facing social engineers ambitious to tailor human nature lies in the vast number of factors that enter into the formation of adult personality. We are able to isolate, and predict for, only a few of these variables. Many more conditions, ranging from the geographical habitat to the pressure of threats from enemies outside the group, which are all probably associated with personality, remain practically untouched by social scientists.

A concrete, if purely illustrative, example may clarify the problem. Although evidence from a series of cultures enables us to predict that rejection of the child is accompanied by anxiety and hostility in the maturing individual, it does not follow that eliminating the pattern of rejection (if that could be done so simply) will get rid of the hostility component in personality. Both these correlated facts—rejection on the one hand and the hostility-anxiety syndrome on the other—may be influenced by a third determinant, say economic uncertainty. In such an economically marginal community, women by being forced to produce food or other forms of wealth, or through their employment in agriculture or industry, cannot freely attend to their maternal role. The conflict between roles leads women to treat their children as though the latter were responsible for the dilemma in which women find themselves. Removing the element of rejection in such a situation merely eradicates one of the channels through which the mother's emotions convey themselves to the child. Other and hitherto unused channels may replace the one that has been excised. Obviously, attention must be devoted to altering the economic patterns of the hypothetical community so that women may quit production. Economic conditions, in turn, are determined by many conditions. Of course, it is likely that modification of any aspect in a social situation will lead to change in others. The difficulty, we suggest, lies in being able to create precisely that change toward which our efforts are aimed.

Childhood and motivation do not exhaust the determinants of

personality, even though social scientists often talk as though these factors are sufficient to manipulate. Multiple determinism makes clear that if any aspect of personality develops out of a plural number of determinants then it will be difficult to predict the result of altering only one of those determinants, say child training, while leaving the others unaffected. Gorer realizes this clearly when he points out that a change in socialization methods does not promise that the modal personality will also change[4] (Gorer and Rickman, 1950:129). All of which is to say that culture and personality as a science will contribute only in a limited way to the control of human behavior. Realistic social engineering requires the concerted action of many social and even some of the physical sciences.

Illuminating Intercultural Relations

Objective study of the modal personality of a foreign nation may facilitate communication with, and promote understanding of, that community. Many of the habits of a group, ranging from gestures to literary and other forms of creation, are constantly in danger of misinterpretation by neighbors who have been reared in a different way of life. Laura Thompson (*1951a*) points out the danger inherent in the erroneous assumption of administrators, teachers, and social workers "that members of other groups perceive the world as they do." She illustrates how three Indian tribes of the United States, the Papago, Navaho, and Hopi, perceive the world differently and in a manner related to the character structure and other aspects of culture.

During World War II, Margaret Mead (*1947a, 1948a*) undertook to interpret British personality for Americans at the same time that she tried to remove some British misunderstandings of Americans. She wanted to reach the members of the American armed forces

---

[4] Gorer thus stands with Goldman (*1950:153*) opposed to the notion that the pattern of cultural development is, in the latter's words, "decisively shaped by influences acting upon individuals during their first years of life," or that "efforts to change the course of history by alterations in social, political, and economic institutions will be of minor importance as compared to what could be accomplished by modifying specific child-rearing practices."

stationed in England among whom British girls had acquired a reputation of being without morals. Mead explained that the English girl is not brought up like the American girl, trained to look after herself. The American boy knows that girls expect him to make advances but is not surprised that the girl repulses him whenever his advances "are inappropriate to the state of feeling between the pair." In Britain a different relationship links the sexes. A girl is reared to depend on a slight barrier of frostiness to keep boys at a respectable distance. English boys do not make passes regularly with the expectation of being just as regularly repulsed. Confronted by American male brashness, some British girls grow even chillier; they earned Britons the reputation of being very cold people. Others responded to the first Yank wisecrack "with impassioned surrender" that disconcerted the Americans. Still other girls brought the boys home as future sons-in-law, much to the annoyance of the Americans who didn't realize what was happening.

During the war Britons perceived Americans as rather indefatigable boasters. In their turn Americans saw the British as arrogant. Both attitudes, says Mead, derive from divergent family contexts in the two nations. At the American breakfast table junior learns he must keep his parents interested in his skills and successes. To be heard, father has to compete with his son by relating a bigger story than the latter. In Britain, the father stands as a model for the son's future behavior. When he speaks the family listens. He acts as though he were certain of his strength and position; therefore he underplays these attributes, speaking with a slight hesitation that never hides his cool assurance. In the American instance, the family situation encourages overstatement; in Britain, understatement. In each case the respective habits are learned in childhood and each nation's style of behavior is misunderstood and resented by the other community.

Margaret Mead discusses next American confusion promoted by the British readiness to compromise. Each nation interprets compromise behavior differently: ". . . the British, speaking from strength, from the paternal position, do not identify government negotiations as made from a minority position. The government acts from strength, and, being strong, can *include* some of the minority demands in any proposal. To compromise is the act of the strong and the entrenched, an act of graciousness, expediency, and a recognition that the heresies of today become the orthodoxies of tomorrow." Americans remain constantly on the defensive against the government, feeling that everyone is weak compared to the government. We think of compromise as a bad solution in which everybody loses. Americans emphasize losses in compromise without perceiving any gains. Closely related to the American feeling of being weak is the fear of being exploited, of being played for a sucker. "This is . . . deeply seated and has been . . . heavily exploited in discussions of our relationship to other countries, both those who are believed to outwit us in the diplomatic game and those who ask us for help."

Margaret Mead does two things when she clarifies British and American modal personalities to each other. First, she describes affect-revealing behavior using objective language in place of value-laden terms like "boasting" or "arrogance." Second, she tries to indicate the determinants from which the respective behaviors spring. Understanding another nation's customary modes of behavior may, as Leighton (1949:102) points out, enable us more accurately to distinguish between the behavior that it is possible for that country to adopt and, on the other hand, behavior which we might want that country to adopt "but which is impossible given its situation and particular cultural patterns." Such knowledge obviously possesses value for prediction and contributes to our skills in managing human relationships.

Recent study of Russian modal personality reveals the complexity that Americans must manage if we are to manage with skill our relations with that nation (Mead, *1951c,* chap. 3). Russian personality is an amalgamation of many elements; first, those which marked pre-Soviet traditional behavior and, second, the ideals of Bolshevik behavior. The traditional Russian personality contains (1) a tendency for thought and action to be interchangeable so that little distinction exists between the desire to murder and the murder itself;

(2) a need for certain kinds of control which are seen as emanating from outside the individual and which are regarded as necessary lest the individual revert to an original impulsive, uncontrolled state; (3) relative underdevelopment of self-control, measurement, and calculation; (4) slight "capacity to plan, work for, and execute a long series of steps toward a goal"; (5) great capacity to endure adverse conditions; (6) the assumption that both good and evil coexist in all individuals—friends can behave like enemies; (7) slight interest in man's responsibility for particular acts; (8) a diffuse sense of sinfulness in which all men share—all men are guilty in some degree of all human crimes; (9) intolerance of any ambiguity in relations between superiors and subordinates; and (10) a high evaluation of rest and relaxation.

Bolshevik "ideal personality" constitutes a deliberate or planned effort to counteract certain elements in traditional Russian personality standing in the way of the establishment of Bolshevism. It also represents an attempt to introduce or accentuate admired tendencies in Western civilization. The Bolshevik ideal personality includes (1) goal orientation of the individual so that all acts are seen as instrumental to reaching the final goal which is the triumph of communism; (2) a strong, internal conscience capable of guiding the individual without external stimulation; (3) purposeful, measured, and calculated behavior appropriate to the desired goal; and (4) a distrust of rest and relaxation except as means toward more effective work. Actual contemporary Soviet personality, in terms of which our foreign relations may be ordered, represents a compromise between the traditional behavior and the Bolshevik ideal.

One of the most dramatic contrasts between American and Soviet behavior involves relative notions of integrity. Americans regard consistency and sincerity as essential to integrity which we hold as a supreme value (Mead, 1951c:38). Out of this value orientation arises American condemnation of Soviet behavior in response to changes in the party line. Our values provoke us to stamp the Russians as insincere, cynical, and without integrity. Such attitudes fail to realize that "from the Bolshevik point of view the essential virtue consists in being so goal-oriented . . . that no contradiction can arise between changes in the Line and the individual behavior." In the Bolshevik system of morals "all acts commanded by the party are ethical because of the long-term ethical goal of the good society." Americans on the contrary hold that personal integrity must never be compromised to external demands. A realistic American foreign policy will be guided by such insights (Mead, *1951b*; Northrop, *1953*:296–309).

Culture and personality also illuminates the dynamics of our own behavior and how that behavior strikes a foreign community (Leighton, *1949*:105):

> False images of ourselves as a nation produce barriers to understanding our position in relation to oℓ ᵣr nations and the consequences, particularly the indirect consequences, of our acts. Thus, we may think we are being cooperative when actually we appear weak. Or, on the other hand, what seems to us a demonstration of reasonable firmness may strike another country as an overt act of hostility requiring immediate retaliation. What we suppose is a generous effort to give support may be angrily treated as an attempt at exploitation. We are confident that we will never, without provocation, attack any nation with atomic bombs and so we discount the threat element in our possession of the weapon, while other nations with a different view of us never forget it.

Problems in Intercultural Education

What can we hope to accomplish by substituting rational interpretations of behavior for blind prejudice and misunderstanding in intercultural relations? Our knowledge of opinion formation and attitudinal change suggests that successful education depends largely on the circumstances under which information is transmitted. It has been demonstrated that requesting a group to change its attitudes is a relatively less effective means of implementing change than allowing the group to reach its own decisions on the basis of new information (Lewin, *1943*; Cussler and DeGive, *1952*:87). This suggests that the comparative study of modal personality and simply publishing the results of field research in exotic cultures will accomplish little unless they are followed by carefully designed educational situations. Insights into extra-cultural behavior may be difficult to disseminate when language and personality factors limit the opportunities of reaching foreign subjects. For example, the personality of the Arapaho Indian promises to be a formidable barrier in education. Yet, his misunderstanding of white intentions makes him a suitable target for such an attempt. Elkin (*1940:247*) points out that because the Arapaho "lack the flexibility and freedom of behavior demanded by our society, they are baffled and discouraged in their dealings outside their own community." These Indians see whites as too outspoken and aggressive. In contrast to the Arapaho's shyness and reserve this is a fair description of how white American behavior must strike him. The Arapaho themselves say that "they are given to feeling 'shame' in direct social intercourse. When they speak they never look at one another, but gaze at the ground or off at a distance. Dark glasses, serving the same psychological purpose, are worn prevalently even indoors. When they visit or meet one another they show no overt sign of heightened interest." An anthropologist would be hard taxed to introduce an objective interpretation of American white personality among these people.

The writer's study into the effectiveness of the communication of American ideas to rural Pakistanis through the medium of informational films leads to some pertinent conclusions. Such moving pictures are distributed by the United States Department of State throughout a large part of the world. The films try to advise illiterate foreign audiences about life in this country, about more successful ways of avoiding illness or of practicing agriculture, and, finally, about the menace of Soviet Russian foreign policy. Experience in Pakistan provides convincing evidence that we have scarcely learned to communicate such messages effectively across cultural boundaries. A successful program of cross-cultural communication will require specialists in international education who will combine the skills of education, cultural analysis, and psychology. Such persons are not yet available and must first be trained. Any program of promoting intercultural understanding must be both long and costly. In addition it will test to the utmost our developing social skills.

Suggestions for Further Reading

This chapter has been mainly concerned with the possibilities and difficulties in applying the evolving knowledge of socially standardized behavior in order to solve pressing social problems. Added cautions to be exercised in human engineering are given attention in the "Code of Ethics of the Society for Applied Anthropology" (*1951*). For an elaboration of the distinction between pure and applied research see Goode and Hatt, *Methods in Social Research* (*1952*), pages 29–40. The hopes of a practical social science are exhaustively treated by Stuart Chase in *The Proper Study of Mankind* (*1948*). Clyde Kluckhohn's "Covert Culture and Administrative Problems" (*1943*) not only contains material useful to the practitioner anxious to apply social scientific skills but also constitutes an important methodological study into levels of behavior. Work leading toward the understanding of contemporary world cultures that is now being carried on is described in Mead's "Research in Contemporary Cultures" (*1951b*). Embree has produced a fine study of problems faced in trying to implement intercultural understanding in "American Military Government" (*1949*). For an appreciation of how durable national values and moral ideas have guided our foreign policy see Tannenbaum's "The American Tradition in Foreign Relations" (*1951*).

The student should understand that a course on culture and personality can be applied to enable him better to understand his own values and the complex sources from which his socially standardized behavior springs. This aim has been consciously implemented by some teachers. See, for example, Riesman, "Some Problems of a Course in 'Culture and Personality' " (*1951*).

PART TWO

METHOD AND TECHNIQUES

Let us therefore mention this fact, For it seems to us worthy of record.

EZRA POUND

Chapter 5

FACTS AND PATTERNS

Having mapped the scope of culture and personality we turn to how such research is conducted. Our intention is to give, first, a general view of scientific observation and generalization and then to examine actual techniques of data collection, interpretation, and verification. Scientific truth represents only one variety of truth but is the kind of knowledge with which readers of this book are expected to be most concerned.

Concerning science itself it is useful to adopt the basic notion that science consists in the search for verifiable connections between facts. A fact, in turn, refers to any material characteristic of reality, like size, weight, color, movement, or sound (Wilson and Wilson, 1945:61–73). However, there is danger that this simple definition will lead us to overlook the extent to which science is an ideational process. Dampier's definition[1] pictures science as "Ordered knowledge of natural phenomena and the rational study of the relations between concepts in which those phenomena are expressed."

The generalizing process of science involves certain related steps that lead toward understanding and prediction as they at first remove and then return the researcher to his concrete data. Initially the researcher is motivated by a problem or an interest out of which he proceeds to observe concrete phenomena. What he looks for is specified by the problem which guides him. Having collected the data

---

[1] Cited in Freedman, 1950:13.

they must be classified, the facts must be named and pigeonholed. Conceptualization, the third step in the method of science, usually proceeds very closely with the actual observing process. Now come the first fumbling attempts at interpretation or hypothesis formation. The research worker joins together facts in relationships which he hopes are predictable but often with very little awareness of how he is going to test his formulations. Verification, nevertheless, is required. To bear the name, at some point every science must mature to where verification enters as the final step in the process of understanding natural phenomena. Successful verification of his hypotheses rewards the scientist with valid laws or principles.

In terms of this paradigm of science, adapted from Northrop (*1949*), it is of interest to inquire if culture and personality has passed through all the steps and can therefore be called a mature science. Like anthropology in general, culture and personality appears to be entering the interpretative stage of science. It has relatively rapidly outgrown the level of fact collecting and for some time workers in this field have been offering a great number of stimulating hypotheses which relate facts of human behavior. Very little work has been done to test the bulk of these connections and the question of verification remains very difficult.

The model of scientific procedure given above should help the student see how the scientist divides his time between the observation of data and manipulating data in his mind. The familiar images of the chemist surrounded by retorts and test tubes or of the anthropologist working in some native village fail to show the speculative role of the scientist in which he is concerned with manipulating words or concepts. Conant (*1952:54*) even ventures "to define science as a series of interconnected concepts and conceptual schemes arising from experiment and observation and fruitful of further experiments and observations."

LABORATORY AND CLINICAL SCIENCE

Two relatively different approaches dealing with human behavior may be distinguished, that of the laboratory and the clinic. What is

called "laboratory science" studies behavior in a closely limited setting which has as its chief object to keep conditions uniform and
controlled. Clinical science does not try to experiment under carefully
controlled conditions but attends to total and complex situations that
occur in life or are seen during visits of patients to medical and psychiatric clinics. Some sciences successfully move problems from the
clinic to the laboratory, so that Mayo (*1945:18–19*) says: "Science
begins in the clinic and is effectively developed in the laboratory.
In the clinic one uses relatively simple logics to examine complicated
facts; in the laboratory clinically developed skill has suggested the
isolation of certain aspects of the complex fact for separate study
. . . the one method informs and develops the other." Culture and
personality remains exclusively clinical in its approach. Several of its
antecedents, including social anthropology and psychiatry, also represent clinical sciences. One of the collaborative fields, psychology, has
made great strides in developing the laboratory approach for studying
data of human behavior. At any rate, little has been done to carry
culture and personality research from the field or clinic into the
laboratory for closer analysis. It is not impossible to study small
models of community life under carefully controlled conditions. The
feasibility of such a procedure has been demonstrated by the experiments of Kurt Lewin and his group at Iowa State University (Lewin,
Lippitt, and White, *1939*). The laboratory approach allows the
scientist to be much more precise in stating and verifying hypotheses.
From this we can understand better the notable lack of accuracy in
predictions of culture and personality as well as of other social sciences. As students sometimes complain, there are so many exceptions
to the so-called laws of social science! The greater accuracy found in
the laboratory is, of course, related to the fact that the carefully controlled situation found there excludes many complicating features of
"real" life from observation. Pavlov's dogs were trained to salivate
to the sound of a bell under conditions that almost completely protected the animals from any danger of distraction. The circumscribed
conditions of the laboratory, however, also limit the researcher in
what he can predict about the behavior of his subjects under natural

conditions where many stimuli are simultaneously operative and where experimental conditions are not approximated.

Despite the advantages of controlled experimentation dissatisfaction with the limits of the laboratory is sometimes expressed. Maslow (*1946*) points out that clinical workers usually produce more hypotheses than laboratory workers and points to this relationship as holding true for personality studies compared to other branches of psychology. More sharp is the following criticism (Office of Strategic Services, 1948:466): "The main body of psychology started its career by putting the wrong foot forward and it has been out of step with the march of science much of the time since. Instead of beginning with studies of the whole person adjusting to the natural social environment, it began with studies of a segment of a person responding to a physical stimulus in an unnatural laboratory environment. Consequently, after a century of diligent application, psychologists still lack sufficient ordered knowledge of everyday social behavior."

Culture and personality as a clinical science parallels psychiatry in relying for data on observations of living persons and including the observer in the observations taking place. As Mead (*1952a*) points out, no document or questionnaire is allowed to take the place of living behavior for the anthropologist. His own person is the delicate recording instrument with which he experiences life in an alien community. The neglect of the interview schedule is at least partly related to the importance which the anthropologist attaches to experiencing actual rather than "talked about" behavior in the community which he is studying. Claparède writes that the clinical method "is also an art, the art of questioning" that "aims at capturing what is hidden behind the immediate appearance of things. It analyses down to its ultimate constituents the least little remark made" (Piaget, 1952:xiv).

FACTS AND PATTERNS

Observation that underlies culture and personality research is concerned with aspects of socially standardized action, thought, and feeling. The investigator directs his attention to (1) nonverbal, socially patterned motor behavior, like walking, kissing, or dying; (2) verbal behavior, because spoken words constitute an important class of facts; and (3) material results of, and aids to, behavior, including embroidered designs, tools, films, and printed paper. Observation may be made on these facts by the scientist himself or by somebody whose evidence the researcher deems trustworthy; for example, a native assistant. Hallowell utilizes observations about Ojibwa Indians made by seventeenth-century travelers, traders, and missionaries.[2]

Technique of Observation

Observation has been described as a process that tries to preserve events "as though they were immediate data of observation" (Nadel, 1951:20). That is to say, the anthropologist does not merely look at behavior but makes records of what he sees. He tries to preserve his data in a form as closely as possible identical to the form in which they were originally seen. There is no question then about a notebook and pencil being essential instruments for field work! Yet, largely because notebook data are difficult to separate and sort, anthropologists rarely leave their notes in the form in which they were originally made. Normally the field worker transfers his observations from notebook to slips, an occupation demanding many hours of daily toil that is best left for a time of the day when opportunities for observation are limited. (It scarcely exaggerates to say that field work means a twenty-four-hour-a-day job!)

Each slip (or note) will usually contain only one relatively specific item as may be seen from the illustrations below. The reader will observe that provision is made on each slip for the date when, and the community from which, the item comes. It is also a good idea to indicate in the upper right-hand corner of the note whether contents represent information secured by observation, from a living informant (in which case his name would be given), or from a printed source (in which case the title will be placed on the slip). It is extraordinarily easy to become confused about whether an incident contained

---

[2] See below, p. 150.

in field notes actually happened or was spoken about by a friendly informant.

Here are two examples of actual field notes collected by the author:

8:4:50   Gr. Whale Eskimo   Observation

In the middle of unloading the boat Simon Tukaluk seized a moment to rest. He sat on the lumber piled near the wharf. As he sat there he was playfully pulled by the collar by another Eskimo youth who was in the act of working.

8:4:50   Gr. Whale Eskimo   Observation

Sara fretting and clinging to mother's knees in the tent as the mother looked for something. Then mother sat down and nursed Sara briefly. Put Sara's hat on. Sara fretted again and mother told her of the boat that was down by the wharf. She also offered the breast again, briefly. Then she picked Sara up and carried her outside the tent. She returned shortly for her shawl, Sara following, wailing loudly. She packed Sara in the shawl and hoisted the child on her back. All this time Sara's sister, Rhoda, remained in the tent playing by herself.

Two bodily senses primarily operate in making anthropological observations—sight and hearing. The social sciences make little use of smell, taste, and touch as sources of data. While the natural sciences use instruments to amplify the senses in order to locate objects in space or in order to manipulate phenomena, culture and personality research employs few or no instruments in this sense. The camera, however, serves as a useful means of recording significant behavior and very likely the use of other recording devices will increase as adjuncts to observation (Rowe, *1953*).

Whether equipped with a prominent motion picture camera or inconspicuous pocket notebook, the observer must always keep in mind that his presence in the research situation probably exercises a modifying influence upon the behavior he is studying (Freedman, *1950*:108). A social scientist may not be able to control this influence but he must at least remain aware of his impact on the group so that he may be in a position to account for modifications in behavior induced by his presence. Most of the time, of course, the researcher will behave so as to reduce the effects of his presence or will encourage the group to become habituated to his nonthreatening existence.

Check lists, questionnaires, and observation guides serve to assist in observation and help insure that pertinent areas of social life will not be overlooked.[3] John W. M. Whiting has prepared but not yet published "Socialization Scales" designed to assist an interviewer to measure a mother's responses to her child. For example, with regard to nurturance, the scale reminds the investigator to note if nurturance during infancy is of the character in which the mother shows high enjoyment of nursing and caring for the infant; always holds the child when feeding him, or always holds and walks with the child when he is upset, etc. Presence of these signs warrant a high nurturance rating. At the opposite extreme is the mother who dislikes nursing and caring for her infant; props the bottle up when feeding; dislikes and tries to avoid bodily contact with the infant, and uses techniques other than feeding and care when the child is upset. Other situations specified as useful for studying nurturance include bedtime (mother reads, sings, talks to the child at bedtime; snuggles and kisses him); when mother is busy (mother arranges work so as to be near child; always stops what she is doing to praise, answer, or give attention to the child); when child is sick, upset, or injured and the agent of distress is somebody other than the mother (mother always comforts, reassures, and stays with child as long as he wants when he is sick, upset, or injured). A similar scale is provided to study frustration of the child and directs attention to parents' concern about neatness, cleanliness, danger, health, eating, and toilet training. Still other scales will help the field worker attend to the amplitude, frequency, and duration of punishment and specify types of punishment (like denial of love, denial of privileges and rewards, and physical punishment).

From Facts to Patterns

Observed facts may be described on two levels of specificity. The initial results of observation, contained in notebook or on slips, are

---

[3] See, for example, Ackerknecht, *1945*; Murdock, *et al.*, *1950*; Saslow and Chapple, *1945*; Simmons, *1945*. Many other guides have been prepared for specific purposes and remain unpublished.

usually particular. That is, the researcher observes Johnny hitting Peter, who is a younger sibling. By grouping or generalizing such facts of individual behavior (i.e., particular facts) patterns, or regularities, are derived. Patterns, it is well to remember, do not exist in nature but are constructed by the observer out of a series of similar events and are at least one step removed from data (Weakland, *1950, 1951*). Any pattern constitutes a generalization which the scientist makes because he believes that it is warranted by the number of cases he observed. Thus, from observations similar to the one made of Johnny hitting Peter, the pattern is established that elder siblings (sometimes, frequently, nearly all the time) behave aggressively to younger siblings. Further facts may help to refine this generalization, for example, by allowing the conditions under which aggressive acts make their appearance.

Pattern generalizations, like culture itself, constitute predictive statements. Clyde Kluckhohn (*1941:111*) points out that "awareness of a 'pattern' (often subliminal) . . . sometimes enables the field worker to 'know' how his natives will react to a set of circumstances before he observes the reaction. Familiarity with the Navaho 'pattern' of generalized economic reciprocity between clansmen justifies my anticipation that, if a Navaho journeys into a portion of the Navaho Reservation which he has not visited before and where he has no acquaintances, he will seek out a hogan belonging to someone in his (or occasionally his father's) clan and there obtain lodging and food. Observation shows that this is factually the course of action followed in 13 cases out of 15."

Although patterns enable prediction, culture like its constituent patterns is not rigidly stable. Patterns alter when the conditions to which they are related change. Thus, the disappearance of the horse as a means of transportation in many parts of America has been associated with the loss of equestrian patterns, corraling, and others. Culture is dynamic, it always is changing in some degree. Hence the patterns out of which culture is largely comprised are also being modified all the time. The fact of modification, which may be progressive through time, somewhat limits the predictive value of patterns and makes them of less scientific value than dependable hypotheses that have been cross culturally tested.

Although the emphasis has been on the derivation of patterns from discrete incidents or observations, obviously there are cases where the field worker obtains ready made patterns from informants. That is to say, a parent may inform the researcher that in the particular community elder siblings frequently attack younger siblings. Similar statements from a sufficient number of other informants will verify the pattern. Pattern generalizations may also be derived from printed sources. For example, when an authoritative Pakistani newspaper quotes public officials complaining against corruption, graft, and bribery in the government bureaucracy we are at liberty to infer a pattern of corruption for that country. Verification of the ready-made pattern may then come from the reporting of specific individuals who make the headlines when they are prosecuted for having taken bribes. This, however, is not the place to discuss verification in detail.

All of the examples of pattern generalization given so far have been qualitative. Quantitative patterns represent a more precise type of generalization. They are illustrated by Davis and Havighurst (1953:312–313) who report that 54 percent of white middle class, 17 percent of white lower class, 29 percent of Negro middle class, and 15 percent of Negro lower class children are reported by parents to have masturbated. Those authors generalize these patterns somewhat when they sum up saying "Three times as many white middle-class as compared with lower-class children are reported as masturbating. Twice as many Negro middle-class children as compared with Negro lower-class children . . ."

For present purposes it is most important to be clear about the difference between particular facts on the one hand and patterns on the other. Unfortunately there is no easy answer to the question of how many particular facts are required before a pattern may be generalized. Certainly the series of cases might be as large as possible but this merely begs the question and we are left with the problem: what is "as large as possible"? The time available for research in a practical way limits the number of cases that one can hope to collect. Type of action must also be considered. There are instances about which a pattern may be relatively quickly established and repeated observation then amounts to a waste of the ethnographer's time. For example, a couple of days in an Eskimo village in summer may suggest the pattern that among these people the sexes play ball together. Once we have constructed such readily ascertainable patterns, time may be devoted to discovering the circumstances which modify the pattern. Once having hit upon a regularity the field worker will keep watch for exceptions to the pattern and note these explicitly. "It means that in order to say that a necktie is a part of conventional male attire in the United States the anthropologist does not count men in neckties, but having once observed the regular appearance of the necktie, he does notice carefully when, by whom, and under what circumstances neckties are not worn, jokes about neckties, suicides with neckties, girls who wear neckties, at what age little boys wear neckties, who can go without neckties, etc." (Mead 1949f:453–454).

Alternative Patterns

The pattern, although always derived from overt action, designates a standardized bit of overt or covert behavior. Obviously an act can be carried out, an idea formulated, an artifact manufactured in a number of different ways. Yet in any community there will usually be one or a relatively few standardized modes of behavior (Sapir, 1927:136). On the other hand, every individual executes a particular pattern in a more or less individualized fashion. These personal variations, however, interest primarily students of individual, rather than group, behavior.

As already pointed out, patterns need not be universal in a particular community; that is, they need not be part of the behavior of every person. A pattern may be restricted to a discrete segment of the population or may represent one out of a number of possible modes of doing a task. David Levy (1948) describes the German family as dominated by a father who uses corporal punishment in the discipline of his children. The child holds the father in awe and the two do not converse freely. Furthermore, the German family reveals a pattern by which, stated negatively, the mother "does not display affection for her child in the form of kissing or embracing past early childhood." Now, there are alternatives for all of these patterns. Some fathers *do* talk freely to children and neglect corporal punishment. This may be designated as a minor subpattern in German culture. Some mothers manifest demonstrable affection toward children. That is another option. Such alternatives may be related to significant structural features of the community. For example, Levy found that a group of anti-Nazi males who had, and rejected, a chance of affiliating with the Nazi party had also not been socialized in the typical German fashion. They missed being brought up by strong fathers and undemonstrative mothers! ". . . it appears clear that as a group the anti-Nazis, in comparison with typical Germans, have escaped the conventional and rigid family structure. They have been brought up with more affection and less restraint. Their world is a broader one, less limited in terms of religious, social, and intellectual boundaries."

Covert Patterns

Let us be clear about the process that is involved in constructing covert personality or culture patterns. Patterns of overt behavior cover only immediately apprehended events. Covert patterns, on the other hand, refer to unseen events that are inferred from immediately apprehended actions. Often this is done after the latter have already been generalized into a pattern. Clarity about this process is essential for understanding how to verify the existence of covert patterns, a problem to be taken up later. Even when an informant tells the field worker about his regular feelings or aspirations, and the latter accepts the statements as evidence of a particular covert state pattern, the process of moving from the immediately apprehended to the theoretically postulated must take place.

The method of covert pattern derivation may be illustrated briefly by referring once more to the Kaska Indians, with whom we introduced this book. A pattern which we observed while living with several Indian families during the winter of 1945 was of men delaying their return to the trap line. We inferred from their wavering tactics a motivational state of procrastination. Then we went further. The question we asked ourselves, in effect, was: "What does delaying their departure to the bush achieve for these men?" In answering this question another covert pattern, in addition to procrastination, came to be postulated. We inferred that delaying the return to the trap line results in a sense of relief from an arduous and unpleasant necessity—having to go into the cold unpredictable forest to make an uncertain living. If this unpleasant necessity could be postponed then the men felt pleasure. However if they delayed too long then still other covert phenomena would arise to undermine the feeling of well-being.

Kluckhohn (1941:125) prefers the word "configuration" instead of covert pattern. He offers another illustration of the process by which such descriptive generalizations are developed.

Unacculturated Navaho are uniformly careful to hide their faces and to see to it that no other person obtains possession of their hair, nails, sputum, or any other bodily part or product. They are likewise characteristically secretive about their personal names. All three of these patterns (as well as many others which might be mentioned) are manifestations of an abstracted *configuration* which may be intellectualized as "fear of the malevolent intentions of other persons." Only most exceptionally would a Navaho make this abstract generalization.

Propositions Concerning "Typicality"

Nathan Leites (1948:111–113) warns that the technical sense in which patterns are employed in anthropology may be misunderstood by some readers. The following propositions advanced by him concerning "typicality" deserve careful study.

1. When a pattern generalization implies or states explicitly that a certain behavior is typical in a certain culture at a certain time, it does not imply or deny that the behavior is equally typical at other times.

2. When it is asserted that a certain behavior is typical in a given culture at a certain time (e.g., American culture) there is no implication that it is equally frequent or emphasized in all subdivisions of this culture.

3. When it is asserted that certain behaviors are typical in a certain culture, it is not denied that certain subdivisions of this culture may show substantial similarities with corresponding subgroups in other cultures. Thus there may be international class-linked patterns that are shared by upper or lower classes all over the world.

4. When it is asserted that a certain behavior is typical in a certain culture there is no implication that there is no other culture in which it is, at the same or some other time, equally typical. Caudill (1952: 65–68) demonstrates that despite extensive cultural differences between communities there may be continuity of values and adaptive mechanisms. He found this to be the case between the Nisei and Chicago white middle-class communities.

The importance of pattern generalization scarcely needs elaboration. Culture and personality finds little significance in discrete behaviors and like anthropology deals primarily with regularities of behavior common to most members of a social group.

Levels of Generality in Patterns

A little experience with pattern generalization soon indicates that a pattern may reach more or less comprehensive levels of specificity. Some formulations remain closer to the level of the concrete fact than others. The high point in abstraction comes when practically an entire culture is expressed in a single pattern, as in *Patterns of Culture* by Ruth Benedict (1946b:42 ff.). As a practical exercise in constructing such superpatterns let us consider the following relatively specific overt and covert northern Chinese behavior patterns:

1. Girls and women are excluded from certain family rituals, notably the feast of the ancestors on New Year's Day.
2. Ideally a man is believed to be superior to a woman.
3. The birth of a girl baby is regarded as unfortunate. She will be a "burden on the family" because, said an informant, "The family has

to bring up the girl till she reaches the age of marriage. Then she will not be good anymore to the family. The boys are much more useful."
4. Social intercourse between the sexes is accompanied by some tension or embarrassment.
5. Sexual intercourse outside of marriage is regarded as indecent and wrong.[4]

Our object now is to generalize from these five relatively specific patterns. Let us focus on the emotional emphasis of each to see if they can be summed up in any single, general ethological pattern. What common emotional note runs through these five generalizations? Undoubtedly particular readers will express the linkage in different terms and obviously a ready phrase does not quickly come to mind. Students in one of the writer's classes have suggested "ambivalence" as a label for this overall pattern. Putting this in other words, it may be said that "intersexual contravention" constitutes a note of northern Chinese ethos.

As might be expected, the greater the degree of generality involved in a pattern, the larger the intuitive element. Also, the more possible will it be for observers to disagree regarding the pattern and the greater the problem of verification (Kroeber, *1948*:317; *1949*:1; Irma Honigmann, *1951*). Bennett's analysis (*1946*) of the controversy over the patterns of Pueblo interpersonal behavior makes this clear. He sees two diverse Pueblo viewpoints in American anthropology. One group of students regards Pueblo culture as Apollonian—highly integrated, harmonious, homogeneous, and "sacred." The modal personality is gentle, nonaggressive, coöperative, modest, and tranquil. Ruth Benedict and Laura Thompson have done most to develop these patterns. The second viewpoint characterizes Pueblo personality as compounded of suspicion, anxiety, hostility, and ambition. Esther Goldfrank and Dorothy Eggan have sketched such a picture.

Neither group of Pueblo researchers is wrong. Each comprises highly qualified field workers. Bennett points out that these dif-

---

[4] These patterns of action, thought and feeling were secured by interviewing two northern Chinese students at Yale University in the winter of *1944–45*.

ferences with reference to the "same" data derive from "personal-cultural differences between the respective workers." A separate, inexplicit value orientation underlies each group. The underlying preference of the Thompson-Benedict workers is for cultural homo-geneity and gentle, nonaggressive, coöperative people. Underlying the Goldfrank-Eggan interpretation is a value of individualism and free, spontaneous, outgoing behavior. The latter see Pueblo people as initially inhibited and tyrannized into coöperation by the powerful native theocracy. From this suppression of spontaneity arise patterns of mutual suspicion, anxiety, and hostility.

The solution is not the impossible ideal of erasing personal biases and preferences. The human recording instrument with which the anthropologist studies people in communities must remain a feeling and a valuing creature. The field workers must learn to be aware of their biases and realize the limitations they exercise. As Wolff (*1945*) says, the investigator's "cultural and personal sensitivity enriched and sharpened by theoretical thinking puts the limit on what he can perceive and interpret." Pattern generalization reorders in subjective or theoretically logical terms phenomena which most of us assume to have external order. As the pattern recedes further and further from the specific, concrete instance, more and more of the personal equa-tion tends to be injected in the process which is essentially creative. Knowledge of the preferences and biases with which the operator approached his data will also facilitate the eventual verificatory proc-ess.

THE FRAME OF RELEVANCE IN OBSERVATION

Scientific observation is never haphazard. No matter how much of a dragnet or catchall technique the observer may develop, facts are always observed according to some theory of relevance.

Frames of relevance vary enormously, however. At one end of the scale lie problems of extraordinary generality which have sometimes given the impression of not being true problems at all. An anthropolo-gist whose interest sends him into the field to know as much as pos-sible about the way of life of a certain community has been accused of poorly planned and relatively unfruitful research. His frame of relevance encompasses a wide range of behavior, including food production, cooking, ritual, child training, social organization, and recreation. The objection that such general problems are unfruitful appears to be denied by the wealth of ethnographic detail which anthropologists have acquired and which is now available in libraries for more intensive comparative study.[5] The more specific problem-oriented approach enjoys a greater possibility of filling aggravating gaps in knowledge and testing hypotheses. For examples of this method we may take Whiting (1941) who went to the Kwoma in New Guinea to study the process of how the person learns his culture or Hsu (1948) whose frame of relevance called for information on Chinese class structure and the personality concommitants of class membership. However, whether the problem is general or specific, scientific observation is disciplined rather than wholly random.

The problem which has guided the selection of the contents of this book is the relationship between modal personality and community membership. More specifically our problem may be refined as follows:

With Reference to Modal Personality	*With Reference to Ethos*
1. How do individuals differ in socially standardized modes of action, thought, or feeling from one community to another?	1. What are the emotional aspects of the culture? (Theoretically, the emotional emphases of a culture refer to those features of culture that reveal emotion.)
2. How are socially standardized modes of action, thought, or feeling acquired?	2. How are the emotional aspects of culture perpetuated from one generation to another?
3. How are particular patterns of socially standardized action,	3. How are the emotional aspects of a culture related to each

[5] Murdock's *Social Structure* (1949) is an example of the kind of book facilitated by the ethnographic richness of anthropology. Whiting and Child's *Child Training and Personality* (1953) is another cross-cultural study drawing on a wide sample of communities.

With Reference to Modal Personality	With Reference to Ethos
thought, and feeling related to each other and to facts of social structure and technology?	other, to the covert personality features of the behaving individuals, or to other classes of facts?

Frame of Relevance for Studying Child Training

A more explicit example of a frame of relevance, related to the problem of how socially standardized patterns of behavior are acquired, calls for the observer to perform the following operations (Kardiner, 1939:20–21):

1. Attend to facts concerning socially patterned interpersonal behavior which interferes with one or more impulses of the child (for example, the sexual impulse).
   a. What are the rationalizations of the people who impose these interferences?
   b. What are the formal characteristics of the interferences (their regularity, age at which imposed, manner of imposition, etc.)?
   c. Note the emotional aspects of the interference. That is, what emotions or feelings are revealed in the behavior of persons who impose the interference? (For example, shame, shock, or digust might be revealed in parents' attempts to prevent a child's masturbatory behavior.)
2. Attend to facts concerning the effects of such interference on the child.
   a. How does the interference alter the child's perception of his impulse?
   b. How does the interference modify exercise of the impulse-satisfying activity?
   c. What unconscious constellations are formed by the interference and the effect of such constellations on the individual's behavior? (For example, sexual disciplines imposed by parents may be accompanied by unconscious, repressed hatred of the parent or to conceptions of the parent as frustrating and dangerous.)
   d. What is the relationship between these constellations and other

patterns of behavior that the individual adopts? (For example, the constellation arising out of sexual disciplines may be associated with childhood behaviors like finger-sucking, playing with toy guns, or, in later life, alcoholism.)

e. What affects (for example, anxiety, frustration, jealousy, feeling of insecurity) accompany a particular interference?

f. What is the relationship between such emotional states on the one hand to attempts to defend against them? (Thus, in the case of sexual disciplines, early insecurity associated with these restrictions may in turn encourage erection of an enduring and socially standardized defense system. Anxiety about masturbation makes many adults in America particularly hostile and intolerant of masturbation in children. The hostility represents a defensive attitude that not only denies masturbation to the self but brings relief from the guilt and anxiety which the child was taught to associate with masturbation.)

Use of this frame of relevance, as Kardiner points out, requires some knowledge of normal and abnormal psychology before it can lead to productive observation and logical or fruitful hypotheses.

The individual researcher's frame of relevance draws on many sources. The psychological theory he has studied, as already pointed out, remains a fecund source of observational directives. Students also learn what to look for in field research through the original field-work monographs they study and from published studies in culture and personality. Through the influence of these sources one generation of scientists is followed by another, the latter carrying on but refining the interests and problems of the older, contributing new insights into the manifold complexities of human behavior in social life.

Expectations Versus Facts

One caution in connection with observation has already been emphasized: The observer must remain aware of his values and how they are likely to enter into the pattern which he constructs out of the social world he studies.

The scientific or common-sense theory of relevance with which the

anthropologist attends to his data presents a similar danger that recommends the vigilant exercise of caution. At the same time that it
specifies what is significant the frame of relevance may determine
what the researcher sees! We must beware of expectations determining data—something not unknown in the annals of social science.
For example, Bougainville and other early travelers in the western
Pacific "found" free love in Tahiti. Later observers dismissed this
pattern as an instance of very inadequate reporting. Karl Polanyi has
pointed out that economists who assumed that markets existed in all
communities also found them everywhere they looked. It has been
left for later observers, using more rigorously defined concepts, to
disprove the existence of markets in relatively simple communities.
In these cases the observer expected to find certain behavior. Instead
of being governed by a rigorous and explicit definition of that behavior he moved into research with a vaguely formulated notion of
what he meant. This, of course, helped him to find what he expected.
The very facts became construed to fit expectations. Philosophers can
teach social scientists much about the value of rigorous definitions.

Related to the dominance exerted by theory is the danger of a
"crisis orientation" distorting the objectivity of the observer. Being
preoccupied with abnormality, conflict, struggle, and disharmony the
field worker may neglect instances of contrasting behavior and
emerge from observation with a partial or skewed picture of community life. Certainly there is no reason why an observer should not
choose especially to attend to phenomena of personal and social conflict but he is a poor scientist if he believes that these phenomena are
dominant in social life when actually he has not tried to estimate their
frequency even qualitatively. Maslow (1950) points out that much
current psychological theory, influenced as it is by psychiatry, focuses
attention on maladjustment, psychopathology, and conflict rather
than on factors of health in personality. This very theory, in turn,
orients many anthropologists working in the field of culture and personality. Perhaps we have here an explanation for why so many
studies in culture and personality depict predominantly anxious, apprehensive, hostile, and insecure people. Perhaps the unconscious

dominance exerted by such an orientation explains why a well-known writer, discussing the continued survival of a suspicious, hostile, and egocentric people, can, in answer to the question "Are they happy?" say, "It is certain they are not aware of their wretchedness" (Kardiner, 1945:253).

Suggestions for Further Reading

Stimulating introductions are available to the field of science in general. Usually, however, they have nothing to say about social science and the reader is left to make his own connections. Two such limited introductions to the scientific process are especially recommended: Gregory's *Discovery* (1949) and Conant's *On Understanding Science* (1951). For a tougher but more explicit guide to method consult Churchman and Ackoff, *Methods of Inquiry* (1950). A very different, short introduction to anthropological method will be found in chapter 2 of Mead's *Male and Female* (1949f).

Are the social sciences scientific? What this question really means is whether they can predict human behavior. Some historians deny the possibility of valid laws for social behavior—at least they do not expect to find them by examining history. Anthropologists, psychologists, and other social scientists usually believe that verifiable laws of human behavior can be discovered. These questions are discussed in Gruenbaum, "Causality and the Science of Human Behavior" (1952). Argyle considers some of the advantages and limitations of the laboratory method of studying social groups in "Methods of Studying Small Social Groups" (1952).

A good discussion of pattern from the standpoint of culture and personality will be found in Weakland's "Method in Cultural Anthropology" (1951). In a challenging paper on "National Character" (1953a) Margaret Mead has written that the anthropologist's interest in pattern does not extend to the number of people who manifest a pattern. Her position seems to abandon both the search for quantitative patterns and the rigorous methods of sampling developed in sociology and social psychology. Mandelbaum's "On the Study of National Character" (1953) takes up the latter point in some detail. Alexander Lesser became convinced over a decade ago that anthropology has outgrown purely descriptive interests and must focus on the level of specific problems. The argument he advances in "Problems Versus Subject Matter as Directives of Research" (*1939*) appears to have caught popular attention in American anthropology so that, with a few notable exceptions, an alarming dearth of general monographs now issues from the presses. A valuable observation guide for students of culture and personality may soon be available when Whiting and Associates revise their preliminary *Field Manual for the Cross Cultural Study of Child Rearing* (*1953*), now available only in limited supply.

As a counteraction to preoccupation with conflict and psychopathology in social behavior the student might study Sorokin's *Explorations in Altruistic Love and Behavior* (*1950*). Here he will find a contrasting but currently hardly popular point of departure.

Chapter 6

TECHNIQUES FOR RESEARCH

Qualitative research differs from quantitative investigation by virtue of the absence of systematic operations for measurement. As Allen H. Barton says, the results of qualitative research are reported in descriptions, lists, and verbal assertions rather than in statistical tables. Culture and personality employs predominantly qualitative procedures. The techniques are mainly adapted to securing verbal data which can then be presented in descriptive monographs.

Eight main techniques are available to research workers in culture and personality. Although these procedures sometimes overlap and more than one may be employed simultaneously—like observation and interviewing—each will be discussed here under a separate heading. The techniques to which we now turn are: (1) sampling, (2) observation of behavior in its natural setting, (3) interviewing, (4) testing, (5) communication analysis, (6) product analysis, (7) empathy, and (8) mapping.

SAMPLING

A serious criticism of culture and personality arises from the fact that the results obtained in this field rely on data secured without adequate regard for sampling. We have already referred to this problem. The omission of sampling more and more is believed to seriously reduce the validity of the results obtained in field work. Signs of an awareness of this limitation are available. It is not too daring to predict that the emerging generation of anthropologists will soon be responsible for introducing this technique in the several fields of cultural anthropology.

Streib (*1952*), while not employing rigorous sampling procedures, utilized the questionnaire among the Navaho. The schedule of questions is often associated with sampling as an aid designed to yield comparable results between informants. Streib claims his work shows that survey techniques can be utilized in communities unlike our own. Sampling, however, does not require giving up other traditional anthropological techniques—like participant observation. Rather, the anthropologist must adapt these procedures to the intensive study of the members of the sample universe, using other persons in the community incidentally for information about the range of patterns.

In the latter half of 1952 the author used sampling procedures while studying the effect of presenting American informational motion pictures to rural Pakistani audiences. Some of the incidental results of this experiment show glaringly the errors which may result when willing and accessible informants alone serve as sources of data. For example, in one large village of North-West Frontier Province, 54 percent of the sample subjects denied familiarity with Urdu and 16 percent claimed to understand the language excellently. Among selected subjects only 34 percent admitted ignorance but 40 percent claimed perfect understanding. When it is understood that Urdu represents a language spoken by the officials of Western Pakistan and is closely allied to nationalistic sentiments, then it is easy to see that our selected subjects represent the more sophisticated members of the community. We have excellent reasons for believing that the sample group more adequately reflects the distribution of cosmopolitanism in the population. To take another example, 36 percent of the sample audience understood the message communicated by one particular motion picture while 69 percent of the selected subjects who attended revealed adequate understanding. Obviously, selecting informants on the bases of congeniality and coöperativeness leads to the danger that very capable but also atypical members of the community will become sources of more or less distorted information.

A brief discussion will explain the bare mechanics of sampling. At the end of the chapter suggestions will be given to further reading. Sampling consists essentially of finding members of the population who are representative of the community as a whole and from whose behavior one can validly predict for the entire population. The sample may be selected from a census of individuals. In the simplest form of random sampling the names are put in a hat and a selected number drawn by chance. Then each sample subject is sought out for study or interrogation—no substitutes being permitted for those who don't answer the doorbell. In Pakistan we spent many weary and unproductive hours marching across dusty, fallow fields looking for farmers whose names had turned up in the sample. For a community that is known to be stratified into social classes or other divisions, a stratified sample may be employed. If it is known that town dwellers constitute 70 percent of the population, then 70 percent of the sample subjects will be town folk. Also areas may be selected for sampling in a variant procedure known as area sampling.

Many new problems of creating rapport and winning coöperation will face anthropologists who select informants on the basis of random sampling. More than ever before, the cultivation of skills for handling interpersonal situations will be required of students who are going to work with this technique.

BEHAVIOR OBSERVED IN ITS NATURAL SETTING

The observation of on-going behavior in its customary setting remains the basic technique of culture and personality. It probably takes up a greater proportion of field time than any other single technique. The behavior studied by the researcher may be directed against the geographical environment (an attitude about the weather), toward material products of behavior (as when a frustrated man kicks a piece of furniture), or it may occur between people. The latter we refer to as interpersonal behavior and is illustrated by Kaska boys chasing girls or by a mother feeding her infant. Culture and personality research pays a great deal of attention to interpersonal behavior. When the genetic emphasis predominates in such research then interpersonal behavior between parents and children holds the interest of the observer.

Participant Observation

The field worker often wants to observe behavior when the members of the community out of shyness or politeness cease what they are doing in the presence of a stranger. Two procedures help to cope with this difficulty. Both involve participation of the observer in the life of the people he is studying.

Participant observation refers to carrying on field work while participating in a group's customary activities (F. Kluckhohn, *1940;* B. Paul, *1953*). The field worker creates for himself a role that facilitates his participation in the community. Then he proceeds to learn while doing. He coöperates with the natives, joins in their daily tasks, and is ready to enter their dances, feasts, or games. Sometimes there is danger that too intense participation may reduce time for note taking. Margaret Mead tells the story of a young anthropologist who spent a summer on an Indian reservation where he obligingly fixed so many cars that he failed to complete his field work. Participation enables the observer to acquire firsthand familiarity with activities about which he wants to know a great deal. Through participation he also acquires strong rapport that later becomes useful in interviewing. Participation strikes most field workers as far more preferable than remaining on the sidelines getting only an indirect knowledge of behavior.

A second and related technique designed to cope with the disturbance created by the observer's presence in a social situation calls for maintaining awareness of the observer's stimulus value and noting the style of response which he engenders. Like the psychiatrist, the anthropologist studies how the subject behaves toward him, using such behavior as part of his record. To use such data in gauging personality, careful record must be kept of what transpires in the relationship of field worker and community. An example may clarify a possible line of study. The qualities of deference and lack of authoritarianism in Kaska Indian personality were twice quite dramatically revealed to the writer in 1945. On one occasion our host, Old Man, spoke at some length about a nearby place in the forest where spruce hens usually abounded. He reminded us that these fowl are rather easy to kill. On another occasion the same man wondered aloud how news of a death in the isolated winter settlement could be conveyed to his absent son-in-law. In the first instance Old Man indirectly encouraged the anthropologist to go out and hunt the birds in order to replenish the supply of fresh meat which had been depleted in the settlement. In the second case he again indirectly suggested that the field worker might carry a message to the distant camp. No direct order was given. Nothing was said that might lead to outright refusal or hostility. It may be worth while stating that the author's wife had been made a classificatory sister of Old Man's daughters. Hence the writer occupied the position of a classificatory son-in-law. Other evidence indicates that similar "kid-glove" treatment is reserved for actual sons-in-law (Honigmann, *1949a*:265).

Special problems are connected with the observation of on-going behavior for culture and personality research. Such observation must acquire depth. It is not enough to report only the formal details of men's actions without taking steps to learn something about the underlying feelings and values which people invest in their actions or the anxieties associated with routine behavior.[1] Only by such efforts can we learn the psychological meaning of behavior. To obtain information about the way in which behavior is experienced by the actors, interviewing remains an essential technique.

INTERVIEWING

When interviewing accompanies observation of on-going activity the observer relates what people feel and think to what they do. At other times a relatively artificial interview situation is created in

---

[1] It is true, however, that some writers in culture and personality, including Kardiner in his early work, have based their interpretations on data that did not include very much information concerning underlying psychological states. Meaning, then, is only later imputed to the behavior. Kardiner is aware of the limitations in this type of data (Kardiner, *1939*: 411–412).

which the subject may be isolated from distracting circumstances. Several types of interviewing are possible. These we will refer to here as passive interviewing, active interviewing, life history recording, and dream recording.

The Passive Interview

Also known as expressive interview, the passive interview method resembles the method of free association in psychoanalysis in that the individual is encouraged to talk with a minimum of direction from the interviewer. The theory behind this technique holds that such spontaneous communication yields customary patterns of feeling and thinking relatively unmodified by the demands of the social situation. Unconscious material appears in the passive method when a person verbally reveals his thoughts and feelings without regard for grammar, logic, or convention. Several interview sessions will usually be necessary to induce sufficient relaxation and rapport for the subject to verbalize freely. Rapport may be far from easy to create with members of exotic communities who do not understand the interviewer's object. Even in psychoanalytic sessions free association requires considerable encouragement.

The following quotation is from a passive interview with a young Kaska man. Much of the material is given as originally recorded.

[The subject expressed great pleasure at having refused to accompany his brother to the father's winter settlement. He said that eventually he would secure a new wife and then would sing "like hell." Perhaps he would even win his wife back from his brother, John.]

I want to go up this way. My missus, John hold it. She don't want to come up this way. That's why John hold her. I tell him, Charlie [the wife's father]. He boss that kid. What he say I never know. [The subject broke into a spontaneous song.]

> I get my mama, this year,
> I don't give a damn.

My missus like a mean man all right. Good. Make mistake sometimes, my missus. Last time I left my place my missus tell me . . . "Me, you

won't give [to] him. Your brother tell me.that!" That's what my missus
tell me. I don't want to do that. You want to get woman, you marry.
"Why don't you? . . . John he want me." I told him no. I wouldn't go
for him down. [I] tell him "Go get girl. Get married." First time he keep
that Mrs. Harry. He leave him. Second time he keep Mamaza. He leave
him. I don't think so wife good for John. . . .

Familiarity with the informant's dialect and problems makes it
clear that he is in conflict over his wife's desertion but tries to shrug
off the pain. Because of the woman's absence he delays moving up-
river for the winter, where his wife doesn't want to go anyway ("I
want to go up this way. . . . She don't want to . . .). The woman
is living with the subject's brother, John. Allegedly she wants her
husband to share her with John ("Me, you won't give [to] him").
John, apparently, also requested sexual access to the woman. Inasmuch as the pattern of wife sharing persists in attenuated form among
the modern Kaska, it may be that the informant feels a bit ambivalent about his refusal. At the end the subject comments on his brother's previous two unsuccessful marriages. In both cases the women
quit John, who does not treat women well ("I don't think so wife
good for John . . .").

The Active Interview

We are all familiar with the interview in which our responses are
guided by questions or suggestions originating with an interviewer.
The technique of active interviewing has a place in field work. The
interviewer should always keep a record of what he says in order
that the degree and direction of guidance will be clear when the
data are later analyzed.

Active interviewing relies on two broad types of prompting—open-
end and straight questioning. The difference between these two techniques lies mainly in that the former follows a nondirective approach
and so resembles passive interviewing more than does direct questioning. Open-end directions aim to guide and encourage a spontaneous
flow of speech around some particular topic that interests the field
worker. A portion of an active interview using open-end direction is
given below:

[Interviewer: "Tell me about your childhood."] I'm scared when I see new man coming. I'm scared when I see new man sit down my camp. I'm scared of everything. I'm scared of rabbit too in trap. My mother catch rabbits. She chase me back. I run home. I get a stick. I come back. I knock 'em down. Just first time. I'm little kid. . . .

Straight questioning, on the other hand, usually pursues more specific information:

[Interviewer: "You know heaven and hell?"] People die, you mean? They go to heaven, good, they say. Good man go to heaven. On Jesus ground, good looking, live good. Somebody say that.
[Interviewer: "Who goes to hell?"] Some people. Good man go to heaven.
[Interviewer: "Bad man go to hell?"] You damn right. Good man good for Jesus. Man he mixed up, no good. He go to hell, he die. Man's a good men . . . good for Jesus. Some man say, man bother girl, can't go to heaven.
[Interviewer: "Will you go to heaven?"] Me good man. Sure I go to heaven. Nothing trouble for me. I never bother my friend too. I never fight nothing. . . .

As already suggested, interviewing provides an essential device with which the researcher can probe for motivational and other covert states that are not susceptible to direct observation. It may also enable the investigator to secure facts about actual behavior that is not amenable to direct observation. An interviewer who uses this technique for information about actual behavior must remain aware of a possible discrepancy between what an informant says on the one hand and, on the other, what he feels, believes, or actually does. An informant's verbalization often constitutes a concession to convention. Also he may be experiencing a far more complex motivational state than he can grasp or express. Requests for a statement of covert behavior may be met by giving ideal patterns—he may tell how a husband and wife *should* coöperate rather than the manner in which he and his wife really get along. Interviewing may provide slight ground for accurately predicting how people will behave in actual situations.

This is the criticism which has been leveled against polling techniques (Mosteller, *1949*).

Considerations of another order that limit the use of the active interview are raised by Clyde Kluckhohn (*1941:119*), who points out that "The trouble is that the ethnographer has a limited time in the field. He cannot see everything. Hence he takes to posing questions in the hypothetical mode, 'What would the Navaho do in such and such a situation?'" Many an ethnographer wastes his own and the informant's time by bringing up situations that are formally patterned in the anthropologist's culture or in some other culture with which he is familiar but for which the native knows no established routines. Another problem arises when an abstract question is presented to a people who lack experience in generalizing. Most Cree informants did not comprehend when in Attawapiskat we asked: "What do people like you eat every day?" A few Indians gave the community's ideal not necessarily accurate view of the food situation saying: "Every day there is nothing to eat and everybody is hungry."

Life History Recording

Interviewing intended to secure a long-range record of personal experience in a given community constitutes the life history technique (C. Kluckhohn, Gottschalk, and Angell, *1945*; C. Kluckhohn, *1949b*). At the same time that life histories vividly demonstrate how the members of a community grew to be as they are they also illustrate the range of an individual's experience in culture and how various experiences connect with each other. For example, do pressures against masturbation in childhood appear at the same time as weaning and are both pressures applied by the same person? The life history technique also lends itself to learning about the subjective experiences of people.[2]

Aberle (*1951*) has analyzed *Sun Chief*, the autobiography of a Hopi Indian, to gain further insight into the divergent interpretations

[2] The student interested in inspecting autobiographical and biographical materials should see Ford, *1941*; Simmons, *1942*; DuBois, *1944*; Kardiner, *1945*, chap. 12; Honigmann, *1949a*, Appendix A, and Devereux, *1951*.

of Hopi community life referred to in the last chapter.[3] Readers will recall that one group of anthropologists sees Pueblo life as integrated and coöperative while another stresses interpersonal relations characterized by hostility and suspicion. Aberle concludes that the truth does not lie "somewhere in between" but in understanding how these two aspects are bound together. The Hopi Society exists in an unstable equilibrium. Under certain conditions the Hopi world view promotes security. Given any increase in misfortune and it produces "everything from psychosomatic disease to community fission." The generalization of patterns thus depends on whether one is studying a demoralized or integrated community. Neither aspect is ever completely absent in any community. Aberle urges that his life history—based on psychological analysis—be validated through empirical field study.

Children of Bondage, by Davis and Dollard (1940), demonstrates how the life history approach yields a wealth of modal personality data. The subjects are eight adolescent Negro children in the Deep South. The aim of the authors is to show the effect of color caste membership on the personality of Negro Americans. Private interviews were obtained several times a week over a four- to seven-month period. This information was supplemented through interviews with parents and teachers. The authors arrange the cases to illustrate three class levels in Southern Negro society.

The life histories of lower-class children reveal a familiarity with violence. They have either participated in violence or have seen it manifested at home. Their education includes teaching to fight back when they are attacked—instruction of great value in a community where children are often left without the protection of parents. Discipline of lower-class youngsters remains largely in maternal hands since the father is not a stationary member of the household. Employment of the mother outside the home leaves nobody to supervise the child's activities. Discipline is primarily restrictive, children being often beaten but seldom rewarded. Incentives like economic privileges are not held out as rewards for "respectable behavior." Mothers also

---

[3] See above, pp. 100–101.

do not expect great achievements from children in school. Youngsters themselves find school distasteful. Masturbation receives punishment but much sexual behavior is openly apparent in a family where the mother receives lovers, the father has girl friends, and a sister may be promiscuous. Lower-class children grow up to satisfy sexual impulses as readily as they release aggressive impulses. Actually in this class rewards for sexual restraint are very unlikely. Behavior with reference to the white caste is learned through punishment, insults, and threats received from whites; from training by parents; and through rumors of violence directed by whites against Negroes. Within his own caste the child learns the meaning of color gradation, often from jibes directed against darker-skinned folk and approval of those with light complexions.

The histories of middle-class Negro children reveal the latter to meet practically the same caste pressures, being taught proper behavior toward whites under conditions of segregation. The children of the middle class grow up refusing to associate with "niggers" (lower-class and dark-skinned Negroes). From parents they learn to strive for upward mobility and believe in trying to improve their social position through schooling. Mothers maintain an alert interest in school performance, rewarding study and punishing truancy or poor performance. Discipline is harsh, consistent, and persistent. Children are expected to learn to behave like ladies and gentlemen. Pressure toward control of sexual behavior comes early, constant and vigilant discipline serving to preserve the reputation of the child and his family. Middle-class children are not allowed to explore their environment freely, parents prescribing and proscribing movies, designating where friends may be found, and so on. The Negro child in the middle of the class pyramid learns a great dread of tangling with the law, an experience which might ruin the family's reputation. He also learns that loss of income might halt social mobility by blocking the acquisition of the symbols of class position. Middle-class Negro youths come to value a steady job, clothes, a home, an education, and a mother who does not work.

Davis and Dollard present one upper-class life history. Judging from this case the upper-class Negroes of Deep South also learn the desirability of upward mobility even though the family may enjoy fair economic security. The boy described was antagonistic toward his mother. As a child he had identified with a lower-class nurse and learned certain elements of lower-class behavior from her. This experience mitigated the family's strict discipline and brought the boy into conflict with his mother's upper-class values.

Davis and Dollard's work illustrates how patterns may be generalized from a series of discrete life histories. The biographical method also lends itself well to the genetic approach in culture and personality study. The case of Julia, for example, allows us to see how in the lower class parental rejection in early childhood may be related to strong aggressive tendencies which in adolescence are channelized into gang fights.

Dream Recording

Two main considerations underlie the collection of dreams in culture and personality research. First is the assumption that dreams represent socially standardized behavior. That is, the dream of an informant is partly determined by the community to which he belongs and hence is part of the culture. We would not expect an Eskimo who has never even heard of television to dream that he is televising an ice skating tournament. In the second place, dreams reveal ideas, feelings, and motivational states which people find it difficult to verbalize—they are relatively unconscious. If these covert states are also socially patterned, then it follows that dreams are an essential avenue for reaching important areas of the modal personality.[4]

For purposes of interpretation recorded dreams should be accompained with dreamer's associations. Such associations may be secured by active or passive methods of interviewing. That is, the informant may be asked: "What do you think this dream means?" Or the subject may be invited to verbalize passively after he has finished report-

---

[4] Dream materials from various communities are increasing. See Morgan, *1932*; Lincoln, *1939*; Róheim, *1947* and *1949*; Kluckhohn and Morgan, *1951*. Many life histories contain recorded dreams.

ing his dream. The ensuing communication will then be inspected to see whether it continues the chain of thinking contained in the dream. Researchers should also note carefully the circumstances in which the dream occurs or the life situation of the informant. This requires knowing something about the dreamer including his "felt age" (e.g., Does he regard himself as an old man?), conflicts, family status, aspirations, and prestige. Such information helps to elucidate the language of the dream. These points may be illustrated in connection with the dream reported by a Kaska Indian who said: "I dream Peter give me revolver. . . . I dream one Carcross Injun wants to fight us. So we scared. No use somebody kill us. Maybe I just worry about gun. So this Peter Tom give me revolver to kill this man. 'No use have trouble till I die,' I say. 'What you want to give me gun for?' " (Honigmann, *1949a*:327).

The dream acquires meaning in the light of certain events observed on the preceding evening. A drunken girl, who originally came to Kaska country from the area around Carcross, in Yukon territory, attempted to shoot her husband's brother with whom she was living adulterously. Old Man, the dreamer, is a mature, somewhat depressed, unagressive man. The informant's immediate associations to the dream are significant. He opined that Peter Tom might soon visit the winter settlement where we were staying. He characterized Peter as a hard-working youth, a good moose hunter, and an important source of meat and general assistance for another Indian with whom the boy was living. To proceed now with interpretation, the dream probably represents the old man receiving power or aid from this youth. The revolver symbolizes power. Hostility toward a stranger points to hostility toward the adulterous girl, for whom the dreamer in reality had little respect. He had less use, even, for her paramour, with whom he had fought seriously some weeks earlier. The girl and her lover are fused in the "Carcross Injun." The dream expresses Old Man's deep-seated reluctance to use violence—he rejects the gun. At the same time, however, he is filled with hostile impulses. The hostility gets itself displaced on Peter upon whose helpfulness and strength the dreamer wishfully leans.

The essence of testing is to confine the subject to highly standard-ized situations (test situations) in which his behavior may be sys-tematically observed. Test situations approximate laboratory condi-tions; the number of variables influencing behavior are regulated as closely as possible.

An important limitation on testing in culture and personality re-search is imposed by the fact that oftentimes the people we study are unable to speak or read English. Hence, many psychological invento-ries demanding use of that language cannot be used in field work. Another limitation restricts the employment of tests whose content re-flects Western culture. Such instruments would be meaningless to people who follow another way of life. Even if such culture-bound tests could be translated, questions like "How do you prefer a man to be dressed? Very carefully, carefully, casually, somewhat carelessly, carelessly" would sound very mysterious to the Eskimos, who mini-mize dress symbolism and do not rate each other on the amount of attention paid to garb. Questions which depend upon a high degree of introspective awareness will not bring meaningful responses from people who introspect little or about different subjects. Examples of this sort could be continued almost indefinitely.

Students of culture and personality use tests primarily to reveal socially standardized states of motivation, valuation, and feeling. In-telligence has also been tested cross-culturally but will receive little attention here. The following instruments will be described briefly: Rorschach's Inkblot Test (Hallowell, *1945a*), Murray's Thematic Apperception Test (W. E. Henry, *1947*), Bavelas's Moral Ideology Test (Bavelas, *1942*), Piaget's guided interview for studying im-manent justice (Piaget, *1929;* Thompson, *1948*), Stewart's Emo-tional Response Test (Joseph, Spicer, and Chesky, *1949*:173, 191–207), and the Interest Finder (Sarhan, *1950*:7).

These devices fall into two categories. Whereas the Rorschach Test has been presented in unmodified form in culturally quite distinct communities, the remaining instruments have been modified in varying degrees for particular cultures. Special problems of verification arise when instruments, like the Thematic Apperception Test, are altered. These will be discussed in the succeeding chapter.

The Rorschach Test

In Rorschach's Inkblot Test an individual receives a series of ten cards, each containing a standardized but indefinite inkblot. Many experiments indicate that the Rorschach Test can be applied to subjects with different cultural backgrounds. Responses to the cards can be secured in exotic communities even though the people may be unfamiliar with illustrated materials. In anthropological field work the Rorschach Test has always been administered to individuals, group norms then being computed.[5] The subject is invited to tell the interviewer what he "sees" in the blot (Frank, *1939*). These responses are recorded and later will be scored and analyzed. "Because of the nonpictorial and unconventional character of the blots, they are open to practically unlimited variety of interpretations, especially since the cards on which they are printed may be held in any position by the subject and either the blot as a whole or any part of it may elicit his attention. . . . Whatever is seen, therefore, is bound to be a highly individualized product; the responses given must necessarily have reference to the subject. For it is *he* who projects his meaning into objectively meaningless forms" (Hallowell, *1945a*:199).

Like the Thematic Apperception Test, to be discussed below, Rorschach's Inkblot Test is sometimes referred to as a projective test. Could not interviews achieve the same end as projective tests? The question has been answered in the negative. "The reasons why they could not," says Korner (*1950*:620) referring to instruments like the Rorschach, "lie in the fact that interviews are more diffuse and less predefined situations, which have an infinite number of variables, in both subject and observer. The prime advantage of tests consists in their being standard sets of stimuli against which characteristic ways of thinking, speaking and perceiving are easily detected and com-

---

[5] For an illustration of how such group norms may be derived see Billig, Gillin, and Davidson, *1947–48*.

pared. Because of this standard screen, fine nuances of behavior, which in a free situation easily get lost, stand out very clearly."

Before responses to the Rorschach Test can be analyzed, they must be scored. In that process the number of responses, proportion of various types of responses, and the configurations of particular responses are computed. From such scores interpretations are obtained.[6] Interpretation yields insight into the motivational states of subjects and into the way he customarily behaves in real life situations. More specifically, Klopfer and Kelley (1942:195–290) point out, the test reveals information concerning the individual's customary responsiveness to external or internal stimulation; the degree of "control" exerted by the subject to regulate his behavior; his creative or imaginative capacities, as well as the use made of these resources; the adjustment level—whether he is secure or anxious; the nature of the anxiety, and, finally, the degree of maturity enjoyed by the personality.

Abel and Hsu's report (1949) on Chinese personality illustrates the kind of data yielded by skillful interpretation of Rorschach Test responses. They administered the test in the United States to American- and Chinese-born males and females. Analysis remained primarily concerned with contrasting these groups. They found American- and Chinese-born males to be less expansive or free in giving responses to the test than American- and Chinese-born females. Other differences include:

1. The males, whether American- or foreign-born, give somewhat more form responses than females but not to the degree where rigidity would be indicated.

2. All the groups are about in the middle as far as of introversive and extraversive tendencies are concerned. However, the Chinese- and American-born females show more extraversive responses; for example, their ratios of movement to color responses are higher.

3. Chinese-born males and females offer color-utilizing responses to which the form of the blot also plays an important determining

---

[6] Several manuals of interpretation are available, for example, Beck. *1944* and *1945;* Klopfer and Kelley, *1942;* Ames *et al.* (*1952*).

role (FC) more often than responses in which color determines the form (CF). This indicates that, compared to American-born Chinese, the foreign-born possess "greater emotional control." To allow color to determine the form is equivalent to letting emotion run away with the response.

4. Inanimate movement is more frequent in responses of American- and Chinese-born females, especially for American-born females. This suggests subjective awareness of some kind of inner conflict.

5. Human expression is projected into cards by American-born females. The nature of these expressions indicate guilt feelings in the respondents.

6. American-born females give responses utilizing shading and texture more frequently than any other group. They thereby reveal their sensitivity to the opinion of others.

Now let us look at the overall picture which the authors derive of their subjects. In general, they see the Chinese as characterized by a control of impulse. Chinese personality is pliant but disinterested in interpersonal relationships. There is evidence of a spontaneous enjoyment of nature and food plus an ability to express that enjoyment. In place of the control exercised by Chinese-born males females reveal greater flexibility. The anthropologist points out that they also "have a less rigid status role to maintain." American-born females show far more sign of adjustive difficulty than do women of Chinese birth.

Thematic Apperception Test

Comprising a series of pictures of people in various groupings but indefinite circumstances, Murray's Thematic Apperception Test is administered by inviting a subject to tell a story about each image. Unlike the Rorschach cards, which retain their contents changed as they are transported from one cultural milieu to another, TAT cards may be selected for use in a particular community from the standardized series. Selection usually utilizes pictures that most readily fit into the community and physical environment. Sometimes, and this is another point of contrast with the Rorschach, pictures are considerably modified to make them suitable for a particular milieu (Leighton and

Kluckhohn, *1947*:174). It is assumed that the individual will project into the picture and reveal in his response his own way of acting, thinking, and feeling. Analysis of TAT responses takes note of the description which the subject offers of each picture and how he interprets the content. In addition attention is devoted to "intraceptive comments," which imply individual needs or feelings, and "press comments," which reveal external pressures acting on the subject.

Caudill (*1949*) has produced a study of Ojibwa children that should allow the reader to understand how the TAT is interpreted. Caudill reports that these children relied largerly on description and interpretation but little on intraception in responding to the cards. In description they paid careful attention to detail but revealed little more "warmth or involvement with a human detail than with an inanimate detail." Content interpretations dealt largely with emotionally neutral or even aimless everyday activities. Aggressive situations, emotional crises, deprivation and illness, were frequently seen. Also they interpreted signs of generalized insecurity and apprehension. All in all, little positive feeling appears in the content interpretations. Those intraceptive comments frequently given indicated hostility and insecurity in interpersonal relations but, as already stated, few such comments were offered. Press comments frequently showed restraints on the part of cultural surrogates (parents and adults) meeting with resistance or failure. From these and similar responses Caudill (422–423) sums up the Ojibwa youngster's personality as isolated, emotionally unresponsive, wary, apprehensive, and liable to explosions of immature hostility.

The Ojibwa child at Lac du Flambeau, then spends his early life in a family situation that gives him neither love nor hostility. He develops a peculiar infantile anxiety that expresses itself in a passive longing for protection and care. While hostility is not directed toward him, he must early become aware of the large amount of unpredictable aggression and violence occurring around him. He is necessarily concerned with the outer world of people and nature because the instability and danger found there directly affect him, and in this sense he is "extroverted," but his relationships with the outer world are not warm and open. In such a situation he has little chance to develop inner resources whereby he might find reassurance within himself. When he tries to reach out for support and guidance from other individuals he is thwarted by the unpredictability of the emotional response he will receive and by the lack of a social structure which would focus his interaction with others for him. Out of this dilemma, only vaguely sensed by the individual and operating unconsciously, arises a frustration that is released in immature emotional outbursts which, in adults, take the form of drunkenness and random aggression.

The projective character of the Rorschach and Thematic Apperception tests imposes one limitation on their use. Interpretation must be largely concerned with reference to internal dynamics and relatively little reference can be made to the overt behavior of the subject under normal situational conditions. This suggests a limitation on the power of projective instruments to predict specific overt behavior in everyday situations.

Other Tools for Testing

The remaining tests, adapted from Bavelas, Piaget, and Stewart, although carefully structuring the relationship of subject and tester, are more like active or vigorously guided interviews than projective instruments.

In the moral ideology quiz the subject, frequently a child, is asked what he thinks are good and bad things to do. The device brings out the official or public moral standards of the individual. The observer learns how the respondent thinks and is supposed to react in given situations. Then the informant is asked *who* would praise or blame him for the good or bad deeds which he has reported. This allows the investigator to learn those rewarding and punishing agents who most concern the subject.

The test for immanent justice is designed to reveal evidence of a belief that the universe automatically punishes wrongdoing or that punishment emanates from things themselves. In the interview a series of fictional situations are created. The subject reads or hears these together with a crucial final question. An affirmative answer to that question indicates belief in immanent justice. Here is one such narrative:

> Once there were two children who were stealing apples in an orchard. Suddenly a policeman comes along and the two children run away. One of them is caught. The other one, going home by a roundabout way, crosses a river on a rotten bridge and falls into the water. Now what do you think? If he had not stolen the apples and had crossed the river on the rotten bridge all the same, would he also have fallen into the water?

Generally speaking and disregarding the effect of socioeconomic status, in Euro-American society the more youthful the child the stronger is his belief in immanent justice. In other words, a magical attitude toward antisocial acts declines with the age of the child (Piaget, 1952:250–261). Research among the Sioux, Hopi, Papago, and Navaho Indians reveals a different distribution. In none of these communities does the belief in immanent justice decrease with the child's age; as a matter of fact in several the belief increases significantly with age up to adolescence (Thompson, 1948).

Stewart's Emotional Response Test requests the subject to recount occasions when he felt happy, sad, angry, afraid, or ashamed. He is also asked to relate the best and worst things that could happen to him. The interview designates those life experiences that are associated with particular emotions.

While tests like the Moral Ideology or Stewart's Emotional Response are administered to individuals, culture and personality research seeks experiences which are common to a large portion of the community. Experience indicates that these instruments can be used to derive modal personality patterns. For example, among Navaho children, Leighton and Kluckhohn (1947:164–173) report, emotional responses reveal how firmly happiness is linked to "property or possessions of various kinds. Having or receiving property is an occasion for happiness or a 'best thing that could happen' to a large proportion of the Navaho children." Comparative research among American Indians indicates that Navaho children definitely exceed other tribes tested in preoccupation with property and even exceed Midwestern white children, who in turn may be more concerned with personal achievement. Coöperative activities involving the family and visits from relatives furnish another source of happiness to Navaho children but health is never mentioned as a reason for happiness nor as a "best thing." On the basis only of such tests as Stewart's and Bavelas', the authors believe they can describe certain definite characteristics of the Navaho child's personality. These devices reveal the Indian child to be practical, fond of kin, but inclined to see persons from outside the family as something of a threat. Great dread is attached to supernatural creatures whom youngsters regard with a concern that far exceeds the white child's fear of bogeymen.

THEMATIC ANALYSIS

Before anthropologists began to work in literate communities we rarely dealt with written materials.[7] Ethnographers, however, have long recorded myths and folk tales for analysis. Folk tales may be compared to those other expressive products of modern communities —short stories published in popular magazines, fairy tales, popular poetry, films, and popular songs. All reveal emotion and offer information about covert levels of personality. "Thematic analysis" designates the process of examing these vehicles of expression for clues to modal personality.

Several experiments indicate that thematic analysis is possible. La-Barre (*1948, 1950*) demonstrates how Japanese poetry written in American relocation camps during World War II echoes personality tensions and how Aymara folk tales, full of violence and treachery, reflect the Aymara Indian world view. The Indian is shown as picturing himself in a hostile world, prepared to secure himself against threat by whatever means are available. Of course, all such interpretations demand verification, a topic to which we return in the following chapter.

Popular works of imagination in a certain respect resemble projec-

---

[7] Sociologists have developed a number of techniques for analyzing the content of modern mass media of communication. See Berelson, *1952*; Jahoda, Deutsch, and Cook, *1951*:235–244, 539–560.

tive devices. They reflect a community's needs, wishes, fears, sources of stress, and ideal norms of behavior. The emotion revealed through popular stories, films, poetry, or songs provide clues to character structure and motivational states. But, somebody may object, folk tales that are contemporarily narrated among nonliterate people go back to earlier times. Are we then interested in the people of that time, if indeed, the inventors of these stories could be identified? A further objection cites that folk tales and Hollywood films are widely and easily diffused cultural items. If a work of imagination has been borrowed, obviously the borrower did not project his aspirations into creating the story. To these two objections we reply that the maintenance or recounting of a tale or the showing of a film are the significant activities. People retain, tell, and find pleasure in works of imagination that possess meaning in terms of their own modal character structure (Asch, 1952:109–113). People may also invest (reinterpret) a borrowed tale with familiar meaning. Integration of any borrowed item into the texture of a culture is always expected.[8] This theory of thematic expression explains why mass-produced magazines, films, and similar products, created by professional productions, may also be used in personality research. Professional works of imagination do not only reveal the character structure of their creators, as might be thought. Successful stories, plays, films, and similar creative products contain themes that appeal to existing needs and aspirations of the community. Popularity indicates that the expressive product satisfies audience needs and suggests a relationship between that product and character structure.

The role of Western films in the life of the American child will

---

[8] This elementary principle of cultural anthropology may be illustrated by Kardiner's discussion (1949b:73) about the diffusion of religion. "You know what happens to a religion when it diffuses. It never preserves its pristine quality. It is always modified. And it is always modified in the direction that happens to suit a particular personality. One of the clearest cases on record is that of Alor. They have the usual stereotyped family gods and all the rest. You can't evaluate their religion on the basis of form, but rather on the basis of how they practice it. They practice it *with neglect*. . . . It means nothing to them because they expect nothing from their deity, just as they expect nothing from their parents. So it's not the form that counts; it's the actual way in which it is practiced."

illustrate these claims for thematic analysis (F. Elkin, *1950*). Westerns allow a child to identify with some powerful hero, thereby to allay insecurity and inferiority feelings. Further, they relieve a youngster's tensions by encouraging him to vicariously release aggression that has been engendered through social frustrations. By allowing the youthful audience to vicariously fight for justice and goodness, these films allow children to symbolically earn the love and admiration of teachers and parents. Western films enjoy especially great popularity in rural areas where they serve a different function. By mirroring the rural way of life they assist rural adults to bolster their sense of pride. This is important in a nation where country people are considered backward "hicks" by their urban contemporaries.

The Analysis of Drama

Thematic analysis of German and American drama by McGranahan and Wayne (*1948*) presents evidence of personality differences between those people. Forty-five German and American plays performed in 1927 were studied to learn the "needs, assumptions, and values" of the audiences. The differences between the plays of the two nations "lend support to the theory that there are real and persistent German-American psychological differences." Unfortunately the authors do not offer any more explicit statement concerning the linkage between the dramatic themes and modal personalities.

American drama is heavily concerned with themes of love and personal morality. When the subject is love, the problem is generally whether two lovers or would-be lovers are going to be united despite the opposition of parents, career ambitions, or personal misunderstandings. In the case of personal morality, the individual must choose between good and evil paths of action. In contrast, German plays are more concerned with themes of idealism, power, and the outcast. Idealism guides the revolutionary or humanitarian hero who sacrifices some personal value in pursuit of principles or else commits an unconventional act to realize his ideals. The power theme involves two individuals or groups in conflict over the same object, position, or influence. When the theme is about an outcast, an individual because of some handicap (color, poverty, or criminal tendency) comes into conflict with the normal members of the community. German plays are also more concerned with social and political problems than American drama and more often use the unhappy ending. While virtue consistently triumphs on the American stage, the unsympathetic side often comes out on top in the German theater. These and other differences between the dramatic styles of the two countries which reflect divergent values are summarized below:[9]

American Plays:	*German Plays:*
1. Dwell more on private problems, like difficulties in achieving love and virtue in daily life.	1. Are more ideological, philosophical, and social-minded.
2. The hero tends to be an ordinary person from the community's midst.	2. The hero tends to be an individual who stands outside the normal community. For example, he may be a visionary pursuing a cause.
3. The emphasis in love plots falls on solving a crisis arising from external opposition (parents, criminals, etc.) or from misunderstandings.	3. In love plots two individuals are united by virtue of sharing common ideals. But the lovers may be cut asunder by "deeper" values.
4. Are essentially moralistic; for example, the hero is shown struggling against immoral tendencies in himself.	4. Are basically idealistic, the hero pursuing an ideal and often having to struggle against the average members of the group.
5. Personal ambition and satisfactions are implicitly approved.	5. Personal ambition and satisfactions are often the root obstacles, constituting the "materialism" against which the idealist must fight.

---

[9] By way of a practical exercise the reader might regard the following eleven pairs of statements as contrasting patterns of German and American dramatic art. Themes are, after all, patterns. Can the reader then use his training in psychology to infer from these patterns some attributes of covert behavior? In other words, relate these patterns to a few highly generalized personality motives or values.

American Plays:	German Plays:
6. Show that conventional moral standards are capable of promoting success and happiness.	6. Demonstrate that conventional moral standards are often petty, hypocritical, and confining.
7. Personal crimes and sins pose basic problems, for which the individual is responsible.	7. Personal crimes and sins are frequently excused, justified, or else society is held responsible for them. The crime may also be warranted by high ideals.
8. Virtue is regularly triumphant—right makes might.	8. Success in wordly conflicts can be won through power and ruthlessness. Even idealism if unsupported by power is doomed to fail.
9. Revolt against authority is expressed against parents and others who interfere with the individual's happiness.	9. Revolt against authority is directed against political superiors, classes, or society itself.
10. The protagonist rebels in the name of his personal right to happiness. The forces opposed to this right are portrayed as immoral, evil, ill advised.	10. The hero rebels not in self-interest but in the name of an ideal—some set of values superior to those of the authority.
11. As a solution to rebellion the person who is wrong (either the rebel or authority) can admit his guilt and reform.	11. The rebel cannot reform, since his is the superior position. The authority also will not reform. Hence the solution does not lie along the path of reintegration. The losing side is deported, silenced, or dies.

Thematic Analysis and Observation of On-going Behavior

Themes like dreams may also be studied in relation to the on-going social situation in which they occur. A folk tale told by an informant may be related to current difficulties in his family or village relations.

A fad in movie plots may be related to features in the national or international situation.

One day Old Man, a Kaska Indian, spontaneously repeated a folk tale that he had already related to the anthropologist during the previous year. In this tale a man's wife cheats her blind husband out of food. The old man is befriended by his medicine animal, the loon, and climbs on the bird's back to be flown across a lake. The bird dips the old man into the water. When he emerges, the man can see a little. Once more the loon dives. This time upon emerging the man discovers he can see perfectly. The loon now directs the man to go to his wife but warns him to avoid trouble. Upon reaching home the man in anger kills his wife. Old Man told us this tale just after he had explained that his weak eyes sometimes improve for brief periods. At about the same moment his wife left the camp. Almost immediately her husband began to narrate the popular Indian folk tale. Interpretation indicates that Old Man identifies with the passivity of the leading character. The folk tale expresses the anxiety and hostility engendered in him by his growing debility and dependence. Old Man resents becoming increasingly dependent on his relatively dominant and older wife (Honigmann, *1949a*:327–328).

Thematic Analysis of Plastic Arts

Relatively slight attention has been devoted to studying plastic arts for clues to personality. As might be expected most such experiments have been conducted by archeologists, who have only the material remains of vanished cultures on which to base inferences. Thus, Flinders Petrie, the Egyptologist, deduces a love of nature to have been characteristic of the predynastic Egyptians. He derives his interpretation from the variety of plants adorning the pottery vessels of those people. It has also been pointed out that in Egyptian sculpture the king is nearly always the dominant figure and largest in size. In battle scenes the ruler is always represented as conquering. In Mesopotamian art, however, the king is not essentially different from his subjects. Frankfort (*1948*:10–12) relates these different modes of depicting royalty to different emotional attitudes toward the king in the two countries. Written records corroborate his interpretation that the while the Egyptian pharoah was regarded as an immortal god descended among men the Mesopotamian *lugal* represented rather a great man among men.

Another example of thematic analysis applied to plastic forms makes use of Renaissance portrait busts. The Renaissance was a period when individualism found strong expression in economic life, which now freed itself from guild and church ties (Simmel, *1950*: 15). At the same time there appeared "an immense spread of naturalistic and individualistic portrait busts. Thus the general attention appears to have shifted from what men have in common . . . to what must be left to the *individual*. Attention is focussed on the significance of personal strength. . . ."

PRODUCT ANALYSIS

An inspection of material culture may also contribute insights into character structure and reveal emotional qualities. Product analysis entails examining utilitarian constructions, like houses or toboggans, to determine the values they embody, as revealed, for example, in careless or perfectionistic construction. The proportion of nonutilitarian objects to utilitarian objects in a culture may also be meaningful. Type and number of possessions may reveal drives and aspirations in a class structured community. Hsu (*1948*:36–41) for example, finds it significant that the houses of West Town are much larger than is needed by the families which built them—rooms often remaining unused. Much more care is lavished on the appearance of the house than on the comfort features of the dwelling. He concludes that the houses "give evidence of a high degree of competition for superiority. Worldly residences are not so much places to house the individual members in comfort and ease as they are signs of unity and social prestige for the family group as a whole." A lack of creativeness in the personality of the Tepoztecan is reflected in the scarcity of handicrafts, weaving, and basketry techniques in his village

(O. Lewis, 1951:288). Among the Kaska Indians (Honigmann, 1949a:260):

The strongly developed practical interest in adaptation leads the Indian to neglect beauty and to be unresponsive to perfectionism as an end in itself—that is, above and beyond the degree required for utility. Embroidery on moccasins, mittens, and gloves is reduced to a minimum or often lacking. . . . Oars are particularly crude and unfinished. Experiments made to deduce the emotional aspects of cultural products in connection with clothing and housing consistently revealed qualities of simplicity and nonperfection. Mittens, moccasins, and children's underwear, without being fitted to the wearer's dimensions, are cut with a general impression of size, allowing a little extra so that the final product is always somewhat larger than necessary. The style is baggy, the garment only crudely shaped to the body. Analysis of several log cabins reveals a striking lack of perfectionism. In one cabin some roof poles are partly hewed while many are not hewed at all. Where the logs join at the corners they are often not all sawed off to equal length. Another cabin is only half floored. The interiors of most houses are not painted or otherwise finished. Such housing style permits the inference that the people's primary concern is with utility, adequacy of a structure being defined primarily in terms of the building's use for the obvious function of weather protection.

Tschopik (1951:185–187) reports that among the Peruvian Aymara Indians "there is little or no interest in such aesthetic qualities of the objects as form, line, and design. Aymara dress in Chucuito is notoriously drab; the decoration on textiles, when present, is limited almost entirely to simple stripes. Even the fiesta costume, although somewhat more colorful, is singularly lacking in ornament and attention to detail." No attempt is made to make houses attractive and the interior characteristically stands unfinished. In other words, the Aymara (who, like the Kaska Indian, lives in a difficult geographical environment) remains "preoccupied with the useful aspects of his culture and environment. . . . Utilitarianism . . . serves to channel the individual's interests and to concentrate the attention of the society's members on the very real problems of survival in a difficult environment."

EMPATHY

Empathy as a technique of behavioral research designates the process whereby an observer identifies himself with the subject who is being studied. The term does not refer to the naïve inference of another person's covert behavior, a detour to knowledge about which Asch (1952:144) has written critically. Scientifically managed empathy requires the deliberate use of a construct of personality which serves as a guide to another person's more or less complex behavior processes. By aid of theory we then infer the thoughts and feelings of the subject and vest ourselves in that pattern.

Rigorousness must characterize the use of empathy, otherwise there is danger that the observer's temperamental biases will be projected into the lives of the people being studied (Mead, 1947c:300). Gorer warns against this danger when he says that behavior which strikes an American as deliberate cruelty may actually arise, as among the Great Russians, from a tendency to ignore physical suffering (Gorer and Rickman, 1950:145). Americans, however, cannot as easily remain indifferent to pain or suffering. Hence our readiness to imply cruelty.

To safeguard against the projection of personal and culture bound biases knowledge of one's own cultural position and deeper layers of personality is helpful. Mead (1952b) points out that we explore the culture of others through our own culture, which we must know with a disciplined awareness. Students of culture and personality, however, explore also the inner life of individuals. It follows that a knowledge of one's own personality will also be of considerable value. "While a full psychoanalysis is undoubtedly an important addition to the training of the anthropologist," says Margaret Mead, "psychoanalysts are only trained at present to analyze an individual with a definite nonprofessional need for analysis or an individual who intends to become an analyst." She suggests work with children, the mentally sick, or projective tests as devices to increase the psychological insights of the anthropologist.

MAPPING

Richardson (1950:31) emphasizes that social scientists who collect data about interpersonal relations "need to describe the *time when* and the *places where* these relations occur." Mapping is a technique for showing how human relationships occur spatially and in what physical contexts. As used in anthropology, mapping includes outlining the plan of a village or other natural region as well as diagraming the arrangements of building. The position of furniture is useful, for example, if it delineates the hierarchical relations of people. There is little virtue in mapping for its own sake but students of culture and personality may discover added meaning in their descriptions of, say child training, when the physical circumstances affecting such sequences are clearly shown.

Suggestions for Further Reading

General summaries of field techniques include Bennett's "The Study of Cultures: A Survey of Techniques and Methodology in Field Work" (*1948*) and Goode and Hatt's *Methods in Social Research* (*1952*).

A short introduction to sampling will be found in Doob's *Social Psychology* (*1952:134–138*) while more systematic discussion occurs in the second volume of Jahoda, Deutsch, and Cook's *Research Methods in Social Relations* (*1951*). See also Parten's *Surveys, Polls, and Samples* (*1950*). Benjamin Paul has written the most comprehensive discussion of participant observation and interviewing in "Interview Techniques and Field Relationships" (*1953*).

The still classic introduction to dream analysis is Sigmund Freud's *The Interpretation of Dreams* (*1938*). In reading this one must not overlook the possibility that to some degree the symbolism of dreams may be culturally relative. Writing on "The Manifest Content of Dreams" Dorothy Eggan (*1952*) presents an analysis of 254 dreams of a Hopi individual.

To study the application of tests in recent culture and personality research the reader may consult the monographs of the Indian Administration Research Project: for example, Leighton and Kluckhohn's *Children of the People* (*1947*) or Joseph, Spicer, and Chesky's *The Desert People* (*1949*). W. E. Henry's "The Thematic Apperception Technique in the Study of Culture-Personality Relations" (*1947*) and Caudill's *Japanese-American Personality and Acculturation* (*1952*) are notable applications of the TAT in this field. An outstanding application of combined life history and Rorschach techniques occurs in Vogt's *Navaho Veterans* (*1951*). A summary of the use of projective techniques in anthropological research appears in Jules Henry and Spiro's "Psychological Techniques: Projective Tests in Field Work" (*1953*).

Content analysis "to determine the psychological state of persons and groups" is discussed in Berelson's *Content Analysis in Communication Research* (*1952*:75–80; also 90–98, 213–214, and 217–218). The latter four pages give bibliography for this topic. That the heroes and heroines of American magazine fiction express American values is the hypothesis successfully tested by Johns-Heine and Gerth in "Values in Mass Periodical Fiction, 1921–1940" (*1949*). This work provides a justification for using mass media as sources of personality data. Two stimulating papers on film analysis have appeared. One, by Bateson (*1949b*), deals with a Nazi motion picture, while Wolfenstein and Leites' *Movies: A Psychological Study* (*1950*) interprets many aspects of American movies in the light of American character structure.

Chapter 7

VERIFICATION

Undoubtedly much work in culture and personality not only remains unverified but there exists little likelihood of it being validated in the foreseeable future. Many patterns of action, thought, and feeling are published every year with nobody repeating the observations which underlie the generalizations. The same is true of the hypotheses which research workers advance and that may remain untested through the course of a lifetime. Several reasons for this state of affairs may be suggested.

1. There probably exists an implicit convention in anthropology that a field worker's descriptive patterns shall be accepted on the assumption that he possesses those characteristics of a scientist—honesty and objectivity—that give his work validity. Certainly we have reason to suspect that the subjective element quite unknown to the observer sometimes escapes management and affects results. But if verification were to be insisted upon in the case of every monograph, then very little material would be considered capable of comparative use. After all, most of the investigators in culture and personality are well-trained scientists, capable of careful observation and critical self-consciousness.

2. Many of the particular hypotheses in which a field worker relates facts in a particular community need no verification because their truth is implicit in wider already tested postulates of psychology,

sociology, or common sense (the latter not being too trustworthy). Thus, the predictable relationship between frustration and aggression sustains the validity of holding a child's tantrum to be related to some restrictive discipline imposed by a parent. To give another example, we maintain that the Kaska Indians experience an increase in the feeling of adequacy with grandiose planning (Honigmann, *1949a:* 272). For cross-cultural testing such a hypothesis can readily be formulated in more general terms. The proposition that "people project grandiose intentions into the future to bolster their feeling of adequacy" represents a principle validated by psychiatry as well as in common sense. In other words, assuming the veracity of the patterns with which the hypothesis is constructed, the relationship of the two events is predictably indicated by previous work in psychological research.

3. Neither personnel nor money is available to permit revisiting communities with the intention of verifying patterns. Similarly, few funds and little coöperation are forthcoming for the construction of experiments in which the degree of subjective involvement in pattern generalization could be studied. Available funds are more readily channeled into new research by researchers whose ability is often taken on faith rather than rigorously tested. Few communities have received the frequent revisits accorded to the Hopi, Zuni, and other Pueblos. It is among the Pueblo peoples that subsequent workers have made most contributions to the problem of pattern verification and observer reliability.

4. For some hypotheses we lack even the ready means of verification. For example, more comparative data in culture and personality are needed before we can test the correlates of cradleboarding or swaddling. We do not have the facilities of the laboratory in anthropology. The procedures of a science are always limited by the kinds of facts or the type of phenomena with which it deals.

With these introductory thoughts we turn to examine the role of concepts in the verification process. Then the procedures of validation will be more directly examined.

CONCEPTUALIZATION

Dampier's definition of science as involving "the rational study of the relations between concepts in which [natural] phenomena are expressed" reminds one that the scientist does not deal with raw facts. Rather he works with concepts derived from, and designating relationships between, facts. Pure facts *can* be immediately experienced but no science deals directly with raw sensory impressions (Northrop, 1949, chap. 3). In Western culture at least we are not accustomed to observe pure facts, consisting of sensory impressions. Instead we automatically infer common-sense objects from our experience. A description of a fact, therefore, is something more than a pure experience.

Conceptualizations vary in degree of abstractness. Certain concepts get their meaning by pointing to facts which can be experienced with relative directness. The meaning of *bookcase* may be conveyed by photographing or sketching that piece of furniture; the meaning of verbs like *run, throw,* and *smile* also derive their meaning from observable phenomena or observable relations between such phenomena. These may be called low-order abstractions or, for our purpose, concepts by inspection. Further removed from empirical reality and more abstract are "concepts by postulation" which stand for entities and relations that cannot be directly sensed. The existence of these entities and relations is postulated and they are defined in terms of a general theory that gives them meaning. For example, "guilt" is a state which cannot be directly observed but from its definition behavioral manifestations are deduced. Use of concepts by postulation in science requires that students pay careful heed to the way such high order abstractions are defined. Daily conversation between scientists sometimes ludicrously fails to be communicative because while each uses the "same" word—say *personality*—but uses it with a somewhat different meaning—one worker limiting or extending the other's meaning according to the theory in which the term is integrated.[1]

---

[1] Students in the author's classes have complained about Clyde Kluck-hohn's tendency to alter his definition of *personality* in successive writ-

The following quotation (Thompson, *1950*) will illustrate the difference between these two classes of concepts:

> During the first stage of the Hopi project investigation of social phenomena and, to a considerable extent, investigation of psychological phenomena proceeded mainly by inductive, natural-history methods of observation, description, and classification. During this phase the emphasis tended to be placed on concepts by inspection of observed behavior and on observed social relationships, especially by the social anthropologists and psychologists. A society was defined as a group of mutually interacting individuals. Since the concepts of "culture" and of "personality" in the field of social science, like the concept of "life" in the field of biology, were considered to determine the subject matter of the research, no attempt was made at the outset of the project to define them. The predominant, implicit conception of "culture," however, seemed to be a traditional one in terms of sum-totals of behavior patterns and culture "traits." There was a marked tendency to conceive "personality" in behavioristic terms: for example, as "social stimulus value." This working definition of "personality" was recognized as unsatisfactory, but no systematic hypothesis was postulated in terms of which the personality concept might be defined more adequately. Indeed, the formulation of such an hypothesis was avoided as premature, and psychological techniques based on several different hypotheses were employed experimentally. Failure of concepts by inspection to define the scientific problem involved in the Hopi problematic situation, and of predominantly empirical, natural-history methods to solve it, forced the present inquiry to move definitely and explicitly out of the natural-history stage of social theory to the stage of postulationally prescribed theory.

Two questions arise. Why does science need concepts by postulation? How do we know whether the unsensed events designated by such concepts are "worth" postulating?

---

ings. They feel that such inconsistency deprives them of ever getting to know what personality "is." They fail to see that different problems and different theoretical viewpoints suited to those problems lead a scientist to order his data differently. If one is using psychoanalytical theory the word *personality* may usefully and logically refer to the covert relations between ego, id, and superego. Utilizing behaviorism, however, will result in a much more objective definition of personality. For further light on concepts by postulation see Wisdom, 1952:25–26.

Like any science, culture and personality needs concepts by postulation because they afford better comprehension of the phenomena under analysis. Thus, the concept "character structure" explains why behavior is often repeated in the face of apparently unwarranted external conditions. The concepts "motive" and "unconscious conflict" help to explain why people say one thing but act in an opposite fashion. The most important (because they are the most useful) concepts in social science are of this postulated order. Consider them: "culture," "need," defence mechanism," "security," and "world view," not to mention "social norm," "opposition," and many others. Each of these notions, representing covert behavior, extends our understanding of overt behavior. Let us take the example of sexual impotence.[2] Through a concept by postulation we are able to connect two overt actions which, because they do not occur simultaneously, could otherwise not easily be assumed to be significantly related. These actions are, first, a harsh discipline in childhood that punishes a sexual transgression and, second, a later life failure to act in a sexual situation. Concepts like "inhibition" or "repression" serve as intervening variables to explain the enduring linkage between the early sexual discipline and the later failure. Another example of the utility of concepts by postulation involves those unsensed entities called "values." Prediction of group behavior in a wide variety of situations is facilitated when we have postulated a relatively few embracive values that guide the behavior of the members of the group.

How do we know whether such postulated entities or relations are worth retaining? Any concept is valuable only as long as it remains useful for solving problems. There is, of course, a way in which concepts by postulation may be tested. This involves knowledge of their consequences. If such postulates allow us accurately to predict behavior in relatively unknown situations, then we may accept them as true or as operative forces. Writing with the laboratory method of natural science in mind, Northrop (*1949*:60) says that concepts by postulation "designate unambiguously what is proposed to exist" and

---

[2] See below, pp. 273–274.

"formal logic is then applied to deduce theorems of consequences . . . which define experiments that can be performed." If the experiment gives the expected results, the predicted consequence is confirmed and the postulated entity or relation has a claim to validity.[3]

While the process of verification will be discussed more extensively below, concepts by postulation may be made clearer if we illustrate in some detail how such concepts are tested. It has been postulated that Americans are motivated by a *sense of guilt*. The postulated abstraction here is a covert, driving force named "guilt." What is guilt? Let us define guilt rather simply as an anxious state which follows a delict, has the character of remorse, and anticipates displeasure from the community (Fenichel, *1945*:134). Verification of a high-order abstraction, as was pointed out above, requires, first, deducing consequences from the concept and then ascertaining whether the deduced predictions are fulfilled. If guilt is indeed a motivating force of Americans it can be predicted (in terms of the definition) that anxiety, remorse, and fear of displeasure will follow behavior in which an American departs from a mos of his group regardless of whether anybody else knows of the delict. Unfortunately, these feelings and sentiments are themselves covert and must be translated into empirically recognizable signs. We know that words can be directly experienced by an observer, so let us interview the subject. Having made these deductions we can perhaps save time if, instead of waiting for a defaulter to come to the clinic, we construct an experiment to create defaulters in the laboratory. To do so we structure a situation in which theft is made easy and then interview both the subjects known to have stolen and those who did not. We inquire about their feelings. Our prediction is that thieves more often than nonthieves will give verbal evidence of anxiety, remorse, and evidence of anticipating

---

[3] Compare Margenau: "Having translated a particular set of data into constructs, the scientist transforms these constructs, within the context of a particular theory, into others by logical and mathematical rules. He then translates the new constructs back into sense data and sees whether these, under the conditions implied by the theory, are found to be present. If so, he says that he has verified the theory . . . in this particular instance" (Margenau, *1943*:68).

displeasure from their community. Furthermore, and this is essential, if guilt is to be distinguished from shame there must be evidence that guilt appeared in the personality immediately after the delict and not only with the beginning of the interview. If these consequences are made manifest by the subject then the state of guilt is indicated to operate.

The reader may have become uneasy reading through this example. Are we saying that it is sufficient to test a hypothesis in the community from which it was derived? For the anthropologist to remain within a particular community is to remain without the kind of universal knowledge to which science aspires. As anthropologists we must make the universal prediction that guilt-motivated people everywhere will react to situations of default in a common way. This way may include the states manifested by Americans but may also include other consequences. When this universal proposition has been widely tested then "guilt" acquires a universal currency and usefulness.

HYPOTHESIS FORMATION

A hypothesis consists of a verifiable connection between facts. Speaking more precisely, however, students of culture and personality do not relate facts but rather work with conceptualized patterns that have been derived from facts. It is necessary, then, before a hypothesis can be tested to make certain of the validity of the patterns constituting it. But whether we connect patterns of overt culture or personality to each other, overt to covert patterns, or covert to other covert patterns, the process of hypothesis formation fundamentally implies the predictable association of facts. Only by once more returning to the facts of experience can the connection be verified. We shall see that the problems of verification grow very complex as one moves from overt to covert pattern levels.

Particular and Universal Hypotheses

Hypotheses are usually constructed in the light of theories that give ground for assuming the correlation of particular facts. Two types of hypotheses may be distinguished. At the one extreme we have statements connecting two or more facts of a particular cultural context. At the opposite pole stand universal hypotheses that are predicted to obtain in a large number of cultural contexts. Goldschmidt (*1950*: 518–522) expresses the distinction as being between "permissive" and "requisite" functional relationships (Honigmann, *1952b*). The aim and very nature of science is to transcend particular hypotheses and to derive universal generalizations. For, as Northrop (*1949*:29) says:

If one restricts a theory solely to the evidence for which it is confirmed, then obviously the theory will seem to be true without qualification. But to extend it to all relevant evidence is to find as quickly as possible the point if any at which the theory is inadequate. When this new evidence appears, indicating the particular facts with respect to which the theory does not permit of unqualified generalization, a new theoretical problem arises, and a later Galilei must come forth to carry through its analysis. Thus the solution of one problem and the subsequent generation of new ones goes on endlessly, lifting science from problem to problem . . . with greater and greater generality.

The relationship of particular to universal hypotheses may be illustrated with Erikson's work (*1939*) on the Sioux Indians. First, we said, that particular hypotheses relate facts within a particular cultural context. Erikson posits that among the Sioux disallowance of biting tendencies of babies gives rise to the habit of playing with the teeth (132).

Universal hypotheses, however, are obtained by generalizing the interpretations constructed within particular cultures. Erikson goes on to say that frustration of an organ system fosters compulsive habits with reference to that organ system (138–139). The implication is that this may happen in any community.

By this time it must be obvious that to verify a hypothesis like the second one above, the meaning of frustration must be clearly defined and the concept of compulsive habit more clearly specified. Then it will be possible to collect data (in field work or from published ethnographies) which will prove, disprove, or commend the revision of the connection which is predicted to obtain between a certain kind of frustration and compulsive habits. Various disciplines are currently engaged in testing Erikson's proposition, at least further within the American community. It is somewhat disconcerting to report that the psychologists appear to find little evidence for the predicted relationship while many psychoanalysts feel they have already substantially established the validity of the hypothesis!

Here are a few more hypotheses entertained in current culture and personality research. No attempt has been made by us to define the concepts that appear in these statements or to deduce the experimental conditions necessary to test the propositions. The student may, by way of an exercise, wish to do this himself.

1. A group imposing little self-discipline on the individual is marked by a high incidence of overt external conflicts and a high incidence of aggressive behavior.

2. A group imposing little self-discipline on the individual is marked by a low incidence of internal conflict and neuroticism.

3. A group imposing much self-discipline on the individual is marked by a low incidence of overt external conflicts and a low incidence of aggressive behavior.

4. A group imposing much self-discipline on the individual is marked by a high incidence of internal conflict and neuroticism.[4]

5. The stability of a socially transmitted behavior system is inversely proportionate to the emotional stress accompanying its acquisition.[5]

6. Those individuals who support and protect a child or adult will retain the dependence and obedience of the person whom they protect or succor (Kluckhohn, *1949a*:211).

7. ". . . if children adopt a certain reaction in certain emotionally important—usually but not always, familial—situations, they are later

---

[4] Jenkins and Hewitt (*1946*) derive the first four from their clinical experience.

[5] In other words, destabilization of behavior under stress occurs in those areas where socialization has been most intense or severe—in American culture, for example, with reference to sphincter control and feeding. Stress tends to be accompanied by difficulties in the exercise of those behaviors (J. Henry, *1948*).

on apt to adopt a similar reaction in structurally analogous political situations" (Leites, 1948:103).

8. ". . . the way in which parent-child relationships are patterned in respect to such behaviors as: succoring-dependence, dominance-submission and exhibitionism-spectatorship, provides a learning situation for the child which patterns his subsequent behavior in situations where these behaviors are involved" (Mead, 1948a:213).

Problems in Genetic Hypothesis Construction

Genetic hypotheses are often unprecisely stated. They frequently fail to specify clearly the conditions under which subsequent behavior that is linked to childhood will appear (Leites, 1948:108). Thus it is predicted that "effort and optimism" will mark character structure following a childhood in which love rewards a child who fulfills readily achievable performance standards. But we are not told under what later life circumstances or in connection with what tasks "effort and optimism" may be expected.

While genetic interpretations are often inadequately formulated in culture and personality, such hypotheses are often misunderstood by critics. Leites (1948) has formulated some propositions intended to clarify the nature of the work being done in the field of genetic studies. Here are six propositions adapted from that author:

1. Many of the statements which are made to connect child training acts with adult character structure are supported by little available proof. In part this state of affairs arises from the difficulty of verifying hypotheses in social science.

2. The basic assumption of culture and personality goes something like this: "There tends to be a transfer of feeling and behavior that is 'learned' in early intimate relations" with adults. This assumption also has not been proven.

3. Genetic hypotheses never imply that sequence A in childhood acts as the sole cause of an adult behavior. Other childhood experiences probably always contribute to the same adult trait. "It is a frequent fallacy in the human sciences to believe that if somebody at

a certain moment talks about the importance of factor A, he is running down the importance of factors B, C . . ."

4. "It is not implied that only intimate ('psychological') childhood events determine adult behavior to the exclusion of various wider (economic, political, social, etc.) aspects of the adult environment. On the contrary the presumption is that any adult act is motivated by" (a) the residual effects of previous experiences of the individual from birth (at least) to the present and (b) is also determined by features of the biological organism and geographical environment.

5. Psychological analysis of adult cultural situations does not imply that childhood is "all important" but it does affirm that it is "important."

6. While patterns of child training are regarded as important in the explanation of cultural behavior, it is not implied that these childhood patterns in their turn are uninfluenced by other areas of socially standardized behavior. That is to say, child rearing patterns are determined by other aspects of culture—economics, technology, ideology, and so forth.

VERIFICATION

Scientists agree that the most acceptable statements are those which lead to successful prediction. This formula for scientific truth (other kinds of truth need not concern us here) applies to pattern generalizations as well as to hypotheses. The process whereby any such statement is verified will now be examined.

Pattern Verification

Patterns purport to describe how the members of a particular community regularly act, think, or feel. Overt patterns (Americans brush their teeth vigorously; German mothers are undemonstrative) are verified when an independent observer visits the community or consults the expressive material products from which they were obtained. He thus makes certain that the predicted behaviors really occur.

Covert patterns and highly abstract superpatterns can be verified only after particular, observable or verbalized signs of the concept by postulation have been stated clearly. The more vaguely a covert pattern is described, without the evidence of overt behavior from which it was originally derived, the more difficult or impossible will be its verification. On the other hand, if a particular type of anxiety, for example, is defined as manifesting itself in (1) frightening dreams of being attacked by large animals and (2) avoidance of color responses in the Rorschach test, then one can readily test for the occurrence of these signs and establish the veracity of that covert pattern.

Any fairly complex bit of socially standardized behavior occurs under a variety of simultaneously determining conditions—motivational, geographical, technological, and social. If the situation ("field") of determinants alters between the time when the pattern was constructed to the time when observation recurs, then the predicted behavior may actually not materialize. For example, the Kaska Indians frequently demanded gifts of food, cigarettes, and other favors from American troops stationed on the Alaska Highway in 1943 and 1944. When Canadian troops replaced Americans in this part of northwestern Canada the Indians reduced their demands. They learned that the new troops were not in a position to be as free with favors. Therefore demandingness as a pattern could scarcely be verified as easily in 1944 as in 1943.

On the other hand, certain overt and covert patterns show great tenacity in time. They are retained even when people move in space, exchanging one set of geographical, technological, or demographic conditions for others. To illustrate, in the seventeenth and eighteenth centuries explorers and missionaries visiting the Indians of northeastern North America found them chronically apprehensive, individualistic, suspicious, and their community relatively devoid of close emotional ties. Under the influence of alcohol these Indians showed a tendency to release carefully concealed interpersonal animosity through overt physical violence. In sobriety a surface amiability characterized them. Nearly three hundred years later Hallowell (1946:204–218) reports that "the same emotional structure remains characteristic of some of the Indians of the Eastern Woodlands at the present time." He documents this generalization from direct observation of on-going behavior and further cites Rorschach data to support his observations. Thus, the patterns inferred by early visitors to America have survived to the present day. In the intervening period, however, the Indians have undergone major cultural changes.

It is happily possible to add that the patterns obtained by Hallowell and before him by the early missionaries and traders have been verified by still other field workers in this area. For example, Ruth Landes (1938) describes the Canadian Ojibwa ethos as characterized by separateness, aloneness, and self-sufficiency. By the first concept she refers to the lack of strong interpersonal ties among the Indians, a pattern clearly made by seventeenth-century observers. Affectionate demonstrations, says Landes, are taboo even in the family and especially toward males. "Social aloneness" refers to the isolated residence during a large part of the winter and the uneasiness possessing people when they join together in the "crowded" trading post during the summer. "Self-sufficiency" is demonstrated by the way the Indians try to stand unaided. The community is "saturated with anxiety. . . . To alleviate this anxiety an Ojibwa may not depend upon the support of his fellows, whom he characteristically regards with envy and suspicion and from whom he expects similar unfriendly emotions." Another investigator who confirms previously established patterns of Northwestern Indian personality and ethos is William Caudill (1949). He worked with acculturated Wisconsin Ojibwa children. Interpreting the Thematic Apperception Test, Caudill sees social cohesiveness in the Indian community to be almost nil; each individual spends his life pursuing personal ends. Emotional ties within the loosely and casually organized family are so weak that children fail to identify with any person in that group. Children reveal weariness and frustration, the latter motivation frequently exploding in undirected violence. Caudill sums up saying that the Ojibwa child finds it difficult to develop any affective interpersonal relations—warm or hostile—because of the atomism marking the social structure.

The northeastern Indians illustrate how successive studies in an area contribute to pattern verification and confirm the reliability of previous observers. A word of caution is in order. Imbued with the prestige of a previous investigator or the appeal of some pattern, an investigator may lose his objectivity. Instead of testing the reliability of the earlier observer the subsequent field worker may actually standardize his predecessor's errors. Scientists must insist that the evidence meets the specifications of the pattern. Otherwise the pattern must be revised or discarded as unproven.

Caution must be exercised in trying to verify a pattern for which the subgroup to which it applies in a heterogeneous community is not explicitly stated. For example, Americans are supposed to be eager for educational advantages, mobility up the class ladder, and possession of prestige marks like a new house in a "good" neighborhood. These values, although they may be ideals to all Americans, are not demonstrably revealed by all segments of the American population in the way that the presumably overt pattern suggests. Increasing evidence indicates that the picture of an education-hungry, socially ambitious America applies best to middle-class Americans and is not so true among lower-class citizens.[6]

Hypothesis Verification

Proceeding to the validation of hypotheses, what procedures are employed to test connections between facts? Appeal is once more made to prediction. Is the expected relationship repeatedly encountered with a probability greater than chance? The following rather lengthy example should make clear the procedure that is involved.

Hallowell (1946:222) correlates the anxiety of Northeastern Indians with their atomistic social organization. Sorcery, he holds, by its threat divides the people. "This is the psychological explanation, it seems to me, of the 'atomism,' or individualism, of the Ojibwa society and of Indians with comparable cultures in the past. It is impossible for people to get together when their outlook is colored by the possibility of malevolence, particularly when there are no social institutions that demand a high degree of cooperation." Carrying Hallowell's

---

[6] See below, pp. 319, 323.

analysis further we assume that the relationship between sorcery and atomistic social structure is probably mutual. That is, the absence of cohesive behavior patterns, like chieftainship and a sense of group allegiance, leaves the community without the means for controlling, arresting, or obviating sorcery behavior. Before people can form a tight organization, they must not only trust one another but there must be some provision for keeping down divisive tendencies of which sorcery is an example.

We pointed out above that hypotheses cannot sufficiently be tested in the community. Anthropologists seek to establish generalized hypotheses cross culturally, that is, through the so-called comparative method. We therefore take Hallowell's statement and deduce the following generalized hypothesis: *There is a direct relationship between the degree of ingroup sorcery and the degree of organizational atomism in a community.* Verification of this proposition calls for information about a representative series of communities. These would then be divided into two categories, one representing communities with considerable ingroup sorcery and the other those with little or no ingroup sorcery. Our prediction is that the first category will also contain a significantly greater number of communities with atomistic forms of social organization than the second.

Fortunately, a very similar "experiment" has been attempted by Beatrice Whiting (1950:82–91). She first selected two categories, communities in which sorcery was an important explanation of sickness and those in which it did not figure importantly as an explanation for illness (it being deduced that communities where sorcery is prevalent frequently use it as a cause of illness). She then discovered that 60 percent of the communities where sorcery was important also *lacked individuals or groups of individuals with authority to punish offenses between families.* The presence of such individuals may be taken as an operational criterion of corporate rather than atomistic social organization. Beatrice Whiting's work reveals a dependable but not invariable relationship to exist between the importance or unimportance of sorcery and the presence or absence of superordinate punishment (see Table 1). The correlation obtained ($r_{tet.}$ + .85) is

TABLE 1. Association of Sorcery and Superordinate Punishment

	Sorcery Important	Sorcery Unimportant
No superordinate punishment	60%	6%
Superordinate punishment	10%	24%

high. Statistical calculation indicates less than one chance in a hundred that the association discovered is due to chance. This becomes significant when it is understood that statisticians are impressed whenever there is less than three chances in a hundred that associations are due to chance. Thus, on a universal scale we have derived what may turn out to be a principle, namely that sorcery is dependably or functionally related to social atomism.

Correlation between two facts does not fully explain how two or more facts are related. In this case we are further told by Hallowell that fear of sorcery is the covert state keeping people unorganized and at a distance from each other. It would now be desirable to design further hypotheses or cite partially verified hypotheses from psychiatry and psychology that would help to test the hunch that fear of magical malevolence contributes to social atomism. The work of science is never done!

Hypotheses can never be completely verified. Despite our use of the term "universal" no hypothesis is every fully validated for the universe for all time. If an experiment is performed once or a number of times—if fifty or a hundred communities are examined—we cannot, except fallaciously, reason with certainty to all other cases which have not been examined nor even come into being! The number of possible cases is indeterminate. We may expect the events to continue to recur together in future or unexamined cases but "expectation . . . is a psychological attitude; it is not a demonstration of proof" (Crissman, 1943:435). Even though it were possible to test a hypothesis using all the communities in the world, some day a community might develop that would deny the principle. Science is always provisional. Concepts, hypotheses, and principles are in a state of continual flux.

Even objective observations may have to be reëvaluated when new knowledge comes to light or as new techniques of observation appear. Science accepts nothing as invariable or permanent (Freedman, 1950:81).

There are no short cuts to scientific truth. To obtain predictable knowledge particular hypotheses must always be generalized for universal testing. The process of testing may take much time and often it becomes difficult or impossible to find the evidence in ethnographies that will permit cross cultural validation. Under these circumstances some research workers are willing to accept tentatively hypotheses that *seem true by experience*. Acceptance of statements on a basis of plausibility may be motivated by personal prejudice or desire. On the other hand, the "test of reasonableness" resembles a modified form of prediction. Statements that sound reasonable because they accord with scientific and other experience are presumably predictive. Without a thorough knowledge of world cultures, however, it would be highly incautious to extend the test of experience beyond those cultural limits within which one is on familiar ground. Applying the test of reasonableness to hypotheses difficult to verify is similar to what Erikson (1950:122) means when he makes the capacity of a hypothesis to explain facts an index of validity. "Our proof must lie in the coherent meaning which we may be able to give to seemingly irrational data within one culture and to analogous problems in comparable cultures."

The Verification of Interviews

When the subject in an interview says something, how do we ascertain that what he said is true? Of course, any communication by an informant is a fact. The question asked really implies a desire to know if the interview statement corresponds to other forms of behavior. To test the truth of an interview statement we deduce or predict the relevant forms of behavior from the statement and look for those predictions.

For example, when it was autumn some Kaska Indians told the writer that winter meant a time of hard work, a period when men were constantly on the go, always "rustlin' " for a living. Observation in the early winter secured little data corroborating this statement. Our prediction, based on the earlier statements of informants, that in the winter people would work hard, was thus proven false. We still have a significant datum in the communication—one perhaps deserving further analysis—but in one sense it lacks validity. Other data about Kaska personality soon suggested that our informants had voiced an ideal pattern in stating the hard work of winter. They expressed what they should do rather than what they would do. Ideal patterns which do not conform to real behavior deserve careful study. Analysis may reveal, for example, that the subject had no intention of acting according to his verbal pattern. He lied, perhaps, for some material or intangible advantage expected from his neighbors or from the interviewer. This inference again must be validated before it can be accepted. Or, it may be that instead of expecting external advantages to accrue through misrepresenting, the informant derived some covert gain from the act. Kaska Indians place great stress on self-sufficiency and personal independence. Promising himself to work hard and to pursue success in winter gratifies the Kaska's character structure. Planning unrealistically constitutes an act of self-glorification, a testimonial of resourcefulness, that gratifies the ego. If circumstances interfere with carrying out such plans then people who are perfectionistic or compulsively inclined will become very anxious, frustrated and depressed. But a flexible people, like the Kaska, find little difficulty allowing their plans to go unfulfilled.

Our discussion concerning verification of interview statements has emphasized correspondence between verbalized intention and real activity. Similar confirmation, secured through independent evidence, is required before a covert pattern may validly be inferred from a subject's oral communication. In validating covert patterns an investigator frequently compares data secured via different techniques —for example from passive as well as active interviewing, dream interpretation, standardized interviews like the Piaget or Stewart tests, or from the Rorschach. Independent confirmation of a covert pattern through different instruments of course fulfills the test of prediction. We thus feel warranted in accepting the unseen pattern. Using any instrument involves an implicit or explicit prediction that the covert material will motivate an expected type of response. Appearance of the response therefore supports the postulated covert state.

Verification of Dream Interpretations

Psychologists usually interpret dreams by regarding them as symbols of covert personality patterns—wishes, ideas, or feelings—which the individual finds difficult to verbalize. Dreams may also be interpreted as indicating overt action patterns characteristic of the dreamer. In any event, the associations to the dream (or the observer's knowledge of events antecedent to the dream) provide valuable aids to interpretation. This still leaves the question, how do we know that dream interpretations are true?

A program for scientifically testing the validity of any dream interpretation must be an extraordinarily complex matter, one rendered more confusing because so little actual work has been done. Two phases of the problem may be distinguished straight off—an individual and a group phase. In brief, the covert pattern which (through interpretation) is linked to a particular dream (or portion of a dream) must be tested like any concept by postulation. Dreams held to reflect characteristic modes of observable action are verified by looking to see if the overt behavior actually occurs.

The gap must be bridged between individual and group, however. The information gained about an *individual* in the course of dream interpretation has value equivalent to a communication made by one subject in the course of an active or passive interview. Knowledge derived in this fashion contributes to knowledge of modal personality only if similar data obtained from other subjects are generalized into a pattern.

Three steps can be distinguished in the verification of dream interpretations:

1. If some feature of a subject's dream is interpreted as referring to a postulated state of motivation, then validation of that interpreta-

tion requires correctly predicting the overt consequence of the postulate. But this makes it valid for the particular individual alone!

2. An interpretation will be valid for two or more individuals in
the same community if the same dream feature can be related to the
same concept by postulation which in turn has similar observable
consequences in each individual.

3. An interpretation will be valid for two or more communities—
and thus approaches universal validity—if the same dream feature
can be related to the same concept by postulation in each community
and that concept by postulation is in turn related to similar predictable, observable consequences in each community.

With the experimental verification of dreams in its initial stages
(Mazer, *1951*), it is not surprising that psychology and anthropology
should still be far, far removed from a universally valid system of
dream interpretation. Theoretically such a system of dream analysis
is possible. It demands the establishment of dependable relationships
between certain dreams (or portions of dreams) and verifiable behavior patterns. From one point of view it makes little difference if
dream interpretation starts from a priori universal interpretations
(the classical psychoanalytical method) or if interpretation and validation start with a particular case in a specific community and then
widen out toward universal interpretations. The latter method appeals to the writer as being less dogmatic and more in keeping with
scientific procedure.

Let us see how the anthropologist actually operates when he interprets a dream. For this exercise we again turn to the Kaska Indians.

It has been suggested that in dreams protrusions symbolize the
male sex organ and the male's normally assertive role in copulation
(Schilder, *1942*:153). Aware of this clinically derived interpretation,
we implicitly predicted sexual inadequacy or impotence for a young
Kaska man who reported a dream in which he was attacked by a
grizzly bear. "My gun stick. I get nervous. I try to take shot at him.
My gun got no power. Goes šššššš—goes out quick . . ." (Honigmann, *1949a*:162). When interviewed, the informant rejected the

interpretation equating gun and penis. Our prediction was nevertheless confirmed when on two subsequent occasions, according to reliable testimony, the informant experienced acute impotence. Previous discussion makes it obvious that we have scarcely begun verification of this particular interpretation (hypothesis) by remaining with one Kaska Indian. The same or a similar dream associated with similar consequences in a representative series of Indians and later other communities would constitute satisfactory proof for the validity of the interpretation. Psychiatry helps us now. Evidence from a variety of communities indicates that weapons and similar protrusions are dependably associated with the penis in the dreamer's mind (Kluckhohn and Morgan, 1951:123; Lincoln, 1939:118–119; Mazer, 1951:270). In other words, previous research into dream interpretation in exotic communities, although limited in quantity, suggests that we are correct in equating penis and gun in the informant's dream. Our interpretation of impotence is based on the inadequate performance of the weapon. For this portion of the hypothesis we are on much less certain ground. And what has the grizzly bear to do with all this? Common in Kaska dreams, we interpret the animal as symbolizing dread of sexual or other intense interpersonal relationships. Such a hypothesis has also been cross-culturally validated in some degree (Róheim, 1950:13–18, 22–23, 30–33).[7] Of course, patterns of acute impotence or dread of intense interpersonal relationships cannot reasonably be generalized for most men in the community. We need similar evidence from other informants to obtain some idea of frequency. Only scattered evidence of impotence came to light in the course of field work with the Kaska Indians. Hence we assume this symptom to be a rare alternative pattern in the community.

Symbolism that is analogous to dreaming may be found in other areas of culture—in plays, fiction, decorative design, etc. Valid interpretation of such symbolism requires the same process of cross-cultural prediction which has been outlined for dream analysis.

---

[7] We need not agree when Róheim says that symbolization of the dread of human beings by ferocious animals is unlearned.

Verification of Test Interpretations

When an investigator wants to learn about group characteristics from a test he first interprets the test results and turns to find out if the interpretation is borne out in on-going behavior, in the responses to other tests, or in interview data.

Let us at this point limit ourselves to a discussion of the Rorschach. The responses given to the cards are valid (1) if the concepts by postulation inferred from the responses are warranted or (2) if any overt behavior which may be predicted from test results actually appears in daily life or in an interview situation. So, for example, an individual whose test responses are interpreted as indicating "opposition" can be expected to show opposition in other areas of life. If the predicted behavior does not appear the particular interpretation proves to have been false. Similarly if a subject gives responses interpreted as indicating creativity, then we can predict that creativity —operationally defined—will appear in other areas of life. Fulfillment of the prediction connotes some degree of validity for the particular individual in that community.

Prediction in culture and personality research often has more of the character of hindsight than foresight. Thus in the work of Abel and Hsu (1949) Rorschachs given to Chinese indicated such personality patterns as control of impulse, a pliant and disinterested role in interpersonal relationships, and spontaneous enjoyment of nature and food with the ability to experience such enjoyment. We might think that prediction demands revisiting the Chinese to discover if they indeed manifest these tendencies on an overt level. Abel and Hsu, however, look back upon their previous experience with Chinese and say that these patterns are consistent with their knowledge of Chinese personality. Field workers do this in more controlled fashion when, after the field trip is over, they match test interpretations against field notes.

The problem of test verification becomes more complicated when connections between test response and personality patterns are extended across cultural boundaries. A verified relationship between

Rorschach responses and other behavior in a particular community constitutes a particular hypothesis. To be universally valid, the hypothesis must be true in a large series of communities. Testing ascertains whether the same interpretations can indeed be employed in culturally distinct communities. Such testing is only now beginning for the Rorschach test. The results *promise* that in general this instrument will be useful for cross-cultural research. However, very much more work remains to be done before any significant claim to validity can be made. Hallowell (*1945a*) and Oberholzer (*1944*) are two investigators who have given explicit attention to the cross-cultural validity of the Rorschach. Both agree that basic principles of interpretation can be applied to data secured from nonliterate people.

Obviously the task of validating the Rorschach or Thematic Apperception tests cross culturally is being carried forward every time that a research worker applies the test in a particular non-European community. For example, the present author collected Rorschachs among the Kaska Indians and discovered a relative absence of color responses (Honigmann, *1949a*:300–302). On the basis of Rorschach analysis done in Europe and America, low frequency of color responses suggests emotional anergy, repressed spontaneity, and a distrust of external situations tinged with strong emotion. Such an interpretation turns out to be warranted by the emotional isolation observable in Indian behavior. The people seek to preserve emotional aloofness and social detachment. They are unable to tolerate affection or to express any considerable warmth in the majority of their interpersonal relations. Now, among the Chippewa, Barnouw (*1950*:19, 22–23, 27) secured Rorschach protocols also distinguished by a relative absence of color responses. If the test be valid then the low frequency of color in Chippewa responses must also be related to repressed spontaneity and emotional anergy. Validation requires prediction that Chippewa overt behavior will reveal signs of emotional isolation similar to those recorded among the Kaska. Data confirm this expectation. Both groups strive to suppress overt emotionality. Barnouw reports that mother and child among the people he studied interact without intense emotion. Interpersonal relations are generally undemonstrative in the community. Such correspondence contributes modestly to the cross-cultural validity of the Rorschach instrument.

Much of what has been said about the verification of Rorschach interpretations applies to the Thematic Apperception Test. One may question whether redesigning the pictures of this instrument to make them locally meaningful permits successive workers to operate with the same or a readily comparable test. Logically it would seem that under such circumstances the TAT will not be cross-culturally verified unless the changes are extremely minor.

The process of verification applied to tests like Piaget's for immanent justice, the Moral Ideology, or Emotional Response, is best understood with reference to the previous discussion of interview validity. These devices correspond to highly standardized, guided interviews which make use of a variety of open-end questions or directions.

It is worth stressing that psychology customarily verifies test interpretations between individuals belonging to a single community. Thus, a Rorschach test interpretation is validated by seeing whether the response—say, one which focuses on inanimate movement—is, when given to a series of subjects, indeed regularly associated with internal conflict. Culture and personality verifies test hypotheses between communities which often differ considerably in culture. From this it follows that culture and personality is in a position to test on a universal scale the particular hypotheses of psychology and other social sciences.

Verification of Thematic and Product Analysis

Works of imagination and products of socially patterned behavior may be interpreted to reveal emotion, patterns of overt behavior, or covert motivational states pertaining to the individuals of the community. Two phases are associated with verifying such interpretations. We may ascertain whether the theme inferred from the products, say a collection of short stories, is to be found in *real* or *ideal* personality. Does the theme reflect the way people actually behave or how they fancy themselves behaving? If the latter, then a second question occurs: What use does the group make of such an ideal? By the second phase of verification we refer to covert patterns inferred from works of imagination or material products. The problem lies in determining whether the postulated motivational state is warranted—whether it really operates. The question demands deduction of hypotheses from the definition of the postulated state and then extending the verification of such hypotheses as widely as possible. The procedure may be illustrated with reference to film analysis.

Siegfried Kracauer (1947) surveys German films which appeared between 1918 and 1933. He interprets their contents and sees the themes and images to reflect a view of the world as a topsy-turvy place, lacking order and stability. In the twenties, for example, films exhibited a rash of realism and featured small bits of real life. Street scenes became popular as well as fairs or carnivals. These images, Kracauer sees related to a German character structure that perceived the Germany of Weimar Republic days as confusing and anarchic. Here and there themes in the films suggest a note of longing for authoritarian protection and security. In *Die Strasse* a middle-class citizen flees off the street to security represented by his wife and home. In the picture's final scene the returning adventurer rests his head on the wife's shoulder while she caresses his arm as if he were a child. In 1927 an American film reviewer contributed to Kracauer's interpretation when he wrote, commenting on the last scene, "Better stay where you are. Life in the haunts you are unused to is dangerous. Romance may always be around the corner, but the effort to find it is hardly worth the candle." Kracauer's analysis postulates German character structure as dependent on props of authority and security. Without these props the world looks terrifying, lacking order or plan, and is as confused as a carnival. A number of other authors offer similar interpretations of German character structure without deriving them from films. Verification demands specification of the observable signs of this character structure and then checking for the overt manifestations of those signs. However, are we **not** assuming without evidence that the German character of Weimar Republic days persists to the present? Another task of verification requires ascertaining whether the symbols and themes of the film are dependably linked with similar character structures in a varied series of communities. Such work has still to begin.

Gregory Bateson (1949b) also analyzed films in the course of carrying out research on the character structure of modern nations. He describes his work as involving inferences of "significant themes" derived from the moving pictures, i.e., concepts by postulation. To verify these in a particular community he proposes to interview members of the group and also to study their interpersonal behavior. What Bateson suggests, of course, is to verify through interviews the observable consequences deduced from the covert themes.

CONCLUSION

This chapter has probably left the reader with the belief that science is in a rather constant state of uncertainty but striving always to move toward greater certainty. Such a picture is accurate in the main. Science is process, activity, hard work. There is a relatively more glamorous view of science, in which the researcher handles ideas, makes guesses, and constructs conceptual systems. Unfortunately each bright hunch carries with it some obligation on somebody's part to follow through with verification. Any guess or hypothesis presents science with an unsolved problem. "It is not scientifically immoral to play freely with ideas. Scientific guesses, amenable to test, are in the last analysis what makes science move. Speculation is legitimate, and heuristic, when it is presented as speculation. When it is presented as fact . . . it is not legitimate . . ." (Gittelson, 1950:609). If for any reason a particular hypothesis is not amenable to wider testing it remains, from the standpoint of science, suspended at some point between truth and falsity or at some level of probability.

Suggestions for Further Reading

A highly stimulating discussion of hypothesis formation occurs in the first chapter of Wisdom's *The Foundations of Inference in Natural Sci-*

ence (*1952*). Here the author also makes clear that no entity (concept by postulation) incapable of being related to some kind of perception has a place in science. However, such entities may be relatable to perception both directly and indirectly, as we have indicated. The initial chapter of Abegg's *The Mind of East Asia* (*1952*) deals with the very difficult problem in cultural science of finding words to capture the concepts and experience of people who in personality are different from us. Fruitful too is Znaniecki's *Cultural Sciences: Their Origin and Development* (*1952*), chapter 6.

Literature concerning the verification of cultural hypotheses is scarcely rich. Sociologists have been far more self-conscious about the scientific status of their discipline and methodological guides like Goode and Hatt's *Methods in Social Research* (*1952*) or Furfey's *The Scope and Method of Sociology* (*1953*) contain good discussions of hypothesis formation and testing. No comparable text by an anthropologist exists nor do the textbooks in the field carry their discussion of method to the level of hypothesis construction. The reader who wants to read further in this important subject has much material available on the psychology shelves of his library. Recommended are Stagner's *Psychology of Personality* (*1948*), 36–63; Newcomb's *Social Psychology* (*1950*), chapter 1.

Perhaps cultural anthropology in general may soon pay the same close attention to the logic of its scientific procedures that it has given to historical method. Concern with the latter is far more dominant in *Anthropology Today* (ed. Kroeber, *1953*), a book that grew out of an international conference called to summarize the state of learning in the field.

PART THREE

PATTERNING OF PERSONALITY

The cultural pattern of any civilization makes use of certain segments of the great arc of potential human purposes and motivations. . . . The great arc along which all the possible human behaviours are distributed is far too immense and too full of contradictions for any one culture to utilize even any considerable portion of it. Selection is the first requirement.

RUTH BENEDICT

Chapter 8

LEARNING

From the standpoint of the individual in a community, culture, excluding material artifacts, is reducible to individual regularities of activity, thought, and feeling. Truly, there are questions concerning cultural development and change that can never be answered in terms of such reductionism (White, 1949:77–79, 125–126). On the other hand, certain sociocultural problems may be explored very usefully from the perspective of the individual. This is true if we wish to know how cultural behavior is acquired and standardized over successive generations. We can afford to repeat, however, that anthropology does not study the individual as a unique personality but as a member of a group. Brown (1951:173) says: ". . . the role of the sociologist and of the social anthropologist is to study this social component of personality, leaving it to the psychologist to study the totality of personality and the individual differences."

With this chapter we begin to inquire how the individual acquires the socially standardized patterns of activity, thought, and feeling which constitute a portion of the community's culture or make up his personality. For a term to designate the operations shaping behavior we will use *patterning*.

PATTERNING

Patterning is used throughout this book as an active verb designating the process, originating with a group or a community, whereby an individual's personality is modified, limited, or standardized. Behavior is also standardized by the constitutional endowments of the person—some of which he shares with all other persons in all communities—or by demographic and geographical determinants (Gillin, 1948b:198–206). As students of culture and personality, however, we are not as much interested in the overall aspects of personality formation as we are in the way in which group linked factors operate in that respect. We want to study "social patterning"—a phrase which may sometimes be useful to indicate specific exclusion of other determinants which influence behavior. Nevertheless, it is well to keep in mind that considerable information about individual patterns of activity, thought, and feeling may be gained by studying the other factors which operate on the individual at a given point in time.

As the word will be used in this book, patterning refers to any force or item of group or community origin which operates to shape personality, i.e., to standardize behavior. "Group membership" (to use the felicitous phrase of Kluckhohn and Murray, 1953:57–58) exposes the individual to certain tools which help standardize his actions; to a diet, which influences covert and overt behavior; to interpersonal behavior patterns, which encourage and fix certain behavioral responses; not to mention: apparel and shelters, silence or din, binding or a richness of tactual stimulation—all effective, we believe, in standardizing individual personality within set limits, thus making possible the derivation of modal patterns by an observer.

This definition of patterning is neither primarily psychological or sociological—neither exclusively concerned with the dynamics of learning or with the effect of social relational factors on the standardization of behavior. Admittedly, however, the present approach to personality formation is as specialized as those others. It is anthropological. Cultural anthropology, it may be well to recall, differs from the other social sciences—economics, political science, or sociology—in seeing culture as a whole (Mead, 1953a:652). If an anthropologist studies political behavior (no matter in what kind of society) he does so differently from the political scientist in that he studies power relations as a part of the total cultural configuration in which those patterns presumably bear a systematic relationship to economic behavior, nursing behavior, and so on. The anthropological approach applies also to study of the development and standardization of personality. As anthropologists we inquire how personality is related to extant patterns of socially standardized behavior and to the products of behavior (food, tools, even noise) of the group or community in which the individual enjoys membership.

The reader is reminded of earlier definitions which he met in this book. The definitions of personality and culture given above are, of course, very closely dependent upon the notion of patterning. Personality refers to an individual's socially standardized patterns of action, thought, and feeling. Culture denotes the socially standardized patterns of activity, thought, and feeling of some enduring social group. These definitions warn or cue the reader to regard as data of primary significance only those behaviors that can be linked to group or community factors. The purely idiosyncratic is specifically eliminated from the referents of personality or culture.

Patterning we hope to demonstrate is influenced by more than social relationships. Oscar Lewis (1951:296), for example, speaks of "the brutalizing, isolating nature" of a farmer's work in Tepoztlan which has "far-reaching effects on his personality and his relations with others. One of these effects is to make him an individualist with faith in his own power alone and with reluctance to seek or give economic aid, to borrow or lend, or to cooperate . . ." The relationship between certain patterns of technology (White, 1949:364) and features of personality is an area deserving further investigation. On the other hand it must not be supposed that the farmer's tasks pattern personality in isolation from other influences. The picture is far more complex. The Tepoztlan peasant also responds with an idea that the world is a dangerous place in which security lies "first and foremost" in the economic independence of the biological family.

Personality is patterned by many factors of group membership, by the emotional quality of interpersonal interaction, the content of that interaction, and other activities which people in groups perform.

SOME BASIC POSTULATES

A postulate is an embracive proposition, difficult to fully verify because it is widely embracive, from which specific deductions are drawn for investigation. One proceeds from postulates to more manageable, verifiable hypotheses that guide the collection of data.

Patterning is an initial postulate in culture and personality research because it defines the universe from which data will be obtained. We postulate that individual behavior is shaped by the socially standardized patterns of the group or community as well as by the material products which the members of a community manufacture or use. From psychology, psychiatry, and sociology anthropologists derive other basic postulates that guide their research. The following propositions may repeat things already mentioned in earlier pages but such repetition should help the reader to reorient himself after our lengthy preoccupation with method.

1. Human behavior can be explained or understood. It is amenable to scientific investigation. (The necessity of such an assumption is obvious. It is a logical premise from which stems the whole field of psychological research.)
2. Human behavior is largely learned. Such learning depends on the fact that every human being matures in a social environment and for a long period of maturation is dependent on other individuals whose rewards and punishments produce modifications of behavior.
3. In all communities people of the same age, sex, and status show relative uniformity of behavior in similar situations.
4. All communities recognize an ideal personality (or, when sex and status differences are emphasized, personalities). Ideal personality types constitute a value orientation (Vogt, 1951:7) that guides parents and other adults in directing the behavior of children.
5. Many patterns of behavior become established through the more or less deliberate use of reward and punishment meted out by other members of the community.

6. Many patterns are learned early in life and remain to influence all further learning. From this postulate derives the importance attached to early experiences for an understanding of human behavior.

7. The learning process consists essentially in an individual modifying, shaping, encouraging, or suppressing his innate tendencies and potentialities. An understanding of adult behavior demands explicit knowledge of the modifications which the organism has undergone.

8. Since in all communities it is primarily the parents who reward and punish the child, the attitudes and relationships of the child to his parents become prototypes of his attitudes towards people whom he subsequently meets. If the parents are assisted by other individuals in training the child then the attitudes and relations to these others are also important for understanding subsequent patterns of interpersonal relations. Siblings relations may also act as prototypes.

9. Most human activity is motivated by covert patterns, called motives, which are superimposed on primary, universal drives.

10. Motives may be conscious or unconscious. If they are unconscious then they cannot readily be verbalized. Hence people have difficulty in expressing all of the motives which impel them to act.

11. When secondary motives are shared by a majority of the community, the culture of that community will include standardized means for gratifying such needs in ways that do not threaten the continuing existence of the group.

12. Particularly in a relatively homogeneous community, social relations, rituals, and other patterns of behavior will be linked by emotional qualities. From such linkages derives a feeling of consistency and an ethos which may be described by an observer.[1]

LEARNING—DIRECT AND INDIRECT

Regularities of behavior become established through learning, a process whereby reward and punishment are instrumental in modifying organismic potentialities and capacities. It is scarcely our intention to review the enormous literature that has accumulated around the topic of learning. Instead we may content ourselves with the salient aspects of learning approached from the standpoint of personality development.

---

[1] The list is adapted from Gorer, *1949b*:274–275.

Learning occurs when an organism, by virtue of some particular experience, acquires a tendency to perform a given overt or covert response under stated conditions. A member of the Air Force, for example, through training acquires the readiness to salute when he perceives a uniform carrying certain insignia; a Muslim responds to the Quran with a feeling of respect; a motorist learns to respond to red, green, or orange lights; experience teaches a Kaska youth to estimate the age of a moose track by the freshness of the torn soil; a Samoan adult male becomes accustomed to occupy a particular seating position at a village council meeting, and so on. Once more we perceive how culture patterns fundamentally represent regularities of individual activity, thought, or feeling.

It is fallacious to assume that because learning depends on the interaction of the organism and its environment that learning inserts anything wholly novel into the individual. Although we may use terms like *inculcate, instill,* and *contagion,* such language must be regarded as merely figurative. We postulate (see proposition number 7 above) that "if the organism is a tissue system undergoing changes partly because of its own dynamics, partly because of interaction with the outer world, it is 'acquiring' new characteristics all the time, never by accretion but always by modification of what is. . . . What is acquired is just as completely an expression of the inherited make-up of the organism as it is an expression of the outer forces" (Murphy, 1947:51). Personality, considered as an end product of learning represents the fusion of inherent capacities or dispositions and external stimuli. "New tendencies, habits, traits are not acquired, plastered on, or stuck on as one affixes a postage stamp to a letter," continues Murphy. Patterning liberates some organic potentials but "what is liberated is as much a function of environing pressures as it is of the latent or potential disposition."

Learning and Reinforcement

Learning from the psychological point of view, arises as a consequence of reward or reinforcement (Gillin 1948b:221–249). A response made by the individual under given conditions comes to be repeated under similar conditions because of the promise of gratification. The tangible or intangible satisfaction forthcoming from a given mode of behavior helps to reinforce the behavior. Rewards for socially patterned behaviors are, of course, manifold, including a father's smile; the "warm glow" that accompanies the trimming of a Christmas tree; the satisfaction of finding a moose where one calculated the animal to be; the gratifying accompaniments of eating moose meat; and the reduction of tensions like anxiety, sexual tumescence, or hostility. For the sake of such rewards human beings repeat the acts they have learned. To be sure activities sometimes remain unaltered although the rewards they produce alter. A father's approval may be replaced by a feeling of triumph in skillfully tracking a moose. Failure in the systematic appearance of reinforcement, however, can with high probability be predicted to result in the extinction of that response. Conversely, learning may be restricted by fear of punishment. A study of school children revealed that they avoided behavioral innovations in response to fear of being penalized for venturing too far from the group norm (Riley and Flowerman, *1951*).

Content, Form, and Emotion in Learning

Any particular learning situation or, approaching the matter from the accomplished learning, the acquisition of any specific pattern of personality, may be analyzed from three points of view: the content of learning that occurs, the form of the learning process, and the emotional quality associated with the learning. Attention to these three factors has assumed great importance in recent culture and personality theory.

The *content* of learning refers to the substance of what is taught or acquired. For example, in America boys learn in school to shake hands, tip their hats, stand when a woman enters or leaves an intimate group, and so forth. Thousands of more patterns are acquired; their complete listing would exhaust the content of American learning. Content refers to the *what* of learning—the skills, manners, postures, feelings, sentiments, ideals which people are given to assimilate in the course of lifelong membership in groups.

Form refers to the social and biological circumstances accompanying learning, including such conditions as the age, sex, and health of the learner; the readiness of the pupil for a particular bit of learning in terms of his previous experience; the age, sex, and pedagogical orientation of the teacher, and nature of the learning process, whether, it encourages trial and error, uses rote, relies on imitation, or involves passive manipulation as in Bali (Mead, *1953b*:655). The learned significance of any particular bit of content will vary for the individual according to the form of the situation in which that content was acquired.

The *emotional quality* of learning refers to the affective circumstances accompanying the relationship of teacher and pupil in a learning situation. Fear and rigidity may mark an authoritarian situation; a relaxed, curiosity-motivated, permissive atmosphere will characterize "experimental" or progressive learning; while casualness characterizes learning in which there is little concern whether the pupil quickly and faithfully acquires any particular pattern. A moment's reflection will indicate that we have all been affected by the emotional quality of learning situations. Many of us may have forgotten the formal details of a childhood discipline but we can vividly recall the emotional nature of the situation in which it was administered.

The emotional quality associated with a particular situation reflects the general ethos of the culture. Devereux (1951:46) asserts that "the decisive force in personality formation is the ethos, which gives meaning to discrete culture traits, rather than the culture traits, e.g., training techniques, themselves. The determining force of the latter depends primarily on the extent to which they reflect the overall ethos and pattern of the total culture." The acquisition of any pattern of modal behavior may profitably be analyzed by reference to all three factors. Genetic studies in culture and personality have recently tended to emphasize the form and quality of learning situations in studying the acquisition of particular patterns of response. Critics have properly objected to this procedure by asking whether content is not also essential in understanding personality development. Anthropologists have probably neglected paying consistent attention to content because the "what" of learning is relatively obvious or apparent. Their interest has gone into studying the less apparent and hitherto neglected aspects of learning to discover, for example, how the father's role in the family is related to the child's later response in leadership situations. The misunderstanding that often greets this kind of research may also reveal a failure on the part of the critic to recognize that the formal and emotional circumstances associated with learning exercise a dynamic influence in personality formation.

Direct and Indirect Learning

The distinction of content, form, and emotional quality in learning implies that to account fully for the facts of personality formation it is necessary to consider not only direct content transmission, or instruction, but also the often unintended consequences of instruction which may be related to the form and quality of the learning situation. For the latent consequences of learning Bateson (*1947*) proposes the term *deutero learning*. While direct learning refers to the successful transmission of specific content indirect or deutero learning designates the acquisition of certain unintended patterns. Such patterns may be as important for adjustment as the consequences of direct learning. Deutero learning, or learning from learning, impinges especially on the character structure of the individual, shaping the world view and other value orientations of the learner (Ruesch and Bateson, *1951*:215–216).

Psychiatrists and anthropologists stress the importance of attending to these two kinds of learning. Kardiner (*1949a*) says: "There is a limit to the sort of culture content which can be transmitted by direct learning process . . . learning processes do not account for the integrative character of the human mind in so far as the emotional relationships of the individual to his environment is concerned."

Murdock (1945:141) points to the distinction when he says that "whereas behaviorists look primarily to the inherited mechanisms of learning for the interpretation of behavior, Freudians look to the conditions of learning, and in particular to the structure of the family relationships under which the earliest human learning occurs in all societies."

Direct and indirect learning may reinforce each other. A view of the world as a hostile place which derives from learning that takes place in an inconsistent and ungratifying social environment may be supported by instruction that specifically points out the undependable and dangerous nature of society. Uneven culture change, however, may lead to a more contradictory state of affairs. Instruction in certain values may continue across generations while circumstances of learning implant quite contrary secondary orientations. This is no more odd than the fact that people sometimes teach contradictory beliefs, one set hanging over from an earlier day without being modified for the contemporary situation.[2]

The literature reveals a number of examples of indirect learning.

Indirect Learning and Moral Standards

In a more or less typical Midwestern town the groups in which boys and girls participate offer moral standards. These groups include the family, town, church, and peer groups (Havighurst and Neubauer, 1949). Each of these sources insists on a rigid code of conduct. Disregarding the *what* of learning, it is reported that in Prairie City the teaching of what is right and wrong is not only carried out rigidly but is done with reference to isolated and concrete acts of behavior. Thus, direct learning is characterized by a high degree of specificity. Little attempt is made to give the children an embracive moral philosophy of the type characteristic in an earlier day (Riesman, 1950). One secondary effect of the modern American style of teaching emerges in the statement that ". . . maladjustment rather than adjustment tends to be the stimulating force toward

---

[2] The topic of uneven culture change is well treated in Wilson and Wilson, 1945:132–136.

reflection, criticism, and personal orientation." There is no evidence that "maladjustment" is explicitly inculcated as a guide to conduct. Rather the child in Prairie City learns to depend on "maladjustment" in the absence of an absolute moral philosophy from which to deduce right and wrong. Another unintended consequence of this learning is a strong value on conformity. A rigid code of morals comes to be expected of all with little room for individual flexibility. The data strongly suggest that conformity as a value substitutes for an integrated moral philosophy through which the individual could deduce the consequences of moral or immoral behavior. Without a body of internalized guiding principles, his security comes to reside in insisting that everybody conform to the same norms. The majority is then able to decide right and wrong.

Independent evidence by other social scientists tends to confirm the pattern that American moral standards tend to be piecemeal and particularistic. According to Riesman, "Uncertainty as to social position, combined with the possibility or hope of rapid social advance, leads parents in certain middle class social strata to largely unconscious changes in their child-rearing practices. The child is no longer trained to an unquestioned ideal as perhaps his parents were; he is trained to do the 'best possible' in any situation" (Riesman, 1950: 3–4). The importance attached to conformity by Americans is also attested by the study of Riley and Flowerman (1951) who report that school children oriented toward their peers rather than toward adults maintain popularity as long as they adhere to an easily achieved series of goals. Popularity depends on being "an all around youth who above all shuns uniqueness; 'smart but not too smart,' 'pretty but not too pretty,' 'friendly,' 'gets along well with everybody.'" Because they are easy to achieve, these writers refer to the goals of American youth culture as "mediocre."

Indirect Learning and Anomie

Merton (1949:125–149) traces the dynamics of another secondarily derived modal personality pattern, anomie or normlessness. Every group inculcates its members with goals worth striving for.

At the same time that these goals are offered people receive some instruction in "acceptable modes of reaching out for these goals." Certain means, like fraud and force, may be ruled out as acceptable procedures while other paths may be highly endorsed. Learning may also stress goals far more than making explicit the means for reaching those ends. That is, the prescribed paths may be invested with far less concern or emotion than is bestowed on the ends. "With such differential emphases upon goals and institutional procedures, the latter may be so vitiated by the stress on goals as to have the behavior of many individuals limited only by considerations of technical expediency," says Merton. Anomie follows. The members of the community "learn" (without having been directly taught) that winning the goal is nearly all-important while the means are of relative insignificance. ". . . a premium is implicitly set upon the use of illegitimate but technically efficient means. The star of the opposing football team is surreptitiously slugged; the wrestler incapacitated by his opponent. . . ." American culture in the opinion of a number of observers possesses a high degree of normlessness. We often witness people placing great emphasis on certain success goals, like the possession of money or winning athletic honors, without equivalent consideration defining suitable means for winning. A high incidence of crime is an unintended consequence of this indirect learning. A well-known journalist has connected the nation-wide philosophy of "it's all right if you can get away with it" to the cheating scandal a few years ago that rocked the United States Military Academy at West Point (Baldwin, *1952*). Other government scandals in the fall and winter of 1951–52 also seem to confirm anomie as a pattern.

Latent Consequences of Discontinuity

In a classic paper Ruth Benedict (*1953*) discusses the secondary effects of discontinuity in personality development. All communities prepare individuals for adult responsibilities, for dominance in certain social relationships, and for the adequate execution of sexual roles. Sometimes, however, earlier learning is not directly relevant to adult responsibilities, dominance, or sexual obligations. American society, for example, places a blanket restriction on sex in childhood and later expects the individual to unlearn a well-nigh total inhibition if he is to adjust satisfactorily in the marriage role. We demand submission of children and then expect them to manifest patterns of adult self-assertion or dominance. Children are first shorn of responsibility and later faced with the problem of acquiring an adult's sense of responsibility. *Discontinuous* describes this style of learning. Concerning the unintended consequences of discontinuity Benedict says, ". . . the adolescent period of *Sturm und Drang* with which we are so familiar becomes intelligible in terms of our discontinuous cultural institutions and dogmas. . . . It is not surprising that in such a society many individuals fear to use behavior which has up to that time been under a ban and trust instead, though at great psychic cost, to attitudes that have been exercised with approval during their formative years." Fear of adult roles, while not directly taught in America, comes as a secondary consequence of discontinuous learning.

Secondary Effects of Educational Modes

Piddington (*1950*:179–188) suggests how the educational methods of small-scale exotic communities "contrasts in a marked way with the corresponding system in civilized communities."[3] First, education tends to be a by-product of living. That is, the child is trained through a progressively greater participation in adult activities. Second, continuity exists between educational situations and daily life; "what a child learns . . . is acquired in a context of real as opposed to artificial training situations." Third, educators are primarily parents and kinsfolk although often all adults possess the capacity to instruct children in the basic techniques for living. Finally, the interests of these children "make them active participants in the educational process rather than passive recipients" or unwilling subjects. Exceptions to these generalizations undoubtedly exist but on the whole Piddington appears to have reliably reported some common features running through the educational arrangements of small-scale com-

---

[3] See also Mead, *1950a*:161–162.

munities. In consequence, it would appear that resistance to education is rare in small-scale exotic communities. Anthropologists rarely report children refusing to learn in the communities they visit. In contrast, teachers in American public schools are quite familiar with that phenomenon. Learning is more meaningful as well as smoother when the gap between education and living is reduced

Absorptive Learning

Cora DuBois (*1949*) calls attention to a type of learning apparently related to secondary learning. She points out that children not only learn by virtue of discipline but also acquire behavior patterns absorptively. Absorptive learning occurs when the child models his behavior on patterns "consistently observed in other members of the family." The effect is described as a kind of "psychic osmosis" or what has been also called "contagion." On the level of individual psychology, H. Flanders Dunbar (*1947:5–7*) shows how quickly food aversions or preferences may be absorbed. Attitudes to the self are also readily "caught." "Just as the infant is sensitive to his elders' likes and dislikes in food, even when concealed, so he reacts to like or dislike of himself. No amount of dramatic acting can prevent the unwanted child from getting a pretty good idea of his real place in the family affections." Symptoms of illness are also catching. The rewards of absorptive learning may be subtle without being consciously presented to the dutiful pupil. What the psychoanalyst calls identification and introjection are probably concepts similar to absorptive learning.

DuBois illustrates absorptive learning in Alor. Here children's experiences with food acquire particular meaning alongside certain adult behaviors. These experiences include irregular periods of hunger and satiation, stealing food, and punishment for wasting food. The Alorese child sees parents being careful not to waste food, hears them refer to regularly recurrent periods of scarcity that have no foundation in fact, and perceives adults acting niggardly with foodstuff. Out of these stimuli the child acquires the notion that food is precious, uncertain, and intensely important.

It is not likely that the Samoan attitude toward presumption beyond one's age is learned solely through adult warnings. True, children are told not to exceed the expectations of their age, but nonpresumption is also absorbed from the example of adults in the community. In much the same way Kaska children acquire elements of their introversive, emotionally suppressed personality when they are dissuaded from "wild" behavior and noisy exuberance but of greater importance is the lesson absorbed from undemonstrative and emotionally constricted adults. Frequent exposure to tales of famine and starvation and expressions, often unrealistic, of fear of food running short play a larger part in developing the anxiety component of Attawapiskat Cree Indian personality than do episodes of actual starvation.

Social Planning and Deutero Learning

Successful planned social change requires an awareness of the dynamics of secondary learning. The evidence presented indicates that simple adjustments in the content of learning cannot be counted on to alter patterns of behavior that are motivated by characterological needs. Democracy does not come about by substituting the forms of parliamentary rule for authoritarian government. Repetition of the word *democracy* in textbooks and in propaganda will not develop the psychological readiness to operate in that governmental process or realize changes in world view and self view, because the character structure is largely a product of indirect learning. Administrators must provide conditions that will give the pupil "a repeated and reinforced impression of his own free will" (Bateson, 1947:125). Successful social change often requires alterations in the content of learning accompanied by constructing new learning contexts. Attention must be paid to the character of discipline, structure of the family, and the emotional quality in the learning situations. Bateson suggests combining the insights of the experimental laboratory and anthropology when he urges taking "the contexts of experimental learning in the laboratory and asking of each what sort of apperceptive habit we should expect to find associated with it; then looking around the world for human cultures in which this habit has been developed."

The raw materials upon which learning plays include the drives, the relatively plastic motor system, and those uncountable potentialities for response with which the human being is born. Not all communities make identical use of these resources; in any group many are neglected, a few encouraged, and others suppressed to varying depths. Ruth Benedict (1946b:219) expresses this idea clearly in her "arc" concept.

The culture pattern of any civilization makes use of a certain segment of the great arc of potential human purposes and motivations, just as we have seen in an earlier chapter that any culture makes use of certain selected material techniques or cultural traits. The great arc along which all the possible human behaviours are distributed is far too immense and too full of contradictions for any one culture to utilize even any considerable portion of it. Selection is the first requirement. Without selection no culture could even achieve intelligibility, and the intentions it selects and makes its own are a much more important matter than the particular detail of technology or the marriage formality that it also selects in similar fashion.

Basic Conditions of Learning

Two basic conditions underlie learning, two features by which man differs from his nearest primate cousins—an embracive capacity to learn and the ability to think symbolically.[4]

Man's great potentialities for learning and symbolic thinking do not mean that his responses are completely unlimited. The degree of fixation is certainly much less than among other animals. Man does not have many responses frozen in the form of instincts. Because the human being lacks innate equipment for survival he comes to be extremely dependent upon learning for living. It is through learning —direct and indirect—that most of his responses are acquired.

---

[4] The relationship of man's psychobiological nature to the invention and acquisition of culture is well discussed in Spiro, 1951:26–31; Hallowell, 1950a.

Some observers maintain that man's capacity for symbolic thinking makes him unique in the animal kingdom (White, *1949*:23, 31). However unique this may be, human learning and behavior closely depend on the manipulation and understanding of symbols. Small children learning to associate different responses to particular words become transformed into social beings. Words are not the only symbols. Any kind of physical form may come to enjoy complex meanings in a group of people, as well as colors, sounds, odors, and movements. The power of symbols to evoke patterns of response is illustrated in the fact that any community is partly held together by these devices. Associations attached to the flag, for example, act as a powerful stimulant to maintain social solidarity (Honigmann, *1953a*). The great volume of trade, essential to the survival of a modern complex nation depends on other symbols, coins. The list could be extended lengthily. As White (33) points out, "All culture (civilization) depends upon the symbol. . . . Without the symbol there would be no culture, and man would be merely an animal, not a human being." Asking what would happen if speech could somehow be excised from culture, White answers that forms of social organization would disappear, although some form of the family might remain. Incest prohibitions, rules of exogamy, and other regulations would be unknown. Preferred forms of marriage could not be realized without speech symbols that designate preferred mates. Churches, nations, schools, missions would drop out of a speechless community and so would theology, literature, science, and philosophy. Games would become very simple, rituals would become meaningless, most tools would cease to be significant. "In short, without symbolic communication in some form, we would have no culture. 'In the Word was the beginning' of culture—and its perpetuation also" (34).

Recurrent Physiological Drives

Among the raw materials exploited by learning are those recurrent tensions whose satisfaction, except in the case of sex, is nearly always imperative if the organism is to survive. Among such tensions psychologists often specify the following "primary drives": hunger, urination, defecation, fatigue, and the need for oxygen. These do not, however, exhaust the list. The exact number of recurrent tensions common to man and other animals cannot be stated because there are varying levels of specificity at which these needs may be described. For example, fatigue can be broken down to various biochemical conditions in the organism, each state of imbalance constituting a particular "drive."

These adaptive needs must be attended to if individual and group will survive (Malinowski, 1944:15). Satisfying the primary drives of the child also encourages the development of clear-cut patterns of modal personality. For example, a middle-class young American learns not only to use foods and utensils in satisfying his hunger; he is also taught to experience hunger only three or four times a day. In addition, and now we approach character structure, he is conditioned indirectly to associate hunger with some feeling of crisis that in itself motivates behavior. Hunger, almost by definition is always in some degree painful but the ability to endure pain is variously distributed in a given population. Likewise groups differ in their learned ability to withstand hunger and other tensions. The Kaska Indians, like other people accustomed to recurrent episodes of near starvation, experience hunger with far less excitement, impatience, or sense of crisis than a middle-class American. Through the operation of different patterns of attending to a child's hunger the significance of hunger comes to vary in different groups and foods come to enjoy a variety of meanings. Not only does the subjective perception of the drive develop through patterning but agents and objects relative to the tension—people who feed or serve, foods themselves, and utensils —also come to acquire specific meanings.

Now it is time to reintroduce the distinction between primary and secondary drives. Physiologically rooted drives constitute the ground plan on which many of the tensions or motives come to be structured. The secondary drives or motives represent learned ways of satisfying, experiencing, or interpreting the primary drive. In Gillin's language (1948b:229–230), "Acquired drives are elaborations of the primary drives which serve as a 'facade' behind which the functions of the underlying drives are masked. They are also anchored to the conditions of life in a particular place and time . . . each culture has the effect of developing acquired drives, in some sense peculiar to itself, in the physiological system of the members of the society to which it pertains."

Sex Patterning

The sex drive is another primary tension upon which a variety of secondary motives come to be based.[5] Unlike the case of hunger, man can survive without sexual satisfaction. Persistent sexual dissatisfaction may, of course, complicate his adjustment in some communities. Communities vary considerably in the degree to which they encourage sex expression. Some groups blanket both the aim of sexual satisfaction as well as an extensive range of objects through whom to obtain gratification (Kardiner, *1939*:23). Perhaps such nearly total blanketing of sexual pleasure is most fully developed in monasteries where strenuous efforts are made to help members resist distraction by sexual feeling. Rewards are consistently provided to make the struggle worth while and to reinforce continence. For example, periodic stimuli reiterate the value of chastity and extol its merits. Such conditions serve to reduce the pain of sexual deprivation which probably rarely becomes frustrating.[6] It may well be that the pain attached to unsatisfied tension is less in such a group than in one that does not regularly reward abstinence and in which constant pressure to gratification competes with inhibition. Few communities compete with the monastery in totally forbidding the sexual aim with a complete range of sexual objects. On the other hand no community can be found at the opposite pole—that is, allowing the full gratification of aim without prohibiting any objects as sexual choices. Anthropologists, however, have described communities in which people accept

---

[5] Sex patterning is particularly useful for demonstrating the interplay of primary and secondary tensions. For further reading see Stagner, *1948*: 309–313; Fromm, *1943*; Fenichel, *1945*:477–496; Honigmann, *1947*; Mead, *1949f*, chap. 10.

[6] For the distinction between deprivation and frustration see Maslow and Mittelmann, *1941*:109.

sexual tension and satisfaction with nearly the same equanimity that Americans reserve for eating. In Samoa, for example, "Sex is a natural, pleasurable thing" (Mead, *1950a*:201). Nevertheless, in Samoa as practically everywhere else people learn to expect privacy in sexual matters and come to understand that certain relatives must be avoided for sexual partners. Furthermore the community demands that the village princess, or *taupo*, avoid any premarital sexual relations. Students tend to exaggerate the extent of sexual opportunity in communities that allow premarital coitus. Goodenough (*1949*:617) points out that in a small community on Truk, despite "a relatively free and easy approach to sex" sexual drive is not easily gratified before marriage because incest taboos are apt to be widely (bilaterally) extended. "There were only ten women and eleven men aged fourteen to twenty in the community studied. With such small numbers, it is likely that at any one time some young men may have several girls who are unmarried and not taboo available to them, and others may have none at all."[7] The selection and rejection of sexual partners is, of course, learned. Such behavior is motivated by secondary drives erected on the primary sex tension.

The Pilagá place relatively few restrictions around sex and these are primarily rules to avoid certain relatives. Children of six or younger engage freely in homosexual behavior, masturbating against each others' bodies. Heterosexual play, including attempts at intercourse, is common among even youngsters. We have already referred to the functions of the very restrictive attitudes toward sex found in the American middle class. Jules Henry points out that the attitude contributes toward the disciplined character structure of the middle-class American and serves to emphasize the gap between adults and children (J. Henry, *1949*). The Pilagá, who expect that children will make an economic contribution to the family from the age of six, feel no need to emphasize the gap between adults and subadults. "Sexuality, far from being a brick in the wall between child and

---

[7] For a somewhat technical discussion of "incest taboos" that points out the survival value of such avoidances and also makes clear the logic with which, in any group, the regulations are extended from parents and siblings to other relatives, see Murdock, *1949*:284–313.

adult, as it is in our culture, is a bridge between them" that structures symmetry between the generations. Pilagá character, in contrast to the American middle-class orientation, is also not tightly disciplined. Thus, learning with respect to sex is shown to bear a relationship to other aspects of culture. Diverse motives may be instituted in personality through the way in which children learn to handle primary drives.

Anxiety

To repeat, the utilization of man's plasticity and capacity for symbolic response to direct the expression and satisfaction of basic drives develops secondary drives or motives. Such motives come to comprise a large area of the covert personality. They represent conditions of disequilibrium, consciously or unconsciously experienced, and direct both covert and overt goal oriented behavior.

An important motivating state which governs a wide range of responses is anxiety. Specific anxieties are acquired from the earliest days of learning. For example, the child who learns to satisfy hunger in a socially patterned fashion also comes to learn to anticipate hunger in the future. If he is himself made responsible for alleviating such anxiety he may respond to the motive by putting aside some food for future consumption. The act relieves his anxiety, induces a measure of security and so becomes reinforced. The same is true with respect to sex. As he matures a Kaska Indian adolescent comes to learn that he cannot depend on regularly securing casual female partners to help him satisfy his sex drive. Experience shows him the many advantages of being associated with a girl permanently. Marriage seems to be the answer to his anxiety. Every culture provides a solution to this problem. Of course, each spouse enters marriage prepared to have the other partner regularly satisfy other tensions than sex, including needs like hunger and self-esteem. Similarly the kind of a girl a man seeks to achieve anxiety reducing and other ends is partly defined by his motivational make-up. The most glamorous Powers model will leave an Australian Bushman cold but she promises to satisfy many needs of an American youth.

Although examples have been kept relatively simple, the reader should realize by this time how any moderately complex bit of human behavior may simultaneously be motivated by many primary and secondary needs.

Modal Personality and Secondary Drives

Some of the strongest differences between modal personalities stem from contrasting secondary needs. To illustrate, American education is at least partly a system of social relationships in which students are pitted to outdo each other. We sometimes talk of this as encouraging talent to come to the fore. Such education helps an American to feel most adequate in those tasks that he can perform better than— or at least as well as—other individuals in his group. His self-esteem has become conditioned to excelling. Excelling is a secondary drive in his personality. On the other hand, in the village of Zuni the ideal man "sees his activities in those of the group" and avoids both leadership as well as the competitive execution of tasks. Asch has several times been quoted as observing Hopi children to consistently belittle their own work (Murphy, *1947*:806). Of course, Pueblo Indians do not fail to encourage a desire for self-esteem or prestige in their children but the means for achieving the goal are very different from what we prescribe. Apparently the Zuni and Hopi modal personality lacks an acquired motivation of competitiveness.

In individualistic Attawapiskat, the Cree Indian is always alert for public approval but has also learned to avoid open competition. He strives for favorable recognition by muted "competition." He takes care to see that nobody becomes hurt or ridiculed while he strives to excel. Even bragging is disallowed to the Cree Indian. Instead, someone other than the successful person, perhaps his wife, assumes the role of the advertiser, carrying the news of a successful wild goose hunt through the neighborhood as she distributes geese among relatives and friends. The concept "competitiveness" by itself is not adequate to designate Attawapiskat covert behavior because we are used to applying the same notion to American modal personality which lacks any such high regard for a rival's feelings. What concept we do apply to the Cree Indian's behavior does not matter too much. We could borrow a technique from physical chemistry and label one motive "Competition-A" and the other "Competition-B." The main point, however, is that different patterns for realizing self-worth distinguish the two communities and these patterns are in turn related to different secondary needs.

Psychologists agree that not all behavior is motivated. Maslow (1949:262) points out that coping behavior, oriented toward need gratification, is always motivated. Expressive behavior that "simply mirrors, reflects, signifies or expresses some state of the organism" while it is always determined is "generally unmotivated" by needs. Expressive behavior, like the hopeless cast or benevolent mien, is usually nonpurposive; it lacks any aim or goal. Maslow contends that to know character structure one must study the expressive rather than coping behavior of the individual. On the other hand expressive behavior cannot be a subject of modal personality study if, as he says, "ideal expressive behavior is characteristically unlearned." We believe that at least some expressive behavior is unconsciously learned or patterned. It is therefore part of modal personality. Absorptive learning probably facilitates the patterning of expressive behavior.

PATTERNING VERSUS LEARNING

Personality, by the definition adopted earlier, includes the actions or motor responses of the organism. Some of these motor responses are visceral or internal and cannot be seen by easy inspection. Nevertheless, most students of behavior would hesitate to apply the term *covert* to such directly verifiable internal physiological responses feeling that it is better to limit covert patterns to postulated constructs. Physiological responses are often and through particular techniques (x-ray and surgery) amenable to direct observation. The so-called "internal diseases" of medicine illustrate one type of internal behavior and the digestive process another. Evidence indicates that both of these types of behavior are in part socially standardized.

The learning concept, with its reliance on reward and punishment to explain the development of behavior, is inadequate to explain the acquisition of these internal behaviors as well as of certain other motor behavior patterns to which attention will be directed in a few moments. Realization of this difficulty makes it necessary to fall back on the larger and less explicit, concept of patterning. It seems to be the case that some internal and external physiological personality patterns become standardized nondeliberately, unconsciously, or so casually that the ordinary notion of learning does not apply. Yet the acquisition of these patterns is nevertheless dependent on factors of group membership. Their appearance can be predicted from certain patterns of interpersonal behavior, physical arrangements, and ideas of a community; hence they are group-linked. Of course, one can deny any interest in such responses and, despite the fact that they are often significant features of modal personality, refuse to study them. Attention to the group factors related to the acquisition of such patterns, however, promises to be particularly useful in view of the fact that their control, as in the case of disease, is of great interest to mankind. It is possible that anthropology can contribute to such control by studying more fully than has hitherto been the case how these processes are socially patterned. More specific knowledge should lead to valuable contributions to preventative medicine. "It will be possible to assemble evidence to show that certain types of psychosomatic modification, carrying with them definite possibilities of pathology which becomes in time structural and irreversible, are associated with our whole way of life and so are circumstances with which we must reckon" (Mead, *1949c*:538). Therapy may then come to include "developing compensatory cultural forms" to relieve somatic strain or alter the social environment. Society also becomes the patient.

Evidence of Internal Patterning

Margaret Mead (*1949c*) presents some of the evidence for believing that group membership patterns physiological processes. For example, the healing of wounds is apparently related to the values and ideals which the individual acquires in his community. Among the Balinese, who emphasize the perfection of the body and the importance of keeping it unimpaired, the healing of wounds is more rapid than in other communities. Another example involves that group of infantile responses collectively called "summer complaint." Here is a behavior pattern related to growing up in a house the windows or walls of which are open to admit insect carriers of disease from the outside and in which food is left in exposed circumstances. The group-linked nature of summer complaint and other diseases may be revealed only when a group's way of life changes and the ailment becomes less frequent. Many pathological responses of the organism in a particular community may be related to living conditions, state of knowledge, or some other aspect of group life. Even the degree of pathology in the society may be correlated with the degree of cultural homogeneity and heterogeneity that is present.[8]

Digestive and metabolic processes hinge on some as yet unknown social factors. The Chinese reveal remarkable little hypertension in comparison to Americans. An American who lives in China for a time, adopting the tempo of Oriental life and increases his consumption of rice, will come to show a reduction in blood pressure. The degree of constipation or looseness of stools may be socially patterned. "The Iatmul of New Guinea, who expend a great deal of energy teaching their children not to step in feces, human or animal, but are uninterested in points of extreme prudery or rigid routine, have loose and frequent stools. The Manus, living on approximately the same diet, of sago, yams, and fish, and in the same climate, as the Iatmul, have hard-formed stools and defecate only once a day, at a fixed time and place in the early morning. This behavior is consistent with their prudery, rigidity, with their general character structure" (Mead, 1949c:531).

Posture also becomes patterned. The Samoan learns to sit cross-legged on the floor without fatigue or discomfort and finds it difficult—though not impossible—to sit on chairs. Navaho Indian children when they first sit on chairs feel ill at ease and fear they will

---

[8] See discussion, p. 355. It should be obvious that when such behavior patterns are related to group membership factors it is not denied that they are also related to factors of constitution or bacteria. Our analysis is not in terms of any single cause but implies multiple correlations.

fall down. Great Whale River Cree Indian men habitually walk with their legs bent at the knee and the shoulders hunched forward. In this posture they find themselves relaxed and comfortable.

Suggestions for Further Reading

Several educational films suggest themselves as useful in connection with this and subsequent chapters. "The Feeling of Rejection" (National Film Board of Canada, 21 minutes) gives the life history of a twenty-three-year-old girl who learned early not to risk social disapproval by taking independent action. Scenes from childhood show her early attempts to gain attention and the gradual suppression of normal competitive activity. "Preface to Life" (Sun Dial Films, 28 minutes) shows a boy growing up influenced by parents, neighbors, teachers, and playmates who through their treatment of him inculcate socially approved and disapproved patterns of human behavior. The subtleties of learning are well treated and personality formation illustrated.

To get a fuller grasp of the dynamics of learning the student is recommended to consult Miller and Dollard's *Social Learning and Imitation* (*1941*). Slotkin's *Personality Development* (*1952*) takes up personality growth from the standpoints of the biological organism, group, and culture. A social psychologist who interestingly inducts the reader into learning theory is Doob in *Social Psychology* (*1952*), chapters 2–5.

Of considerable interest to students of culture and personality is the research into absorptive learning (or behavior contagion) now being carried on in the laboratory. For an early report on such research see Lippitt's "An Experimental Study of the Effect of Democratic and Authoritarian Group Atmospheres" (*1940*). For a more recent study see Polansky, Lippitt, and Redl's "An Investigation of Behavioral Contagion in Groups" (*1950*). Lewin's *Field Theory in Social Science* (*1951*) should certainly be consulted by any reader interested in the laboratory approach to group dynamics, especially pages 155–169.

A strictly anthropological approach to the psychosomatic theory of disease has been little developed apart from the paper by Mead (*1949c*) referred to in this chapter. The relationship of mental illness to group membership factors will be discussed in a later section of the book.

Chapter 9

GROUP MEMBERSHIP

Anthropologist and psychologist, working in a productive partnership, view personality as the product of five interrelated determinants (Kluckhohn and Murray, 1953). These are: (1) the constitutional factors with which the individual is born; (2) the groups of which the person is a member; (3) the role in which the individual operates —whether as father, boss, or husband; (4) the accidents which befall him; and (5) the geographical milieu. The last category is included although the authors point out that we know little as yet about the direct relationship between geography and the system of action, thought, and feeling characteristic of an individual.[1]

---

[1] Indirect relationships are not difficult to discover between environments and personalities. Thus, the persistent fear of starvation of the Attawapiskat Cree Indian is certainly related to a habitat poor in a variety of food resources. Tschopik relates "the hardships of life on the *altiplano* and the endless toil required to make a living in so inhospitable a region" to the utilitarianism of the Peruvian Aymara (Tschopik, 1951:187). However, conceivably there is a possibility of discovering behavior patterns which would allow more successful adaptation to these milieus. In other words, the relationship of the environment on personality is mediated by the fact that the Cree Indians do not possess behavior patterns permitting more successful adaptation. Culture intervenes between the individual and the geographical milieu, making the dynamics of the latter indirect rather than direct.

Of course, a great deal of intuitive speculation has tried to link modal personality and environment. Hermanns speaks of the free and individualized personality of the Tibetan nomadic herders as formed by the open spaces of the high pastures and "heaven scaling mountains." More

At any moment of its career a human personality represents a response to the coöperative action of these five sets of factors. To ignore any determinants in giving an explanation of behavior means to present a relatively partial statement. On the other hand, how widely functional relationships are traced depends partly on the problem under analysis and the frame of relevance of the particular researcher. One's frame of relevance usually reflects in some degree the division of labor existing between the sciences. Culture and personality represents a fusion of certain areas of psychology, psychiatry, sociology, and anthropology but has no ambition to duplicate the approaches of these specializations. Hence this book contains next to nothing about the influence of endocrine, neural, or other constitutional factors on behavior; pays relatively passing attention to role influences on personality; and ignores the influence of accidental situations, like parents' divorce, on personality development. On the other hand, these pages stress topics that other social sciences either ignore or develop only marginally. In particular our object is to learn about the relationship between group membership on the one hand and characteristic modes of action, thought, and feeling on the other.

INFLUENCE AND NATURE OF GROUPS

As we have already said, the members of any enduring group tend to manifest certain relatively common personality characteristics. Such a postulate allows the hypothesis that removing an individual from a group and joining him to a new group will be followed by the modification of particular behavior patterns. Illustration of both statements comes from an examination of gesturing or delinquency. Typical patterns of gesturing distinguish "traditional" Jews and Italians living in Manhattan ghettos. These patterns disappear when the people become assimilated to the larger community (Efron, *1941*), Delinquent behavior, too, is typical of the members of certain gangs but may be displaced from the personality of a gang member who assumes membership in, say, the Y.M.C.A. (Shaw and McKay, *1942*;

plausible is a relationship between the emphasis on individualism and the isolating demands of a pastoral technology (Hermanns, *1949*:233–236).

Brown, 1947:75–76). These simple examples demonstrate how forcefully groups define the behavior of members.

Often personality patterns maintain themselves through rewards provided by the group. Putting the same thought conversely, fear of punishment makes the members of groups adhere to certain ways of acting, thinking, and even feeling. These rewards vary, of course. One reward that frequently reinforces behavior is being allowed to remain in the good graces of an organization. This desire not to be cut off from relations with other members gives rise to the social solidarity of cohesiveness of groups. As we have already seen, reward and punishment do not provide a sufficient explanation for the maintenance of all personality patterns.

Groups Distinguished from Categories

The term *group* is often loosely employed to cover human aggregates ranging from the family or nation to a subway crowd. Social scientists employ the term in a more precise way to designate a unit comprised of people whose social roles interlock or who interact with each other. A subway throng is not a group to the same extent that a factory composed of interacting managers, accountants, engineers, assemblers, and shipping clerks meets this definition. The various positions of a factory interlock like gears; the result is an organization. Members of an Air Force bomber squadron constitute a social unit which we can examine more closely to see how overt and covert behavioral modifications follow from close-knit interpersonal association.

The commanding officer and his staff are explicitly charged with effecting certain modificatory behavior, like shaping the morale and performance of the flying personnel and ground crew. These officers conduct briefings and make work assignments that are calculated to achieve the desired ends. Meanwhile regulations operate in the squadron which demand punishment for behaviors that are expressly prohibited. In consequence of these regulations men become careful not to appear on duty while intoxicated, are careful to salute and to use the term "sir" with a commissioned officer, and observe many other cautions in their activities. A quality of formality comes to enter the behavior of enlisted men and officers. On the other hand, close working together (for example in an aircraft) helps to pattern a certain familiarity and ease in the behavior between officers and airmen that is said to be lacking in the Army or in the Marine Corps. Covert behaviors are likewise acquired through association of squadron members. Air crew members who fly the planes come to respect the judgement of capable crew chiefs who make the aircraft ready and fit to fly. Enlisted air crewmen learn to resent the fact that higher flying pay is received by officers in the same organization. They argue that all the members of a bombing team share the same risks and should therefore be compensated in the same way for taking those risks. Many additional patterns which help make up the personalities of squadron members could be provided. We have probably said enough, though, to indicate how living and working together in a group standardizes activities, thoughts, and feelings.

Now, the word *category* refers to any aggregate of people sharing one or more characteristics in common but who do not interact as a group. For example, all eighteen-year-old American males comprise a category as do all men, women, farmers, crew chiefs, and bombardiers. It is interesting to note that although all eighteen-year-old males do not form a unit of interacting social roles, they nevertheless share a number of common elements of personality. For example, they nearly all manifest an ambivalent attitude toward the responsibilities of adulthood (Farnsworth, *1951*). They look back to childhood with "its many attractive features." Frequently the eighteen-year-old lapses into childish behavior, and more frequently feels a desire to do so. In an attempt to emancipate himself from parents and other external authorities the eighteen-year-old tries to substitute "his own built-in controls in the form of self-respect, reliability, ambition and awareness of the needs of other people." Grumbling, fault-finding, cynicism, antagonistic emotional outbursts are a part of his rebellion against parents, school, and church. The rebellion also engenders a sense of isolation which incidentally makes eighteen-year-old American youths "easy prey" for the propaganda of movements that simultaneously further revolt while offering a stable meaningful doctrine. Sexual conflicts complete the picture of the eighteen-year-old male personality.

What do these facts mean? Do they indicate that personality depends on category as well as group membership? We look to another explanation. If we took all eighteen-year-old males in the world we would find that they shared very few distinctive traits apart from those closely related to constitutional factors. The characteristics given in the preceding paragraph are not universal but can be traced to American youths' experiences in a single national group. In part these characteristics can be traced to the discrepancy existing between the way in which boys are reared by American parents and teachers and the roles expected of American men. Originally, at least in the middle class, boys receive few responsibilities, are taught highly restrictive behaviors with regard to sex, and remain subordinated to adults. Then after puberty these emphases begin to be reversed. Responsibility, dominance, and the ability to participate in sexual relations come to be expected of a healthy, normal youth. The contradictory expectations surrounding the eighteen-year-old boy in the United States are related to these modal features exhibited by that category. Below we shall see that American executives and business leaders are also distinguished by relatively recurrent patterns of personality which derive from their membership in the same national community. Put in other terms, the homogeneity exhibited by American eighteen-year-olds stems from the role expectations that face the members of this category.

Any individual is simultaneously a member of several groups—perhaps family, school, factory, and others. Does all group membership affect personality so that the members of each unit come to resemble each other more than they do the members of other similar organizations? Are the Smiths more alike as a family (making due allowance for individual differences) than they are like the Greens? The little evidence that has accumulated around this point suggests only that the members of every group acquire certain habits—including tastes, gait, habits, and speech mannerisms—by virtue of belonging to the particular association (Roberts, *1951*). That differences between family groups have not been more attended to is related to the fact that people are more concerned with individual differences between persons than they are in the characteristics people possess by virtue of common family membership. Greater interest has attached to personality differences between cities, towns, and neighborhoods, although observation of these differences is often far from objective. Actually, the differences between family groups are probably slight compared to the similarities existing between families who belong to larger, distinguishable groups, like a nation. Between different nations values tend to be more sharply defined and goals are relatively dissimilar.

When two or more groups, whether families or nations, share one or more distinctive characteristics in common they fall into a category. Thus Northrop (1946) has pointed out that Orientals have a systematically different way of conceptualizing experience than do Occidentals. He categorizes together China, Japan, and India because of this common mode of perception. Similarly one may categorize the Indians who live north of the Rio Grande as possessing certain common attitudes (Thompson, 1948).

Interpersonal Relations and Group Membership

Interlocking roles allow the group to exert much of its dynamic influence on the individual through interpersonal relations—i.e., mutual perception and response (Newcomb, 1950:21). The social interaction through which patterning is accomplished may be of three varieties. It may be (1) direct, i.e., face to face; (2) indirect, that is, through intermediate persons; or (3) mediated, as in modern complex nations, by forms of communication like writing, radio, or movies (Slotkin, 1950:11–12).

We must now examine the culturalistic fallacy, which, incidentally, we hope to avoid by adopting an emphasis on interpersonal behavior as a vehicle of patterning. Interpersonal relations provide the mechanism through which is acquired a large part of the individual's system of action, thought, and feeling. In other words, a great deal of patterning occurs through human relationships. This is different from saying the group or culture shapes human behavior (Spiro,

1951). It is relatively useless to refer questions concerning instigations to action or the derivation of action patterns to "the culture." Such an explanation was once more useful than it has become today when with new and more precise concepts we can discover the efficient mechanisms of behavioral transmission. Personality is largely a product of the expectations, actions, or suggestions of other people transmitted and perceived directly, indirectly, or mediationally in social interaction.

Experimental evidence reveals that interpersonal influences in patterning are closely related to the subject's status in the group. Unfortunately, this question has never been examined in clinical or field work situations. Polansky, Lippitt, and Redl (*1950*) report that popularity promotes learning in distinction to unpoularity. The prestige of the initiator also affects patterning. In acculturation situations the prestige of a missionary, trader, or government administrator may bear a clear relationship to the amount of diffusion which he promotes. The readiness of the initiator to act in modifying behavior must also be taken into account in estimating the success of patterning through interpersonal relations.

ENCULTURATION AND SOCIALIZATION

Two aspects of the patterning process as mediated by people are distinguished by Herskovits (*1948*:40–41): enculturation and socialization. Enculturation refers to individuals acquiring socially standardized overt and covert responses like counting, reading, driving a car, mixing drinks, dressing for dinner, choosing members for a county school board according to certain criteria, and trusting in the validity of majority rule. Such shared behaviors not only make up the culture of the community but, as in the present instance, they may also be viewed as part of the modal personality in a community. Enculturation in personality development may be illustrated by referring again to an American Air Force bomber squadron. A member of this group, by virtue of having undergone training and also because he has become enculturated through living and working with other airmen, shares with them a disdainful attitude toward the capabilities of the mess hall staff, a certain pride about his role in the nation's defense program, and an evaluation of the Air Force as possessing certain advantages that largely outweigh particular disadvantages when membership in it is contrasted to a civilian career. Reservists who were called into the service during the Korean emergency resisted becoming enculturated with some of these sentiments. In some cases, if their civilian job had rewarded them highly they never responded positively when their colleagues talked of "staying in" for twenty years or until retirement. The modal personality of reservists is different from that of career airmen and officers. Sometimes habits which were once dutifully learned need to be unlearned in response to changing circumstances. The acquisition of more appropriate responses is still enculturation. Thus a reservist who is recalled to any branch of the armed services may unlearn certain civilian ways of doing things, often at the cost of severe frustration or nostalgia. Over a period of time he adopts new patterns congruent with the military milieu and that are expected by the group which he has joined. The concept of enculturation makes it clear that culture cannot grow, continue, or change apart from people who learn to behave in standardized fashion.

Socialization bears the same relationship to enculturation that social organization bears to culture. By the term *social organization* the anthropologist refers to those patterns of behavior through which people relate to each other in a particular community. Social organization refers to the manner in which interpersonal contacts are channelized or structured in a community. The term *socialization,* as used by Herskovits, designates approved interaction patterns for customary social relationships. Included are the behaviors that a boy learns to reserve for his parents; the privileges he may be able to take with his mother's brother's daughter; the qualities he must demonstrate in play groups; and the duties he owes to his wife and children. An airman in a bomber squadron is socialized for his relations with officers.

Not all anthropologists find it useful to distinguish between enculturation and socialization. There is a pronounced tendency to use the term *socialization* to encompass both aspects of patterning through interpersonal relations but to restrict that term to the early portion of the life cycle. Although the distinction between enculturation and socialization may prove useful for certain purposes, readers must remember that the latter word has long been current in anthropology to designate "all those factors, influences, and processes, formalized or implicit, which the culture of the group acting through parents, elders, or other children brings to bear upon the neonate and continues through maturation to adolescence in order gradually to mould the raw stuff of human nature into conformity with group patterns of thought, feeling, and behavior" (Beaglehole and Beaglehole, 1941:282; Slotkin, 1952:45–263).

THE SCOPE OF GROUP INFLUENCE

Membership in a series of groups provides the individual with the skills for adapting and adjusting to many of the problems that will confront him and his larger community. As Kardiner (1939:10) points out, the child not only acquires patterns for winning acceptance, approval, support, esteem, plus approved channels through which to release hostility. He also learns the wisdom of, and techniques for, acting with other individuals to preserve the group from dangers to its physical existence and social integrity. The comprehensive role of group influence in personality development is also clear to Durkheim (1938:6) who notes that

. . . all education is a continuous effort to impose on the child ways of seeing, feeling, and acting which he could not have arrived at spontaneously. From the very first hours of his life, we compel him to eat, drink, and sleep at regualr hours; we constrain him to cleanliness, calmness, and obedience; later we exert pressure upon him in order that he may learn proper consideration for others, respect for customs and conventions, the need for work, etc. If, in time, this constraint ceases to be felt, it is because it gradually gives rise to habits and to internal tendencies that render constraint unnecessary; but nevertheless it not abolished, for it is still the source from which these habits were derived.

Groups and the Overt and Covert Level of Personality

Group membership affects both the overt and covert areas of personality (Fig. 2). On the overt level the motor, including speech habits, of the members are shaped in a specific pattern—as well as the internal physiological responses. Great Whale River Indians come to walk with a characteristic gait in which the knees are hardly straightened out while the back and shoulders remain stooped. Such a manner of walking presumably comes through imitation of adults but in part perhaps also through the custom of carrying heavy loads on the back. Membership in an Air Force bomber squadron results in the modification of speech habits to include a stock series of profane expressions (cf. F. Elkin, *1946*). College youths come to dress in a fashion distinctive of the campus they frequent. On the covert level they learn to value the dress and other customs of the college com-

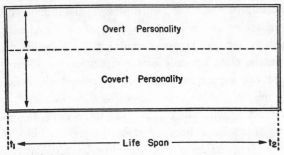

FIGURE 2. Scope of Group Influence.

munity. As an illustration of how values are patterned, Belo (*1949: 37*) reminds us that Europeans and Americans are brought up to value courage and to be ashamed of fear. Balinese, on the other hand, consistently frighten young children in the process of socialization, thus helping them avoid dangers in the surrounding world. Balinese children who demonstrate fear win the approval of parents and fear continues to be a useful technique till adulthood. A Balinese admits fear complacently, "as if he expected approval for his lack of daring.'

Group influence on character structure may be illustrated with reference to the Kaska Indians' learned need for "emotional isolation,' a syndrome that includes a distrust for intense affective stimuli, a desire to avoid close interpersonal relationships, and a simultaneous craving for affection but with an accompanying inability to accep or reciprocate love (Honigmann, *1949a*:287). Closer to home, by way of example, are the playground warnings offered to middle-class American children not to hit somebody who is smaller and not to strike the first blow in a quarrel. Such training leaves a lasting distaste for aggression in middle-class Americans plus a deepseated (nuclear) inability to originate aggression (Mead, *1942a*, chaps. 9–10).

Patterning in Time

The lowermost arrows in Figure 2 extend from birth to death. The human infant is born into a community and joins a series of groups each of which follows certain traditional forms of behavior. Patterned behavior in the family—the first of these groups—features attitudes and actions undertaken toward the newborn infant while attending to its demands. Thus, from the moment of birth interaction occurs between the infant and others. The influence of group membership on the overt and covert levels of personality continues to occur through the life cycle, although, as already pointed out, there appear to be differences in the amount and intensity of learning at different ages. In Gorer's words, "Learning probably never stops, but the increment of new learning, the rate of growth in the strength of new habits, steadily decreases with repetition. It is for this reason that the experiences of early life have such (apparently) disproportionate effect on later development" (Gorer and Rickman, *1950*:7). Haring (*1950*:131) says the same thing in different words: "Conspicuous in the behavior history of every individual is the primacy of habits of emotional response learned in infancy and childhood, a primacy never quite overcome by subsequent learning. The analogy of the tree that changes its growth pattern in a new environment but cannot undo previous growth, is pertinent if recognized as merely an analogy." Mead (*1950b*:52) illustrates the thought concretely: "By the time the Arapesh child is seven or eight, its personality is set" with a "happy, trustful, confident attitude toward life," an unfamiliarity with aggression, expectation of generosity, little experience in organizing the social environment, and a quick vulnerability to offense.

There is a difference in saying that "the increment of new learning declines with age" and to claim that "the character structure becomes fixed through the group experiences of infancy and early childhood." Knowledge gained from comparative cultural studies indicates that in communities where experiences between early and late childhood are inconsistent, there the years of late childhood may be of great importance for understanding the derivation of character structure (Goldfrank, *1949;* Underwood and Honigmann, *1949*). The achievements of psychoanalysis in reëducating adult character structure also demonstrates how inaccurate it is to say that early childhood fixes the nuclear patterns of personality. Horney (*1939:132–133*) points out that in the United States at least the increment of changes in character structure may vary for different individuals: ". . . the sum total of childhood experiences brings about a certain character structure, or rather, starts its development. With some persons this development essentially stops at the age of five. With some it stops in adolescence, with others at around thirty, and with a few it goes on until old age."

The inverse relationship that seems to obtain between new patterning and age is probably explicable by other factors than biological incapacity for the old to learn. Learning theorists suggest that as long-established responses continue to be rewarded new learning, which involves the modification of those responses, will be reduced. Since socially approved responses by definition have reward, their very efficacy serves to reduce the amount of new learning assimilated by the mature individual whose status undergoes no drastic change. Unless successful habits are extinguished by changes in the social or geographical situations which render previous habits unworkable it is likely that resistance to the accumulation of incompatible new responses will be maintained. Dollard and Miller (*1950:45–46*) sum up this aspect of the problem when they say that dilemmas facilitate learning. It is also likely that as people mature they become highly selective of the groups which they join; this reduces the likelihood of becoming exposed to further patterning. Finally, the aged may have relatively little opportunity to alter their statuses. Their static position in social structure of course reduces need and opportunity for learning. A constitutional factor enters the picture if incapacity limits the participation of oldsters in new positions.

Patterning and Persistence

The influence of group membership on learning decreases with age, but maturity is a period when much early learning tends to be transmitted to children and pupils. Such transmission, of course, helps to maintain patterns of personality across generation lines. Modal personality comes to persist in the same way that culture endures from one generation to another. Not everything that an individual acquires in the course of his experience will be passed on to the next generation. Few American mothers or home economics instructors any longer teach the method of grinding coffee beans, although they may have learned such a routine in their childhood. Other, mainly covert patterns, are more tenacious.

Laura Thompson (1948:201) discovered that although Dakota Indian rituals were officially banned from 1881 to 1933, a period during which far-reaching changes occurred in the technology and social life of those people, in 1942, 100 percent of the Dakota adolescents in a less acculturated community and 92 percent in a more acculturated group retained the traditional Dakota cosmological dogma. The aboriginal Dakota had conceived of the world as pervaded by a great and mysterious power from which life and all the good things of existence derived. In order to win this power men had to humble themselves ritually in supplication. In 1942 Dakota children believed that a principle of immanent justice operated in the world. Lacking rituals to supplicate this power the children also manifested apparent signs of insecurity and anxiety, and perceived the world as a dangerous place. Thompson mentions not only the Dakota Indians but other Indian tribes too where people retain certain basic attitudes which she believes to be continuous with the aboriginal world view. The aboriginal outlook persists despite white influences and accompanying changes in culture. The source of the stability puzzles the anthropologists who have so far only suggested that it may be bound up with the language or other symbol systems of the tribe or that it may be conveyed through indirect learning associated with nursing and child care.[2]

Persistence does not deny change. At the same time that certain personality patterns persist others reveal a large element of instability. Communities could not survive if new habits were not adopted when old ones prove ill suited in the face of changes in the natural environment, new technological devices, or the encroachment of a foreign culture that contains new demands (Kroeber, 1948:374–376, 378–382; Gillin, 1948b:208–209). Thompson (1948:210–211) discovers that some American Indians did modify their world view when they abandoned a hunting and fishing technology to adopt one based on agriculture. The technological shift was accompanied by man altering the concept of himself in relation to power sources. From being a helpless supplicant, the farming Indian of pre-Columbian times became a power entity himself, able to influence the superhuman world of forces. Nevertheless these changes often did not destroy the basic religious conception, namely of a cosmic force able to punish and to bless.

Group Membership and Uniformity

Interpersonal relations affect every individual who maintains relatively enduring membership in a group. Because practically every human being is raised in a social milieu and learns to adjust his responses to the expectations and responses of other members it follows that all of us reflect some patterns of action, thought, and feeling acquired through group participation. Through much of our remaining lives we will continue to join groups, the members of which will offer rewards for appropriate responses and punishments for uncongenial responses. Social isolation is rare and practically no person escapes being influenced by group centered interpersonal relations.

This is certainly different from saying that the members of any group are precisely alike.

---

[2] For further evidence concerning the persistence of modal personality see above, pp. 150–151.

Is there any uniformity in the effects that institutions [i.e., patterns] have on individuals in the same culture? There cannot possibly be any uniformity because there are always the differentiations of sex, age, and status, as well as constitutional differences in strength, beauty, and intelligence. This, however, does not contradict the fact that in any culture all individuals are subject to certain disciplines, as is true of religion, and of prescribed attitudes to members of the family. In other words, a culture creates an orbit within which move all the individuals comprising the culture. This orbit is made up of institutions [patterns] to which all individuals in a society are subject. Within this orbit sharp differentiations appear for the sexes, primogeniture, and status. It is as untrue to say that all women or all oldest sons in a given culture have the same 'character' as to suppose that all chiefs from different cultures have the same character (Kardiner, *1939*:86).

Uniformity cannot be attained in even the most authoritarian group or community by virtue of the following somewhat overlapping factors:[3]

1. Certain standardized differences, like male and female roles or occupational specialisms, are systematically shaping behavior of group members at the same time that pressure to conform to group standards is exerted.

2. Every individual enters group life with unique experiences that continue to affect the way in which he as a distinctive person participates in socialization. Some of these unique experiences (like intra-uterine experiences) trace back prior to birth.

3. No two individuals undergo exactly the same postnatal experiences or participate in precisely the same social relationships. The peculiar experiences of each person encourage diversity at the expense of uniformity. For example, each of two identical twins may not only have enjoyed unique intra-uterine experiences but following birth will pursue somewhat different careers. Very likely each will develop not only a somewhat distinct character structure but distinct total personality.

---

[3] For a more extensive discussion of "cultural heritage and behavioral diversity" see Spiro, *1951*:36–42.

4. Persons who share at least one group in common, for example the tribe or nation, also enjoy membership in diverse constituent groups of more limited participation. These groups differ from one another in what they expect, punish, and reward. Membership in diverse subgroups contributes personal diversity between community members.

5. Uniformity is further reduced to the degree that any individual resists specific patterns of behavior. Resistance often expresses itself in the refusal of a person to enter a particular group or he may reject particular community patterns of behavior that are enunciated in many groups—like belief in God, sense of community responsibility, and others.

6. Finally, individual diversity is maintained by anything that prevents the person from receiving the intended messages transmitted by other members in a group. Deafness is a physical liability that retards socialization but the unintelligibility of communications or the use of unfamiliar symbols—foreign language in the case of a resident abroad—may act in the same fashion. Research in the social class structure of the United States presents evidence suggesting that the values and standards which a child brings into the school group can facilitate or block the success with which the values of that organization become communicated to him. The values previously acquired by lower-class children in the home and neighborhood, for example, are relatively incompatible with the middle-class values of the school. Hence lower-class children tend to do more poorly in school and are a great disappointment to their middle-class teachers.[4] The result, of course, is that the standardized educational system of a particular community does not succeed in turning out a perfectly homogeneous crop of graduates.

Considerable time has been taken to emphasize the fact that socialization in groups fails to produce uniformity in any community. However, culture and personality remains much less concerned with individual differences in personality than with the modal elements of action, thought, and feeling—those patterns which the individual

---

[4] For further development of these points see below, p. 331.

shares with many other members of his group or community. Just as no individual can completely ignore the interpersonal pressures of his environment so no group can completely overcome individual differences among its members.

The Social Deviant

One cannot discuss personal diversity in relation to group patterning without considering the problem of deviance. If everybody retains the stamp of personal uniqueness then how do we distinguish the deviant? Deviance is probably always the product of those half dozen determinants of individual diversity which have just been discussed. The social deviant, however, is a person who develops extreme uniqueness. He is conspicuous and stands out in the group by virtue of his behavior patterns. The deviant in any particular group is not radically different from the conformist. His uniqueness is a matter of degree rather than of kind. To the degree that our behavior is conspicuous or outstanding in any group, to that degree we exemplify deviance in a particular association of people. Note that nothing is implied about the goodness or badness of deviance. Although the term is often used to designate deplored uniquenesses of behavior, logically a deviant personality may be characterized by approved as well as by disapproved outstanding patterns.

Let us examine further the idea that deviance is always relative to the group in which it occurs. In New York City a person can participate in many groups the members of which will not be concerned with whether the individual neglects attending religious service. We can generalize and say that New Yorkers are not concerned with church attendance as a behavior pattern. If the same individual finds a job in a small Midwestern town he may find that his nonattendance at Sunday service excites much attention. Church going is strongly valued in the latter community and failure to adopt the pattern leads him to stand out as a deviant. Even in New York City a child of nonchurchgoing parents who belongs to a playgroup of churchgoing children may be stamped as a deviant. His failure to conform to a strongly approved behavior pattern arouses interest or attention. Conversely, an intensely religious New Yorker may be admired by her differently oriented office group at the same time that her atypical behavior excites attention and makes her conspicuous. However, she scarcely arouses the same emotions as the nonchurchgoer in the small town. In other words, the character of the attention aroused by deviation from modal behavior is not pertinent to the present definition of social deviance. The relativity of deviance is well illustrated when we learn that among the typically gentle Arapesh the deviants "are the violent, aggressive men and the violent, aggressive women" (Mead, *1950b*:107–108). Among the violent Mundugumor, however, the mild mannered men, who do not make trouble, excite attention. Mundugumor deviants play a useful social contribution. Among them refuge can be obtained by the proud polygynist who has quarreled with his son, or the son can escape his father's wrath. "The atmosphere of struggle and conflict would become unbearable and actually impossible to maintain if it were not for them, for each man would have only an army of one to put in the field." Deviants, instead of making life unintelligible, "actually make possible the violent competitive life that is really so uncongenial to them" (159).

There is another relationship between deviation and social patterning. The deviant may be a person who has taken over group patterns but overplays, underplays, or otherwise distorts some bit of modal behavior which he in company with most of his contemporaries has acquired through learning. Ruth Benedict (*1946b*:–256) gives the example of the policeman who, for whatever reason, overplays his role, manifests too much arrogance, and spreads frustration wherever he moves. We recognize that such law enforcement officers are not typical of policemen in general. Such men are reminiscent of those Mundugumor men who are so violent that even the Mundugumor can find no place for them (Mead *1950b*:159). Another example of deviance through role distortion is furnished by the rate-buster in a modern factory. The term refers to the worker who, in the face of his group's demand that individual production be limited to a stated amount in a given period, exerts himself to exceed that quota. Even the management of the factory may not be pleased with the effects which rate-busting generates in the group (Dalton, *1948*:5–18;

Homans, 1950:60–61). Underplaying role behavior is illustrated by the Crow Indian who shrinks from physical danger. He fails to espouse the goals that most Crows hold important.

It is quite likely that any deviant shares hundreds of personality patterns with the majority of his community. He stands forth as a deviant merely because of one or two specific departures from the norms. Group expectations of an important kind have failed to take hold although in other respects the deviant represents a relatively enculturated and socialized person. Even the very deviant behavior may bear some relationship to group membership factors—for example, the deviance may be socially standardized. Margaret Mead (1947b) maintains that the deviant can be understood only from a knowledge of his culture plus his physical make-up. She stresses the standardized nature of deviance when she says that "there is no item of behavior of any human being reared in contact with other human beings which may not be referred to the concept of culture." Individual variation is limited by standardized interpersonal expectations and controls. The mother who, contrary to the mode, rejects her infant, does so in a patterned fashion. "The language in which a mother may express rejection, the speed and tempo with which she thrusts the baby from her breast . . . the extent to which she attends to what she is doing, the likelihood that she will remember her rejecting an hour afterward—these and a thousand other comparable qualities of her behavior will be found to vary systematically with the culture to which she belongs." The types of deviance are also limited (Mead, 1949f). A Manus may conceivably grow up to be a rapist "but he will not grow up to be a gentle and considerate lover." Both extremes represent deviation but one extreme is impossible in that particular community. Conversely, an Arapesh may become a passive homosexual but, unless he is "completely insane," rape will be impossible for him. In the same sense it is most unlikely that a Kaska Indian, living in a community with a profound dread of the dead, would ever develop necrophilia as a deviation.

One of the few comparative studies of deviance is Tumin's analysis (1950) of a hero and a scapegoat in a Guatemalan community. The hero was a curer and served a basic need in the community which was marked by a great fear and little control of illness. The fact that the hero did not conform to traditional behavior patterns was apparently canceled out by the strong prestige which he earned through curing. The deviations he manifested really enhanced his prestige. He was a young man, Tumin points out, and appealed to the youth of the community who were becoming increasingly insecure due to constant alienation of land. Some youths saw in the curer an appealing kind of a person, "a *type* of possibility," one of the few remaining alternatives facing Indian youth. The scapegoat, however, was in another category. He also departed from traditional behavior patterns, including the rule against caste miscegenation, and was greatly disliked. He threatened the status quo and provided no reasonable alternatives for the norms he flaunted. The author suggests that the deviations of each of these public figures are rooted in "relatively unique and idiosyncratic facts of the individual life histories." However, "difference in the reception accorded to each of them is to be found in the functions of the image which each symbolically represents. The objective characteristics of each man's acts are not nearly so relevant for our understanding as are the subjective definitions of these two men as held by the persons with whom they were in interaction." Tumin offers the hypothesis that the acceptance or rejection of a deviant depends upon securing a favorable definition of his role.

DISCIPLINES

The influence of interpersonal relations on patterning, we have already suggested, depends largely on the attitude taken by the members of the group toward the responses of other members. Attitudes may be expressed as approval or disapproval. In culture and personality literature the concept of "discipline" is used to refer to the manifest attitude taken with reference to particular instances of behavior. For example, Kardiner (*1939*:45) speaks of positive and negative disciplines. The former (also called "training") "encourages or fosters curiosity, enterprise, and activity which the individual accepts or follows eagerly." Negative discipline blocks or interferes with needs, urges, and capacities of the person. Encouragement of, and praise for, an Indian child's hunting birds with toy weapons exemplifies training. The punishment of the same youth for masturbation or sex play illustrates negative discipline. Cora DuBois (1949:196) offers a similar distinction between permissive and restrictive disciplines. The difference between these rests on whether primary use is made of reward or punishment.

We suggest that groups probably differ in the relative use they make of permissive and restrictive disciplines. But it is necessary to point out that little evidence exists to support this assumption. In some cases permissive discipline may be so casual as to pass unnoticed by many field workers. Restrictive disciplines are of such a character as to stand out more sharply and anthropologists must beware lest their incidence or importance be exaggerated. Of course, both elements may be mixed in the socialization process. This is reported to be true of the Czechs where praise of children by parents also frequently carries the connotation of blame. "When a child has behaved well on a visit to friends of the parents, the father or mother may say: 'You see how well you can behave!' According to these words of praise the child has, as it were, unguardedly behaved well on this occasion and thus supplied ammunition in support of the parents' argument that he could behave well at other times. The commendation for this instance of good behavior reminds the child of less good behavior on other occasions" (Wolfenstein, 1949:316–317). The tendency for a positive expression to be followed by a qualifying negative one appears in other contexts of Czech life as well as in the handling of children.

Discipline is not equally required for the acquisition of all kinds of behavior. Kardiner (1939) suggests that the patterning of language and the acquisition of techniques for mastering the environment need relatively little external approval or reinforcement. Learning to control the sexual and aggressive responses, however, demands relatively severe restrictive disciplines.

Permissive and Restrictive Disciplines

Learning with the aid of immediate or delayed rewards illustrates permissive discipline. Communities or subgroups within them probably differ in the degree to which they rely on delayed rewards in an effort to promote learning. Clyde Kluckhohn (*1949a*:211) suggests that "upward mobile" Americans, who generally belong to the middle class, make much use of delayed rewards to encourage the acquisition of certain behavior patterns.

Having chafed in their lowly positions, many lower- and lower-middle-class parents are eager to see their children "rise." But this involves postponement and renunciation, which can be learned and made a stable part of one's character only if, from early childhood on, the individual has continuous opportunity to experience the advantages of working and waiting. And, if parents are economically unable to give their children this kind of training—compensation for renunciation and enhanced reward for postponement, their efforts are almost certainly doomed to failure. Physical punishment for indolence and indulgence, if not conjoined with experienced gains and advantages, will not ordinarily accomplish the desired end. Because of the inability of underprivileged parents to keep their children from experiencing want, such children tend to develop precocious self-sufficiency and emotional detachment. Why, after all, should a child remain dependent upon and obedient to parents who have not really supported and protected him? When the child thus becomes prematurely independent, socialization is ordinarily at an end. And when this emancipation is accompanied by feelings of deep hostility and resentment toward the parents, the stage is set for a criminal career.

College students who have taken careful notes all semester and prepared diligently for final exams need not be shown how the promise of delayed rewards maintains the dependence of learner on teacher and exploits that dependence to encourage learning.

Permissive and restrictive disciplines differ in degree. When does holding out a reward for learning amount to promising the loss of an advantage if the lesson is not assimilated? Restrictive discipline designates learning promoted by punishments ranging from physical violence to withdrawal of approval. As Kluckhohn suggests in the paragraph quoted above, groups rarely rely solely on restrictive disciplines to achieve learning. It is even likely that punishment unaccompanied by reinforcement or the promise of realizable rewards is relatively unsuccessful in promoting learning. Punishments cannot, of course, succeed without the coöperation of the individual. No threat or punishment can of itself force an individual to follow a course of action if he does not value that action—value it either as an end in itself or as a means of escaping punishment.[5]

Kardiner's formulation of positive and negative disciplines is somewhat broader than DuBois's reference to reward and punishment as the primary techniques of promoting behavioral development. If we understand Kardiner rightly, simple permissiveness on the part of the members of a group is sufficient to identify a positive discipline.

The Effects of Discipline in Childhood

The impact of discipline on the child constitutes one of the most important areas in which to study the relationship between group membership and personality. Psychoanalytically oriented workers in culture and personality have paid extensive attention to this question. Kardiner (1939:25–26) offers two postulates that sum up personality correlates of positive or negative discipline.

1. The successful consummation of an activity in association with positive discipline results in a feeling of satisfaction, ego-enhancement, contentment, relaxation, and self-confidence. These covert states tend to maintain themselves beyond the immediate training situation. As aspects of the world and self views they come to motivate many subsequent behaviors.

2. Where a biological drive or an urgent need (especially sex, hunger, and dependency) is interfered with, the result, depending on the age when the negative discipline is instituted, may weaken or interfere with the development of the ego. Sometimes the effect may be ramifying, involving many of the functions of the individual. At other times, however, only the exercise of the particular function may become impaired.

Both these postulates will now be illustrated to show what hap-

---

[5] It is a matter of anthropological interest that Americans do not regard forced compliance as possessing the same validity as voluntary compliance. From a broader perspective, however, both bases of action depend on individual valuation or choice.

pens when parents or other persons responsible for a child permit or interdict autoerotic gratification in childhood. The first column below presents effects correlated with the successful completion of such gratification while the second illustrates the correlates of negative discipline directed against autoeroticism.

Effects of Autoerotic Indulgence	*Effects of Autoerotic Interdiction*
Aids growing up.	The pleasurable activity may be abandoned in order to escape conflict.
Aids in completing weaning from dependency on the mother, hitherto the chief source of gratification.	Anxiety becomes attached toward the sex drive.
By inculcating the idea "I can get pleasure from myself" it contributes to potency in later life as well as sexual adequacy.	As the sex drive comes to provoke anxiety its execution is regarded as hurtful to the individual. Thus pain and sex gratification may come to be associated for the individual.
Instills self-confidence.	
Encourages "a confident, eager, and friendly attitude."	Self-confidence is undermined.
Conditions pleasant anticipation toward the sexual drive when it will again appear.[6]	Encourages timidity and dependency.

It should be understood that not all of the individuals who grow up under a particular discipline react to it in the same way. For example, all Americans who have been punished for autoerotic gratification are not inhibited to the degree of impotence or frigidity. The "very inhibited individual represents the most extreme consequence of what all the others have to some measure," says Kardiner.

Kardiner stresses the manifold correlates of negative disciplines. (1) Overtly they may result in the prohibited activity being stunted or altered in execution. (2) covertly there may develop (a) changes in the perception of that impulse whose expression is prohibited; (b) changes in the perception of the people who interfere with the drive; (c) changes in the image of the self. Such effects are interdependent and simultaneous. In the case of masturbation, for example,

---

[6] Adapted from Kardiner, *1939*:26–29.

the child who is punished for the activity may invent new attitudes toward the sexual urge, toward the parent, and toward himself. His hatred for the interfering parent, although carefully repressed, may in turn promote guilt feelings because he knows it is wrong to hate one's parents. Permissive disciplines that allow need gratification also have their manifold overt and covert correlates.

So far our discussion has remained concerned with the individual. When a childhood discipline is widely shared or employed in a community then the similar correlates will appear in those members who have had experience with that pattern. The covert states resulting from a negative discipline, for example, will find expression in socially standardized ways, for example, in doctrines that equate sin and sex, in folk tales presenting images of cruel and suppressing parent symbols, and so on.

Kardiner (1939:58–64) also points out the correlates of discipline directed against aggression. Aggression may be defined as an expression of hostile tendencies against either the self or the external world with the intention of inflicting pain or destroying. The covert side of aggression we will call hostility. Two conditions favor the appearance of aggression: (1) any interference with, or threat to, the satisfaction of a need or impulse of the individual; (2) any failure of the resources or techniques by which the individual has been accustomed to adapt to the world. Both of these conditions are summed up in the hypothesis that frustration often instigates aggression.

Aggression tends to be one of the most carefully controlled areas of social behavior. As in the case of sex, negative discipline with reference to aggressive acts also effects the perception of the underlying drive (i.e., hostility). Kardiner gives the following behavioral correlates of discipline which interferes with aggression:

1. Changes in the attitude to and conception of the object that aroused hostility (e.g., exaggeration of the importance of the object).
2. Changes in the attitude toward the self. (For example, one may come to feel unworthy as a consequence of experiencing a hostile impulse.)
3. Development of disguised forms of aggression.
4. Inhibition of other activities or techniques. (For example, if blocking

of masturbation aroused the frustration-aggression sequence, then the sexual impulse and its exercise may become inhibited.)

5. Changes in the conception of impulses and activities whose blockage or denial creates frustration and aggression. (For example, the sex drive and its channel of expression, masturbation.)

We shall see below that communities differ in the degree to which they restrict aggressive activities. "In our culture, sanctions exist against only certain forms of aggression: the destruction of life and property of another person or interference with basic rights. Within the domain of rivalry and competition no sanctions exist, but only certain rules which are perhaps not legally specified" (63). In any community prestige may accrue to the person who expresses aggression in conventional or approved forms.

PATTERNING—PREREQUISITE OF SOCIAL LIFE

Why is it that universally groups strive to standardize the activities, thoughts, and feelings of their members? Why so much care to bring about some degree of individual conformity to group norms? What is the function of socialization and enculturation in group life?

1. In any community there must be some congruence between what different people do, believe, and feel, otherwise social order would be impossible (Wilson and Wilson, *1945*:46–48). If everybody were utterly different social relations could not continue. There would be little in the utterly different behavior of Mary to bring John to marry her. She would not understand his needs, sexual or culinary; she could not appreciate his wishes; her views of gracious living would be totally different from his. On the other hand, if everybody were completely identical then also no rewards would issue from social interaction. Group life is founded on complementary diversity, on differences between people that supplement each other. Where complementary differences shade into uncomplementary (nonsupplementing) differences, human life comes to be beset by problems that divide rather than cement human relationships. As examples of how complementary differences support social relations, note how people pay to hear or see artists who interpret Brahms, landscapes, or human

passions sufficiently uniquely to be interesting. At the same time an artist usually restrains his degree of uniqueness to remain aware of what interpretations will attract a paying audience. Trade, discussion, government, teaching, and religion all rest on differences between participants that are neither too extreme nor too limited. Patterning reduces the limits of personal diversity in group life without, however, completely eliminating differences. Positive and negative disciplines inculcate those common values, faiths, aspirations, tastes, and beliefs which allow interpersonal relations to continue.

2. Group patterning prepares individuals for reciprocal functioning in a social order that has not only men but also women, not only subjects but also authorities, not only audiences but also actors, not only readers but also writers. The acquisition of appropriate role behavior maintains the social structure of interrelated statuses.

3. Group interaction provides for the continuity of tradition. The word *tradition* may sound like something better thrown overboard than preserved. A moment's reflection indicates that without the heritage of skills, values, and techniques inherited by one generation from another, the members of each generation would have to learn to speak, secure food, and acquire other behaviors with survival value. Truly this would be a formidable task in the execution of which people would find survival extremely imperiled if not probably impossible. Patterning has survival value. Cottrell (1951:17) says, social continuity depends upon "(a) the development in the young of those basic conceptions of self and expectations in others which enable the individual to perceive and react in his various life situations in a manner which supports the [community's] basic value and institutional structure; (b) the transmission of the specific value orientations and interaction patterns which enable him to integrate his behavior with others in the various roles he may occupy in his life situations; and (c) the development of the specific skills called for in these roles."

4. Group life provides the person with certain behaviors and values that serve to maintain the solidarity of a social group. The feeling we call patriotism and respect for symbols of the national and other

groups are cohesive factors acquired in patterning. The shared values thus acquired link us to one another and serve group solidarity.

5. Patterning supplies the members of any particular group with behaviors through which they become distinguished from one another or through which the group becomes more visible. The policeman's uniform or the dignity of the minister and the sentiments which he utters in the pulpit are examples of distinctive role characteristics. Many ends are served by distinctiveness, including group solidarity, the preservation of social order, and the maintenance of prestige. The dignity of the minister, for example, helps to build up respect for his status. The ministry comes to be set apart as a profession. Differentiation in itself possesses little survival value. However, by enabling the occupant of the status to execute his duties more effectively, differentiation contributes to the functions which he renders to the community. Social visibility helps protect the integrity and cohesiveness of groups. Solidarity, in turn, helps the members carry out the tasks for which the group is organized.

Discipline, it would seem, reduces the individual's freedom of action. Survival invariably depends on standardized behavior and involves curtailment of a theoretical total freedom. On the other hand, without such standardization freedom is meaningless. The fact that an individual has been reared in a particular way of life does not rule out the possibility that he continues to possess a power of choice within a definable range of alternatives. He retains the power to alter established culture patterns in his community. Even a radical innovation springing from a unique idea may take hold provided certain conditions are favorable. Our emphasis on the importance of group membership in personality patterning must be tempered lest it obscure the significance of the individual on which the group basically depends. Patterning and social order are mutually interdependent. Out of social organization emerge the behavioral standards and expectations acquired by new members of the group. By conforming to these standards the individual helps maintain the organization of which he is a part. Each generation perpetuates part of his community's way of life by participating in the subgroups of which the community is comprised. Every individual sustains and perpetuates the group in which he learns to act.

GROUP MEMBERSHIP AND INTERCULTURAL MOBILITY

Enculturation and socialization often come to limit our understanding and appreciation of the behavior patterns of another community. The tendency to respond to a foreign way of life by automatically referring the behavior to one's own enculturative experience is a consequence of patterning. We tend to interpret the foreign in ethnocentric terms and see in the exotic a reflection more or less of one's standards of behavior. If Kaska Indians shrink from exerting themselves to exploit the fur-bearing resources of their winter environment it must be because they don't want to work hard for a living. That more complex motivations may underlie procrastination will rarely occur to the untrained observer who will see the Attawapiskat Cree Indian's reluctance to engage in summer wage labor as laziness (Honigmann, *1949b*:23–28). Now the term *lazy* has a particular meaning which it derives from the patterned glorification of work found in western Europe and America. When the word is used to characterize Cree Indian behavior it is being used evaluatively and not descriptively. We should not be surprised to learn that the Cree Indian also extolls hard work. Obviously, though, he has a different conception of meaningful duties.

Lionel Field (*1950*) has shown how people reared in a particular milieu may react to unfamiliar experiences. Speaking of an Easterner (that is, somebody reared east of Suez and west of Vladivostok) who gains his first glimpse of a western European city, Field says, "The orderliness of a western street would strike him as an irritating regimentation, the buildings would seem monotonous, the dress drab and uniform, and the food tasteless. He would be revolted by such habits as washing in a bath and not under running water and he would dislike using cutlery which had been in other people's mouths. He would be surprised by the excessive indulgence in tobacco and alcohol." The author, who came to know Orientals while living in the Near East and India, then contrasts Western and Eastern thinking.

His description is useful because it illustrates how wide a gap may separate modal personalities.

The Western mind tends to concentrate upon the possession and defense of physical comforts and beautiful objects and sound investments and a general sense of security; the Eastern mind places very little value on any of these things, and though it enjoys making a huge vulgar splash, doesn't fear poverty because it can exist quite comfortably with very little security and comfort. And in this "religion" plays some part . . . I don't mean religion of mere morals or an afterlife . . . but rather a sense that mental (or, if you please, spiritual) happiness may be more important than, and have little to do with, material welfare.

Whereas the West prides itself on a sense of humanity, "an Eastern eye roves carelessly over a dead dog or a dead camel or a dead man: an Eastern body accepts bombs or acts of God, like paralysis or cholera. An Eastern mind tends to regard disease as a part of life: does not connect it with flies or sanitation or slums."

This characterization of an exotic personality appeared in a daily newspaper. Assuming its validity, the description is not essentially different from one that a professional anthropologist might produce. The latter might borrow more from the vocabulary of psychology but he could hardly express himself more clearly.[7]

Another example of how rearing in one community limits one's understanding of unfamiliar or contrasting behavior patterns involves the use of language. Arabs speak with assertiveness and exaggeration, overstressing details as a matter of course. "If an Arab says exactly what he means without the expected exaggeration, other Arabs may think that he means the opposite" (Shouby, *1951*:300). Non-Arabs, however, may misunderstand the exaggeration just as an Arab will fail to realize that the foreigner's unelaborate manner of speech nevertheless means exactly what it says. "To many Arabs any simple 'No' may mean the indirectly expressed consent and encouragement of a coquettish woman." This is illustrated in the English girl who

---

[7] For a critical examination of the thesis that only scientists "can rid their minds of . . . impediments to lucid thought" and objectivity see Bendix, *1951*.

complained "that her Arab friend (a) was pestering with his attentions and declarations of love; and (b) refused to take 'No' for an answer when she made it perfectly clear that she was not interested in him at all. The Arab confided (a) that the English girl was encouraging him to make love to her; and (b) that he had so far shown only a little interest and admiration. Both were strictly honest and truthful even to their conscious selves, but they did not know what a contrast could be created between Arab overassertion and exaggeration and British tact and understatement."

Sensitivity to contrasting modes of standardized behavior and a readiness to look beyond the more obvious aspects of behavior patterns enables one to overcome at least in part the limitations imposed by social patterning. Culture and personality, as pointed out above, involves the acquisition of skills which contribute to intercultural mobility.

Suggestions for Further Reading

Hallowell's inventory paper, "Culture, Personality, and Society" (*1953*), is eminently suitable for further reading in connection with this chapter. Newcomb's *Social Psychology* (*1950*) offers a rich source of accumulated information concerning the general subject of group influence on the individual. More specific studies illustrating the role of group membership as a determinant of personality include Mead's "On the Implications for Anthropology of the Gesell-Ilg Approach to Maturation" (*1949e*) and Lee's "Are Basic Needs Ultimate?" (*1953*). As a critical and cautionary overview to the theory of social determinants of individual behavior Inkeles has written "Some Sociological Observations on Culture and Personality Studies" (*1953*).

How extreme deprivation of bodily needs becomes associated with a brutalized kind of group life that patterns the behavior of even reluctant members is illustrated in the studies of European work and concentration camps. See, for example, Bettelheim's "Individual and Mass Behavior in Extreme Situations" (*1943*) or Herling's *A World Apart* (*1952*). Homans's *The Human Group* (*1950*) constitutes an excellent introduction to the theoretical study of the group and of how social relationships standardize individual behavior.

Chapter 10

AS THE TWIG IS BENT

With this chapter we begin to examine certain concrete interpersonal situations in early life. These have been selected because research workers in the field of culture and personality have pointed them out out as significant influences in patterning. Our interest, therefore, will be genetic. The approach will also be cross cultural, selecting data from a wide series of communities. The hypotheses which we seem to favor are tentative rather than definitive.

ELEMENTS IN EARLY EXPERIENCE

Babies and older children become involved in interpersonal situations with older children or adults that have varying degrees of emotional impact. On the one hand are those that are casual and relatively inexpressive and opposite them those which are highly charged with emotion and significant communication. The latter are probably much less numerous than the former in family life but are more important in personality formation.

. . . within the general framework of biological development the significant specific character-forming elements will be those through which the adults attempt to communicate with the child. This communication need not be an articulate type of "character education" but it is affect-laden and emphatic. Early toilet training followed out for some casual reason of household arrangement will have a very different, and possibly almost negligible effect, while toilet training at an age when it might be conceived to be less traumatic and more appropriate to the developmental stage may, because of the weight given it by the adult, have far stronger effects.[1]

Although the first year or two years of life may not be all-important for patterning the modal personality, they nevertheless constitute a significant period of development marked as they are by the earliest contacts between the newborn organism and its environment. While the very young baby can hardly distinguish between itself and the surrounding world, very shortly after birth gratification and non-gratification are discriminated (Harsh and Schrickel, 1950:35–63). These states of pleasantness and unpleasantness gradually become attached to specific objects, persons, or other stimuli, even though prior to the acquisition of language the child cannot make linguistic discriminations about significant things and people (Stagner, 1948: 89–93).

Considerable question exists concerning the amount of preverbal thought which the infant can manage. At one extreme are those who would say that in the absence of language ability only conditioned motor responses can occur. Opposed to this relatively behavioristic position is a group of psychoanalysts and anthropologists, like Margaret Mead and Geoffrey Gorer, who admit that the precise degree of thought and discrimination in the early years is unknown and perhaps unresearchable but continue to talk as if such discrimination occurs. This position only makes sense if we assume that they treat the baby in terms of an adult model capable of explicit thought and feeling. Their procedure is closely akin to that of the physicist who speaks of space inside of an electron but cannot empirically demonstrate such a meaningless statement. Regardless of demonstrable correctness, the Mead-Gorer approach in company with motivation theory is the more useful for understanding the impact of early learning and the relationship of early experience to personality patterns manifested later in life.

---

[1] Margaret Mead, quoted in Benedict, 1949:349.

There can be no question about the capacity of the baby to experience pleasure and pain (Stagner, 1948:81–88). Emotional states of pleasantness and unpleasantness constitute the earliest signals which the infant derives from its environment. The incidence of early gratification or nongratification provides the earliest direction to the development of nonverbal world and self views. Pleasurable early states, such as may be associated with warmth, hunger satiation, gentle handling, or rocking, encourage relatively positive feelings toward experience. These feelings endure, especially if they are reinforced by consistent subsequent experiences. They gradually crystallize into attitudes of confidence, mastery, adequacy, and security. The positive world and self view, born of gratification, may be summed up in the formula: "This is a predictable, friendly world that I can manage." Persistent nongratification, tension, or exposure to unpleasant experiences may encourage a negative world and self view, one summed up in the phrase: "This is a dangerous and unpredictable world that I cannot control."

Consistency

Evidence suggests that the quality of early experience is often maintained through the years of later childhood. In other words, subsequent experiences tend to reinforce the world and self views derived in early life rather than to reverse the picture completely. As Mead (1949f:63) puts it, ". . . a careful examination of the ways new-born babies are handled—cradled gently against the breast, held up by the heels and slapped, wrapped so close that no light comes to them until they are many weeks old, stood out on the mother's iron-stiff arm to fend, like tiny frogs, for themselves—shows that these early ways of treating them are strictly congruent with later handling. . . ." The element of consistency suggests that the totality of early experience be studied for an understanding of the early patterning rather than particular events.

Two reasons support the view that—especially in a homogeneous culture[2]—early experiences tend to be reinforced rather than counter-

[2] See below, pp. 346–347.

acted by those in later life. First is the self-regulatory nature of character structure which, like any regenerative system, tends to maintain
itself. A favorable picture of the world developed early provides
confidence and leads to perceiving and creating friendly stimuli in
the environment. Thus the child interprets his experiences as security
promoting. He comes to see the world as a friendly place. However,
the child's expectations of kindliness could not persist in the absence
of reinforcing experiences coming from the environment. Hence it
becomes necessary to account further for the reinforcement of early
experiences by those in later childhood. The second reason supporting
the hypothesis of reinforcement holds that consistency in the quality
of patterning follows from the integrated nature of social life. In the
absence of a shift from one culture or subculture to another, the treatment that a young child experiences is determined at successive moments in time by many identical conditions—technological, geographical, demographic, social relational, and ideological. To put it grossly,
if poverty forces neglect of a one-year-old it will also require neglect of
a three-year-old.

Consistency in the early life cycle is never perfect. Discontinuity
must also be reckoned with. For example, as will be more fully demonstrated, the treatment of the child is modified in relation to the
altering demands and capacities of the maturing organism. Also, every
community enforces special demands at particular points of the life
cycle; children under six may be free of responsibility but beyond that
age girls are often expected to help get wood and water and perform
other services for the household. Despite these modifying factors,
early experiences productive of specific world and self views tend
to be reinforced by later childhood experiences as long as the individual's milieu remains relatively constant. Consistency is also reduced by the fact that in the most homogeneous of communities
deviants may be present to distort the ideal plan of life consistently
held out to developing individuals. Among the Arapesh, for example,
the children of deviants as well as youngsters reared close to deviants
may take the conduct of these atypical ones "as pattern and so become
confused in adult life. The picture of a gentle community in which

all men are loving relatives is not quite so vivid to the little boy who has just seen his mother bind up Yaluhaip's wound" (Mead, *1950b*: 117).

Comparative studies by Martha Wolfenstein (*1949*) illustrate what may also be termed continuity in socialization. The Czech mother considers it traditional to use (or threaten to use) the wooden kitchen spoon for spanking children; the American mother supposedly prefers the hair brush, while Soviet and pre-Soviet informants spoke of sometimes tying down and beating children with a whip or a belt that wrapped itself around the child's body. Ear pinching is a technique for punishing a Syrian child at home or in school. "The manifest rationale for this attack on the ear is that the child has not listened to the words of his mentor; the punishment is directed against the refractory organ." Consistency is revealed in that the choice of implement or technique of punishment can be related to earlier experiences between parents and children: ". . . our first tentative guess is that something in the mother-child relation having to do with the giving of solid food is repeated in the choice of the kitchen spoon as the spanking instrument, while where the hairbrush is chosen the antecedent situation is one of cleanliness training." In Soviet and pre-Soviet culture the swaddling of infants stands out prominently on the earlier horizon. The ear pinching of Syrian children is less clear but assertedly relates to a style of nursing and early feeding in which the child has the breast and food thrust into its mouth. "The relation between the immobilized infant into whose mouth the breast is thrust and the school child who is required to receive with equal docility the word of the teacher is indicated by explicit formulations. The child is supposed to receive his character from his mother's milk." Generalizing these particular hypotheses the author says that "punishments tend to repeat some earlier phase in parent-child relations not only in the choice of implements but also (where the punishment is corporal) in the part of the body to which the punishment is applied." Further hypotheses are then constructed to further explain the dynamics of this relationship between punishment and antecedent conditions.

If we suppose that punishment repeats an earlier, premoral situation, we must ask what could be motivations for this repetition. A preliminary hypothesis would be the following. In the early care of the child the mother of necessity imposes numerous deprivations. Her empathy with the child re-evokes in her (probably mainly unconsciously) the feelings of rage and resentment which she felt towards her own mother in similar circumstances and which she now feels are directed towards her by her own child. If later when the child has been "bad" she symbolically repeats the earlier deprivations in the guise of punishment she communicates to the child in effect that it is his own "badness" which has provoked the deprivations and requires that he redirect his blame of her into self-blame. As a result the earlier deprivations are reinterpreted, or, insofar as the child has a spontaneous tendency to feel that the original deprivations were punishments for his bad impulses, this feeling is now confirmed. Hence punishment may tend to re-enact those early experiences which were felt (presumably by both mother and child) to have had a strong deprivational impact on the child. Where this is the case for weaning or the introduction of solid food, a favored punishment would be likely to be withholding, and the spoon might become an instrument of punishment. Where toilet training has been a major focus of interference with impulse, the related punishment which in a moralized way attacks the same body area would be spanking. Where earlier interference with motor activity through swaddling has had a strong deprivational impact, the related punishment may be a renewed immobilization as the child is bound and a lashing of the body in which the whip replaces the swaddling bands.[3] Of course, as we have already remarked, a variety of punishments is usually chosen in any particular family or group which would then commemorate a variety of early deprivations.

The implications of consistency in the quality of the child's early experiences for patterning are quite clear. Consistency means that particular gratifications or nongratifications, specific styles of learning, or concrete lessons in what to expect from, and how to respond to, people will be continued and reiterated in diverse ways as the child matures. The baby fed with an object—the bottle—grows up in a

---

[3] A footnote in the original reminds the reader that the supposed deprivational impact of swaddling has been questioned. See Benedict, 1949. Also see below, p. 242.

world dominated more by things than by people and acquires distinctive attitudes toward possessions. Lessons in strength and self-reliance may similarly be communicated from one point in the life cycle to another.

Discontinuity

Consistency in the quality of total early experience does not deny that discontinuity also finds a place in socialization. Modification in attitudes toward children may reflect those changes in the growing child's development which the community chooses to emphasize. Discontinuities in child rearing, as already pointed out, may have considerable implications for patterning.

The Maori baby is treated with "an easy affectionate indulgence" and receives many more gratifications through food, affection, and cuddling than he receives punishments, deprivations, or frustrations (Beaglehole and Beaglehole, 1946:117–151). Toilet training is very lenient. At about the age of three or four the pattern alters and negative disciplines increase. Punishments tend to outweigh rewards, both parents becoming equally severe in this respect. Threats of ghosts and spirits come to help control the behavior of the child. Children are put off by themselves a large portion of the time and should make themselves neither seen nor heard in the presence of adults. Rewards, notably bestowed by indulgent grandparents, come as capriciously as punishments. The authors hypothecate the latent consequences of this break in the style of socialization. The Maori adult's generous, friendly, coöperative personality, they say, "is ultimately linked with the traumatic anxiety of early childhood when the Maori child after two years of warm, affectionate, friendly care is suddenly cast on his own resources." Generosity and friendliness are used by Maoris to hold on to warm human contacts. "Thus symbolically does the Maori adult ever seek to recapture that golden world of love and affection which he lost irretrievably in the process of growing up." The native's attachment to generosity and what the latter symbolizes help explain the people's resistance to the individualistic acquisitiveness of whites.

It will be noted that the alteration in the style of the parents' behavior toward the Maori child parallels the Kaska mother's emotional withdrawal. Both events occur at about the same point of the life cycle. A similar break in the tenor of child rearing, coming at three or four years of age, is not uncommon in other communities and appears to follow recognition of certain visible signs of maturation. A second perspective from which to understand the shift in behavior toward the two- or three-year-old involves recognizing that a very young baby could not survive except for a great deal of indulgent parental care. The connection between affectionate care and survival may not be explicitly made by native peoples. On the other hand their generous attention to the infant undoubtedly has survival value, a point to be examined more closely below.

In the German Protestant community emotional weaning comes very much later than among the Maori or Kaska (Rodnick, 1948:57, 60–71). It remains for adolescence to change the protected, happy years of childhood. The child "finds that he is to be a lone individual competing for status in a society where there are few opportunities and few places to give him the sense of well-being he had as a child." Many young people in Germany are reluctant to leave childhood and would like to hold on to a state in which they are loved for themselves alone. Adolescence poses demands for resourcefulness and self assertion greater than the child can muster. Youth organizations come to take the place of parents, giving to youth a sense of belonging and of being wanted. They perpetuate some of the security of the earlier years. The qualities in which German children were trained—gentleness, submission to parents, and nonaggression—come to be of little use when as adolescents they are put on their own. The middle class needs qualities that will lead to success and rank advancement while members of the working class expect their children to "build a new world." Working-class children feel harassed by these expectations and draw into shells. Middle-class youngsters come to envy the more successful classes in the community and feel aggrieved at their own handicap. They become pessimistic about the future and eager for a miracle. Rodnick believes that the late emotional weaning of children and the discontinuity it introduces have the secondary effect of encouraging feelings of dependence and insecurity.

Caution must be exercised not to read inconsistency into the life cycle by missing early subtle preparation for changes in the later treatment of children. Thus the ridicule directed at the Pukapukan child who does not wean easily, and the removal of a child at weaning to another village where "feeding parents" will teach it to eat solids and help it to forget the breast, represent a firmness of attitudes directed to early childhood (Beaglehole and Beaglehole, *1941*). The same quality is reinforced when whipping follows failure to achieve toilet control once the child can walk unaided to the toilet area. These early patterns set the stage for the physical beatings that can be expected before puberty. Disobedience, lack of expected skill, and laziness lead to whippings generally administered by older women. The punishment "tends to jolt the child out of an earlier freedom attitude; it also hastens the fuller participation of the young person in adult economic activities. . . ." It does not appear, however, that such treatment is inconsistent with the earlier handling of the Pukapukan child. Parenthetically, it is interesting to observe the outcome of this rearing pattern. The modal personality turns out to be self-assertive ("aggressive," the authors say), keenly engrossed with prowess in love and other undertakings, rivalrous in sport, and violent in war.

The Configuration of Early Experience

A review of the literature reveals how little can be expected by correlating particular variables of early childhood experience to subsequent personality patterns. Attempts at experimental verification of hypotheses connecting particular patterns of child rearing with later motivational patterns, Orlansky (*1948, 1949*) demonstrates, lead only to confused and conflicting results. For example, do breast and bottle feeding relate to different covert personality traits? One study of 109 children in the United States indicates that children who have been artificially fed during infancy experience more feeding difficulties, poorer health, and greater restlessness than the children who drew milk from the breast. Another study finds the highest security scores to be registered by those college students who had hardly or not at all been breast fed *and* those who had been breast fed for over a year. Still another experiment led to no evidence that those nursery school children who had not been breast fed experienced any greater maladjustment or insecurity than those with long records of breast feeding. If these connections cannot be upheld in testing with many cases, then they do not seem worth while to use in cross-cultural research. At an earlier date in the history of culture and personality it was far more logical to borrow from psychiatry, pediatrics, and psychology these kinds of hypotheses involving breast, bottle, regular, or demand feeding and other similar, discrete variables. The choice led to a considerable if negative advancement in knowledge. Researchers summoned these hypotheses to highly critical testing with the result that we may regard many of them as probably false. Now new hypotheses are needed to fill the gap. The new statements which are beginning to guide culture and personality research bear a different character. They emphasize less the specificities of what is done to the child than (1) the interrelationship of discrete early experiences and (2) the form and emotional quality of early interpersonal situations. In place of dealing with isolated variables, like breast or bottle feeding, the tendency is to work with the configuration of early experience. Davis and Havighurst (*1953*), for example, carefully observe patterns of feeding, weaning, toilet training, age of assuming responsibility, and strictness of the daily regime. They then generalize the pattern that "middle-class families are more rigorous than lower-class families in their training of children for feeding and cleanliness habits. They generally begin training earlier . . . place more emphasis on the early assumption of responsibility . . . are less permissive than lower-class families in their regimen . . . require their children to take naps at a later age, to be in the house at night earlier, and, in general, permit less free play of the impulses of their children." Their experiment demonstrates that a consistent quality links successively imposed childhood disciplines. How the quality of rigorousness in American middle-class child rearing can be related to other personality patterns will be brought out below.[4]

Oscar Lewis (*1951:418*) reveals how attention may be given to the configuration of early experience. From his work in the village of Tepoztlan he reports patterns of long nursing; swaddling; restriction on the movements of the child; belief that the child must not be allowed to cry; and absence of preoccupation with training the child to walk, talk, eat alone, and develop sphincter control. The preponderance of adult attention goes to limit and protect the child rather than to stimulate him. Exploration, whether of a motor or a question-asking sort, is not encouraged. Between the ages of two and five much stress is also laid on obedience to, and respect for, adults. Taking these elements as a whole he sees them related to the development of children who are easy to control, that is, children who are submissive, quiet, passive, and dependent. These patterns, however, do not explain why the children in turn grow up to be constricted, negativistic, hostile, detached, envious, unimaginative, and individualistic adults.

One rationale for studying the configuration of early experience comes from the postulate that early life experiences do not operate in isolation upon the child's developing personality. It is more likely that successive experiences with feeding, swaddling, toilet training, and other stimuli blend, whether their mutual qualities are reinforcing or discontinuous. The amalgam of these early experiences comes to be reflected in patterns of action, thought, and feeling—in personality.

THE INFANT'S SURVIVAL

The socially standardized treatment of infants must to some degree be lenient or pleasurable if the baby is to live. Extreme or persistent pain threatens survival. Common sense indicates that a culture which standardizes extreme neglect of infants would soon vanish as its carriers disappeared. Even minimal feeding and protection from the cold are not enough. The poor survival value of child rearing methods that neglect certain tactual satisfactions is shown by Margaret Ribble (*1944*), who reports that absence of mothering (rocking, cradling,

---

[4] See below, pp. 316–317.

stroking, etc.) is associated with constipation, rigidity, and screaming; if the affectionate lack continues the infant drifts into a stupor. Such cases of infantile trauma are not uncommonly encountered in orphanages with inadequate staff or wherever mother and baby are separated for relatively long periods. Such "anaclitic depression" is well described for infants six months or older, who were removed from their mothers for three months or more (Spitz and Wolf, 1946; Spitz, 1945). The babies wept frequently, lost weight, suffered from insomnia, and remained retarded in development. These signs continued during the first three months of separation. Then a "sort of frozen rigidity appeared." Interpersonal contact with the children became difficult. In three cases the mothers returned to the children, reunion being followed by "dramatic" changes in the children who became "friendly, gay, approachable." Development also accelerated (Spitz and Wolf, 1946). Many psychologists and pediatricians recognize that infant mortality rates remain high in the best-run orphan homes, presumably at least partly because busy staffs cannot help each infant satisfy survival-linked demands for mothering.

The Alorese appear to be the closest standardized parallel now known in anthropology to the extreme unsatisfaction of infantile needs described by Ribble and Spitz. Among these Indonesian people a woman in the planting season returns to her gardening duties ten to fourteen days after she has given birth (DuBois, 1944:34–35; Kardiner, 1945:130–131). The mother does not take her baby along to the field but leaves him at home in care of the father, older siblings, or grandmother. Such babies frequently become hungry during the time they remain at home. The person charged with their care feeds them premasticated food but this is often rejected by the infant, who searches for the nipple to which he has become accustomed from earlier contact with the mother. Wet nursing sometimes occurs but is neither dependable nor consistent. We must note that Alorese infants are not denied handling nor are they left to cry without attention. In the evening the baby is fed and fondled by the mother who has then returned from work. The situation of the Alorese neonate is not as extreme as the foundling situation described by Ribble and

Spitz. In commenting on the psychological significance of Alorese infancy, Kardiner (1945:147, 151) infers that the child receives no opportunity to become attached to any person, even its mother (Du-Bois, 1944:176). No person stands out on the baby's horizon as a source of tension gratification. Rather the mother is apt to be interpreted as a "frustrating object." The early child-rearing pattern is held to be related to the Alorese inability for sustained effort, low self-esteem, low aspiration level, and tendency to give up easily.

The Arapesh mode of bringing up children stands in sharp contrast to Alorese child care. Arapesh child rearing probably represents one of the most indulgent in the literature (Mead, 1950b:33–65). Here, where a crying baby is to be avoided at all cost, suckling is generously available. When the mother can no longer easily carry the child to the garden where she works, she becomes concerned with making restitution for her absence. This occurs in the afternoons through prolonging suckling and much playing with the naked body of the baby. A cold bath daily, a pattern initiated a few days after birth, constitutes a discomfort to which the child never quite becomes accustomed. Nor does he adjust to the jerk with which a person holds him aside to urinate or defecate. These are among the rare shocks in the early months of growing up. In early life the baby learns to depend and love widely in a large kin group. Fright, hurts, or falls are responded to with cuddling and attention. "The result is that the child grows up with a sense of emotional security in the care of others, not in its own control over the environment" (Mead, 1950b:44). He develops a "loving trust of all persons whom he sees or calls by a kinship term." But this is security on a narrow base. His loving trust is "an attitude that can be shattered at a blow because no blows are received in childhood to habituate the growing child to the competitive aggressiveness of others" (Mead, 1950b:102).

Kardiner (1939:99) stresses some of the adaptive difficulties associated with a highly permissive childhood. Among the Trobriand Islanders, for example, restrictions on sexual activities are imposed only when the individual marries. The individual who is thus raised with little thwarting of his sexual inclinations does not accept later restriction on his opportunities without protest. Rather he "is under a more serious handicap than one whose activity is restricted from infancy and who has accustomed himself to masochistic adaptations which are socially compatible." The child who lacks sufficient experience with restriction and becomes accustomed to sheer gratification never learns to be strong in the face of trials. Kardiner sees the "readiness with which the Trobrianders commit suicide as a result of failure or degradation" related to the permissive childhood which "gives the individual a low frustration threshold." The same author has also pointed out that overprotection and great indulgence of young babies encourage passive attitudes to life at the same time that they develop a strong capacity for affective response and a tendency to idealize the parents (Kardiner, 1945:345, 347–348; Kardiner and Ovesey, 1951: 28).

To sum up, the matter of pain induction, frustration, and neglect in infancy and early childhood must be considered relatively. That is to say, one community may frustrate more or inflict greater pain than another. Probably no community succeeds in avoiding some pain and frustration in the course of early socialization. The consequences of this universal component of pain and frustration in child development are not clear and, of course, they need not concern us. Our interest lies in the differential patterning of modal personality.

SOME EARLY EXPERIENCES

The role of the future child may be reflected throughout the mother's pregnancy. The customs, avoidances, and other rites practiced by the pregnant woman will reflect ambivalent, fearful, or hygienic attitudes toward reproduction that may be sustained in the later handling of the baby. Mead (1949f:61) says, "It is probable that in different societies, by the attribution of more or less autonomy of movement to the baby, by enjoining upon the mother active or placid behavior, the process of learning may begin within the womb. . . ." After the baby is born the socially standardized ways in which people think of infants and handle, swaddle, cuddle, feed, or masturbate them come to occupy the attention of the student of culture and personality. In the first months of life the world manifests itself to the new baby through the gratifications and frustrations that follow from early handling. These early emotional experiences promote the earliest personality patterning after birth.

Five bodily zones mediate the bulk of the baby's early experiences. Psychoanalysts describe early socialization as a process which sequentially energizes or libidinizes the mouth, gums and teeth, anus-urethra, limbs, and genitals (Erikson, *1950*, chap. 2).[5] As each of these zones becomes involved in patterning, the child acquires certain modes of behavior. Thus in the period of infancy, when suckling makes the mouth the primary zone, the child normally learns his first lessons in giving, receiving, and dependence. Later, when the teeth become primary, the child adds to his earlier learning lessons in taking or holding on. When bowel training is instituted, he takes his first instruction in retaining. As control of the limbs enter the picture, learning intrusive behavior occurs, learning that later attaches to use of the genitals. Regression at any stage to an earlier mode is not only possible but not uncommon. Erikson (140) does not claim the activation of successive bodily zones to be solely responsible for personality formation. Rather, the process of socialization as it affects these areas results in putting additional energy at the disposal of socially provided goals and values: ". . . we are dealing here not with simple causality, but with a mutual assimilation of somatic, mental, and social patterns which amplify one another and make the cultural design for living economical and effective." We will probably find Ruth Benedict's phrasing (*1949*) of the course of early socialization easier to understand. She says, "Identifications, securities, and frustrations are built up in the child by the way in which he is traditionally handled, the early disciplines he receives, and the sanctions used by parents."

Swaddling

Swaddling provides one of the socially standardized ways in which adults and infants interact. Benedict's comparative examination of

---

[5] See the use Margaret Mead makes of Erikson's theory in *Male and Female* (Mead, *1949f*:64–77).

TABLE 2. Some Conceptions and Patterns of Swaddling

Country	Pattern and Conception
Great Russia	Here swaddling is the tightest and longest of any patterns examined. The swaddled baby makes a rigid bundle. Parents say swaddling is necessary to keep the baby from hurting itself through its violence. They also point out that it makes for ease in carrying. "You couldn't carry an unswaddled baby."
Poland	Parents say swaddling is necessary because the baby is fragile, it may snap in two if it is not bound. Swaddling is also said to "harden" the child, just as life hardens a man through suffering. In Poland children are often left to cry themselves out, the rationalization being offered that crying benefits the lungs. Temper tantrums also go unappeased. Swaddling is also important to the Poles because it prevents the indecency of putting the toes into the mouth, a sensitive point to the Poles.
East European Jews	The baby is swaddled on a soft pillow, the bindings loosely wrapped around the baby and featherbed. The aim is to keep the child warm and comfortable. It is regretted that the baby's limbs must be confined, but one reward is that swaddling promotes straight limbs.
Rumania	Swaddling is necessary to prevent masturbation. It is restrictive just as the custom of tying an older child's hands to the crib, or keeping them in clumsy mittens, are restrictions designed to prevent masturbation. Ease of carrying and keeping the legs straight are other reasons for swaddling in Rumania (Benedict, 1943a).

swaddling (1949) shows how childhood disciplines may be variously conceptualized by the people who follow them. Swaddling, she points out, does not mean the same thing in every community where it occurs. (See Table 2.) Swaddling constitutes a kind of communication between adults and children and the content of that communication may often be learned in the rationalization which the community gives for the act.

The relationship of swaddling to personality patterns has been much discussed in anthropology and psychology. Sustained retardation, the developmental psychologists assure us, does not follow from swaddling (Dennis, *1940a*). The question of characterological correlates is left without such neat solution. Use of the cradling board among American Indians has been associated with frustration that generates a fund of lasting aggression (Erikson, *1939*). Such a connection may be warranted among the Sioux and other Plains Indians communities but it is not so readily supported by the data of the Hopi and other Pueblo Indians. Greenacre (*1953*:512–513) refers to the problem of restraints in infancy as "difficult and complicated" but believes that evidence supports her conclusion that prolonged restraint may encourage anxiety, sadism, and masochism. Benedict's work, just mentioned, poses another question. Should we assume the functional equivalance of swaddling from one culture to another? Precisely such an assumption, which neglects the specific meaning ascribed to the action in a particular community, is required to test cross culturally the relationship of the discrete variable, swaddling, with some element of personality. If, on the other hand, we adopt a configurational approach, then not swaddling alone but the pattern in a syndrome of other child rearing activities, especially those which are affect-laden, will become the variable. Thus, among East European Jews swaddling is only one of the channels through which the helplessness and pitiable condition of the infant are warmly stressed. Swaddling is not equivalent to isolation among those people for the immobile child is almost never left unattended. The mother spends much time "talking out her heart" to the baby. Swaddling, like kissing and cooing, is further integrated into a determined effort to hurry the child out of babyhood and into a precocious cleverness (Zborowski and Herzog, *1952*:324–329). On the other hand, no states of personality are correlated with, for example, the syndrome of the baby treated with pitiable helplessness found among East European Jews. The data on these people are given descriptively without genetic interpretation.

Early Feeding

Compared to swaddling, nursing and other forms of early feeding have received far more interpretation from students interested in the problems of personality patterning. Such attention, as already mentioned, has led to realization of the unfruitfulness of connecting specific variables of early feeding—like the use of the breast or bottle, scheduled or unscheduled nursing—to particular attributes of personality (Orlansky, *1949;* Newton, *1951;* Sewell, *1952*). The original interest in feeding experiences derived from psychoanalysis where it is said "that generous suckling and later weaning are related to generosity, optimism, and co-operative, peaceful behavior; whereas ungenerous suckling and early weaning coincide with arrogance, aggression, and impatience, a tendency to collect and hoard food, competitiveness, and quarrelsomeness, and attitudes of acquisition and retention, love of property, hostility, suspicion, and a nostalgic sadness" (Goldman-Eisler, *1953:147*). Psychoanalysts still employ these hypotheses and endow them with greater predictive power than is the case with more eclectic workers in culture and personality. Experimental research by psychoanalysts supports their belief. Goldman-Eisler, using a group of middle-class English adults, discovered a small but significant correlation between early weaning and "oral pessimism" (defined as compounded of pessimism, a passive receptive attitude, unsociability, withdrawnness, a disinclination to be helpful and protective, and narcissistic self-sufficiency). She concludes that "the length of breast-feeding is a significant factor in the etiology of oral pessimism and probably depression, but the size of the correlation also shows that there are other factors involved in oral pessimism which account for it to a greater extent."

In the case of early feeding routines it is again necessary to regard the feeding situation as one channel for affect-laden communication between mother and child. The nursing situation reveals to the child the emotional emphases of people to him as well as of the culture as a whole. The communication aspects of feeding have received little explicit attention.

To see how infant feeding bears a systematic relationship to the cultural configuration and mediates learning we may examine the general pattern in the United States. The decline of breast feeding in this country is related to several features of modern life. In the first place, the majority of births take place in hospitals where routine sometimes recommends bottle feeding (Schultz, *1950*). Especially the 2:00 A.M. feeding may be by bottle, thus sparing the mother's rest. However, any bottle feeding probably reduces stimulation of the woman's breasts so that milk production lessens and breast feeding declines still further in favor of using the bottle. In the second place, the American mother's culturally learned motivations toward feeding and nursing support the high incidence of bottle feeding. An informal poll of hospitals, doctors, and nurses indicates that 50 percent of mothers do not wish to nurse their infants. Several culturally linked motives underlie this reluctance (Mead, *1949f*, chap. 13):

1. Some women fear that nursing will impair their figures. Stress on firm, upright breasts is a valued trait in American life, a narcissistic compensation for femininity. When this narcissistic component in the woman's personality deprives the child of contact with the mother's body the baby begins to learn different attitudes than are acquired by the Arapesh child who sensually cuddles his naked body against the mother's equally naked breast. A direct human relationship is mediated by an object, the first of many objects which will interpose themselves between the person and his social relationships.

2. American mothers are anxious about their capacity to satisfy the baby's hunger through breast feeding. Such anxiety is not only learned but is related to a rapidly changing culture in which one's own parents are no longer automatic models for replicatory behavior. Books take the place of parental models. Stressing ideal development this literature teaches that the child must regularly be weighed, its development needs frequent checking. ". . . the new child," says Mead, "is treated as if its health and well-being depended on the machine-like precision with which it is fed, and on what it is fed.

The mother learns impatience with her milk, which is too rich or too weak, too much or too little, pouring through nipples that are inverted or sore or otherwise unobliging." The rubber nipple, which can be enlarged with a pin, is more reliable; the graduated bottle, able to contain just the right formula, is a more predictable device to insure the child's health. The concern for proper weight and diet will continue through the rest of the person's life. The decrease in the infant death rate reflects the perfect care our children receive but the characteristic learning encouraged by those patterns of care also warrants attention. The first learning against spontaneous pleasure, against following the body's own rhythms and in favor of external rhythms, takes place in these relations between American mother and child.

3. Breast nursing conflicts with the woman's role in community affairs or employment. In other words, as American women have emulated men in taking up careers they have also been forced to make compensatory changes in their relations with children. The substitution of the bottle for the breast has facilitated the employment of a nurse, who adds an impersonal and transitory element to the family, the first of the many impersonal relationships which the child will form.

The Attawapiskat Cree mother is also ready to adopt a bottle in favor of the breast and she is also anxious lest her milk be insufficient to satisfy the baby. Her anxiety, however, is differently grounded. She is less concerned with having the proper food or promoting the ideal pattern of development than she is worried about sheer hunger. Her attitude foreshadows the unrealistic food anxiety which the Attawapiskat child will likely acquire.

Nursing among the Arapesh, it has been pointed out, communicates the mother's cherishment of a helpless infant. Among the Iatmul a somewhat contrasting attitude prevails (Mead, *1949f*:69). The Iatmul child without being rejected is regarded as far less dependent or helpless than the Arapesh baby. The Iatmul baby is seen to have a will of its own. After he is a few weeks old the mother no longer carries the child everywhere or sits with him in her lap. She perches him on a high bench and here comes to feed the baby generously whenever he cries. Quite early in life children receive a piece of hard meat to chew. When teeth appear they cut them on shell ornaments hung from the mother's neck. "In this interchange between mother and child," says Mead, "the sense of the mouth is built up as an assertive, demanding organ, taking what it can from a world that is, however, not unduly unwilling to give it." Toward this world the child acquires the attitude that "if you fight hard enough, something which will treat you as strong as itself will yield."

Margaret Mead (1949f:88) correlates the degree of emphasis on suckling with preoccupation of the community with differences between the sexes: ". . . within . . . those societies which have emphasized suckling . . . there is the greatest symbolic preoccupation with the differentials between men and women, the greatest envy, over-compensation, ritual mimicry of the opposite sex, and so on." Male initiation rites and men's houses also reveal a stress on sexual differentiation in a culture. The explanation for the relationship between an emphasis on suckling and preoccupation with sex distinctions may lie in the fact that if suckling is emphasized then the child is required to spend a considerable time with the mother during which he learns to identify with her and with women. For a boy there comes a time when such identification must at least partly be abrogated. The dramatic affiliation with male adults, ceremonially accomplished and periodically renewed, in turn contributes toward the preoccupation with sexual roles. The Arapesh ceremonially separate men from women even though temperamental differences between the sexes are not admitted. A considerable emphasis on nursing is also characteristic of this community. In the United States, where suckling may be regarded as somewhat indecent, very low affectivity marks the process. Sex equivalence in American culture is also strongly patterned. Strong separation or distinctions between men and women tend to be resisted. Our popular music is written so as to be sung by either a male or female singer, one simply substituting "she" where the other sings "he." The same careers and opportunities are supposed to be open to each sex.

The age and manner in which solid foods are introduced vary considerably between groups. An Umbundu native of Angola, in southwest Africa, gave this account of how solids are fed to young babies (Childs, *1949*:88): " 'From the time the baby is born they set its gruel . . . and . . . feed (it to him). It is difficult to feed a baby because he struggles greatly, and so when they feed him they hold his little arms and legs and put the food in his mouth when he cries. The mother takes the gruel from the pot and first puts it in her own mouth to cool it with her saliva, and then she takes it out and with the crook of her finger puts it into the baby's mouth.' " Force is also used to make the baby drink magically treated beer. Among the Balinese a similar "assault on the mouth" is interpreted as "not unexpectedly, followed by a great tendency to cover up, or plug up, the mouth in later life. Eating is accompanied with great shame, while drinking, the prototype of which is drinking from an upturned breast above which the infant is carried, is a matter of casual pleasure" (Mead, *1949f*:72). Whether the relationship between forcible early feeding and mouth anxiety regularly occur together is not yet clear.

The reader will note that in directing attention to variables like the emphasis placed on suckling attention has been devoted to the ethological aspects of early feeding. Other areas in infancy may also be examined for their ethos. In this way the qualitative patterns linking a number of spatially and temporally separated cultural situations are derived. We have already seen the Arapesh pattern of infant care marked by warmth, gentleness, and indulgence. The child learns that the world is replete with love and trust. The Mundugumor world is a very different place characterized by fight and struggle. Among these people infancy is associated with little sensuous indulgence in suckling. Children "develop a very definite purposive fighting attitude, holding on firmly to the nipple and sucking milk as rapidly and vigorously as possible" (Mead, *1950b*:139). The months before the child can walk are partly spent in a harsh, stiff basket that practically pinions the arms to the sides and shuts out a good deal of light. No warmth from the mother's body penetrates the container where the baby is carried. Babies have to cry before they are fed and even then the supply of milk may be delayed while attempts are made to distract the child by scratching on the basket. Nursing is never utilized here to comfort an injured or frightened youngster.

Weaning

Psychologists and psychiatrists have been especially interested in the consequences of early or long delayed weaning. Early or abrupt removal from the breast is associated by them with unconscious images of the mother as a frustrating object while emotional passivity sometimes stems from prolonged suckling or delayed weaning. Such connections remain poorly verified and increasing evidence of the sort referred to above suggests the unlikelihood of obtaining significant correlations between the time of weaning and later personality manifestations. Like swaddling, weaning is better studied for the way it contributes to the process of communication with small children. "The mother who weans her child harshly by putting red pepper on her breast will express the same attitude toward the child in her every act or tone of voice. If she does not, if in fact the idea of red pepper is a naive importation which she uses in contexts containing no other congruently harsh elements, this weaning method will probably have very little effect on the child because it is unsupported by the details of voice and handling that would reinforce it and give it significance" (Mead, *1947b*:155). Emphasis may be placed on the attitudes accompanying the transition from the breast to solid foods. The Arapesh, for example, believe abrupt weaning to be cruel and feel guilty about having to remove a child from the breast. This guilt develops extra parental solicitude. Weaning then becomes a very gradual process, the child becoming accustomed to more and more solid food as the breast comes to serve more and more for affection and security (Mead, *1950b*:38). The Mundugumor, however, do not try to mitigate frustration in weaning (141). The haste formerly associated with nursing is replaced by the blows and cross words of weaning "which further accentuate the picture of a hostile world that is presented to the child." In Poland, where people believe that a twice weaned child will die, weaning comes suddenly. Somewhere at

around eighteen months the mother selects a day and, with no previous experience in eating solids, the child is expected to make the
transition from the breast. Weaning among the Poles serves as one
more means of urging the child to adulthood. The mother, not una-
ware of the unpleasantness of her actions, communicates to the youngster her own belief that persistence in the weaning situation is necessary for "hardening" him (Benedict, 1949:346).

SYMMETRICAL, COMPLEMENTARY, AND RECIPROCAL PATTERNS

From the moment of birth contrasting emphases can be distinguished in the mother's and other adults' treatment of the child
(Mead, 1949f:64–77). The relationship to children may be compared according to whether the dominant pattern of the mother's
behavior is symmetrical, complementary, or reciprocal (cf. Bateson,
1949c).

1. The symmetrical relationship appears when people treat the
baby as though he were a finished little individual, able in some
degree to oppose the mother's will with his own, or as if he were endowed with rights similar to those enjoyed by any adult member of
the community. Adult and child are conceived of as basically similar
when symmetry marks the relationships. The Samoan treatment of
children evidences symmetry and the same quality appears in attitudes toward Kaska children after they are about three years old.
From that age the Indian child is treated with the relatively unintense
behavior that marks interpersonal relations among these people. The
description of socialization among the Mohave Indians also appears
to illustrate symmetry (Devereux, 1950). While Mohave adults out-
rank children in prestige, people feel that children are "incomplete"
rather than inferior human beings. The adult represents the completed person. Children—even the unborn—are open to reason or
argument and "amenable to moral suasion." In keeping with these
attitudes, adults relate to children in a personal, "man-to-man" fashion. A considerable measure of equality prevails; standards of good
conduct tend to be the same for grownups and youngsters and adults
cannot claim immunities or rights which they will not grant to chil-

dren. Mohave also do not regard rearing a child as an expense which places the latter under obligation to the parents. American visitors to the Mohave reservation perceive the difference between such treatment of children and their own when they complain that the Indian child is "not looked after properly." Symmetry also marks Navaho parent-child relations: ". . . in the old Navaho way, children and adults do not belong to two separate worlds. The same set of standards prevails in most things for all ages, from the child (as soon as he can talk) to the very old people. Generalizations were really 'general' and easy to apply in the old Navaho world, and the child was taught a way of thinking suitable to such a world" (Leighton and Kluckhohn, 1947:74).

Symmetry in child rearing is, of course, related to other elements of culture. The Mohave and Navaho children do not, like American children, grow up in multi-roomed houses in which walls separate them from parents. The work of the father is not wholly removed from the routines of the home. Mohave children have opportunities to obtain an "undress" view of parents, something we do not encourage (Riesman, 1950:44).

2. A complementary relationship calls for an emphasis on the different but complementary roles played by parent and child. The mother may act as though the child is essentially different from herself, as though it is weak and dependent while she is strong and able to succor or enjoy it. The relationship of the British father to his children illustrates a basically complementary bond as does the family situation among the Arapesh. Strongly complementary parent-child relations show up in the "Old Kingdom" of Rumania (Benedict, 1943a:44). Here a woman takes keen pleasure in her baby. She does not like to think of the baby as an investment for the future when the child will take care of her. In a folk tale a female partridge drowns two fledglings who promise to take care of her when she becomes old. But the mother bird spares the third fledgling because it says, " 'When we grow up we will also take care of our young children with the same love and devotion.' 'With the same joy and enthusiasm' would translate more accurately the Rumanian attitude."

3. In a reciprocal relationship emphasis falls on an exchange between adults and children. Love, trust, obedience, feces, and tears come to be treated as if they were physical objects. When one person in the relationship gives, the other reciprocates with his offering or reward. American childhood is replete with reciprocal themes. The American mother's attitude to elimination illustrates the emphasis but so do the many other situations in which right performance or achievement are rewarded by the mother's love. The conception which the child learns is one of his own body or personality manufacturing commodities—health, marks, popularity—that can be presented to the mother, who is somehow responsible for all this achievement and who staŕted off the process. The Manus also emphasize reciprocal themes in human relations (Mead, 1949f:154–155).

Margaret Mead suggests that in each community adults make dominant that style of behavior toward children which they value in interpersonal relationships. And so, through early treatment, children learn the major pattern of social relations that they themselves will follow in later life.

Classification of the modal interpersonal patterns of any particular community into one or another of these three categories will be difficult. The definition of the modalities needs to be made more explicit. Students in the writer's classes have not been able to agree whether American middle-class attitudes toward children are primarily complementary or reciprocal. They readily agreed, however, that the middle-class American family pattern was not symmetrical.

MATURATION AND MASTERY

The emotional intensity with which maturation is encouraged carries over into attitudes toward achievement in later life. That is to say, a community which values individual achievement and initiative will begin to inculcate these goals early in life. Maturation phenomena like standing erect, walking, teething, and speaking are likely to be invested with strong emotional significance or children may be compared invidiously to each other for progress in walking, speech ability, or their respective number of teeth.

Among the Navaho Indians the time when a child takes his first steps is also a period when he receives the maximum of attention from others. "Everyone around takes turns in leading the child. The admiring audience murmurs encouragement and approval" (Leighton and Kluckhohn, 1947:31). Additional, gentle encouragement surrounds the acquisition of language and in former times relatives also encouraged training in hardihood. By the time puberty is reached the Navaho child has acquired considerable responsibility in a wide range of activities and can take care of himself. Far more intense preoccupation with development appears to mark the Manus where "Every gain, every ambitious attempt is applauded" (Mead, 1930:26, 29–30). Children are encouraged to do their best, whether in swimming, punting a canoe, or walking, and adults seize upon early differences in intelligence for comment. Parents hold earlier accomplishments before the child and allow no backsliding.

The gratification which a child realizes through increasing capacities—standing, walking, building with blocks, or even masturbation—promotes in him feelings of self-confidence and adequacy, quite apart from any deliberate encouragement he may receive (Kardiner, 1945:26–41). Successful execution of these techniques furnishes early lessons in coping with the environment or with the individual's own emerging needs. Successful coping registers as a sense of mastery. Circumstances that block the exercise of these capacities are equivalent to failure of mastery and such failure, according to psychoanalytic theory, may be followed by dependency cravings. The child adopts a subjectively helpless state paralleling the objective helplessness of infancy. The same sequence may come about in adulthood when an individual's techniques of mastery fail. However, rarely will the older child or adult find his dependency needs gratified as readily as in infancy.

INDUCTION OF AFFECTIVITY

The capacity to give, receive, and feel affects may be encouraged or strangled in early life. Some of the most conspicuous differences between modal personalities lie in the handling of emotional expression. "The ease, the appropriateness of emotional response is a part of training which begins in the cradle, and affective responses can be encouraged, deflected, or completely blocked. Furthermore, affective responses tend to become habitual along the lines of most frequent exercise" (Kardiner, 1945:229). Complete emotional spontaneity is probably not tolerated in any community, but the degree to which affective lability is suppressed clearly varies. Anthropological records contain data about the Kwoma among whom hostility is freely expressed in a variety of situations (Whiting, 1941). Pakistanis, generally speaking, are also emotionally labile and express sentiments readily. The Haitian peasant has been described as volatile, excitable, and able to discharge emotion easily (Underwood and Honigmann, 1949:633). At an opposite pole we have emotional suppressors like the villagers of Tepoztlan or the Hopi Indians. In Tepoztlan the positive emotions are restricted. "The limited expression of affection in Tepoztlan is part of a larger pattern whereby what might be called the positive emotions—love, tenderness, kindness, sympathy, generosity, and joy—are less easily expressed and not as well developed as the negative ones, such as anger, hate, irritability, fear, jealousy, and envy" (O. Lewis, 1951:292). Among the Hopi the negative emotions are carefully inhibited and Dennis (1941:261) indicates that such patterning does not come automatically: ". . . the Hopi child has temper tantrums in which he screams and kicks and throws himself on the ground as no adult Hopi ever does. The child comes into conflict with other children over property, and these conflicts lead to hitting with the hands and with sticks, to pushing and shoving, and to the throwing of dirt and of stones. The pugnacity and aggressiveness of the child must be overcome so that in adulthood the behavior of the Hopi will approximate the Hopi ideal of a person who causes no trouble."[6]

At first glance it may seem odd that the positive emotions, like love, with their capacity to promote good feeling should ever be inhibited through social patterning. Psychologists claim that human

---

[6] Similar difficulty in controlling hostility is experienced by the Great Whale River Eskimo. See Honigmann and Honigmann, 1953.

beings normally crave affiliation and love *provided* that such attachment does not threaten personal security or self-esteem (Allport, 1950). Failure to encourage the capacity to give or receive affection sometimes promotes a personality syndrome known as affect hunger (D. M. Levy, 1937). Then the individual is beset with a desire to receive tenderness but lacks the techniques to solicit or reciprocate such feeling and also the ability to sustain the attention. Levy believes that emotional reactivity and certain other organismic functions are "inherited potentials, fulfilled only within appropriate organic or social environments. Just as the chick who after breaking through the shell, fully equipped with the neuromuscular pattern and response for pecking, will lose the pecking drive if fed from a dropper for a certain period of time, so it is assumed that an infant equipped with potentialities for social response will suffer their loss or severe diminution if no environment exists in which the response can operate. The social object, mother, or mother substitute, who constitutes the infant's first social environment, must presumably give emotional warmth during the process of infant care . . ." (Karpman *et al.*, 1951:250). Affect hunger is not part of American modal personality as it is of the Kaska Indians'. We have seen that the Kaska mother stimulates affective responses in the young child until about the age of three, when she withdraws emotionally in her interpersonal relations. From now on the child is exposed to the prevailing emotional climate of Kaska life which is keynoted by a suppression of feeling. Emotional contagion helps the children to grow up to be emotionally constricted people. They develop into men and women who, although they want the reassurance of being loved, can tolerate little tenderness, passion, or hostility in social relations. The Balinese similarly reveal the importance of exercise for the appearance of affective response patterns (Mead, *1947b*; Bateson and Mead, *1942*).

In parts of Germany, where children receive little or no demonstrative affection from parents, suppression of the positive emotions is also the rule. German children when they grow up continue the pattern of affectional rigidity which they have "caught" from parents. The German's sentimentality is not an exception to this generalization concerning German modal personality. In sentimentality the tender emotions are directed against impersonal or absent objects (like a landscape, a certain period of life, a musical composition) or invested in an intimate group of friends that provides "safety through numbers." Not all Germans neglect inducing some affectivity. Rodnick (1948:17–22, 27, 37), an anthropologist who studied postwar culture and personality in that country, reports that both parents among German Protestants show much affection to the infant. For both sexes the demonstration of affection lasts into childhood. According to Rodnick in this way Germans develop submissive and gentle children who are more dependent and less resourceful than American youngsters.

Allport (1950:26) points out that "each person, through circumstance and training, develops an exclusionist, or an inclusionist, or a mixed style of life that guides his own human relations." We would extend this to say that communities, too, may be distinguished on the basis of the predominant orientation of members to other people. For example, among the Pilagá Indians rewards for love are nil (Henry and Henry, 1953). Warm human relations between siblings are not systematically rewarded or reinforced by parents nor expected by tradition. The child does not owe compulsory love to parents. Interpersonal relations cut people asunder and do not cement them in affectionate ties. The doll play experiments conducted by Jules and Zunia Henry with Pilagá children reveal little expression of warm emotions but reveal a great amount of hostility that merges closely with sexuality. It is possible that the preoccupation with sexuality in Pilagá children—sex being untrammeled by severe restrictions—constitutes a substitute for unsatisfied love impulses and a way of making warm but disguised attachments to people, including parents.

PLAY AND PERSONALITY

Study of any childhood situation may have double significance. It may reveal something about the dominant ideals or values of the community at the same time that it contributes to shaping personality. Play well illustrates this double-barreled function. Children's play is standardized in terms of overall cultural values and by following the modes of playing the youngster receives training in the values.

Arapesh games are consistent with the dominant ideals of Arapesh life in that they encourage neither aggressiveness nor competition (Mead, *1950b*:50). Among such a gentle people it is needless to use games for teaching children to give and receive blows and children never do become accustomed to blows. In the kin play groups among the Mundugumor, on the other hand, play does not neglect habituation to physical punishment. Here we find an "endless display of physical violence, which is returned in kind with no show or resentment . . . a blow given by a 'mother's brother' or a 'sister's son' cannot be resented, and so the small boys grow accustomed to stand a great deal of knocking about and harsh treatment" (Mead, *1950b*: 147). The emphasis on open competition in the play groups of urban American communities is similarly an index to larger values. The style of playing trains children in the pattern of estimating their performance as better or poorer than that of peers. If better, then the child learns to feel pleasure; if poorer, then he is supposed to experience dissatisfaction which may reach the point of intense anxiety. As Ceylon in the past hundred years developed into a dual community with an acquisitive urban élite set off against a more passive rural majority, games from Western acquisitive society have also made their appearance—in the urban localities (Pieris, *1952*). Violent competitive sports have become popular in the areas where individualistic ideas are also accepted. Schools foster emulation and emphasize the importance of the playing field to inculcate self-reliance and independence. Simultaneously the Sinhalese are adopting early weaning and early bowel training thus approaching the pattern of the American middle class, in which early experiences are relatively rigorous for the child (Davis and Havighurst, *1953*:317). The "depressing" picture of a people who refused to pursue capital accumulation and showed little ambition, that struck the British when they came to Ceylon, will decline further as Sinhalese personality undergoes repatterning.[7]

---

[7] See Greenberg, *1932*.

Erikson (1950) contributes another insight into the manner in which play patterns personality. In his theory, play serves as a device by which the child learns to test and master reality through model situations, which copy the real life of the community. Thus Great Whale Eskimo children play at store and the shop occupies an important place in native life. Erikson distinguishes between three types of play: *autocosmic* play, directed to one's own body; *microspheric* play, acted out on toys, and *macrospheric* play, centered on the world of playmates.

SPHINCTER TRAINING

Toilet training rivals nursing and weaning in the attention it commands from social scientists concerned with personality formation. Perhaps the best-known anthropological study emphasizing this area of early discipline is Geoffrey Gorer's (1949b). Working with Japanese informants in the United States and relying on books about Japan for additional data, he derives a pattern of early life in which the infant is welcomed; carried around a good deal, especially on the mother's back; fed whenever he shows signs of wanting food; gradually weaned between two and three years; and carefully restrained in movements around the house. From the age of four months the baby is regularly held over a balcony or road with the intention of completing his toilet training by the time he can toddle. Apparently the aim is realized. Gorer then relates certain patterns of Japanese personality to the strict patterns of toilet training.[8] Among these traits are the feeling of shame associated with eating ("the unpleasant effects surrounding defecation have moved forward to the eating of solid food . . . both aspects of the digestive process are treated almost identically" by the Japanese); an "excessive" dislike of dirt associated with marked cleanliness and neatness of the body, house, and garden; lack of an absolute morality but "very strong emphasis on doing the right thing at the right time"; ceremonial perfectionism; and a fund of hostility with few socially approved channels for its release. The

---

[8] Gorer also traces the interrelationship of these traits to other aspects of early conditioning. We do not present his analysis in its entirety.

author advances two basic hypotheses, the first of which we give in Gorer's own words (*1949b:284*):

Where infantile sexuality is prohibited, it is prohibited absolutely; there are no places and no occasions when a child is allowed to strive for whatever sexual pleasure is physiologically possible for him. Where this prohibition is enforced rigorously there would appear to be moral absolutes in the value system of the society: absolute prohibitions, absolute sins, a concept of absolute evil, a constant contrast between the unreachable ideal (of purity in the first place) and actual mundane practice. Excretion, on the other hand, cannot, for physiological reasons, be absolutely forbidden; all that can be forbidden is excretion at the wrong time or in the wrong place. If this cleanliness training lies at the bottom of the value system of the society, it would follow that there would be no absolutes, no "right" or "wrong," but instead very strong emphasis on doing the right thing at the right time . . . on "correct" or "suitable" behavior, which would be defined by the context in which the behavior took place.

The second hypothesis, derived by Gorer from classical psychoanalysis, holds that compulsive personality patterns (manifested in traits like the intense pursuit of neatness, perfectionism, cleanliness, persistence, conscientiousness, and conformity to rule) correlate with early anal traumata. The hypothesis is concisely stated by LaBarre (*1945:326*), whose observations of Japanese in America corroborate those of Gorer: "The compulsive character is . . . largely the product of severity or cruelty in treatment during the period of cleanliness training, in which the child is forced to relinquish primary gratifications and to take on culturally colored conditioning of the sphincter."

The hypothesis which connects guilt to sex training and shame to severe toilet training remains most poorly untested. One cannot help but wonder what would be the character structure in a group that standardized both severe sphincter and sex training. As far as the second hypothesis goes, many workers in culture and personality feel that severe training is one aspect of a childhood environment consistently oriented toward compulsiveness. In other words, they occur in a configuration of related experiences. It is, therefore, quite logical that severe toilet training should correlate with compulsive trends while lenient or casual training would go along with a flexible personality. Quantification, however, is much needed at this point. Qualitative differences in toilet training appear to exist between Japan (that "Japan" is a homogeneous community remains debatable), the Great Whale Eskimo, and the Kaska Indians. Training becomes progressively more lenient as one proceeds from the first to the last group. Strong emphasis on neatness in clothing and housing is lacking in Great Whale River Eskimo culture, while it is a strong point in Japanese culture as described by Gorer. On the other hand the relative cleanliness of Eskimo clothing and underclothing and the tidiness of their tents reflects greater compulsiveness than is manifested by the Kaska Indians. Disconcerting doubt has, however, been cast on whether early and severe bowel training really occurs modally in Japan. Both Gorer and LaBarre gained their information from Japanese in America. Benedict (*1946a*) also worked with Japanese in America and reports essentially the same pattern. On the other hand, a study of the Japanese in Hawaii (including those born in Japan and in the Islands) reports "a seeming lack of emotional involvement of the Japanese parent in the toilet training practices" (Sikkema, *1949*:591). It may be significant that Hawaiian-born Japanese parents appear to be "adopting Western customs and . . . these customs of child training, toilet training, and so on, are more 'strict' than Japanese customs."

AGE PATTERNING

Drawing upon her own research Margaret Mead (*1949a*) shows that the symbolic richness of a culture is related to the manner in which the community handles growth in the child. For example, the status of a baby may be prolonged, cut short, or otherwise affected by the subsequent birth of a sibling. All through Southeast Asia members of the family show distinctive treatment to a child who has just had a first or second sibling. This gives rise to the terms "lap baby," "knee baby," and "yard baby," although terms are less significant than the treatment which a child receives as he passes from stage to stage. The differential treatment at each stage is also not simply a response to increasing motor development. Comment and posture of parents, relatives, and neighbors echo the special state and goals attributed, for example to the baby. ". . . the series of differentiated treatments through which he passes may be said to have 'plot,' rather than merely form and sequence." Thus, in Bali the lap baby is assumed to be violently anxious to get back to the mother's arms whereas the new baby is a current delightful toy, a center of delight, and an object with which the knee baby is teased. The yard baby, in turn, has major responsibility for the lap baby; he receives little attention from parents and suffers merciless bullying from his young charge. Gradually the yard baby joins the children's world, to tend cattle or work with the mother, and the lap baby moves into the vacated position. In Iatmul the lap baby wanders away from the mother when a next baby is born but returns to the mother when another sibling is born.

By way of developing her hypothesis that symbolic elaboration in a community is related to "the number of positions in which the child is successively placed before he is lumped with a large children's group," Mead says:

In those cultures in which the child passes from babyhood into an undifferentiated children's group, development lacks the plot and structure which it is given when the knee baby remains closely identified with the parental group. When only two positions are recognized, the lap baby as knee baby is dispossessed but remains close to its parents; at the birth of a third baby, he passes over into the children's group, relinquishing any close relationship with the parents. In the third case, where three successive positions are recognized, the child is first, possessor, then dispossessed and while still inside the family constellation, sees the dispossessor in turn dispossessed by the new baby. The new baby is furthermore given into the yard child's charge, so that to a degree he is able to participate with the new baby in the usurping of his own former rival's place. It seems possible that this long period in which the child, still in close contact with the parents and younger siblings and without the strong pressures of the children's group toward conformity and age-grade-oriented rather than parent-oriented . . . interests, makes possible a development of a series of layers of integration which is itself particularly favorable to symbolic elaboration of experience.

As far as degree of symbolic elaboration in art, music, and drama is concerned, Iatmul and Bali stand at the top "in the complexity of their symbolic preoccupations." Arapesh and Manus, where only two positions are differentiated in the early life of the child, stand out "as interested in *acquiring* artistic expressive forms rather than in creating them." The Samoans, Lepchas, and Kaingang, where only a lap baby position is differentiated, stand at the bottom of the scale of symbolic development. Mead does not say that age patterning itself creates "an artistic or symbolic culure." Differential treatment is simply one aspect of early life contributing toward symbolic elaboration.

Suggestions for Further Reading

Infancy, growth, and the child's ever-widening awareness of group expectations and responses are topics systematically treated in Slotkin's *Personality Development* (1952), particularly on pages 57–167. Hsu considers the limits of childhood as a source of personality patterning in "Anthropology or Psychiatry: A Definition of Objectives and their Implications" (1952). Several attempts to understand American modal personality with reference to child-rearing patterns will interest the reader at this point. Most influenced by psychoanalysis is Margaret Mead's chapter, "Expected Childhood Experience in America and its Consequences," in *Male and Female* (1949f). Less specialized are Davis and Havighurst's *Father of the Man* (1947) or Mead's *And Keep Your Powder Dry* (1942a). Kluckhohn and Murray's *Personality in Nature, Society, and Culture* (1953) contains appropriate papers. Davis writes on "American Status Systems and the Socialization of the Child" and Leites on "Trends in Affectlessness," a picture of affect inhibition in modern Western society derived from a novel. Haring's readings in *Personal Character and Cultural Milieu* (1949) offer Goldfrank's "Socialization, Personality, and the Structure of Pueblo Society"—a warning that study of the early years is not sufficient to understand patterning. The point is further illustrated in Underwood and Honigmann's paper, "A Comparison of Socialization and Personality in Two Simple Cultures."

Chapter 11

EMERGENCE OF THE MODAL PERSONALITY

As the child reaches six or seven years, his role in the community becomes more integral and explicitly defined in terms of rights and responsibilities. Disciplines become more varied, pointed, and complex. The increasing scale of social participation intensifies the forces which come to bear on the developing personality. Adults expect the child to show increasing responsibility for behavior and chastisement, scolding, or other penalties are brought into play to hasten conformity so social norms. All communities do not rely equally on these negative forms of discipline, however. Many American Indians deny or minimize the extent to which children are chastised and attempt to secure conformity primarily by "talking to" the child. In distinction some social classes in the American community rely heavily on physical punishment, saying that to spare the rod is to spoil the child. Discipline by "talking to" the child may correlate with relatively symmetrical patterns of relationships to children. Symmetry cannot logically be expected where parents show their strength or authority by beating youngsters. Some psychoanalysts maintain that forms of punishment set up conscious or unconscious associations concerning the author of the discipline, zone of attack, etc. For example, the conception of all women as sadistic or dominant may be related to a severe mother. Punishment by emphasizing parts of the body, like the buttocks, may stimulate the erogenization of these parts. Such connections have hardly begun to be tested with the comparative materials of social anthropology.

The use made of fear and threat to promote learning constitutes a significant factor in personality formation. Here we deal with communities who regularly expose children to the threat of gods or witches, terrify them with masked figures, or instill terror of parts of the environment. Among the Hopi, for example, the inculcation of fear in the disciplinary process was continuous (Eggan, 1953:288). Once a year, or oftener if children misbehaved, the Soyoko descended upon the village, leaving nightmares in her wake. Then the Katcina spirits added their pressure to socialization. Between seven and ten the young Hopi underwent a severe initiation at the hands of these spirits, only to learn at that time that they were kinsmen rather than gods. Speaking of his own mischief-making days a Hopi Indian describes the use of fear in his community (Simmons, 1942:70):

. . . we children were never denied food, locked in a dark room, slapped on our faces, or stood in a corner—those are not Hopi ways. . . . Our relatives warned us that the Katchinas would bring no gifts to naughty boys and that giants would get us and eat us, or the Spider Woman would catch us in her web. My parents often threatened to put me outside in the dark where a coyote or an evil spirit could get me, a Navaho could carry me off, or the Whites could take me away to their schools. Occasionally they threatened to throw me into the fire or warned me that Masau'u the Fire god would appear in the night and cause my death.

Considering these experiences Eggan says that "such fearful beings were a clever device for minimizing parent-child conflict but they brought nightmares throughout a lifetime."

Considerable early emphasis on fear appears characteristic of the Umbundu who are reluctant to apply physical punishment (Childs, 1949:99). They do not hesitate to warn children one year or older against persons, animals, and things that are dangerous. Imaginary dangers also serve as deterrents. A youngster crying at night is told by his mother that a ghost may come to eat him. If he does not go to sleep quickly the mother may say, " 'Look out, the little old woman will come and pour live coals on your head and you will burn up.' " An older sibling may be sent off by the mother to sound like a hyena whose cry is then pointed out to frighten the younger child. Men among the Umbundu claim that they do not like to see children disciplined by fear.

Jewish mothers in New York City reveal a more subtle use of fear (Wolfenstein, *1949*). The most severe punishment they employ is a relatively prolonged refusal to speak to the child. In this pattern the mother acts out her destruction by a disobedient child. "These Jewish mothers are apt to reproach their children with having damaged and weakened them through the ordeal of childbirth, the depletion of nursing, etc. There is some evidence to suggest that this suffering imposed by the child, and the fantasy of being destroyed by the child, is a source of strong gratification to the mother though it may only be expressed in complaints and conscious dysphoria. When the mother, injured yet again by the child's badness, refuses to speak, she is behaving as if dead, that is acting out the fantasy that the child has destroyed her." The suggestion in this quotation that parents may derive gratification from punishment appears well founded. An adult who vents rage against a child may also derive gratification through releasing his feelings.

Margaret Mead (*1942a*) argues that when parents slough off discipline on terrifying bogeymen of one sort or another they provide a favorable condition for the development of a quick sense of shame at the expense of a developed conscience. Most communities appear to make some use of fearful figures to augment parental power so perhaps the intensity and frequency with which such symbols are presented are crucially related to the patterning of a responsiveness to shame rather than to guilt. When fears used as disciplines have to be unlearned in later life they complicate the individual's adaptation in the community. This is the case among the Kaska Indians, where fear of the bush is taught to children to keep them from becoming lost in the forest. But the people secure a large part of their living from the forest and so both sexes, but particularly men, must later unlearn this fear. A number of Northern Forest Indians also use the white man as a bogeyman. The fear of white men engendered in this way may also have to be unlearned. Discipline that uses neighboring tribesmen as symbols of fear effectively restricts the size of the ingroup and perpetuates ethnocentric or hostile attitudes from one generation to another.

Form of Punishment

The form of punishment standardized in a community may constitute the vehicle for nonverbal communication between parent and child. Submission is demanded through harsh and inflexible discipline while deference as part of punishment situations carries a message of respect for the child and his rights. Among the Hopi punishment of a group of youngsters also conveys important meaning. Group punishment is illustrated when the maternal uncle (among the Hopi) punishes a group of brothers, even though he knows that only one is guilty. Dennis (*1941:263*) suggests that this action reinforces the principle that the bad conduct of one person may affect the welfare of the entire community. Thus, the corporate structure of Hopi village life bears a congruency with a pattern of punishment.

ATTITUDES TOWARD THE SELF

The pattern of interpersonal relations in a community helps to shape the individual's attitudes toward himself. Communities offer their members a variety of grounds on which to realize self-esteem —including affiliation with a particular family; possession or nonpossession of wealth, and even self-repudiation. Such props, however, are not the only sources through which self-esteem becomes patterned. The network of interpersonal relations in which the child becomes involved may also help define personal adequacy (Bateson, *1943*). In England, for example, adequate self-esteem is made dependent upon seeing oneself repeating one's image of the parent: ". . . a person can accept himself (or herself) if he comes up to his own estimate of his parent's role and adequacy," assuming that the parent was accepted by the community. In America, however, self-esteem is made dependent on the child realizing the parent's image of his, the *child's* future. "Here the presumption is that the child's role in life will be different from and superior to, the role played by his parents. . . . The parental image of the child's success and advancement may be vague, and in the case of foreign born parents their picture of the child's American success can have extraordinary little relation to reality; but still the picture is there . . ." Other anthropologists who have studied American life also see the focus of reference shifting from parents or family to peers. The reputation which the child establishes in the world is far more important than family orientation for defining the sense of self-worth.

A feeling of self-esteem may also be conditioned upon conformity —"upon knowing that there is no conspicuous difference between oneself and one's fellows." This basis of self-evaluation is probably more important in America than in England. On the other hand, upper-class English life illustrates how self-acceptance may be made to depend on idiosyncracy: ". . . for the English generally, acceptance of self is enhanced by feeling that one is a little different from one's fellows, and reciprocally, an individual is accepted by his fellows a little more easily if he is labelled as rather different."

Various beliefs come to support the feeling of self-worth in a particular community. For example, financial success or martial exploits may be essential criteria of adequacy. Or children may learn that only a limited degree of success is available to any one individual; as a consequence strivings toward self-fulfillment must at least partly be frustrated for most people. It is, of course, equally possible for people to believe that the achievement of success is potentially unlimited. Or a community may inculcate the lesson that one person's success is always at the expense of someone else, thus engendering an extreme degree of competition. Guilt may interfere with the feeling of self-esteem in other communities.

In American life, according to Kardiner (*1939:115*), self-esteem lies in attaining the goal of being on top. Our children learn to value surpassing others, even their own parents. Quite a contrasting tendency prevails in Zuni where the "inflation of the ego is not an end in itself." Personal wealth is without significance, envy and covetousness are not rewarded, and "Property is appreciated as far as its utilitarian character is concerned, but is shorn of its magical properties to command love and respect for its possessor." Zuni represents a group in which self-aggrandizement is as unnatural as the same goal is "natural" among ourselves. In China social climbing is of equally slight importance and parents train the child to succeed them rather than to succeed by rising in the class structure. Riesman (*1950*:40) sees an inverse relationship between stable communities with high birth and death rates on the one hand and social mobility as an avenue of self-realization on the other.

Self-Esteem and Social Inequality

Does a class or a caste system necessarily undermine self-respect or frustrate those individuals who are at the bottom of the pyramid or in the lowest levels of social rank? Bateson (*1943*) shows how persons reared in a stable, stratified community may be taught ways of thinking about class and caste hierarchy. While crude commanding or prohibiting behavior on the part of people in the dominant strata may produce frustration, individuals in a class system may also be taught to "put brackets around sequences of this sort and rephrase them in other terms."

Something of this sort has occurred in England. Still more extreme, and therefore more useful as illustration, is the Balinese caste system. This is a system in which dominance and submission as we know them virtually do not exist, since the patterns of behavior between individuals of higher and low status are conceived of not as enforced by the individuals of higher status, but rather as inevitable grooves or tramlines in the structure of the universe; and these grooves are not merely limiting in their functions, they provide an idiom and a tone of voice in which very full and free communication can occur between one sort of people and another. The English patterning of life has something of the same sort of impersonal structure. The conventions and idioms used by people of lower status in addressing people of higher status (and vice versa) are not seen as directly enforced by the superior person (though the superior is rather sharply conscious of being put back in his place by the inferior if he should deviate from the pattern). . . . The lower status child is taught by lower status parents how to behave towards higher status people; he does not learn this in a harsh face-to-face relationship with the latter; and when the patterns are learned, a very great deal of initiative and criticism can come from the lower to the higher without ever over-stepping the conventions.

Kardiner and Ovesey (1951), however, argue that a slave system is always psychologically degrading. They see the American Negro, especially the lower-class Negro, at the present time still degraded by virtue of his former slave status. The fact that his position subjects him to a high degree of anxiety also helps to undermine his self-esteem. An analysis of twenty-five Negro personalities convinces the authors that the discrimination imposed on the American Negro "means that his self-esteem suffers . . . because he is constantly re-ceiving an unpleasant image of himself from the behavior of others to him." Compensation for low self-esteem is found in apathy, hedon-ism, living for the moment, and criminality. The work of Kardiner and Ovesey does not necessarily contradict Bateson's thesis that social relations in a stratified society may be arranged in such a way as to preserve self-respect or reduce personal frustration. Without doubt American caste relations, particularly in the South, are not structured so as to maintain and reinforce the Negro's self-esteem. His inferiority is often stressed in favor of the white man's superior status. Probably in no social system can people accept without resentment the image of themselves as inferior. The Negro belongs to a national community whose ideology insists on freedom of opportunity and equality of per-sons. These constitutional premises define morality and convince the Negro that his treatment is unfair. Psychologically speaking his social environment is both crippling and degrading.

ATTITUDES TOWARD WEALTH

Cultures differ in the degree to which they make wealth, particu-larly material possessions, capable of enhancing feelings of adequacy. Many monastic communities demand that recruits vow poverty and reject material wealth. Renunciation promotes self-worth. People who live close to a subsistence level, like the hunting and fishing tribes of northern Canada, seldom emphasize the acquisition of wealth. Thus, technological conditions have something to do with attitudes toward wealth. The kinds of wealth that become ego-involved also vary between communities, even between subdivisions of the same community. Books come to have such great value for a scholar and he will sacrifice food for their acquisition. His landlady, however, has so different a set of values that she could conceivably use his books to start the furnace. The gigantic stone discs which represent valuable objects in western Micronesia contrast strikingly to the fine dentalia shells, serving the same purpose for the Californian Indians.

Rights to wealth are also learned. The Eskimo child is made to understand that in event of hunger he has an absolute claim on a share of any food in the local settlement. Conversely rights to his own food dwindle as hunger descends on neighbors. Among the Alaskan Eskimo (where wealth was somewhat more abundant than in the Eastern Arctic) and in many American Indian tribes a man sought not simply to accumulate goods but sought to acquire sufficient possessions to be able to give things away. Thus, the distribution rather than accumulation of wealth may bring prestige.

The sense of possession may be more or less strongly inculcated. An Arapesh child is warned to respect the property of others but without any extreme sense of possessiveness being transmitted. Patterning of this type is produced by parents who often point out that "this is grandfather's" but rarely say, "This is not yours." Also anything in the family will be given to a crying child. Boys are advised that the festival dishes, sago trees, and other wealth which they see around them will become theirs as they grow up. "In such a system no one becomes aggressively possessive about his own" (Mead, 1950b:52). Quite different attitudes are acquired by the Manus child. Despite the importance of wealth in adult Manus life, children acquire few possessions. Collecting shells, seeds, and so on, important activities in American childhood, play no role in the youngsters' lives. What possessions children secure are not hoarded and are readily discarded or lost when their novelty wears off. Parents carefully instill attitudes of caution with regard to material possessions as well as a sense of individual ownership through instructions like "That belongs to Piyap, put it down," or "That isn't yours" (Mead, 1930:32). A Manus boy ready to marry is still without wealth of his own. He even fails to understand clearly how wealth is acquired. This learning begins abruptly when the newly wed youth takes up residence in his rich uncle's house. The transition means that he substitutes the arrogance of childhood for the humility of poverty. Only successful men "dare again to indulge in the violence of childhood . . . stamp and scream at their debtors, and give way to uncontrolled hysterical rage whenever crossed" (209). The young man begins to participate in wealth exchanges, always striving to realize a profit. The importance of individual achievement has been inculcated in him since childhood and he draws upon this earlier learning in order to bring himself up to the measure of men.

The abundance or absence of inheritable property available in a community for whatever reason may affect relations between adults and children. The presence of wealth, says Devereux (1950:492) can "perpetuate the economic dependency of children. Since the Mohave has nothing to transmit to his children—all property being destroyed at the death of a parent—he obviously cannot enforce life-long obedience through compulsory economic dependency." Anthropologists know a number of communities in which the eldest male in the family controls the wealth and thereby his dependents. Such communities generally furnish little opportunity for a man to achieve independence through employment outside of the family. The joint-family pattern of southern Asia imposed such dominance on younger males. Today in Pakistan profound deference to age is still encouraged but as industrial, military, and civil service careers open up, the integrity of the Asian joint family is being undermined and many do not hold together despite the centralized control of wealth.

SEX AND SEX ROLES

An earlier chapter has already touched on how communities demonstrate diverse attitudes toward sex.[1] We say that the range of sexual

---

· [1] See above, pp. 187–188.

expression may extend from an extensive avoidance of both the aim of sexual gratification and of a large variety of potential sexual objects to wide gratification with many potential objects. An extreme blanket on sexual activity in childhood will have to be unlearned at least partly following marriage. While the new learning may succeed in a large number of cases, it does not follow that the lessons are therefore easily absorbed or that such new learning is without stress. Sometimes, as we shall see in this section, the unlearning does not occur.

The Arapesh place wide restrictions on both expression of the sexual aim and the range of permitted sexual objects. A child is taught that "sex is good, but dangerous to those who have not yet attained their growth" (Mead, 1950b:62). Parents warn children to abstain from sex so that they may grow, boys so that their future wives may develop. Girls are even chaperoned to prevent anything happening that might retard their growth. Adolescents among the Arapesh acquire no belief in romantic passion or in the spontaneously flowering of sexual desire. Rape remains unknown as does "any conception of male nature that might make rape understandable" (Mead, 1950b: 81). Sex is dangerous to the yams as well as in certain ceremonial contexts. The husband approaches his wife gently and neither men nor women are preoccupied with the thought of climax or satisfaction in sex relations. The ability to satisfy a partner's sex desire is valued less than the ability to accomplish the sex act with ease. "There is no recognition on the part of either sex of a specific climax in women, and climax in men is phrased simply as loss of tumescence."

The Navaho more readily recognize sex as an acceptable source of personal satisfaction (Leighton and Kluckhohn, 1947). They view sex as a natural phenomena, one likely to make its appearance in early childhood, and do not strongly interdict youthful exploration of the genitals. A mother herself may stroke the genitals of a nursing child. Puberty does not come before the child has become familiar with the "facts of life," either by observing parental sexual relations in the one room dwelling or coitus between animals. Experimentation with other children is also possible but attempts are made to keep children from premature heterosexuality, boys often being warned that promiscuous women may infect him with disease. Girls are lectured concerning the undesirability of unmarried motherhood. Successful marriage, however, does not depend on physical virginity. In other words, mainly practical considerations restrict the sex aim for the Navaho. Among Navaho adults "most sexual matters are discussed in more open and matter-of-fact fashion than among white people." Incest rules, however, must be carefully observed and extend from close relatives to include every person in the sib. The intensity with which incest rules operate serves to associate certain potential sexual objects with a high degree of danger but does not touch the sexual aim directly. Against such a background of child rearing with regard to sex it is significant that adult Navaho are rarely troubled by impotence or frigidity. This reinforces the hypothesis that a sex life free from potency difficulties develops when children become accustomed to sexuality as a natural and normal part of life. Women often manifest active, initiatory interest in sex without losing prestige in consequence. Although the genitals are associated with shame and must never be exposed even to members of the same sex, the nonsexual functions performed by these organs are not strongly embarrassing. So, in an automobile filled with men and women, a woman will unembarrassedly ask to have the car stopped in order that she may urinate. The act itself is carefully concealed. Despite the fact that excessive participation in sex holds danger, ". . . there is much material which suggests that in these days sex, like alcohol, is a measure of escape for some men and women. Especially for those who are caught between two ways of life—who are held by neither the old native restraints nor the white standards which they do not fully comprehend—indiscriminate sexuality takes its place with drunkenness as expression of the felt futility of existence" (89).

Sex in Plainville, U.S.A.

Now let us look at sex training and development in a rural community of the United States. While Navaho taboos on nakedness come into full force only upon puberty, among the citizens of Plainville, U.S.A., they are instituted before the age of five years (West,

1945:177; Kardiner, *1945*:350–356; Kardiner, *1939*, chap. 6).[2] Usually
the rules of modesty hold between members of opposite sex only but
sometimes also between women. There are men and women who learn
the lesson of modesty so well that in married life they will not undress
before each other in a lighted room. Although rural children observe
sexual intercourse among animals and sometimes between parents, in
Plainville they hear no matter-of-fact discussion about sex from the
parents. The taboo on conversation helps to make sex a subject of very
special significance. Parents manage to inform children that sexual activity must be avoided until marriage. Boys are warned that masturbation leads to insanity and weakness. From age mates each sex acquires
a certain amount of information about sexual processes along with
much misinformation. Neither masturbation or premarital intercourse
are completely avoided by the youngsters of Plainville, although fear
of being disgraced deters most girls from sex relations. What kind of
sex life does the adult citizen of Plainville carry on? Sex relations are
"usually unsatisfactory," a condition partly related to the fact that girls
have been taught to believe that sex is predominantly a male interest.
The almost complete suppression of sexual aim in the formative years
probably also contributes to marital dissatisfaction (West, *1945*:193).
According to Kardiner (*1945*:352), "relations to the sexual object and
to the activity have been spoiled. The sexual act has become a crime
and the person who submits to it is a degraded object." He reasons
that when sex drive is blocked in its expression, and comes to be
associated with anxiety, execution of the sex act becomes uncertain.
Early conditioning against sex promotes hostility and disgust for sexual objects. Sometimes ideas of asceticism become associated with the
sex leading, of course, to further inhibition and anxiety.

It will be recalled that Kardiner (*1939*:26–27) associates quite
different consequences with permitted childhood masturbation, which
may contribute to the development of feelings of mastery. "The auto-

---

[2] Indication is that Plainville sex training is not representative of the
United States as a whole but illustrates a relatively severe Midwestern
pattern. The same pattern also occurs in Elmtown or Prairie City (Hollingshead, *1949*:238, 414–424). Relative "free thinking" about sex characterizes the culture of Plantation County (Rubin, *1951*:171–172).

erotic activities of the child have an extremely important function in aiding growth and completing the weaning from the mother. Up to this time the mother is the chief source of gratifications. . . . Uninhibited masturbation adds to the child's mental life an extremely important idea, namely, 'I can get pleasure from myself,' an idea which helps to break that dependency tie on the mother." Kardiner (88) predicts that potency disturbances in adulthood will follow severe sexual restrictions in childhood. Interference with sexual potency is very likely among groups who regard sexuality in anything but a casual fashion. Mead (1949f:207) asserts that when sexual behavior becomes "complicated by sets of ideas about sentimental love, or by prestige, moral qualms, theories of the relationship between sex activity and athletic prowess or religious vocation, or between virility and creativity" then sexual activity becomes less automatic and reliable. Failure in potency is likely. As partial support for her hypothesis she points out that "it is not an accident that in the élite groups—the aristocracy, the intellectuals, the artists—of all cultures there have developed a variety of subsidiary and supplementary practices designed to stimulate male desire, whether these be perversions, a new concubine every night, homosexuality, or dramatizations of obscure daydreams. These occur with startling regularity, while in those portions of a population where there is less choice, less taste, and few confusing ideas, copulation is a simpler matter."

Learning Sex Differences

Boys and girls must learn not only the acts traditionally associated with each sex but also appropriate patterns of feelings. Every community patterns diverse attitudes and feelings for men and women, even though in some respects the character structure shared by the sexes may be relatively similar. Often role differences between the sexes are complementary, that is, mutually reinforcing or supporting. For example, women may be taught to behave as frail, helpless, and yielding, but men to believe themselves strong, capable, and adaptive. While all communities pattern diverse sexual roles, not all attend equally to distinguishing men from women. Some communities emphasize such differences while others avoid stressing the unlikeness of the sexes. Mead (*1949f*:75) suggests that a community which lumps together all children regardless of sex as inferior to adults in status or strength will minimize sex differences in adulthood. Such a correlation seems to hold in the United States where the expansion of women's roles has resulted in a kind of denial of any basic differences. This, of course, explains why sex discrimination promotes so much resentment and confusion in America. Among the Mundugamor, girls are also treated little differently from boys. Here too in adult life temperamental differences between the sexes are not sought after nor expected. Girls "are believed to be just as violent, just as aggressive, just as jealous. They are simply not quite so strong physically. . . . So little girls grow up as aggressive as little boys with no expectation of docilely accepting their role in life" (Mead *1950b*:149). Mundugumor culture, it is worth pointing out, lacks men's club houses as well as ceremonies for reaffirming the solidarity or importance of males over against females. The community quite thoroughly ignores sex as a basis for the establishment of personality differences. Symbolic or ritual devices to emphasize sex distinctions, we have seen, tend to be developed where the suckling experience is marked with great intensity (Mead, *1949f*:88).

Training for sex roles may begin in infancy, nonverbal communication proceeding subtly from the mother to the child as he nurses. Almost everywhere a girl baby is given to understand that she will repeat the mother's role. A boy, however, is told that he faces the task of differentiating himself from the maternal object of identification. Mead (*1949f*:149) believes that the male drive toward self-assertion arises from this situation. "Cultures like the Arapesh show how easily, where parents do not discriminate strongly between the sexes of their children and men take over a nurturing role, this drive in the male may be muted. . . . The mother-child situation at present provides a perfect learning context in which girls learn to be and boys learn the need to act." She stresses the nonverbal character of this learning. Messages to the boy, for example, are conveyed in "his mother's smile, the slight coquettishness or perhaps aggressive tightening in her arms, or the extra passivity with which she yields her breast. . . ." The fact that weaning is a different experience for a boy, who parts quite finally from the breast, and a girl, who will suckle babies as enthusiastically or as distastefully as her mother suckled her, adds another element to the earliest learning of sex roles.

Little attention has been devoted to the possible effects on personality development of a preference for children of one sex or the other. Many groups, like the Eskimo and Chinese, prefer boys and rationalize that these will grow up to be food producers, to continue the lineage, or to officiate in ancestor rites necessary for the welfare of the deceased parents. What does a preference for one sex mean for the development of the opposite sex's personality? Wayne Dennis (*1941*: 268–269) has pointed out that Hopi boys present behavior problems more frequently than girls. The Hopi are a matrilocal and matrilineal people but Dennis explains the phenomenon saying that girls are more under surveillance than boys. Recent research indicates that at every age Hopi girls are psychologically more secure than boys. This may be related to the girl's having a firm place in the matrilocal household while the boy faces an eventual break with his family. This eventual separation begins in childhood when the boy comes to spend an increasing amount of time in the ceremonial chamber or kiva (Thompson, *1950*:109; Thompson and Joseph, *1944*).

Communities not only pattern appropriate sex roles in boys and girls but also instruct each sex in how the opposite category should be regarded. Such learning may begin when a boy learns he has a penis but that a girl is differently constructed. If he can flaunt his male organ he is following along the road of self-assertion. The girl may learn "some bitterness or despair, or sense that it is no use trying" (Mead, *1949f*:153). Often one sex learns about the other by observing sex-linked rituals. Arapesh girls observe their brothers emerge from initiation "plump and sleek . . . their eyes glowing with pride and self-importance . . ." (Mead, *1950b*:60). The menstrual seclusion of girls among American Indians conditioned socially expected male attitudes toward women who were dangerous in certain periods.

Children also learn sex complementarity from peers. Where boys in the evening stalk the length of the village as in Attawapiskat, and girls cling in shy giggling groups, one sex dramatizes its boldness and assertiveness, the other its passive receptivity. The phalanx of predatory females on Main Street on Saturday night passing the male audience in front of the drugstore does not give a similar clear clue about who is the hunter and who the hunted. Each sex may have its traditional stock of myths about the other—girls like candy, any girl can be "had," boys are all immoral. Such items of childhood culture continue into adulthood. Like the popular magazines they help to teach a traditional and approved manner of approach between the sexes.

Physical attraction can outdistance more practical attributes of personality in determining popularity. Women in the "Old Kingdom" of Rumania acquire much confidence in their own charms (Benedict, 1943a). Rumanians conceive beauty to be of the body, not of the face. A proud, slim figure is the narcissistic ideal and a woman retains faith in the idea of her physical attractiveness long after childbearing and into middle age. Physical attraction is regarded as an important feature in marriage and love marriages are common. The evidence suggests how the girl's faith in her attractiveness may be related to her early development. The baby is always regarded as "just too lovely" and full of "pretty ways." At adolescence the girl uses "endless rituals and magic to attract the boys to her; some she uses every morning, some before every dance, some on special festivals." The rituals consist of charms which ask that she grow "dazzling in the eyes of man." From our point of view such magic cannot create beauty. Like training in the use of cosmetics or in the choice of perfumes, magical charms support the girl's morale and increase confidence. The presence in Rumanian culture of a prominent body of folklore relating to physical attractiveness also helps to focus the attention of each generation on the meaning and desirability of beauty. Girls learn that they must make themselves irresistible to men. Conversely boys come to believe that women should be irresistible and learn to respond to the enticements of a belle. By their behavior they again support the value that the culture sets upon feminine charm. Each sex acquires its own socially standardized role patterns and learns to support the contrasting but complementary role of the opposite sex.

In America the girl's role vis-à-vis boys is marked by a competitive element such as does not appear in Rumania. Not unsurprisingly in a community where the baby is pushed to competition by the conditional love of its mother, boy-girl relationships also come to have a competitive quality. Prior to going steady the number and quality of one's dates determine the girl's popularity rating and how far she will go in intimacy with any boy. Student term papers written for the present author reveal the regularity with which boys ask, and are expected to ask, for deeper intimacy only to be repulsed by the girl who is secure in her popularity. "Only the unpopular girl has to carry petting to the limits where the reward the boy receives is grossly physical rather than a delicate flattery of his good judgment in having taken out a girl who knows her way around" (Mead, 1946: 348).

Not every male follows the approved course of personality standardized in his community. Among the Arabs of Siwa the boy may pass his youth as the homosexual partner of a father's friend but then is supposed to marry and himself takes a homosexual partner (Cline, 1936). Some men, however, devote the rest of their lives to serving as male prostitutes. Among the Plains Indians, a boy disinclined for the marital role standardized for males could follow the example of the transvestite who dressed and acted like women. At the cost of appearing a little incongruous he might prosper in his deviant profession and grow up to be a relatively contented member of the band.

OLD AGE

Patterning continues into old age and one of the last as well as most difficult lessons an individual may have to learn is to retire gracefully when physical debility no longer permits his strenuous exertion. The lesson may be especially hard when work produces varied and numerous secondary rewards. In America, for example, a survey reports that retirement means being cut off from social contact, deprived of an opportunity to express creative impulses, and loss of social prestige.[3] Hence the reluctance of men to quit work when they reach retirement age.

The Attawapiskat Cree Indians, who live in northern Canada, live by hunting and trapping. Community values expect a man or woman to "always" be doing something. Where social approval depends on strenuous masculine activity, as is the case among the Cree, the increasing debility produced by age may be extremely conflictful unless alternative paths to social approval become available. There are no such alternative opportunities for an old person among the Cree. Children are unable to produce surplus of wealth on which parents may rely; there are no activities reserved for the old that would allow them to realize social worth. Even an old man's chance to express his frustration through sorcery has been largely taken away by the growing disbelief in traditional magic that followed the arrival of Catholic missionaries. The situation is a painful one. Old men tend to remember with retrospective nostalgia the games and activities that they undertook in childhood.

In great contrast is the picture in Korea where to reach the age of sixty puts one practically in the category of the immortals and constitutes one of the greatest possible events in an individual's life (Osgood, *1951*:43).

HOSTILITY AND AGGRESSION

Aggression is an activity that seeks to destroy or deliberately inflict pain upon the object against which it is directed (Kardiner, *1939*:60). Hostility (hate) represents an attitude or motivating state impelling a subject to express aggression (other motives, however, may also give rise to the activity). Both hostility and aggression may be turned against the actor as well as against substitute animate and inanimate objects in the actor's environment. A person who feels no conscious hostility toward an object may nevertheless use that object as a target for aggression.

---

[3] *New York Times,* March 29, 1953, Section 4, p. 12.

Sociocultural Sources of Aggression

Psychologically speaking, aggression may arise from hostility, conflictful dependency, frustration, and various kinds of threat. Anthropologists, however, are more concerned with the social and cultural conditions related to aggressive behavior. A model analysis is one in which Jules Henry (1940) explores some of the cultural determinants of hostility in Pilagá Indians. His theory leads him to examine this South American culture for patterns which conflict with one another or otherwise induce tension. To these he sees Pilagá hostility linked. Among such patterns and conflicts he finds the following:

1. Conflict between the ideal pattern of sharing food and a simultaneous pattern of reluctance to share. At the same time people feel themselves bound by a socially sanctioned norm that one should not beg. Underlying all this is a chronic scarcity of food that converts even the ideal behavior of sharing into a threat.

2. The demeaning attitudes attached to women and their exclusion from most prestigeful activities. These patterns relate to the hostility that women feel toward men which, in turn, undermines the solidarity of the household. Husband and wife are joined by no deep emotional attachments. The family environment among the Pilagá provides the child with little emotional security.

3. The pattern of the Pilagá woman going to her husband's village to deliver her baby may precipitate strong conflict, for she is afraid of the sorcerers who threaten her there. If the Pilagá wife gives in to her anxiety and flees from the foreign village back to her parent's home, "Who would take care of the child?" Sometimes a fearful woman becomes so fearful that she will induce abortion. But women also desire offspring because children guarantee a marital tie.

4. The long period of sexual avoidance beginning in pregnancy and lasting until the child can run around, produces friction between husband and wife. Many communities which demand a long abstinence following birth of a child make some provision acceptable to the wife for the sexual satisfaction of the husband. Polygyny usually allows a man to find sexual outlets and sororal polygyny—the mar-

riage of a man to two or more sisters—is apt to be particularly acceptable to a woman. Polygyny, however, is rare among the Pilagá. Women feel strong anxiety lest husbands develop serious affairs during the period when sex relations need to be avoided. Some women vent strong aggression against their husbands and rivals at this time.

5. The child in the Pilagá family is treated to little security and tends to be rejected after an initial warm reception. Rejection manifests itself in a severe withdrawal of attention. Beginning at about the age of eight months the child is left behind, in the care of an old grandmother, while the mother goes afield to gather food. The guardian can offer little to the dependent youngster. Small children grow up to be fearful but even evidence of pronounced terror does not readily bring parental reassurance. Birth of a sibling intensifies rejection and hostility comes to be directed against the usurper. Doll play experiments confirm the anthropologist's generalization that Pilagá children experience intense hostility toward parents and siblings (Henry and Henry, 1953).

Ruth Benedict has generalized that hostility and aggression correlate inversely with social synergy: ". . . minimal interpersonal hostility, also, is correlated with certain cultural institutions, political and economic as well as forms of the family and methods of child-rearing. The social institutions of such cultures make it possible for an individual to advance the general welfare of the society at the same time and by the same act that advances his own prestige or security."[4] In other words, social synergy is a condition in which almost each time that an individual advances his own welfare he also contributes to the well being of the community. The process is illustrated in Kaska Indian life where killing a moose provides a gain of the entire small winter settlement. The distribution of the meat by the hunter contributes to the prestige of the producer at the same time that it offers food to the group. In other communities perhaps the acquisition of a wife may be a gain for the group at the same time that the individual who acquires her feels advantaged. Synergy denotes careful use of

---

[4] Benedict's theory of synergy remains largely unpublished. See her discussion in J. Henry, 1940:120.

humiliation. People are singled out for humiliation only when they default. Under such conditions aggression is minimal. Benedict believes that synergy and aggression bear no relationship with scarcity or abundance. Communities subsisting on the brink of starvation may pattern synergic interpersonal relations while many communities with relatively dependable food resources show anomie, the opposite condition from synergy. Obviously synergy is closely related to the world and self view engendered in character structure. Synergy appears where people are ready to allocate prestige generously, where they expect to be helped by neighbors, and where the community is seen to be a friendly place.

Benedict argues that hostility can be reduced if frustration and humiliation in social life are kept down. Kardiner (1939:125, 129) points out other sociocultural factors may generate hostility and sees one instigation to aggression in "a shifting economy, which permits no sense of control, and in which skill and hardiness do not always reap their reward, and in which no one can take pride in records of achievement. . . ." In other words, minimal control over the environment arouses frustration or threat and intensifies hostility. His second correlate of hostility is akin to Benedict's concept of anomie: a "social organization, in which mutual responsibility is underplayed, so that there is no expectation of help, but only the necessity of bowing to fate. . . . Dependency is even held up to ridicule." Finally, Kardiner says, hostility will be high when the community offers few rewards for the control of impulses that it imposes.

Training in the Handling of Aggression

All communities that have survived long enough to be studied by anthropologists limit the expression of aggression and give training in approved ways of handling of aggression. The Chinese, for example, are much more inclined to compromise differences rather than resort to force. Chinese children, in whom personal daring and bravery will not be highly esteemed when they are adult, learn that instead of quarreling they should take disputes to older members of the family for settlement. This lesson also inculcates respect for judgment of age. Chinese culture has been described as making interpersonal harmoniousness "an end in itself" (Office of Strategic Services, 1948: 353).

Training in the handling of aggression may insist on practically total inhibition (comparable to aim and object avoidances of sex) or may be closer to the opposite extreme where a considerable amount of, but not all, aggression may be permitted. The first position is illustrated by the Great Whale River Eskimo, the second by the New Guinea Kwoma. Among the people of Great Whale River there is continual fear lest aggression in adults get out of hand, with people running amok and committing murder. They recall with anxiety cases of such behavior out of the past. Parents, while resigned to the fact the children will fight, deeply deplore aggression and brand it as one of the meanest activities. Together with older siblings and unrelated adults they regularly reprimand fighting and order it to cease. Adults and children agree that physical aggression is the "worst thing" that a child can do. By the age of ten or twelve the preceding years of scolding have their effect and aggression is channelized into acceptable forms, like intensely rough ball games or wrestling. The Arapesh, too, intervene the moment quarreling appears in a group of playmates. One or both quarrelers are dragged off. Parents aim not to teach control of hostility but to see that the hostility does not get expressed so that one child injures another. The show of anger in temper tantrums is not restrained. Thus is inculcated a readiness to vent rage upon one's own surroundings that persists into adult life. "An angry man will spend an hour banging on a slit gong, or hacking with an ax at one of his own palmtrees" (Mead, 1950b:45).

The picture changes as we enter a Kwoma village in which aggression is not only a means of venting tension but also furnishes a means of winning attention (Whiting, 1941). The louder a young child cries the more effort his mother expends trying to aid him. Parents provide training in aggression when they readily beat a youngster for stealing, failure to control erections in public, public fingering of the genitals, noncoöperation, and bed wetting. The paths channelizing the expression of aggression are standardized. Older brothers vent hostility against younger brothers as they rough up and tease, kick, and command the youngsters. Such aggression is not uncontrolled; care must be taken lest serious injury be inflicted. A child who receives blows too submissively is scolded and warned to retaliate when he has the right to do so. Nobody who is afraid to fight can hope to amount to something among the Kwoma. Frustration which stimulates aggression piles up throughout childhood but always brings additional opportunities for the discharge of feelings. By the time a youth is initiated he may taunt unitiated boys, doesn't hesitate to express hostility to nonrelatives at the slightest provocation, and always resists being taken advantage of. Aggression is also allowed between a boy and his sister's lover; men demonstrate it before ghosts and spirits, and against natural calamities, like storms. Intertribal warfare and headhunting formerly provided a further channel for aggression. Information from the Kwoma suggests that in a community which rewards aggression interpersonal behavior will tend to accentuate rather than mitigate frustration. Kwoma character structure sees the world as replete with threat and frustration and nobody is supposed to allow himself to be taken advantage of. Of course, the "big" man's chip-on-shoulder attitude succeeds in threatening and frustrating others with the result that another sequence of aggression and threat are generated. Several regenerative circles are revealed by these data. Note that the Kwoma do not give completely free rein to violence. No community can afford to encourage indefinite reliance on aggression if it is to remain intact.

Available evidence suggests that communities cannot afford to suppress too greatly the expression of opposition through aggressive and other channels of behavior. Among the Menomini, for example, quarreling, abuse, criticism, and physical conflict are all punished in a variety of ways (Slotkin, *1953*). Few channelized forms of expression of social opposition exist and even competitive games are nearly lacking. These widespread social controls prove to be ineffective and partly hidden channels of expression, like witchcraft, drinking (with expressions of bellicoseness), and vicious gossip appear in spite of the norms to weaken social solidarity. Similar compensatory forms for expressing hostility also appear among the Hopi, where aggression is also strongly condemned (Eggan, *1953:* Simmons, *1942*).

Witchcraft and Hostility

Anthropological literature contains reports on a number of communities in which harmony in human relations is strongly desired but which are ridden by chronic suspicion of witchcraft. The Umbundu, an African tribe taken by way of example, teach a child not to express anger. Even evidence of the covert state is greatly disturbing (Childs, *1949:124–125*). Nevertheless, people do sometimes experience hostility and also maintain hidden grudges for long periods. Related to this fund of latent hostility is the frequency with which suspicion of witchcraft flares in the tribe. Other African people, the Kaska Indians for a period of their history, and various Pueblo groups illustrate the same connection between emphasis on peaceableness and chronic distrust of neighbors who are presumed to be practicing witches.

Now, there is reason to believe that the incidence of actual sorcery in these communities is not nearly as great as people believe. Quite possibly, communities that strive very hard to eliminate the expression of all hostility in interpersonal affairs also promote considerable guilt or anxiety in members who are unable to avoid hate impulses. The socially patterned mechanism of projection brings belief. The person who is unhappy because he is burdened with forbidden hate, projects hostility on another member of the community, the witch. Witches, then, are projections of the fear of one's own hostile impulses. As Clyde Kluckhohn (*1944b*) notes, in such communities people are able to direct the satisfaction of hostile impulses into oblique channels where the emotion is not socially very disruptive. Witches are a legitimate target of hate among the Navahos and other similar groups. In Kluckhohn's words they serve as scapegoats. "Most contemporary European societies feature such witches quite obtrusively. These 'witches' may be either a minority within the society or an external society. Thus the Nazis have had the Jews; the Fascists have their Communists and their 'plutocratic democracies'; 'liberals' have the

Jesuits (and vice versa)."[5] Witchcraft beliefs provide a channel for displacing aggression. Displaced aggression, in turn, does not lead to punishment as would, for example, the expression of hostility against one's father-in-law. The fact that many accusations of witchcraft among the Navahos refer to distant witches protects the accuser from the anger of the accused.

Why should interpersonal hostility develop at all in communities where there are no open patterns of aggression that may be "caught" or learned by children? If hostility and aggression constitute two related responses to frustration, then it is clear that in any community children are exposed to frustration coming from many quarters. To some extent all socialization techniques used by adults impose some frustration. Dorothy Eggan (*1953*) describes how the socialization of the Hopi child, after it passes through the early period of indulgent infancy, inculcates frustration. At the same time that he learns to rigorously suppress aggression the child finds the pleasant state of early childhood abrogated. "Society, represented by his parents, mother's brothers, and others, now began to mold this relatively unrestrained personality into its conceptually ideal pattern of smooth, selfless, co-operative effort which was necessitated by crowded villages, natural and human enemies, and an irregular food supply; the behavior which had been so pleasantly effective and easy during the first few years of his life was the antithesis of that which was now expected of him." Eggan sees in this discontinuity of patterning an important source of the anxiety that generates the friction which operates in Hopi interpersonal relations. (See also Goldfrank, *1949*.)

Unfortunately, there is no knowledge available concerning whether modal personalities differ in level of frustration threshold nor do we know whether frustration tolerance is differently patterned from one community to another.

Suggestions for Further Reading

The chapter has selected a few areas of social life out of many more possible ones to show how behavior in these fields is shaped in childhood.

---

[5] Recent experimental work in psychology questions whether scape-goating enters prejudice in Europe and America.

In a sense we have been talking about informal education. Tumin illustrates how such education varies between the divisions of a caste structured community in *Caste in a Peasant Society* (1952), chapters 2 and 5. Other good studies in training include Zborowski and Herzog's *Life is with People* (1952), pages 291–360, dealing with East European Jews; Whiting's *Becoming a Kwoma* (1941); Elwin's *The Muria and Their Ghotul* (1947), and Raum's *Chaga Childhood* (1940).

Piaget's suggestive studies in the development of moral judgment (*The Moral Judgement of the Child*, 1929) among European children should be consulted as well as duplicated with children in other communities. His experiments consistently suggest a period in the early years when the child is inclined to think magically. The rules of the game are held to be untouchable, duty is independent of circumstance, and punishments may emanate from things themselves. The latter belief, known as faith in immanent justice, has received a little cross-cultural testing with interesting results.[6]

Several cross-cultural interpretations of the belief in malignant witches have recently appeared. They all attempt to correlate that anxiety pattern with other social conditions. See M. Wilson's *Good Company* (1951a), chap. 5; M. Wilson's "Witch Beliefs and Social Structure" (1951b), and Marwick's "The Social Context of Cewa Witch Beliefs" (1952).

---

[6] See above, p. 127.

Chapter 12

AGENTS OF PATTERNING

The basic family constellation, consisting of a man who helps to provide food for one or more women and children, is found everywhere. Usually the family is built around the man and wife nucleus but sometimes the woman is the man's sister and the children are hers (Mead, 1949f:188–190). Whatever its form, the family represents a fundamental social area of personality formation. We will orient our discussion specifically to the family which consists of father, mother, and offspring because that is by all odds the most common and well described around the world. Nevertheless we must keep in mind that the father's influence on children will become much attentuated in situations where his wife's brother's role includes the training of nephews and nieces. With pronounced avuncular dominance, relations of children with the biological father tend to be quite relaxed and friendly (Homans, 1950:252–259).

PARENTAL INFLUENCE IN THE LIFE-CYCLE

Quite likely the importance of parents as agents of personality formation reduces with the age of the child. In America, for example, this decline increases as the growing child comes more and more to respond to the expectations of peers, club members, teachers, employers, and other associates (Mead, 1953b). The fact that earlier parental functions come to be shared by other members of the community naturally does not deny the enduring importance of the primary contacts between parent and child. Some of the long-lasting influences rooted in the relations of parents and children will be examined in the present chapter.

Independent and Dependent Families

The significance and importance of the parents in the child's life is not the same in all communities. In American cities the pattern of living in independent nuclear families that are largely cut off from relatives[1] serves to emphasize the emotional significance of parents in the life of the child. There is nobody to take their place or supplement their responsibilities. An orphan never forgets the misfortune that death removed his parents before he was grown. In America parents have sole responsibility for many duties which in other communities are shared with grandparents or a parent's siblings. Urban parents' relationship to the child is far more intense than would be the case were additional intimate relationships available to diffuse the child's emotional attachment to any particular relative. It has been suggested that a sense of individualistic responsibility develops modally in children who have been reared under the concentrated affectivity of the independent nuclear family (Mead, *1942b, 1948b;* Honigmann, *1946*:94, 148). Considerable self-consciousness develops and the individual perceives himself as a distinctive person and a vital influence in any chain of action in which he engages.

Contrasting to the independent nuclear family, found not only in the United States but also among certain Indian groups of the northern forest, is the Samoan village of related families. In such a community of two hundred or more kinsmen the nuclear family maintains little independence. A consistent lack of intensity pervades the social relations of the child, and extends from the way he is toileted to his freedom to wander off in a world of relatives, finding

---

[1] For classification of family forms based on rules of residence see Murdock, *1949.* The importance of the nuclear family in America has been discussed by Mead, *1942b.* For the implications of divorce see Murdock, *1950*:201.

welcome in almost any household (Mead, *1950a*). An attitude of extreme dependence on the pair of parental relatives is hardly expected under these conditions. The Samoan child grows up detached in his interpersonal relationships, a style of behavior with antecedents in the ephemeral emotionality of his early interpersonal contacts. The village kinsmen never offer him a chance to form tight binding ties. Strong self-responsibility in the Samoan personality is replaced by the fear of presumption and a shying away from responsibility. The extended families of India and Pakistan would be suitable areas for investigating more deeply the problem of personality regularities associated with this pattern of living. In Western Pakistan the nuclear family is often subordinated in patrilineally extended household where dominance is reserved for the eldest male. On the other hand, interpersonal relations in these units are not detached and considerable emotion is bound up in the father-son and mother-son relationship.[2] Preliminary data gathered without highly focused methods suggest a relatively uncertain sense of responsibility in males, lack of strong initiative, and feeling of limited personal control. An implicit theme of the culture is that one can accomplish little outside the household without support and backing. An interesting "indicator phenomenon" in this connection lies in the value, which men set on chits, or recommendations, from previous employers. Manufactured recommendations are allegedly sold by scribes and used to further the buyer's career. This pattern is reported by Kipling and other writers (Kipling, *1949*:382–383; Knight, *1896*:99–100). Comparison of the Pakistan and Samoan data indicates that extended families are not all of a single type.

Technological Change and Parental Influence

Rapid technological change has introduced other changes in the functions of the American independent nuclear family. Despite the extreme emotional importance still attaching to parents, cultural in-

---

[2] Data on women, who remain in seclusion or purdah, are not easily obtainable.

novations have considerably modified the influence of parents on the development of roles and values. Mass media of communication— radio, movies, comics, and television—reveal to the child social norms for particular ages that frequently conflict with parental standards. Even the behavior expected to be shown by parents is learned by the child through these sources and American youngsters try to set or standardize parental roles! Family relations have not remained unaltered as these influences came to increase in importance. Implicitly recognizing their inadequacy to assure the child's future in a rapidly changing world, middle-class parents carefully prepare youngsters to model behavior on the cues of the social environment (Riesman, *1950*, chap. 2).[3] American parents are installing "in their children something like a psychological radar set—a device not tuned to control movement in any particular direction while guiding and steadying the person from within but rather tuned to detect the action, and especially the symbolic action, of others." The parents' influence in patterning, at least in the later years of childhood, consists in their sending signals which mingle with the signals of others. Sometimes American parents shift the family residence to certain social environments in order that they may control to some degree the signals which the child is able to receive. Rarely they may risk "a very partial and precarious censorship of incoming messages."

Parents and Conscience

People are not born with a wide-awake sense of guilt. Some anthropologists believe that conscience does not even appear in all communities. Benedict (*1946a*:223) and Hsu (*1949*:223–224) speak of guilt and shame cultures, indicating communities governed by conscience and "face" respectively. The term *guilt* refers to a quick sense of wrongdoing that attaches to a forbidden act even in the absence of a disapproving witness. *Shame*, on the other hand, denotes covert behavior that follows wrongdoing when the forbidden act is known to other persons. It is not likely that any people are governed

---

[3] See below, pp. 351–352.

solely by either guilt or shame. It may be, however, that one or the other sentiment predominates and then anthropologists speak of guilt or shame cultures.

Three features in the early life of the child contribute to the development of a sense of guilt (Mead, *1942a*:128–129). First, children come to evidence a sense of guilt when they are brought up by parents rather than by nurses, slaves, or governesses, or in large and relatively impersonal groups. Second, in communities where guilt is patterned parents who resort to punishment are not afraid to chastise their children or to threaten them with the withdrawal of love. In other words, parents accept responsibility for discipline even though it entails the risk of earning the child's hostility. They do not call on the masked gods or use bogeymen as surrogates of discipline. Finally, guilt feelings appear when parents act as if they embodied all the virtues which they wish to see mirrored in the child. Adults parade themselves as paragons of virtue. When these three variables exist, people who default consistently experience a sense of the loss of love and fear of punishment—even when the paragons of virtue are not present to witness "the sin committed or the enjoined act which has been omitted." One further pattern of socialization is held to encourage development of conscience, regular reward or punishment "on the basis of conformity to consistent principles that the child can understand" (Gorer and Rickman, *1950*:137). *Consistency* is very important because it allows the child to predict how the parent would act even in the parent's absence. Among the Great Russians capricious punishment, which is often aroused by annoying behavior as well as by serious infractions of rules, encourages a sense of shame that is added on top of an "archaic" guilt.

The Navaho Indians represent another community governed more by shame than guilt (Leighton and Kluckhohn, *1947*:170–17▶). The phrasing of this pattern indicates not a complete lack of conscience but predicts that the Navaho child will frequently react with "self-consciousness" where a white child will feel guilty. Euroamericans who note the infrequency of guilt in the Navaho sometimes label the

Indians as morally deficient. "The fact probably is simply that he was trained differently," corrects the anthropologist.

Riesman (*1950:45*), writing of middle-class United States, speaks of the disappearing inner-directed person, who took his cues for behavior from within, and the emerging outer-directed person who is primarily responsive to the signals he receives from his social environment. Something of the guilt-shame dichotomy appears in this formulation. Homes in which inner-direction develops show a "lack of indulgence and casualness in dealing with children." Such a family climate, Riesman says, prepares the child "for the loneliness and psychic uncomfortableness" of the inner-directed community where he has only his own standards to rely upon for gauging success and morality. If we interpret Riesman correctly, as America moves to an outer-directed personality we are reducing the role of guilt in favor of increasing sensitivity to shame.

Many unsolved problems have been created by the guilt-shame hypothesis. For example, in a single community there may be diverse forms of socialization. Upper class, royal, or working-class children may be brought up by humble or deferent servants in the one case or in large, fluid families and cordial neighborhoods in the other. Other social classes, however, may have socialization firmly limited to the independent nuclear family, to parents who act as paragons of virtue and manifest the other characteristics said to encourage the development of conscience. Then does such a community contain some members who react primarily to shame and others who rely on conscience? This is a fascinating speculation. If true it would illuminate the operation of heterogeneous communities. On the other hand, the evidence for the hypothesis is practically nonexistent.

Both guilt and shame are concepts by postulation, as the reader will recognize.[4] To test for such covert phenomena one must have a key to their consequences in overt behavior. An operational definition provides such a key. One fundamental difficulty with the guilt-shame hypothesis lies in the lack of satisfactory, operational criteria by which

---

[4] See above, pp. 141–143.

to verify the existence of either guilt or shame. The ability of different observers to agree on the identification of these sentiments while using existing definitions promises to be very low. These remarks are based primarily on the author's own experience in field work. The identification of guilt or shame remains too much a matter of intuition. Perhaps some observers are endowed with greater sensitivity for empathically sensing these covert processes.

Family Relations, Prototype of Interpersonal Behavior

The family circle constitutes a microcosmos in which the individual learns many elements of behavior which will continue to appear through lifelong interpersonal relations: ". . . Freud taught that all our relationships with other people, including the relationship of the mental patient with his doctor, are patterned by our early relationships with the significant people of our environment in infancy and childhood" (Fromm-Reichmann, 1950:4). The lack of intensity characterizing the relationship of the Russian parent and child comes to be reflected in the Great Russian's feeling of a great gap between himself and political leaders. The emotional aloofness between Kaska mother and child conditions the remoteness that mark most interpersonal relationships of the Indian community. The ephemeral social attachments of the Samoan girl appear expectedly in her premarital love relationships and are perpetuated in the relationship she establishes with her own children. The American child carries the exhibitionism he learns in the family into the classroom and onto the lecture platform.[5]

The perpetuative function of socialization, through which many of the less peripheral elements of behavior are effectively maintained across generations despite more or less drastic cultural innovations, explains the consistency between family patterns and interpersonal patterns involving the larger society. The hypothesis may be illustrated by data from the Aymara of Chucuito, Peru. Parents and older siblings demand submissive behavior from the child and dependency constitutes a related note in parent-child relations, especially between

---

[5] See above, p. 79.

father and son. Tschopik (*1951:182*) writes that the Aymara Indian adult like the child "is accustomed to bow submissively to status, rank, and authority." Humility is manifested toward the socially dominant Mestizo caste and dependency lingers into old age. Submissiveness constitutes strategic policy for these Peruvian Indians by which they at first deal with parents and, later, with other powerful figures likely to be in a position to help. "It must be remembered that it is the Aymara view that the world is a hard and unfriendly place in which humility and appeal to strength by a display of weakness are frequently the most appropriate tactics." Such an implicit theme underlies both the behavior of the child and adult. Not unexpectedly the quality of humility in behavior is carried over into relations with supernaturals. Tschopik says that relations with Christian-derived deities "duplicate with remarkable exactitude those that exist between Indians and Mestizos" (209). Again: "The relation between the Indian and these Christian-derived deities appear to be patterned on Aymara-Mestizo caste relationships." But he has already referred the ethos of intercaste relations to the prototype of the family. Hence, a common emotional quality links family, intercaste, and supernaturally oriented relationships. It is reasonable to assume that this quality of behavior is first learned in the years of childhood within the family and that the pattern is reinforced through rewards earned in the role playing of later life.

The postulate that family relations are the prototype for learning appropriate responses in ensuing social relationships lends itself readily to the deduction of more specific hypothesis. For example, it has been suggested that where security in childhood lies in placating a powerful parent, security in later life will also tend to be sought in submission and passivity. If later circumstances make it necessary to resist demands of authority, the resistance will be conceived of as guilt-tinged "revolt" (Dai, *1944*).

Another formulation of the postulate is given by Mead (*1948a:*213) when she says that ". . . the way in which parent-child relationships are patterned in respect to such behaviors as succoring-dependence, dominance-submission, and exhibitionism-spectatorship, provides a

learning situation for the child which patterns his subsequent behavior in situations where these behaviors are involved." Haring
(*1950*) expresses the same thought:

Infants adapt emotionally to the interpersonal "climate" of their homes.
Habitual responses of adult members of the family to each other are felt
by the child who adapts his emotional habits to the prevailing patterns.
This kind of learning is wordless because it occurs before the infant has
either a vocabulary or the ability to reason. Subsequently, as an adult, he
prefers certain kinds of people and certain patterns of human relationships and cannot explain his predelictions. . . . The "soul of a people"
is thus observed to be the typical pattern of emotional interstimulation
that is habitual in the majority of the homes of the people . . .

Using material from the German middle-class community Erikson
(*1948b*:490) illustrates how family relations influence personality development. From parental roles the individual learns the relative
worth of each sex and how to respond to males and females. Cues for
this learning come from cues provided by the interaction of the father
and mother.

When the father comes home from work, "even the walls seem to pull
themselves together.". . . The mother—although often the unofficial
master of the house—behaves differently enough to make a baby aware
of it. She hurries to fulfill the father's whims and to avoid angering him.
The children hold their breath, for the father does not approve of "nonsense," that is, neither of mother's feminine moods nor of the children's
playfulness. The mother is required to be at his disposal as long as he is at
home; his behavior suggests that he looks with disfavor on that unity of
mother and children in which they had indulged in his absence. He
often speaks to the mother as he speaks to the children, expecting compliance and cutting off any answer.[6]

---

[6] Rodnick's study of Germans in the American zone of Germany does
not wholly bear out Erikson's picture. Rodnick sees the father deferring
to the mother in all social classes. Both parents are symbols of authority
to the child. Working-class fathers spend considerable time interacting
with children but do not care to share responsibility for punishment.
Hence they are not even told of a child's misbehavior during the day
(Rodnick, *1948*:24–25, 28).

Schaffner (1948:15–40) gives us further glimpses into the social structure of one type of German family and traces the pervasive influence of family patterns into other areas of social life. Life in the German family according to this author revolves around the omnipotence and omniscience of the father, that paragon of wisdom, source of authority, judge, jury, and court of last appeal. Children owe him *Ehrfurcht*—deferential respect bordering on reverence that that is reminiscent of the filial piety due to the Chinese father. Corporal punishment by the parent is regarded as just and constitutes a sign of manly virtue. The German father never spares the rod through fear of losing his children's love; he expects not love but primarily their *Ehrfurcht*. Nor does he usually embrace or fondle his children, certainly not once they have passed their fifth or sixth year. Despite their undemonstrativeness the German father worries about his children. He makes toys for them and gives them presents. But he can never reciprocate the confidences received from his son lest he reveal his own limitations, indecisions, or inner conflicts and thus damage the son's concept of him as an "all-knowing, perfect father." The father remains equally impersonal with other members of the family. Little open affections appears between husband and wife. The mother also inhibits intimacy and affection toward her children once they are past infancy. Her authority over the children stems from her role as representative of her husband. To avoid conflict within the family she often submerges her individuality and identifies with the father as closely as possible.

From this type of German family stem people who, if they are in positions of authority, cannot graciously admit their limitations and do not readily unbend. Sentiment between adults is rarely displayed and any show of affection is discomforting. Women grow up to feel the same respect for, and show the same compliance to, men that they saw displayed by the mother. Even the sexual freedom of young German women is probably motivated more by passive compliance to the wishes of men than to any search for affection. The respect for men prompts women to borrow masculine values, like physical endurance, ability to endure pain, and the espousal of military strength.

Such borrowing probably equals a degree of identification with males. The qualities of stiffness and emotional restraint in German interpersonal behavior continue the interpersonal style conditioned in childhood. Schaffner's data show how a single ethos links social relations from childhood to adulthood. German children adapt their behavior to the family climate and in their turn transmit this climate to a fresh generation of youngsters.

Family Relations and Political Relations

Another hypothesis logically derivable from the postulate that the family is a prototype of interpersonal relations in the larger society holds that certain aspects of power relations are related to family relations. This is not the same as saying that political relations are wholly patterned after family relations. Such an assumption is obvious nonsense and to the writer's knowledge has never been seriously offered by any anthropologist. Generally it would seem that the quality invested in political relations is related to the quality of family relations. Early learning does little more than transmit the more widely shared tone of social relations anew in each generation to a relatively flexible organism. Support exists for this hypothesis.

When German national organization was strong, attitudes toward the top leaders paralleled the compliance and respect demanded toward the father. Children interviewed by Rodnick (1948:57–58) in the American zone of postwar Germany considered a Fuehrer necessary for Germany and appeared to identify a Fuehrer with the father —"just as a father takes care of the needs of his children, so there must be a Fuehrer to take care of the unfortunates who exist in German society." LaBarre (1945:324) contrasts parentally modeled political relations, like what is found in Germany, with the "sibling society" of America. The latter is characterized by "relatively little of the political parent-child organization of some European societies and most Oriental ones . . . some western societies, notably England and America, have a sense of the law, of equal applicability to all men, which is entirely foreign to India and China and Japan—a sense of law which is a clear outgrowth of siblingism, since it is so uniformly absent from parentally-organized societies." The quality of democratic equality in American family relations is indicated by the ritualistic "joking relationship" existing between father and son (Erikson, 1950:267–272). The American father does not expect to be treated with great consideration or awe. Our radio programs often make "the head of the family" a butt of humor and picture him as a somewhat inept figure. Joking behavior facilitates identification between the father and his child, reducing the opposition and conflict which other communities expect between these relatives. These attitudes toward the father enjoy a certain congruence with American attitudes toward people in authority. In America it is the feminine figure who represents "the principal disciplining and character molding parent" (Mead, 1948b:457; Strecker, 1946).

Osgood (1951:38–39) through his work in Korea reveals how Confucian ideology runs through the relations of subject and king, wife and husband, and younger brother to elder brother. All these "are merely special applications of the father-son unity." Koreans demand that the highest respect be paid by a son to his father. As among many other people where the male parent exercises a paramount disciplinary role, the relationship of the two is cool, distant, remote and often strict. Obedience is enjoined upon the son as well as utter respect. It is these emotional qualities that appear again between the other status pairs which are relations modeled after family structure in which the earliest role learning occurred.

Interdisciplinary study of Soviet model personality demonstrates the congruence between family and political relations in contemporary Russia. In the Soviet Union successive upper levels of the Communist Party enforce their will on each lower level but without a demand for personal loyalty (Mead, 1951c:55–56). Strong personal attachments are condemned and are expected only for the topmost leader. In the Soviet family each individual who is responsible for others looks to the parents as models of perfection. The Soviet mother, who is forgiving, exacting, and proud, demands responsibility *to her* for conduct and deeds. Mead goes on to say, "In this respect, parents in regard to children bear a close resemblance to

Stalin's relationship to every Soviet citizen, as their right to receive love and respect is as explicitly stated as their duty to deserve it." Fantastically perfect model workers or model collective farmers, used to spur on correct role behavior in Soviet citizens, are likewise congruent with the image of the perfect mother or top-flight leader.

Parents and Immortality

Until this point we have been primarily interested in the family as representing a microcosmos of the social relationships of the wider society. We will now turn to examine how family attitudes toward children are bound up with philosophical conceptions about the nature of time and the universe. The general proposition is that adult attitudes are patterned by ideas that children represent either a link with the past or with the future. Such attitudes in turn operate on the developing personality of the child.

Among the Mohave Indians a basic reason why children are treated kindly lies in the fact that they are regarded as representing the future of the tribe (Devereux, 1950:492). Such an orientation toward the future represents the only kind of immortality in which the Mohave believe. Devereux suggests that "there may exist a functional relationship between a lack of deep belief in true personal immortality, and kindness and respect toward children." Such a hypothesis is logically subsidiary to the general postulate given at the end of our last paragraph. An echo of Mohave ideology occurs in America. Our middle-class conception of the future is one of progress or improvement. It is a realm closely bound up with children. Our socialization techniques take pains to prepare children to realize the better future in which we so firmly believe. It is quite likely that American attitudes toward children are appreciably affected by ideological premises like our notion that nature is malleable, that change through time is marked by progress or improvement, and that our children will see as dramatic a change in their life span as our parents and grandparents saw in theirs. The latter conception, in turn, is related to a demographic datum—our greater life expectancy. We have grandparents and parents with us longer than do members of many other communities and these kinsmen gave us a yardstick with which to measure the rapidity of social change. With this yardstick we can estimate how far and how fast our children will travel.

Among the Eskimos it is common to bestow on a child the name of some outstanding individual, living or dead. The namesake may be a deceased relative, for example, the child's grandfather, or he may be an old living person. People sometimes believe that the essence of the namesake is transmitted to the child with the name. Other informants said that this pattern of naming perpetuates the memory of an outstanding person who has died or will soon die. In either case, the naming pattern influences socialization. We heard an Eskimo mother at Great Whale River tenderly address her small child, "Mother." The little girl had been named after her grandmother, i.e., her mother's mother. It is likely that the association of the child with the beloved namesake conditions respect and deference on the part of the parent.

Belief in reincarnation may also be associated with respect for children. Reincarnation implies that the child contains a soul which has already lived. Such a belief is held by the Kaska and other Athapaskan Indians among whom a youngster may inform parents of his status by recognizing the country as a place which he previously saw. The fairly common *déja vue* experience may explain how reincarnation beliefs were originally derived.

THE ROLE OF SIBLINGS AND PEERS IN SOCIALIZATION

Considerable patterning in every community occurs through the socially standardized relations enjoyed with siblings and peers. Individual psychology demonstrates this hypothesis with the case of the only child who is apt to develop self-centeredness in association with failure to learn patterns of give-and-take from siblings.

In the United States, weaning and the development of self-control often coincide with the birth of a younger sibling. On the brink of successful mastery the two-and-a-half-year-old suddenly finds the world very confusing when, having learned to keep himself dry and to feed himself neatly, he sees the new baby receiving mother's love despite the fact that it soils itself and messes with its food. This situation may be the seed "out of which grows the bitterness towards all those who 'have it soft' or 'get away with it' that is typical of American personality" (Mead, 1942a:108).

In some communities peers almost outstrip the parents in their importance for personality formation in childhood. Sometimes, siblings, whether playmates or responsible nurses, constitute a source for the derivation of future behavior patterns in relation to peers. Often being closer to the learner in age and experience peers reduce the great gap existing with respect to parents. They encourage the adoption of appropriate role patterns toward relative status equals.

Peers as Cultural Surrogates

Not only do peers tend to supplement parents as agents of socialization in rapidly changing heterogeneous communities: even relatively stable groups may entrust a large amount of the educative process to age mates. A most striking illustration comes from the Nyakyusa of Central Africa (M. Wilson, 1951a). Among these people villages are formed by groups of boys all about ten or eleven years old. Later they will bring their wives to these villages but at first merely the unmarried youths sleep together and take their meals at the parental home. With marriage and a wife to cook, the village becomes a permanent residence and a "coming-out" ceremony establishes it in a formal sense. The association of boys and men represents a training group in which behavior appropriate to the male—sexual norms, eloquence, manners, and wisdom in general is learned. One can almost expect to hear a Nyakyusa defend the age village as we defend the school, protesting its indispensability for preparing youth for future responsibilities.

These are bare outlines. Let us refine our focus and examine the pattern on the individual level in the manner of culture and personality science. Youth villages are associated with a value on "good company," which stresses the pleasure and knowledge that may be found through living with contemporaries. Good company is a highly specific social value and it is somewhat difficult for us to understand that it can never be satisfied between the sexes or between men of different generations, because of the respect demanded in relations between men of different generations. A Nyakyusa realizes good company through eating together and sharing beer with peers. Ritual eating and drinking constitute techniques for maintaining social interaction and the value of good company. The ritual dramatizes the value on which, in turn, the organization of the village community is founded.

Peers play a considerable role in the socialization of the Japanese child (Benedict, *1946a*). The process of peer influence begins when crying babies are invidiously compared to other youngsters or teased with the threat of being given away. Younger siblings early learn the necessity of deferring to older brothers and sisters. In the lower school, children match themselves against each other to compete in boasting and bitter criticism. Between the ages of six and nine the school does not separate the sexes but at nine years the impropriety of mixed association is inculcated and boys are given an opportunity for forming strong bonds of loyalty with other males. When they are about twelve years old some boys enter middle school and encounter its pattern of hazing. The older fellows treat the younger with merciless ridicule. Boys who do not go to this school may join the army which provides the same experience. Each generation of victims in turn become converted into good torturers. Consistent exposure to peer demands and ridicule helps develop in the Japanese a firm sense of shame. Japanese socialization inculcates reliance on external rather than internal sanctions. Fear of criticism or ridicule and sensitivity to public judgment are strongly engendered, in large part through the ridicule and hazing by age mates. The Japanese male learns to value "face" and the necessity of vigilantly defending his honor.

Riesman (*1950*:48) writes of the peer group's increasing role in socialization in the United States in association with the shift from reliance on inner-direction to dependence on group approval and expectations. Parents, he says, are no longer able to inculcate in the child explicit values and clear goals whose realization will mean success. "Parents in our era can only equip the child to do his best, whatever that may turn out to be. What is best is not in their control but in the hands of the school and peer group, that will help locate the child eventually in the hierarchy." The teacher's role also changes in the other-directed community. Her job is no longer simply to install content into the child's mind but to develop his social skills. The child must be prepared to leave school fully equipped to respond to the signals of the group in which he moves. This pattern of socialization by peers is corroborated by Mead (*1953b*:659) who writes that "the surrogates who carry the cultural standards have changed. They are no longer the parents, omnipotent and belonging to another order of being, but one's everyday companions, with the same strengths and weaknesses as oneself." The consequences in the individual are attenuated self-respect and a weakening of the sense of conscience "upon which the operation of our culture is still postulated." Demagogues are apt to have an easy task in communities where the standards of the crowd assume predominant value.

Continuity between parent-child relations and peer group relations is to be expected in terms of our hypothesis of relatively homogeneous patterning.[7] Maas (*1951*) has demonstrated such a relationship in contrasting the middle-class child's peer group social relations to those of the lower-class child. The latter evidences more submissive, bullying, and hierarchical behavior that reflects similar qualities in the parent-child relations of the American lower class. Lower-class children have more feelings of rejection and unworthiness sustained in family relations than middle-class children. The rigorous quality of the parent-child relations is thus repeated in the rigorousness of the peer group. The learning in one situation is both repeated and reinforced in the second.

SOCIAL STRUCTURE AND PERSONALITY

Despite the varied meanings of the term let us agree that "social structure" will here designate the network of social positions or statuses existing in a community. Participation in this network continues patterning, a point we have already begun to touch upon in

---

[7] See above, pp. 228–229.

discussing peer group interaction. However, it is well to emphasize that important learning continues to occur after the years of childhood. In fact, essential aspects of personality modification or development occur through life. In every community people learn certain regularities of overt and covert response through participation in social relations. Such learning is both explicit and implicit. That is to say, the individual who comes to occupy a certain status is not only formally told what is expected of him in that position but often also sets his behavior according to subtle cues received from other statuses.

The anthropologist, who may have no intention of "going native," nevertheless finds himself playing some of the roles attached to familiar statuses with which he is identified in the culture that he is studying. When the writer studied the Air Force bomb squadron he chose to be identified with airmen rather than officers and found himself unwillingly responding with a certain degree of deference and customary ambivalence to the "top brass." These are, of course, attitudes directed toward military superordinates. An anthropologist among the Great Whale River Indians will at first be treated as though he occupied the status of government administrator. He will be told of troubles, treated with a degree of deference that he doesn't welcome because it interferes with rapport, and find himself adopting a paternalistic air. The skillful anthropologist does not allow such role setting to continue but works determinedly to create a new status for the community to accept—the status of a permissive, curious, and appreciative anthropologist (Paul, 1953:431–434).

Role Learning

To speak of persons occupying social statuses acting out appropriate behaviors is to talk of role playing. When emphasis is put on how these roles are acquired and by what rewards they are maintained we speak of role learning. This is an aspect of personality patterning often neglected by students interested in culture and personality, although Conrad Arensberg has called attention to the omission.

It is quite clear that every community rewards appropriate behavior appearing in individuals who occupy particular social positions. The rewards, however, sometimes come in indirect fashion. The business executive discovers from profits that it pays to cultivate competitiveness or administrative skill. Tips help the waitress to acquire a winning air. In the nineteenth century men won admiration from the opposite sex if they were adventurous, bold, athletic, and somewhat exhibitionistic. Women, however, found approval from men when they remained docile, timid, and unathletic to the point of ill health (Murphy, *1947*, chaps. 34–35). Although male and female roles have changed from the nineteenth century (men and women today behave toward each other in a more symmetrical and less complementary fashion), the principles of role learning remain the same. Growing boys and girls still imitate the roles of like-sexed peers and thereby taste social approval. The imitated response takes hold. Or, people take cues from the occupants of statuses, much as the freshman in college or in Congress patterns his behavior after veterans.

Role learning neither denies modal personality nor wholly offsets the influence of early life experience. Actors enter their social relationships with certain response tendencies that they share with one another by virtue of having been exposed to similar family situations. On the other hand, role learning in a homogeneous culture may be more congruent with earlier learning than is the case in a heterogeneous community.

Appropriate behavior between kinsmen is a common example of role playing. Many communities demand avoidance behavior between a woman and her father-in-law or between a man and his mother-in-law. An avoidance is not purely rational. Although coming relatively late in life it possesses very strong roots in the personality. This is indicated in the difficulty that comes in trying to unlearn rationally such a behavior pattern. The overt action may be dropped but the inner confusion on meeting the specific relative may be very hard to eradicate. Missionary teachings often stress that avoidance between relatives is unnecessary and may even stamp the behavior as unchristian. Nevertheless the tendency hangs on (M. Wilson, *1951a*:85).

Another example of the difficulty in unlearning the role associated with a status is seen in discharged soldiers who find it difficult to adjust to the status of civilian. Here we see that the dynamics of role playing are not automatic. The youth of Israel who fought British imperialism, according to an Israeli radio broadcast, "finds it difficult to fit itself into the order of the law-abiding state. . . . A certain proportion, resorting to various slogans and political ideologies as pretexts, has repeatedly tried to return to the use of physical force, in alliance with the most diverse elements of the scum of society."[8] Apparently these youths selected statuses as nearly similar to their wartime positions as possible. Their motivations for doing so may, of course, have been varied.

Conflicts between parts of the social structure are often associated with rather sharp divergences in personality or character structure, a topic to be discussed further in connection with social class in the United States. In Nyakyusa society Christians and pagans are in conflict, and each has different values concerning the mutually approved goal of hospitality. Pagans believe it is proper to feed *neighbors* while Christians stress feeding *strangers*. The pagans jibe at the Christians for their inhospitability and the latter affirm the worthwhileness of their wider obligation. Structuralization of a community into clans, political parties, social classes, privilege groups, or disenfranchised categories conditions many of the rewards, frustrations, and anxieties that befall people by virtue of the statuses they occupy.

The Yurok and Western Culture

If our postulate that position in a social structure contributes to personality formation is correct then we may predict that two communities with similar social structures will reveal similar personality characteristics. This is different from saying that relatively similar networks of social relations are associated with relatively similar modal personalities! We are simply saying that even though other aspects of culture (including child-rearing methods) differ between two communities, if the social structures correspond in degree then similar role components will be identifiable in the personalities.

---

[8] Broadcast reported in *The Listener,* 1952(49), 292.

The Yurok and other native tribes of northwest California bear certain similarities to Western capitalist countries (Goldschmidt, 1950). A common feature is that individuals are left pretty much to themselves to carve out their own careers and to advance themselves in an open class system. Families are individuated and not oriented to fixed groups like clans or lineages. Western and Yurok cultures are, of course, similar in more than social structure. Both make much of private ownership of wealth, use money as a medium of exchange, and utilize wealth as a determinant of power and an indicator of status. In both areas we find markedly similar values, sentiments, and motives, including a compulsive concern over asceticism and industriousness, a development of conscience, a sense of individuated responsibility, a tendency toward hostility, competitiveness, and loneliness. Erikson (1943:296) speaks of a personality with these characteristics as anal. Goldschmidt sees these traits as suited to a social structure in which one's position is extremely fluid and in which the individual lacks a large body of relatives to support him or to lend security. Security comes from individual effort along prescribed channels, and existence leading to a lonely, competitive existence. Goldschmidt observes that this personality is also related to "an intense parental concern over the behavior of children." In other words parental techniques of socialization are relatively similar between Western capitalist countries and northwest California. This suggests that modes of child rearing will themselves be related predictably to types of social structure and hence capable of reinforcing the role learning of the latter. Once more we see how family relations are congruent with other relationship patterns in the community. The configurational nature of culture, with the parts mutually dependent upon each other, is also illustrated by these observations.

Ritual and Status Promotion

Any status change, whether occurring through giving birth, marriage, growing to manhood, or graduating from college, involves some reorganization of previously learned behavior as well as new learning. Always there exists danger that the transition will not successfully be accomplished, that the proper learning and reorganization will not occur. Elaborate, long, and costly ceremonies are cultural devices by which the community sanctions status progression and helps members to move successfully from one status to another. Ritual helps avoid backsliding and reassures the person making the transition. It mobilizes the energies for change and personality reorganization. Techniques of public procession, flogging, isolation, or emblemization by cutting the skin are commonly associated with the rituals accompanying passage from childhood to adulthood. When a body of boys collectively go through such rites, the ceremony serves to build up in the group a sense of unity with age mates who will pass through life together. The collective initiation, therefore, not only helps individuals to firmly adjust to new responsibilities but also serves to pattern feelings of group loyalty. Any large-scale pageant, ritual, or holiday performance may develop sentiments of group belongingness in the participants who are having a good time together (Chapple and Coon, 1942, chap. 21).

Margaret Mead (1949f:102–103) points out another aspect of male initiation rites. A woman's basic distinction, she points out, lies in the fact that she can bear children. This capacity makes her social role clearer and better defined than the man's. "By a great effort man has hit upon a method of compensating himself for his basic inferiority." This method is the widespread becoming-a-man ceremony, or initiation, which in many communities remains concealed from the opposite sex. Thus the male initiation ritual is a device to compensate for deep biologically derived, characterological insecurity and bolsters self-esteem. Absence of the initiation ceremony in Euroamerican culture does not indicate an absence of these personality needs in that society. The lack is rather related to the fact that members of this society employ other means for exalting the achievements of men while at the same time depreciating the role of women.

Suggestions for Further Reading

Piaget has written on the consequences of movement from the constraining influences of the family in early childhood to the freer cooperative relationships that increase with age and membership in peer groups. He has particularly correlated this movement with a decline in magical thinking and a tendency to see social norms as rationally derived through group decision. His book, *The Moral Judgment of the Child* (*1929*) deserves careful reading. Congruence between family relations and wider social relations is revealed in Haiti. Rhoda Metraux in her paper "Some Aspects of Hierarchical Structure in Haiti" (*1952*) indicates how Haitians are early trained to be competent and self-sufficient in subordinate positions yet able to assume roles of leadership. Hsu's *Under the Ancestors' Shadow* (*1948*) provides another useful study of structural influences in personality patterning and is mainly concerned with the dynamics of social status in China.

Concerning structural conflict in a community and attendant value conflict, students will be interested in Godfrey and Monica Wilson's brilliant discussion in *The Analysis of Social Change* (*1945*). They conceptualize conflict between irreconcilable values as "radical opposition." One of these authors, Monica Wilson, has written a paper, "Witch Beliefs and Social Structure" (*1951b*), describing how anxieties that become focused in witch-fear have their genesis partly in social structure. The Nyakyusa, living in villages of non-kin, are anxious about their wealth in which only kinsmen and not neighbors may share but which neighbors covet. The Pondo, living in kin villages with their large exogamous clans and widely extended incest rules (including either grandmother's clan), are made anxious by limited sexual opportunities.

PART FOUR

SOCIAL DIFFERENTIATION
AND PERSONALITY

I have gone at dusk through narrow streets
And watched the smoke that rises from the pipes
Of lonely men in shirt-sleeves.

T. S. ELIOT

Chapter 13

PERSONALITY IN CLASS, CASTE, REGION,
AND OCCUPATION

Personality literally gets its start in the cradle and for many years continues while the child figuratively remains in the cradle of the family. More or less subtle forms of communication between parents and offspring mediate the expectations of the community with reference to the developing individual. What is communicated, of course, depends in part at least on the world outside the household door. As soon as the child steps through that door other interpersonal stimuli contribute more vigorously to the work of patterning begun by the family. For example, teachers or peers may come to replace parents as the dominant influence in determining immediate behavior and in influencing motives that will control future behavior. Throughout life and into old age role playing inculcates new response patterns that keep personality constantly shifting and adjusting.

In the last three chapters we remained primarily in the family circle and closely examined the elementary mechanisms of personality patterning. We saw personality emerge as a product of group membership. Family, peer group, adult work team, tribe or nation—all are groups the members of which transmit cultural expectations to other members and so come to channelize human behavior and make behavior predictable.

In this chapter, however, we will look at more loosely organized social divisions. Interest will be directed to finding dependable relationships between individual behavior on the one hand and, on the other, class membership, caste participation, regional affiliation, rural or urban environment, and, finally, occupational categories.

It is not difficult to predict some of the ways in which personality will correlate with participation in such loosely organized social divisions, the members of which never associate as a body.[1] A carpenter performs different actions and holds different occupational standards than do barbers; a farmer has at least part of his personality occupied by roles unlike those of a city dweller. A more useful aim would be to find out how deeply such correlated variables of personality extend. Do they, for example, affect the character structure?

Students who have done previous work in sociology and anthropology know that communities which possess fairly dependable food supplies capable of supporting dense populations are often stratified. That is, social interaction takes place in and between ranked levels of people. When such strata are loosely demarcated and easily crossed by marriage, diligent cultivation of the "right" people (upward mobility), or association with the "wrong" people (downward mobility), they represent *social classes*. American communities frequently reveal classes, that is, social categories comprised of people who enjoy intimate access with each other. Pakistan and Bharat (Indian) villages, towns, and cities, on the other hand, are stratified more complexly into loose and more rigidly demarcated, endogamous hereditary strata between which mobility is very difficult and rare. These strata we call *castes*. In addition, the Pakistan village, for example, also reveals a class structure that divides gentry from common people. Between these there is only limited social intercouse even though the

---

[1] A purely technical problem occurs in this connection. By "social division" we refer to unorganized social classes, economic categories, castes, regions as areal aggregates of people, or other plurels (Dodd, 1947:62). We assume that such divisions will generally be found unorganized and will not operate as groups. If a region, for instance, does organize then it acquires group structure and its behavior can be directly analyzed with the theory of group membership instead of moving to the level of social division. In some South Asian cities a caste also occasionally forms an organization of its members.

members of different classes sometimes belong to the same caste. According to some social analysts, America shows a caste organization to a certain extent based on color (Davis, Gardner, and Gardner, *1941*). Following this theory, which is useful for certain purposes, we will speak of a white and Negro caste. Crossing the line between these two categories is extremely difficult.

One of the interesting discoveries of contemporary American social science is that class and caste structure interferes with the distribution of a uniform personality throughout a stratified community. In other words, class or caste in a community is associated with distinctive personality patterns which may be called varieties. These varieties, according to our theory, reflect different ways of bringing up the young, different social expectations on the part of functional groups within each strata, and variation in other conditions responsible for patterning. We cannot forget as we talk more or less abstractly about personality being correlated with class, caste, or other social division that personality is primarily a product of interpersonal relationships or of group life.

SOCIAL CLASS AND PERSONALITY

In a class stratified community, the evidence indicates clearly, techniques of socialization vary between the ranked categories. Hence the social classes come to be associated with differences in personality.[2]

Our definition of social class follows W. L. Warner who regards such a category as an aggregate of people with similar rank (prestige) in the community who may have intimate social access with one another (Warner, Meeker, and Eells, *1949*, chap. 1). Unless specifically indicated, we will not be talking about income, occupational, or educational classes of persons.[3]

---

[2] The literature includes the following pertinent studies: Ericson, *1947*; Davis, *1943, 1947, 1948, 1953*; Davis and Havighurst, *1953*; Davis, Gardner, and Gardner, *1941*:3–251; Brenman, *1940*; Kardiner and Ovesey, *1951*; Myrdal, *1944*:956–994.

[3] For studies of the relationship of income to personality see Stagner, (*1948*:420–430). Kinsey, Pomeroy, and Martin correlate sex behavior with occupational and educational class (*1948*:327–393).

Early Care of Infant and Child

Davis and Havighurst (*1953*) attempt to quantify differences in childhood experiences between social classes and castes in Chicago. They discover that more Negro than white children in all classes are breast fed without a supplementary bottle and more Negroes receive the breast for as long as three or more months. In the Negro lower class, children tend to be nursed at will rather than by schedule and lower-class whites more frequently than those in the middle class also feed the child when it is hungry rather than when a proper time has elapsed from the last feeding. Thus "demand feeding" emerges as a pattern of the lower class, both white and Negro, and exists as an infrequent alternative pattern among the middle class. However, only 35 percent of lower-class whites follow demand feeding compared to 50 percent of the lower-class Negroes.

Negroes of all classes begin bowel and bladder training earlier than whites. Bowel training is completed earlier by middle-class Negro children but Negroes generally complete bladder training before whites.

With reference to age expectations and sex role patterning, Negro girls are expected to dress themselves earlier than white girls and are expected to go to the store earlier. Negro boys are permitted to attend the movies alone earlier than white boys but white girls may do so earlier than their Negro age mates. White children of both sexes must be in the house earlier at night.

More of the authors' data are summed up in Table 3. Here we want to give their conclusions in greater detail. Davis and Havighurst point out that middle-class families, both white and Negro, tend toward greater rigor in their training of children than lower-class families as far as feeding and cleanliness habits are concerned. The middle class also emphasizes the early assumption of responsibility and earlier individual achievement. The evidence points to the hypothesis "that middle-class children are subjected earlier and more consistently to the influences which make a child an orderly, conscientious, responsible, and tame person." These are the very traits destined to be rewarded by the schools of this country (Davis, *1953*). The Chicago

TABLE 3. Class Differences in Child Rearing

	Lower Class	Middle Class
Feeding and weaning	Children are more often breast fed only, are fed on demand, and, in the case of Negroes, for longer than three months. Pacifiers are more frequently used. Weaning in the case of Negro children tends to be sharp.	Children are more often given supplementary bottle feeding; feeding tends to be on schedule and, in the case of whites, weaning occurs earlier than in lower-class families. Children in this class tend to be held for feeding.
Toilet training	The tendency is to delay onset of bowel and bladder training more than in the middle class.	Bowel and bladder training are begun earlier and, in the case of Negro children, are completed sooner. The mode is to begin bowel and bladder training earlier than in the white caste.
Father-child relations	Fathers more often discipline children (Negro caste only).	Fathers spend more time with children, especially in educational activities like reading and taking walks.
Occupational expectations	Occupational status expectations are lower.	Higher occupational status is expected of children.
Educational expectations	College not expected by most.	More often expect children to go to college.
Age of assuming responsibility	Children are not expected to work around the house as early as middle-class children, but may cross the street earlier, are expected to get a job after school earlier, and expected to quit school to go to work earlier than their middle-class peers.	Child is expected to help at home earlier and expected to go downtown sooner. Girls are expected to help with younger children earlier, and, in the case of the white caste, parents look for girls to cook and sew earlier.
Strictness of regime	Child is allowed to go to the movies earlier and can stay out later.	Children take daytime nap more frequently and must be in the house earlier at night.

Source: Adapted from Davis and Havighurst, 1953:314.

study also indicates that "middle-class children probably suffer more frustration of their impulses" than lower-class children.

Negro middle-class children receive more permissive treatment than their white peers except with respect to toilet training. In comparison to white parents, Negroes of all classes are more permissive with regard to such things as feeding and weaning. "Negro babies have a markedly different feeding and weaning experience from white babies," although their course of toilet training is more severe. Psychoanalytic theory suggests that thumb sucking and masturbation may be connected with severity of socialization. In support of this hypothesis the authors point out that thumb sucking is reported three times more frequently for white middle-class than for white lower-class children. Also, almost twice as many Negro middle-class as compared to lower-class children suck their thumbs. Thumb sucking may be a response to frustration on the part of middle-class youngsters. Masturbation, reported more frequently for middle-class children, may also be a "palliative to frustration."

Davis and Havighurst's work demonstrates vividly how very unsafe it may be to assume the existence of homogeneous patterns of child rearing in a complex modern nation. In America different pressures impinge upon the child depending on the social class and color caste to which he belongs. Their work also demands admiration for the fruitful use made of quantitative methods in a field hitherto largely restricted to qualitative research. Finally, the conclusions concerning thumb sucking and masturbation allow us to see how feeding and toilet training are quite insufficient in themselves to explain personality development. We know that very likely both thumb sucking and masturbation in the middle class are punished. From this blocking of the substitutive gratificatory sources further dynamic consequences upon middle-class personality development may be expected —guilt and anxiety, for example, attaching to sexual actitivies in general (Fenichel, 1945:75–76).

Values and Social Class

Sentiments or value-tinged beliefs also vary with social class. All the people of Prairie City respect such general virtues as honesty, responsibility, loyalty, and kindliness (Havighurst and Neubauer, 1949). Different strata in the community, however, variously interpret, extend, or limit these values.

In the lower-lower class of Prairie City it is important to be honest in dealings that take place within the family and the small neighborhood group. Lower-lower-class people feel little compulsion to tell the truth to everyone. They similarly restrict virtues of responsibility and of loyalty to a small sphere of action—the family, neighborhood, and friends. Stealing from outside these ingroups will more likely be overlooked or condoned by members of this class who, in comparison to middle-class people, also bring less pressure against fighting, sex play, and sex exploration.

Middle-class parents in Prairie City actively inculcate in children values like self-reliance, initiative, and good manners. They encourage loyalty and responsibility to the community as a whole. Sentiments of responsibility and loyalty to community, expressed in things like community betterment drives, are largely limited to upper-middle-class persons who sometimes even subordinate their roles as parents to the responsibilities they feel as citizens. The middle class generally values education highly and sometimes regards it as the solution for all social problems. Parents in this strata exert strong pressure against stealing, property destruction, sexual immorality, bad manners, and carelessness in dress and speech.

The values of the upper class differ from those of the other classes of Prairie City. Its members place great stress on family history and value spending money for things which will not produce a profit, like philanthropy, fine houses, and fine horses. Of course the poverty of lower-lower-class people would prohibit conspicious consumption and uneconomic spending even if they came to endow such goals with high value.

The research conducted in Prairie City reveals how children of all classes in a community may learn to pay lip service to ideals like responsibility, citizenship, and kindliness. Nevertheless these sentiments may not be reinforced equally in the various social strata. When the lower-class people are compared to members of the upper middle class with respect to the overt execution of these ideal patterns considerable differences in personality become evident. Such differences reflect the varying expectations to which the developing individual is exposed in the various social strata.

It is of interest to note that the experiment of Hieronymus (1951) also leads to a conclusion reinforcing the Prairie City research findings. Working with Middle Western children Hieronymus' work reveals that quite apart from intelligence social class is closely related to the meaningfulness of social goals or goal striving. Goals as objectives which the individual pursues in a given situation are values in our sense of the term. Hence social class is closely associated with the value orientation of youngsters. How well American schools act on this knowledge will become clear later in this chapter.

From such studies we learn the necessity of being wary when pattern generalizations are offered concerning universal American values. Such generalizations may sometimes be true when they refer to ideal values, like loyalty to the nation, but may have little reality as far as the customary action patterns of people are concerned. As a result of careful research like this we may well question how generally Americans feel attached to possessions, or deem it desirable to sacrifice anything for the indulgence of animal appetites, especially sex (Bell, 1952:40–47). All such values may be predicted for *some* strata or elements in the population but the chances are that all will not truly characterize the personalities of most Americans.

Conceptions of Parents and the World

Eugene Lerner (1937) studied Montclair, New Jersey, school children and discovered that the conception of the parental role as well as belief in immanent justice differ between economic classes. Such classes were identified on the basis of housing type and area.[4]

Some 380 children ranging from 6 to 12 years were interviewed. They came from two contrasting socioeconomic areas in the city. Area A is described as an Italian ghetto containing also a large Negro popu-

---

[4] Perhaps his results will hold between social classes for social classes are partly related to differential housing and areal patterns. See Warner, Meeker, and Eells, 1949:21.

lation and marked by dilapidated dwellings. The parents of the children who lived here largely engage in unskilled, semiskilled, and skilled manual occupations. Eighty-three percent of such parents were foreign-born. Area B is a "fine, restricted residential district." The parents of children from this neighborhood are mainly professionals or engaged in business and technical tasks that demand "leadership qualifications." Ninety-one percent are native born. In Area A Lerner discovered that the "definition of parental role as a matter of authority clearly prevails . . . over its definition as a matter of goodness; whereas, just in the opposite fashion, in Area B, the latter prevails over the former." It may be that the authoritarian conception of parents in the economically depressed section reflects a European pattern but this is questionable in view of the large Negro population. Each of these conceptions of parents may be associated with the fact that the belief in immanent justice appears more frequently in children from Area A than in those from Area B. The belief persists longer in the former group, despite the fact that these children are a little older on the average. Table 4 makes clear the relationships.

TABLE 4.   Percentage Distribution of Belief in Immanent Justice

Mean Age		Percent of Believers		Difference in Percent
Area A	Area B	Area A	Area B	
7.3	7.1	82	62	20
9.3	9.1	70	50	20
11.3	11.1	31	15	16

SOURCE: Lerner, *1937*:86.

Lerner's work might be considered together with the evidence of the belief in immanent justice, or the "power pool," of contemporary American Indian communities (Thompson, *1951b*:41, 79, 111, 146). The Montclair data indicate that membership in social divisions, like class, may be associated with characterological differences not essentially different from those occurring with tribal membership. Future investigation will probably indicate further significant differences in the nuclear world and self views of members belonging to divergent social divisions in modern nations.

Anxieties and Social Class Membership

One of the most striking descriptions of personality differences in an ideal urban American community is drawn by Allison Davis (1948). His analysis takes note of attitudes toward eating, anxieties about housing, handling of wealth, and social sources of anxiety.

Lower-class people have patterns of eating different from those of the middle class. Owing to greater security of their food supply middle-class people eat more regularly as well as more sparingly at any given time. They have developed a conscientious taboo against "overeating" and feel guilty about getting fat. Slum people, on the other hand, face an uncertain food supply and become anxious about not getting enough to eat. This anxiety begins to develop shortly after the child's nursing period. When food happens to be plentiful lower-class people eat all they can hold. They "pack food away" in themselves as though seeking protection against the shortage which may appear before next payday. They don't mind becoming fat for they regard fat as protection against tuberculosis and physical weakness.

Lower- and middle-class folk differ in their anxieties about housing. The middle-class person who buys coal by the ton or five-ton lot is relatively certain that he will not run short of coal. He enjoys similar security about light and burns five or ten electric lights in the evening. The lower-class family's security about heat is on a day-to-day or week-to-week basis. It buys coal by the bushel, five-bushel, or one-ton load. Every week or so the lower-class person may have to face anxiety about cold for himself and his children. Lower-class people spend their evenings in a gray light because if they burn too many bulbs or bulbs of a high wattage they may not be able to pay the light bill. "Therefore the fear of not having so basic a necessity as light—a fear which middle-class people escape . . . is recurrent with the slum individual. Walk into any slum housing at night. People are crowded together in a dingy twilight world. Their streets and alleys likewise are full of darkness, so that their chronic expectation of assault or rape is increased."

Against this background of lower-class anxieties, Davis points out, we can understand what happens when the slum dweller gets a relatively large increase in income, such as happened during World War II. Under such circumstances slum dwellers spend their money "extravagantly," or at least that is the judgment of middle-class members of the community. The slum dweller's spending for fur coats, expensive clothes for children, or new furniture represents an attempt to increase self-esteem and security. He is acquiring some of the prestige symbols attached to middle-class status. He is striving for upward mobility in traditional American fashion. Extravagant spending also serves as a defense against anxiety. "When one has money, he buys things which he will be able to buy only once or twice—such things as expensive, respectable warm clothes, and a 'decent' bed. He burns all the lights he wants; he eats great quantities of meat." Lower-class homes are apt to be stiflingly hot when their owners have fuel because the latter remember what it was to be cold. "Just as their deep anxiety about starvation leads them even in good times to glut themselves, as middle-class people view their eating, so does the learned fear of deprivation drive lower-class people to get all they can of the other physical gratifications, 'while the getting is good.'"

Lower-class and middle-class persons feel anxious about different social as well as physical dangers. Whereas the middle-class child learns not to receive poor grades in school; not to show aggression to teachers; not to fight, curse, or have sex relations, the slum child dreads quite different situations. His gang teaches him to fear being taken in by the teacher, of being a softie with her. To pursue homework seriously brings disgrace in the eyes of lower-class peers. Instead of boasting about good marks lower-class children conceal high grades if they ever receive them. The slum child also fears *not* acquiring a reputation as a street fighter. He cannot afford *not* to curse. "If he cannot claim early sexual relations, his virility is seriously questioned."

Slum people are frequently deprived of sexual outlets which in turn conditions particular attitudes toward sex relations. They lack sufficient housing space and beds. Mates or lovers being frequently separated and the hard work of a mother who must care for from six to fourteen children help to make lower-class sexual life less regular, secure, and routine than is generally true for the middle class.

As already indicated, slum dwellers take a view of aggression that differs from the middle-class pattern. People in the latter strata clothe aggression in "the conventional forms of initiative, or ambition, or even of progressiveness." In the lower class aggression "often appears unabashed as physical attack, or as threats of and encouragement for physical attack." The parents of lower-class children may teach the latter to fight, defend themselves, or strike first. Social relations in a lower-class family accustom children to aggression. Boys may strike the father, husbands and wives stage quarrels in the presence of children, or a husband may break down the door when his wife locks him out. From such experiences the slum child gains the impression that aggression is a necessary and appropriate form of social adaptation.

Davis' conclusion is a bit startling to those of us who were brought up with the fiction of a relatively homogeneous American culture. So vast a difference does he see between lower- and middle-class behavior patterns that he believes American personality is marked by few common traits "in comparison with the great variety of cultural acts, beliefs, and values which have been differentiated by the various social strata in the United States." Final conclusions concerning the extent of behavioral homogeneity between the social classes await further careful investigation. Such study will better define the extent to which common acts, beliefs, and peripheral values—the bricks of personality—allow one to talk of a representative American personality. It is well to note that Davis does not proceed into the area of character structure as we have defined the term.

In a recent study Maas (*1951*) observes that lower-class children enjoy greater physical and social freedom than middle-class peers but he fails to find this climate associated with more "psychological freedom." He reasons that in lower-class culture rigid parent-child relationship patterns lead children to more often fear parents. Children in lower-class families more often feel rejected and unworthy, partly as a result of lacking the equal access which the middle-class youngster enjoys to both mother and father. Such closer parent-child ties in the middle class also reduce fear of the potential danger of adults. Especially interesting is the correlation drawn by the author who connects family culture on the one hand, the intervening motivational variable of psychological freedom, and the expression of the child's personality in play. Greater psychological freedom in the middle-class child, the product of relaxed and close parent-child relations, is associated with less submissive, bullying, or hierarchical behavior in the middle-class play group. The quality of peer relations in turn probably has further dynamic significance for the patterning of the middle-class personality. With psychological freedom we approach the nuclear region of personality. Maas' evidence indicates that class factors may have a relatively deep impact on the person.

Social Class Outside the United States

There is no reason why only members of American social classes should systematically vary in personality. Class-linked personality patterns appear whenever structural factors mark community organization.

In the British West Indies aggression correlates with position in the class hierarchy (Hadley, *1949*). Three social classes are delineated for the British Caribbean: lower (the "Proletariat"), lower middle (the "Unestablished"), and an upper middle (the "Established"). Members of the first category are deferential, accommodating, and dependent in much of their behavior. Greater aggressivity has come to distinguish lower-class people as their position in the social structure subjects them to more intense frustration. The "Unestablished" are upward-striving people, self-assertive and competitive. Their aspirations earn for them considerable frustration which, in turn, motivates aggression. Upper-middle-class people occupy an assured position in the community and manifest self-confidence, a sense of security, and relatively little overt aggression.

Rodnick (*1948:*105–106) relates patterns of relationship between German girls and American soldiers to the class position of the former. In general, German girls are accustomed to being put on a pedestal by lovers but American troops in the occupied western zone of the country failed to respond properly to this expectation. Rather they often treated their feminine companions contemptuously. Girls of the middle-middle and upper-middle class would not put up with this treatment and quit associating with Americans both for this reason and through fear of losing prestige in the eyes of friends if they continued. Lower-middle and working-class girls, however, saw rewards in meeting American boys and did not resent the treatment of the soldiers. Most of the girl friends of American troops in western Germany came from these lower strata of the community.

CASTE AND PERSONALITY

Evidence has already been offered indicating that caste membership is also associated with distinctive patterns of socialization and correlated with systematic variations in ways of acting, thinking, and feeling.

Within the last few decades social scientists have made many close studies of color castes in the United States. One of the most recent, by two psychoanalysts, is based on the deep study of twenty-five American Negroes (Kardiner and Ovesey, *1951*). All but one subject were analyzed for at least three months and each case continued long enough to show the dominant style of behavior. In general the cases, which are further arranged by social class levels, show that the American Negro, even in the North, has his personality affected by the discrimination which he suffers. His life style is powerfully influenced by the discriminatory patterns exercised by the dominant white caste against Negroes. In his relations with whites, the Negro receives an unpleasant image of himself that causes him to devaluate himself. Such devaluation in turn motivates behaviors like unrealistically high aspirations, self-abnegation, caution, and idealization of whites. The Negro also becomes exposed to frustration in intercaste relations and such frustration stimulates hostility which he fears to express. As a consequence, the Negro becomes hesitant, irritable, submissive, compensatorily affable or good-humored, and passive in his approach to problems. The Negro male is often disinterested in sex, an attitude that the psychoanalysts relate to the ambivalence felt toward female sex objects. Many Negroes retain a memory of the mother as a frustrating figure that conditions their relations with women. Women in the Negro caste also often enjoy better economic opportunities than men. Hence the male comes to be dependent on and at the mercy of women who also become threatening to his masculinity.

A great deal of energy in the Negro personality goes toward disposing of the hostility that must not be released in retaliatory aggression against the sources of frustration (304–305). In some individuals who were analyzed the only manifestation of rage turned out to be fear. Other persons replaced hostility by compliance and ingratiation, the latter sometimes serving as a subtle form of exploitation. Hostility is also denied or replaced by gaiety or flippancy; sometimes it ricochets back on the person to engender masochism and depression. Hypertension and headaches are other expressions of repressed rage.

Membership in a caste that lacks many comforts and opportunities does not leave unaffected the socialization of the child. Instability in the lower-class Negro family interferes with the development of strong affective ties to parents and with the induction of those emotional responses most conducive to social cohesion. And so the instability of the Negro family maintains itself in the pattern of a regenerative circle. Insufficient food in the house contributes to an image of the mother as a frustrating object and scarcity also instigates rivalry between siblings. "The result of continuous frustrations in childhood is to create a personality devoid of confidence in human relations, of an external vigilance and distrust of others. This is a purely defensive maneuver which purports to protect the individual against the repeatedly traumatic effects of disappointment and frustration. He must operate on the assumption that the world is hostile. The self-referential aspect of this is contained in the formula, I am not a lovable creature" (308).

Minority Group Attitudes Among Negro Girls

Feelings of insecurity are not equally distributed throughout all social classes of American Negroes. A study of lower- and middle-class Negro girls aged twenty to twenty-five living in Syracuse and

Harlem shows consistent social class differences in security feelings between these categories (Brenman, *1940*). Middle-class girls show more insecurity regarding their membership in a minority group than lower-class girls. The latter not only demonstrate little feeling of insecurity but seem to accept the white man's dogma of Negro inferiority to a greater degree than do their middle-class peers. In spite of accepting this dogma, the lower-class Negro girl remains more secure because, Brenman thinks, she lacks the dilemmas faced by the middle-class person. The latter enjoys an economic position that permits participation in social situations on a par with whites. Yet middle-class girls cannot move freely in the white caste because of the discriminations imposed. Such conflicts escape the lower-class girl who has neither means nor, generally, inclination to participate in social situations with white people.

The girls in Brenman's sample also differ in attitudes toward sex. The middle-class subject follows the standards of her white middle-class contemporaries: "No sexual relations before marriage and strict monogamy thereafter." Should she engage in premarital relations with a fiancé the fact must be carefully concealed and rationalized, as is true also of white girls. Lower-class Negro girls tend to reject this ideal standard in practice and also often in theory. Their attitude is understandable when we recall that renunciation of sexual gratification does not reward the girl. In the absence of any likely reinforcement there is little incentive to practice self-denial.

Caste in Latin America

John Gillin (*1951*:1–5, 119–126) has analyzed the distribution of psychological security between the Indian and Ladino castes of San Carlos, a town in Guatemala. He defines security as a "state of affairs in which an individual or group may anticipate with confidence that wants will be satisfied (that is, that goals will be achieved) according to expectations." Security means a minimum of tension and anxiety. Any culture provides security for community members but at the same time also contributes to insecurities (Honigmann, *1950*).

Indians and Ladinos respond differently to the problems that face members of each caste. The Indian, generally passive, remains intent on seeking a peaceful adjustment between man and with the universe. His function as an individual is to promote the prosperity of the group. On the other hand, the Ladino approaches problems of living assertively. He believes that the universe is amenable to a good deal of human manipulation—"Even God can be forced to favor the strong." The group exists to promote the individual's welfare (F. Kluckhohn, *1950*).

By observation and from Rorschach testing (Billig, Gillin, and Davidson, *1947–48*), Gillin concludes that the Indian is relatively more secure than the Ladino, providing that the cultural routines of the former are not interfered with. This preoccupation with an undisturbed way of life suggests a compulsive element in the Indian personality that also appears in other areas. Compared to the Ladino, the Indian inhibits emotion, including aggressiveness. Not surprisingly, alcohol dissolves this inhibition. Characterizing the Indian as relatively constricted in behavior, Gillin wonders how such a trend relates to a relatively permissive type of child rearing which lacks swaddling and minimizes spectacular traumas, including punishment. Actually, the Indian remains a relatively outgoing person until he is about eighteen. Then a personality change is instituted whose dynamics extend to the caste structure of the community. On top of the security given in childhood, pressure from the caste structure stimulates the Indian to adopt a series of inhibitions. These give rise to a "constrictive and relatively rigid character structure." Here we are once more reminded that early childhood does not fully pattern the adult personality or character structure and that social structure may be highly significant for understanding the developmental process.

Less constricted than the Indian, the average Ladino goes through mood swings ranging from depression to euphoria. He remains uncertain of the ability of his culture to satisfy his needs, hence more insecure in his outlook on life. Ladinos are far more aggressive than Indians and also more frustrated. Ladino child training is "fairly permissive" but "probably more authoritarian than the Indian system" and marked by earlier weaning. In recent years upper-class Ladinos have also adopted scheduled infant feeding and rigid cleanliness training. Being sent to school at the age of six for six years of compulsive discipline is an experience which few Indians share with the Ladino child. Whereas the former adopts adult work patterns early, the Ladino still lacks practical knowledge when he leaves school, although he has acquired literacy. A greater variety of occupations is open to Ladinos but the choice which the boy makes when he reaches maturity "usually does not appear to be entirely satisfactory to him." Some Ladinos leave the community to seek their fortunes in the outside world: ". . . those who remain suffer from feelings of anxiety, frustration, and insecurity that is probably related to the fact that they also become drunk more frequently."

Class, Caste, and Ethos

Our evidence clearly indicates that different motivational systems, divergent aims, and varying world and self views characterize the social divisions of a complex community. Each of these divisions thus comes to reflect a distinctive ethos, very likely an ethos which cannot be appreciated fully by the members of another class or caste. Life is familiar and proper to the members of one class when the streets bustle with life, neighbors call one another cheerfully, and children play with impetuous shrillness. The quality of this scene contrasts strikingly with an atmosphere in another class of quiet sedateness, restraint, and self-effacement. People accustomed to one mode of behavior may not only find another quite strange but also very difficult. This leads us to the problems of interclass and intercaste adjustment faced in complex modern communities.

SOCIAL DIFFERENCES AND SOCIAL OPPOSITION

Multiplication of the standards, values, and activities attendant upon social stratification multiply misunderstandings and conflicts in community life. We have already seen that enculturation in one way of life to some degree deprives a person from fully understanding another set of customs and values. As a result, when people who have been enculturated in different systems of belief are required to live and work together their relations frequently show signs of conflict and are productive of personal distress. Intercultural tension need not be limited to international or intertribal relations. Class-structured communities encourage the same type of stress and probably do so to a greater degree than caste-organized social systems because in the latter social interaction between the divisions tends to be sharply limited.

Weckler (*1949*) examines the consequences of class-linked value conflict upon the lower-class child in Prairie City. The youngster derives his earliest learning through the agency of parents. In the family, however, he derives those values that are shared and approved by the parents' social class. Eventually, the lower-class youth enters school where he becomes aware of other expectations of his teachers and peers. That is to say, his patterning is partly taken over by a heterogeneous group of people some of whom belong to social classes other than his own. Quite likely his teacher conducts lessons from the standpoint of middle-class values. The lower-class child inevitably feels pressure to modify certain aspects of his behavior. Failure to meet the school's expectations leads to punishment. The teacher, for example, will find the child making insufficient progress. Her judgment comes to be reflected in the child's grades. Also, if a lower-class youngster fails to modify behavior in response to middle-class demands his reputation with middle-class peers suffers. Consequently he is thrown back on the friendship of those who like himself are from lower-class families. Lower- compared to middle-class parents do not give children very much direction and guidance in school work. Hence such youngsters enter school disadvantaged in comparison to their middle-class peers who earn higher grades.

Social scientists point out that American schools teach behaviors that possess far greater significance for middle- than for lower-class children. From parents the former learn the importance of goals like higher education, etiquette, leadership, and responsibility. The same values, therefore, are held out at home and in the school. Middle-class children experience less conflict between the values of home and school than do lower-class youngsters. The former students receive higher grades and enjoy wider popularity. Lower-class pupils often find school dull, meaningless, and difficult. They remain inadequately motivated toward the kind of performance which most teachers reward. Such children tend to play truant and often drop out of school as soon as they can. Such behavior brings them into further conflict with the dominant middle-class values of the community.

Margaret Mead (*1949f*:203–204) points out that the multiplicity of norms and symbols in class-structured communities facilitates errors in judgment as well as crime. The situation that prevails is essentially similar to what happens when a person reared in one system of behavior finds himself unable to understand the cues and symbols of a foreign way of life. In open class communities it is often inevitable that persons with different norms, who express sentiments differently or use the same symbols differently, should come into contact. An interest in classical music or an unfamiliar accent may then come to symbolize affectation, wealth, or homosexuality. The charge of statuatory rape (that is, sex relationship with a female partner below a certain age, usually eighteen) often stems from the fact that one strata of the community is determined to enforce behavior standards which another category does not recognize. Premarital relations are far more customary in lower economic strata of American society than among college youth (Kinsey, Pomeroy, and Martin, *1948*:347–351) but the pattern is regarded with little tolerance by middle- and upper-class citizens. A wife from a lower-income stratum is unlikely to appreciate the considerable variety of erotic stimuli that appeal to an upper-level husband (363–364). Kinsey and his associates have discussed the social implications of the different sexual patterns associated with different social divisions. They write that "most of the tragedies that develop out of sexual activities are products of this conflict between the attitudes of different social levels. Sexual activities themselves rarely do physical damage, but disagreements over the significance of sexual behavior may result in personality conflicts, a loss of social standing, imprisonment, disgrace, and the loss of life itself" (385–386).

REGIONAL PERSONALITY AND ETHOS

Region refers to a loosely bounded geographical area. To be useful in sociology and anthropology a region must be distinguished by homogeneous social and cultural as well as geographical features. Generally regions are homogeneous with respect to only a certain number of the aspects that interest social scientists, for example, in density, housing, or animal domestication patterns. We then deal with culture areas, regions possessing relatively common cultures. The culture area concept in turn, gave rise to inquiry into the determinant relationship of environment and culture (Kroeber, *1939;* Wissler, *1922*).

Environmental Factors in Personality

On first glance it would appear that environment exerts no clear deterministic control over any large segment of behavior. To demonstrate this take two successive occupants of what is roughly the same region and compare nuclear and peripheral areas of personality between them. The Plains Indians encountered by the westward-moving pioneers and explorers were men who enjoyed the chase and warfare. Sensitive and with low frustration tolerance they were as likely to direct the aggression derived from frustration against themselves as against an enemy. Ruth Benedict has emphasized the quality of tightrope walking in Plains personality; they seemingly walked a narrow edge between devastating experiences. Attracted to sexual satisfaction they expected a stringent chastity from girls and honored virgins as well as parents who delayed resuming sex relations after the birth of a child. Easily aroused they chose men of unfathomable calm to be their chiefs. Benedict (*1946b*:72) refers to these Indians as Dionysian, meaning that they pursued the values of existence through annihilation of the ordinary limits of experience. The most valued moments of living came to them when the boundaries of the senses were escaped and some sort of psychological excess achieved. The fact that we can speak of an area in this fashion obviously indicates that there is a degree of validity to the hypothesis of areal personality and areal ethos.

When we look at the Great Plains today, however, it is equally apparent that the geographical environment is not consistent in its operation on personality. A type of mechanized culture capable of exploiting many new facets of the geographical milieu occupies the Plains today. With accent on success, Anglophobia, and isolation, with a passion for uniformity, curious, and possessing great trust in their own destiny, Midwesterners of European ancestry are systematically different from the Sioux and Cheyenne in most areas of their personalities (Hutton, *1946*). With the aid of a long tradition of invention in the arts, sciences, and philosophy, Euroamericans have constructed a very different kind of culture from that which flowered in the area during the eighteenth century. We do have evidence, though, that homogeneity in some areas of personality, including character structure, coincides with the region.

Theoretically there is little question but that any behavior manifested in a given environment bears a meaningful relationship to the geographical features with which it coincides. Generalizing such relationships and testing for predictability is a job that remains to be attempted. To illustrate, barren Eskimoland supports few people. Low density in turn subjects people to a tight ingroupness that colors values towards strangers and conditions security to familiarity. These relationships warrant the generalization that low density is indirectly related to distrust of strangers and preference for familiars. This hypothesis implies that low density is a predictable concomitant of so-called barren environments.

Research on northern forest Indians by Barnouw (*1950*), Caudill (*1949*), Hallowell (*1946*), and Honigmann (*1949a*) suggests that a relatively homogeneous personality can be discerned in the vast coniferous forest zone extending from northeastern Canada to western Alaska. Briefly, such a personality is marked by strong emotional constraint and the inhibition of strong emotions in interpersonal relations. Emotional indifference is maintained through avoiding investing any great emotion in anything. When deep feelings are aroused they are put aside as quickly as possible. Reflecting the individualism or atomization of social structure (which, in turn, rests on the hunting and gathering technology that requires little coöperation and supports low densities) is the independence or self-sufficiency of the individual personality. Impulses of one person to tell another what to do are suppressed; parent-child relations are accompanied by considerable deference and respect. Probing for the dynamic significance of these traits we come upon a deeply rooted anxiety that colors the people's whole outlook on the world and the capacities of the self. Anxiety is aroused by strong emotional stimuli, so that danger and fear are often denied rather than pragmatically handled. Deference in interpersonal relations is guided by the fear of arousing hostility or resentment in others. The mutual confirmation which anthropologists working in the North have given to each other's conclusions is among the outstanding examples of validation in culture and personality research.

The Areal Ethos

Devereux (*1951*:37–44), speaking of a Plains areal ethos, lends further support to the hypothesis that areas are distinguishable in terms of the emotional aspects of the behavior manifested by populations. Citing the fact that early travelers also perceived a generalized Plains Indian modal personality related to uniform areal culture patterns he goes on to label the areal component as "the most important constituent of any given Plains Indian personality." The constant, formally patterned contacts between the Plains Indian tribes represent one mechanism through which common values were inculcated in the region. Homogeneous elements of personality in turn facilitated communication between Plains Indians of various tribes, even on the battlefield. The behavior of an enemy could be understood by empathy at the same time that one's own aspirations were made articulate. In contrast to the type of communication prevailing within this area the raider type of contacts between Plains tribesmen and Pueblo people rested on another type of communication that relied not so much on empathy as on projection.

Devereux believes that just as the areal culture pattern survives longer than tribal patterns so the areal personality pattern also maintains itself. For certain purposes, it is more important today to know that a given Indian is a Plains Indian than to know, for example, that he is a Crow Indian.

Dynamics of Areal Personality

The mechanisms for engendering the areal personality are several and interlinked. In first place stands the group to whose expectations the individual becomes sensitive and according to whose wishes he modifies his behavior. In other words, interpersonal relations pattern personality in the region as well as in the tribe. If a region shows some degree of personality homogeneity it is probable that socialization techniques in the area are relatively similar in certain respects. Other foundations of such similarity need to be studied but we suggest that similarity of personality is conditioned by (1) a community of interests within the region which directs learning and facilitates borrowing; (2) diffusion of values and the patterns of interpersonal relationship between tribes contributes to uniformity of areal personality; (3) barriers to diffusion from outside the area; (4) the common elements in personality, which may represent common occupations or other interests which in turn reflect the homogeneous distribution of physical resources and other physiographical features.

To illustrate how physiography secures patterning through occupational and other interests we will consider the pastoral technologies of Central Asia. The choice of pastoralism is related to the character of the environment. The technique of animal husbandry was invented in the region or diffused into the area and flourished, partly because it was well suited to the natural resources. In turn mobile tribal communities (the patterns of mobility and tribal social organization are in turn related to pastoral routines) condition particular kinds of interpersonal relations to which personal development responds in childhood and adulthood. Forde (1949:395) has written on the integration of pastoral technologies to their habitats. He goes on to speak of the hostile and disruptive relations that pastoralists frequently enjoy with adjacent, settled, cultivating peoples. Then he adds: "It is not pastoralism and cultivation as such that face each other in hostility, but mobility with poverty as against sessile and vulnerable wealth. That the pastoral nomad who travels light mentally and aesthetically as well as materially may have little immediate appreciation for the intellectual and artistic superstructure that an advanced agricultural economy can support is also manifest" (405). Such are the dynamics of regions!

Whether children are really "the same everywhere" is a question seriously challenged in the Cumberland research. The study, which involved the comparison of rural Tennessee and New York City youngsters, finds the rural children to be generally more placid and easygoing and less rebellious than those who grow up in the metropolitan community (C. Lewis, *1946*). These characteristics of the child in Cumberland County, Tennessee, are related to his prolonged infancy as well as to the ready acceptance which he receives from parents and other adults. The rural youngster may accompany adults during a variety of their activities. The country environment recommends fewer restrictions or frustrations in the life of the growing child who at the same time is saddled by fewer aspirations projected upon him by parents. In many ways the relationship of adults to children in this southern region is more symmetrical than the relationship of urban middle-class parents to children.[5] The metropolitan community excludes youngsters from many activities so that considerable areas of adult life cannot freely be understood.

The unruliness of the city child may partly stem from the fact that urban adults spare a minimum of time and reserve little place for children. The urban environment with its many restrictions offers inevitable temptations for the youngster to test his growing capacities for mastery. Such testing often brings fresh parental and community disapproval and thus encourages a pattern of unruliness that rural circumstances are less likely to encourage.

---

[5] Premature universal generalizations concerning rural patterns must be avoided. A study from Israel reports punishment to be more severe in small rural towns of that country than in large cities like Jerusalem and Haifa. See Merzbach, *1949*.

Sex Differences in City and Country

Rural-urban personality differences are also evident in adulthood, membership in city or country being associated with quite diverse patterns of behavior. Rural males, for example, engage in less frequent sexual activity than their city cousins (Kinsey, Pomeroy, and Martin, 1948:452–464). Rural males are not accustomed to obtaining orgasm through petting as frequently as city boys, perhaps because girls are not as readily available for dating. Rural males also visit prostitutes rarely and do not engage as much as urban males in premarital sex relations. Among ranchmen, cattlemen, prospectors, lumbermen, and farm groups, however, there exists a pattern of unaffected homosexual relations that finds little counterpart in urban areas. The pattern is conditioned by a shortage of women and is based on "the attitude that sex is sex, irrespective of the nature of the partner with whom the relation is had." The study by Kinsey and his associates also points out that more rural than urban boys have sexual relations with animals. For most individuals these contacts remain isolated occurrences.

OCCUPATION AND PERSONALITY

Different occupational categories in a community because they consist of people who pursue different technical skills are necessarily distinctive in at least a few aspects of personality. There is very little information on hand concerning whether members of occupational categories also come to develop more extensive differences in behavior.[6] Dexter (*1949*), describing the personality of professional class Puerto Ricans, suggests that white-collar occupations in the Islands are filled by individuals with certain common response patterns. The professional male, whether a politician, businessman, or academician, is notable for flamboyant and dramatic behavior that serves to win him respect and deference. Characterologically he is rather insensitive to other people's needs and reactions. He furnishes unfavorable criticisms with great frankness. This quality of the professional class gives

[6] See, however, the summary of studies in Stagner, 1948:412–419.

Puerto Rican culture something of its ethos of relative "disorder" and uncompulsiveness.

Special qualities characterize leaders among the mild mannered Arapesh, whose group norm is gentleness (Mead, *1950b*:31). Leaders there are needed only for large-scale ceremonies and boys still in their teens are selected for this status. Training begins when the youth is assigned to a *buanyin*, or exchange partner, whose role is modeled after that of an elder brother. The two partners exchange feasts and insult each other whenever they meet. This competitive, boasting relationship provides a "training-ground in the kind of hardness that a big man must have, which in an ordinary Arapesh is regarded as undesirable." It is worth pointing out that Arapesh try to select youths with appropriate qualities for jobs as leaders. Hence the community is able to incorporate potential deviants into the social structure in positions where, instead of being condemned, their characteristics will prove useful merit rewards.

Several studies have probed into the attributes of American executives (Stagner, *1948*:413–414). One researcher found high ranking executives to be very egocentric and characterized by desires for "ego-expansion," power, and philanthropy. Stagner points out that such traits would help an American secure an executive position. They would also continue to be rewarded in industrial practice. Another study found eighteen top executives frankly rejecting "humanitarian values." A third research, covering fifty executives, found American businessmen to be "highly authoritarian."

Quite likely successful executives in the United States are recruited from members of the population who possess particular personal characteristics. Other behaviors are added to the personality in the course of role playing (W. E. Henry, *1949*; Newcomb, *1950*:408–409). Henry's study reveals American executives to be marked by strong drives toward achievement and a powerful desire for upward mobility. The modern captain of industry has won relatively complete emotional independence from parents. He regards superiors as persons with helpful experience but conceives of authority as neither destructive nor prohibitive. Along with these attitudes a successful executive identifies emotionally with his superiors. The American businessman possesses the ability to make decisions. He has a firm and well-defined sense of self-identity, knows what he wants, and possesses techniques for achieving his goals. Yet the executive lives with the anxiety that he may not really succeed, that he may fail to accomplish the things he wants to do.

Leadership in Culture

Anthropological studies indicate that leadership manifests itself variously in different cultures. Leadership is related to the kinds of jobs that must be done in a community as well as to the value system shared by the group. The Assessment Staff of the Office of Strategic Services (1948:351) points out that the Javanese leader "played the role of helping others to accomplish their special duties rather than directing them." When such a leader discusses a problem with followers, the parties do not debate but try to overcome differences and win agreement. The Karens of Burma, on the other hand, follow leadership patterns more akin to those of Americans. The Chinese pay deference to the oldest man in the group regardless of whether he shows leadership ability. Deference increases if the oldest man possesses more than an average education. Among the Indians of northern Canada leadership when it is required appears muted or oblique. That is, the man who directs an undertaking expresses his request only indirectly and, like the Javanese, helps his followers to realize a goal rather than directing them toward it.

Craft Specialization and Personality

Craft or occupational specialization of labor refers to the division of tasks between a number of workers according to functions. In a complex community, like that of the United States, some men spend all of their working hours making hats, driving trucks, designing houses, or organizing the labor of the men who build houses. Division of labor according to skill, as this type of specialization is also called, is not a universal feature of culture but appears in association with food producing techniques capable of producing large surpluses and able to support relatively large populations (Chapple and Coon, 1942: 253–256; Jacobs and Stern, 1947:141–142).

A culture marked by craft specialization possesses a wide basis for the allocation of prestige (Kardiner, 1939:49). The various tasks, especially as they are divided between planning or organization of work on the one hand and actual production on the other, may become endowed with differing prestige values. The prestige of a job may then be expressed in the amount of money it pays. The individuals occupying the various positions in a craft specialized community come to enjoy different degrees of economic and social power. Their unequal earnings furnish men with differential access to the finished products of labor. Conflicts between the specialists over rewards or other issues may have psychological repercussions and the entire system promotes particular anxieties and insecurities in workers and executives alike. The regulation of such anxieties and derived hostilities becomes of paramount importance because if they get out of control the whole intricate system of collaboration may break down. Even a partial breakdown promotes intense distress to the individuals whose survival thus becomes imperiled.

A large degree of craft specialization with many job roles from which to select means that children may no longer safely take their parents as finished models of future years. Especially is this true for males.

Character structure undergoes modification as specialization increases. With the emergence of the Protestant ethic the traditional-directed personality of Western man gradually gave way to guidance by the gyroscope of inner direction (Riesman, 1950:41).[7] Man came to strive toward ideals and learned to master himself in order to retain those ideals. Today the orientation of inner direction is once more changing; outer direction is beginning to replace the gyroscopic inner orientation.

---

[7] See below, pp. 351–352.

The Scientists and the Public

It is possible to conceive of the American community as comprising a vast circle of population in the center of which stands a core of innovators. At work in laboratories, universities, and libraries the scientific elite engage in an unending pursuit whose consequence—scientific knowledge—stimulates a constant series of changes in social life. The meanings by which members in the outer sectors of the circle live are frequently being altered through the activities of this core. Scientists introduce "a continuing process of change . . . into the primary symbolic systems which help integrate the life of a society, and into the structure of the situations in which a large part of the population must carry on their activities" (Parsons, 1947:177).

Clearly, relatively diverse personalities characterize the core and fringe sectors of the community. Between the two extremes there is probably a continual gradation in the frequency of certain attitudes. At the core are the "emancipated" people, who are relatively untraditional, rationalistic, capable of making objective generalizations about many segments of sociocultural life, possessed with a thoroughgoing relativity of belief that encompasses either the timeless universe or else world society with its diversity of cultures. These men and women are often agnostics, liberals, and have little patience for the compromises and blunders of national and international political life. Their model for problem solving comes from science and includes the experiment, cold and dispassionate observation, and decisions undertaken without fear or compromise. The fact that they may not carry out this laboratory model in personal or day-to-day behavior does not deny that it is a powerful symbol of right behavior in their hierarchy of values. The core thrives on change, in fact these elite make their living through stimulating the process of unending change.

At the fringe of the community we encounter another kind of personality. Here is the fundamentalist, the compulsively traditionalistic person. The emotional biases of his thinking have no check, scientific models possess no relevance, and observation is undertaken from the standpoint of personal bias and a belief in the necessity of common sense and conformity.

Now, between these two social areas there is conflict. The constant stream of change coming from the core of the circle increases the anxiety level in the fringe. A reservoir of aggressive impulses is maintained at a constant high level in the outer edges of the circle. Sometimes the fringe produces patterns that represent a compulsively distorted exaggeration of traditional values. Such patterns may become incorporated into fascistic movements. These exaggerations are to be understood as instances of revivalistic or perpetuative nativism designed to arrest change. Parsons distinguishes a marginal element of the community—the compulsively emancipated person, who distorts the nontraditionalistic culture patterns and by his behavior further provokes the fringe who strike back indiscriminately at all "longhairs." A vicious circle of mounting antagonism gets started which in 1952 entered the presidential campaign. The core-fringe tension in American life is an instance of the disequilibrium that possesses most societies which undergo rapid culture change (Wilson and Wilson, 1945). This aspect of the problem need not concern us here but the role of such conflict in building up sources of latent hostility in social life must not be overlooked. The latent hostility becomes channelized into other types of social opposition—anti-Semitism, antilaborism—as well as into anti-Negro, anti-Catholic, and antiforeign feeling.

Suggestions for Further Reading

The essential concepts encountered in class and caste analysis will be found in Goldschmidt's "Social Class in America—A Critical Survey" (1950). The paper clarifies systematically conceptual difficulties that have entered this area of study. Research exploring cultural and personality differences between social classes appear constantly in the sociological and psychological journals. The field is currently a popular one. If any one introduction should be recommended let it be Warner and Lunt's classic *The Social Life of a Modern Community* (1941).

Three additional volumes in the Yankee City series have also been published. The opening chapter of Warner, Meeker, and Eells's *Social Class in America* (*1949*) is a much briefer and very useful guide to the subject of social class. See also Mills's *White Collar* (*1951*) and the very readable and dramatic study of learning as related to social class, *Elmtown's Youth* by Hollingshead (*1949*). Komarovsky and Sargent take up the relationship of occupation, caste, and class on personality in "Research into Subcultural Influences upon Personality" (*1949*). Several of J. P. Marquand's novels illustrate class-linked behavior patterns.

The restlessness and rebelliousness of urban children is dramatically revealed in Martin's *Why Did They Kill?* (*1953*). The author finds it difficult to answer his own question, partly because he has no explicit theory and hypotheses in terms of which the data can be made to yield an answer. The book is a nice illustration of the difference between excellent newspaper reporting and social scientific analysis. Erasmus interestingly explores the relations of leadership to community values in "The Leader vs. Tradition: A Case Study" (*1952*). Another novel, *Executive Suite* by Cameron Hawley (*1953*), gives nice insight into common and idiosyncratic elements in the personalities of executives in a single company. Analysis of these elements should provide students with a useful exercise. Anne Roe has reported on a careful study of the scientist's personality in "What Makes the Scientific Mind Scientific?" (*1953*).

Chapter 14

HOMOGENEITY, HETEROGENEITY, AND CULTURAL CHANGE

The student by this time will have become familiar with a number of cultures several times referred to in preceding pages. Many of these—Arapesh, Samoa, Kaska, Umbundu, Eskimo, and Manus—share a quality in common. Members of the community follow a highly coherent set of behaviors that change little between a particular individual's birth and death. On the other hand, Germany, the United States, and the British West Indies confront us with communities that have undergone drastic social and cultural changes in the past two or three centuries. The very fact that of England we can speak of a Victorian Age which contrasts with something called The Postwar Years indicates the instability of behavior patterns in the western world. Anthropologists think of isolated, slowly changing communities like the Arapesh as possessing homogeneous cultures. Modern nations and exotic communities that come within the orbits of these nations show highly heterogeneous cultures. These concepts have skillfully been used by Margaret Mead, much of whose work is devoted to analyzing the fate of personality in these diverse types of social environment.

CULTURAL HOMOGENEITY AND THE INDIVIDUAL

Culture and personality, it has been said, is a method of social research that focuses observation on the single individual—his development, satisfactions, and perplexities in a given cultural milieu. If America possessed a homogeneous culture each of us individual readers would be dwelling where his forefathers had lived through several generations. The moving van would scarcely be a familiar trait. Change in the way of life would proceed gradually and at such a pace that it could readily be assimilated between the time an adult is a parent and a grandparent.

The anthropologist is one of the few persons in our complex society who has participated in life in homogeneous environments. On the basis of such experience, Mead (*1949d*) describes the distinctive process followed by personality development and expression in an atmosphere of consensus and gradual change. In a homogeneous community (that is, a community with a homogeneous culture) every individual carries the same basic assumptions. This is true if he is someone who carefully observes normative patterns of behavior or somebody who flouts and ignores them. Conformists and deviants recognize the same conventions, "the man who is admitted to the ceremony, and the woman who is excluded; the chief who sets his foot on the slave's neck, and the slave who kneels to receive the stepping foot." The expectations with which the developing individual becomes confronted are mutually compatible and complementary. Cultural and ethological patterns anticipate and support one another in the life cycle so that "the gentleness of a grandmother may be contrasted with rough handling, or even cruel practical joking on the part of the grandfather, but the grandmother's gentleness allows for and in a sense contains the joking of the grandfather. She can be gentler because his harshness will prevent her grandson from being too softened by her behavior. He can be harsh because the solace of her gentleness can be relied on."

It is an operational definition of a homogeneous community that in such a setting the child can theoretically prefigure his future experiences for as long as he lives. At any point in life the adult can consolidate previous experience in the light of current roles. A youngster sees his probable future career in the activities that others of his sex perform in the village. They are going through sequences that he too will go through when he is older. In this way the present con- stitutes a dependable training situation for the future. Past experience can always be consolidated as growing children or even adults under- stand their contemporary roles and prospects in the light of what they have already experienced. "The trembling hand of old age, as it strokes a child's feverish skin, contains in it a promise not only of the bearableness of illness, but also of the bearableness of death itself, or of the unbearableness of both."

Growing old in a homogeneous community brings increasing con- fidence in one's ability to predict with some precision other people's behavior. The longer a person has lived the more he becomes aware of the dependable regularities in his social environment. Simultane- ously with the increase in such assurance with reference to the be- havior of others, the individual's own behavior can become safely automatic in regard to such things as "who should enter a door first and who second, when will the ceremony really begin . . . when people mean what they say and when their speech is only ceremonial self-depreciation or shrewd bargaining." Habituation not only reduces fatigue and enables the aged to conserve their energies but provides compensation for the decline in spontaneity and zest which usually accompanies aging.

In general, then, a homogeneous culture changes so slowly that the past continues to be a reliable guide to the present. This is not the same as claiming that development in a homogeneous community insures a smooth, painless, or untraumatic socialization process. The matter is better expressed by saying that no matter how traumatic or frustrating experiences may be between infancy and death, life "can nevertheless be presented to each individual as viable and to that ex- tent bearable." The "tough" demands of Japanese culture when they are universally shared do not exceed human tolerance, Mead points out, no matter if to us they appear to be unbearable.

CULTURAL HETEROGENEITY AND PERSONALITY

Cultural heterogeneity is closely associated with an open class system, ethnic diversity, and other forms of social mobility. Mobility from one subculture to another exposes the individual to frequent contact with disparate values, expectations, and behavior patterns. Rapid change also characterizes a heterogeneous community. Such change may take place between generations as well as between successive cultural environments in which previously learned patterns must be unlearned and new ones assimilated (Mead, *1949d*:549).

Modern American culture with its profound heterogeneity contrasts sharply with the homogeneous communities so frequently studied by anthropologists (Mead *1949d*:552–553):

> The carefully fitted together internally coherent sequences of behavior and the implications for learning of their presence in the behavior of others, the prefiguration of the future and the consolidation of the past, or finally, the increase in automatic behavior and sureness with age—all these are missing. The rapidity of social change alone during the last few decades has, for most people, eliminated all of these features. Each person who approaches an infant is likely to approach it with behavior which embodies sequences to which the child will not otherwise be exposed. The behavior of the adults is discrepant and confused because of the breaks in continuity in their own upbringing. . . . Instead of being able to develop more and more automatic behavior, he must learn to be increasingly on the alert for lights that turn off differently, lavatories with a different flushing system, games which have the same names but are played with different rules. . . . On the social level he meets ever-changing standards of manners and morals. . . . There is no chance for relaxation, for, even as he becomes adept and in part accustomed to the ways of his adult contemporaries, his own children begin to display new forms of behavior to which he has no clues. By the time grandchildren arrive, the gap is so great that many grandparents are refusing even to bridge it.

All cultural heterogeneity is not of a kind. There is first the *primary heterogeneity* that confronts an individual who passes from one homogeneous community to another. The children of such a migrant then find themselves being reared under a diversity of incongruent stimuli approaching the heterogeneity described in the preceding quotation.

More familiar to urban readers will be the *secondary heterogeneity* to which the migrant must adjust when he leaves an Italian or Puerto Rican village and settles in New York or Detroit. The same type of change is represented, albeit in less dramatic fashion, when the transition is from a rural to an urban environment or from a culturally independent, small-scale tribe to a culturally dependent colony. In all these types of transition a person reared under homogeneous conditions is transposed to a heterogeneous setting. Two contrasting types of adjustment are employed to cope with secondary heterogeneity. First, the immigrant or tribesman may seek to preserve the coherence to which his personality had been conditioned. Experiences which differ in external form from those to which he was accustomed become reinterpreted to make them congruent to customary expectations. For example, if the migrant marries a wife from the new community he may appreciate mainly those points of her behavior that can be interpreted in terms of his prior conception of the wife and mother role. If her cultural background leads her to expect him to carve the roast while in his tradition honors go to the man by never letting him serve a spoonful of peas or even ask for salt, then her expectation will to him denote lack of respect. He may perpetuate memories from out of the past, persistently produce these memories in conversation, and in other ways also manifest a pervasive nostalgia for the homogeneous environment. If the migrant can manage to live in an enclave community that preserves the language and customs of another culture in the middle of the heterogeneous scene then he is aided in maintaining continuity with the past. In such a community ritual patterns of the old culture will likely be "invoked for weddings, funerals, and all high holidays" so that "the new culture becomes invested with the aura of the ordinary; the old keeps a nostalgia-invoking quality."

At another extreme the migrant or tribesman caught in secondary heterogeneity instead of hanging on to the past tries to overcome his earlier socialization by ridding himself of traditional expectations. A serious struggle is waged in order to fit into the demands of the new community. Quite likely haste and eagerness will lead to an overplaying of the roles of the new culture. The immigrant acts in too American a fashion, goes too native, and finds that his sincere efforts earn him laughter and ridicule. Where he masters the external forms of new behavior he may nevertheless run into difficulty by missing their meaning. In this way adjustment becomes complicated.

The children born after parents have experienced the transition from a homogeneous to a heterogeneous environment confront what Mead calls "full secondary culture contact" but which might also be labeled *tertiary heterogeneity*. Sometimes the child continues to live in the past, identifying himself with his "old-fashioned" parents. More likely he will leave parents behind to "migrate" into the next generation, culturally speaking, and assimilate the manners and attitudes of his peers. The process of adjustment often requires suppressing completely all of the values learned from parents. This child reveals a characteristic pattern of development, whether he be an American Indian attending a missionary boarding school, a Kibei in San Francisco, or a Puerto Rican growing up in New York City. Life for him lacks the consistency felt by the youngster who grows up in a homogeneous community (Mead, *1949b:27*):

Each act which the child encounters as he is fed, bathed, dressed, hushed to sleep, and wakened again may stem from some different background, and there may be no consistency between any two of them. Gentleness of touch and ferocity of corrective methods alternate without meaning, and rewards and punishments follow no recognizable sequence. Clothes are unadapted to activities, furniture unadapted to ways of sleeping and sitting. . . . A hand held out for help may meet instead a slap, a pinch, a lollipop.

In underdeveloped countries, for example in West Africa, rapid culture change creates a gap between generations similar to that which occurs in the United States. On the modern Gold Coast a schoolgirl confronts her illiterate mother with problems the like of which the older woman has never encountered. The traditional patterns of childrearing, a native observer points out, were designed to teach the child approved ways of the community. "These approved ways do not always meet the new situation, and the lack of definite standards makes parental supervision diffident. Parents blame the teachers, and teachers the parents for the 'misbehaviour' of school-girls, though sometimes a 'misbehaviour' just means non-conformity to the ways traditionally approved by the community" (Busia, 1950:38).

Character Structure and Heterogeneity

In a heterogeneous community people with diverse personality attributes come into frequent contact. Industrialization and colonization in all parts of the world have led to the intermixture of persons representing highly disparate cultural traditions. "Character types that would have been well adapted to their situation find themselves under pressure from newer, better-adapted types" (Riesman, 1950:32). New values are introduced to these "cultural migrates" and they strive for goals even though lacking culturally prescribed means for attaining such ends. People who can't learn or relearn quickly enough find themselves deprived of jobs and opportunities because their personality is "not right."

In America the rapid culture change of the nineteenth century has promoted a plight for the inner-directed individual trained to respond to steady, internalized values and a personal sense of discipline. The inner-directed person, who possesses a relatively inflexible gyroscopic standard for judging success and morality, finds himself in a diversified social milieu that calls for something else. The other-directed personality came into being in response to the problems presented in this new social environment. Other direction means a personality possessing something like a radar system, "a device not tuned to control movement in any particular direction while guiding and steadying the person from within but rather tuned to detect the action, and especially the symbolic action, of others" (Riesman, 1950:55). The other-directed personality has been socialized not so much to rely upon his own rigorous standards and values but is trained to respond flexibly to the standards of whatever group he finds himself in. Skills of gregariousness and amiability become of paramount importance in other direction. In our heterogeneous world we have learned to train our children always to do their best—whatever that best may turn out to be. In fact, judgment of what is best is largely left up to the group rather than built into the character structure.

Riesman believes that the modal American personality in general is steadily moving toward increased other direction. Inevitably such development implies an interim when inner- and other-directed people will interact in the same situations. This is the case in our heterogeneous communities today where other-directed canons of success conflict with the values held by inner-directed people. Often the inner-directed type is forced into resentment and rebellion. He refuses to adjust to the behavior held out to him because of intense moral disapproval. Inability to hold jobs under such conditions is frustrating. Parents who are inner directed run the risk of failing to train their children for successful cultural participation. "Under the new conditions of social and economic life parents who try, in inner-directed fashion, to complete the internalization of disciplined pursuit of clear goals run the risk of having their children styled clear out of the personality market." The inner-directed person finds himself not sufficiently flexible "for the rapid adaptations of personality that are required . . ."

Margaret Mead (1949b) defines some of the consequences for personality development under conditions of tertiary cultural heterogeneity. Mainly she is concerned with those nuclear areas of the personality called "character structure." Some of the characterological signs accompanying growth in a highly heterogeneous environment appeared also in Plains Indian children in the seventeenth century. Their rearing took place in an era after the arrival of the horse, an era of great dislocations in the way of life of those former hunters and gardeners. Among the personal consequences of intense heterogeneity the following appear to be most significant:

1. Children grow up with a situational or tentative attitude toward life. They neither seek nor expect coherence. Situations are sharply polarized and unrelated. The relationships of home to school, of work

to play have become so unclear in America that these topics have become the subject of numerous conferences and papers. Such meetings are designed to restore some feeling of coherence and unity between sharply polarized segments of community life.

2. Cultural heterogeneity is associated with a tendency to reduce values to some simple quantitative scale, like dollars and cents, or the size of one's name in neon lights, or the number of points accumulated toward demobilization. In such ways the incommensurableness of diverse and relatively unfathomable values, careers, and goods are superficially reduced. A measure of common order and experience appears. The immigrant mother who cannot understand what her daughter is learning in school can nevertheless use a scale of letters extending from *A* to *F* to estimate and compare her child's performance. Among the American Indian the introduction of the horse led to new ways of warfare. A simple solution for evaluating performance in war became "counting coup." A man kept a careful mental record of heroic deeds which were themselves standardized in order of significance.[1]

3. The capacity to organize experience in a heterogeneous community is replaced by an interpretation of the outside world as something atomized into thousands of unrelated bits. Atomization can be understood as following from an education in which the child no longer learns "a coherent set of culturally interrelated experiences to guide his perception." Remember how moral beliefs are learned in Prairie City (Havighurst and Neubauer, *1949*)? Readers will recall that the meaning of right and wrong is taught with reference to concrete acts of behavior and is characterized by a high degree of specificity. No embracive moral philosophy exists that would relate specificities to a single system of value. We live at a time when philosophers are looking for new systems of coherency to relate such things as the dozens of varying kinds of ritual in churches, associations, and ethnic groups; the diverse philosophies that compete with one another by stressing their diversity, and incongruent styles in

---

[1] See also Mead, *1942a*, chap. 7.

dress, writing, and architecture that are often completely unintelligible to, or violently rejected by, their partisan followers.

4. Just as the American child in consequence of the heterogeneity of his milieu learns to see the world as fragmented into unrelated bits so the covert areas of his personality are unsystematically fragmented, incoherent, less secure in their integration, less able to resist strain, and responsive to the propagandist who promises a coherent world. It may be that the recent spread of fascism as well as the incidence of schizophrenia in the modern world are related to the atomization of the inner world.

American culture reveals some patterns of behavior that function to reduce the strain of internal fragmentation and aim to cement together the subjectively perceived, atomized bits of the external world. Reduction of values to a quantitative scale constitutes such a device, one recommended by the process of rearing unknown children for an unknown world. Allowing self-demand to govern feeding, weaning, and other maturation habits represents a philosophy well suited to a world where representatives of different cultures living side by side are uncertain about adhering to any schedule. The child's physiological rhythms and emerging capacities serve as a guide for instituing various types of training. It is possible, of course, that self-demand may increase the insecurity and incoherence of the child's world. This is an objection sometimes raised to self-demand scheduling. Progressive education abandons to a large extent the authoritarian direction of the teacher for the self-direction of the pupil and takes the child's interests as a reliable guide to his readiness for learning. It is a movement that may be regarded as another product of a relativistic world. The point system of demobilization followed after World War II developed as a result of asking soldiers how they thought they ought to be treated. In other words, self-admitted proprieties guided the traditionally authoritarian military system (Stouffer *et al.,* 1949:7). Social science itself, finding regularities in diverse systems of human behavior and relating geographical, technological, sociological, and other variables also functions to restore coherence in modern heterogeneous society, reducing subjectively perceived fragmentation. The rise of social work and psychiatry can be similarly understood.

Heterogeneity and Disease

Margaret Mead (*1949c*) suggests that the degree of pathology in a community is related to the extent of cultural heterogeneity. Homogeneity, however, does not mean an absence of disease. "In the most homogeneous culture we may expect to find consistent slight pathologies, as well as consistent and systematic somatic modifications." Particular individuals who are subject to unique and severe pressures or who are constitutionally more vulnerable to strain than other individuals will demonstrate some aggravation of the consistent pathology.

Under conditions of heterogeneity, on the other hand, there appears "an exuberance of somatic expressions of varieties of psychic conflict or peristent character strain." Mead explains the increase in varieties of psychosomatic disorder asserting that "in a heterogeneous culture, individual life experiences differ so markedly from one another that almost every individual may find the existing cultural forms of expression inadequate to express his peculiar bent, and so be driven into more and more special forms of psychosomatic expression."

IMPERSONALITY AND THE INDIVIDUAL

Carrying on a large part of one's activities among strangers may contribute to a personality characterized by feelings of being misunderstood, unappreciated, and of lowered morale. In such an environment people may come to channelize intense affection on a few intimates who then become very essential in the individual's life (Honigmann, *1949c*).

There is little point in condemning impersonality. Too many of us value the privacy it affords and many of us in cities would not readily surrender anonymity for the curiosity, gossip, and intimacy of a small town. An unwalled Samoan house would fill many New Yorkers with dismay. Many urban people feel content to live without knowing the producers of the goods they buy, the administrators on whom they depend, or the artists whose performance stimulates them. Impersonality remains essential to a modern industrial community and if it were done away with, then our system of mass production would become impossible. It is facetious to think of a factory in which people are treated as distinctive individuals all the time rather than as the assembly room, repair shop, or office force. Production would slow down tremendously if tasks were assigned specifically to John Smith and Fred Brown. How could the administration of modern nations be accomplished unless planning were done for large, unknown categories of the population?

Impersonality, however, has consequences that complicate our living together and often, like strikes, interfere with maintaining the supply of goods on which social organization depends. Life holds special difficulties when someone is forced constantly to try to gauge the character of strangers. We are familiar with the child who, through error in his judgment of strangers, is led into a traumatic episode but it is perhaps not so evident how often the adult is also inexpert in his appraisal of character. Partnerships in business, teamwork with management, and marriages dissolve when a person discovers that he has been taken advantage of by someone whom he too late came to know. Perhaps we don't yet possess the required skills for living in an impersonal world. The popularity of psychology in colleges and lending libraries may be related to the American's groping toward such skills.

Marriages need not be the implementation of chicanery and exploitation in order to fail. Freed from families, young people in this country arrange marriage on other than grounds of deep mutual understanding. Infatuation and the excitement of romantic love have become guarantees against the danger of mismating. That they actually do not serve this function shows up in statistics of divorce. No culture gives perfect protection against temperamental differences cropping up and leading to divorce. It has been left to the rising tide of impersonality (in which the parents of the bride and groom, if they meet at all, meet as even more remote strangers than the contracting parties) to add new hazards to family unity. Living in isolation against strangers, the problems of the couple become magnified when they lack close knowledge of other couples who are weathering similar storms. The demand for privacy in our world, which is merely another index of impersonality, effectively keeps our troubles from becoming the concern of friends whose accumulated experience might help to solve dilemmas for which no one person's experience is wholly sufficient.

The factory represents an organization which contributes to the impersonality of the Western world. In the factory the impact of anonymity on personality can be studied as in a laboratory. The prodigious development of efficiency in these industrial establishments allows the most refined calculations about such things as the effect of absenteeism on production. But when the individual absentee has become a statistical point he also ceases to exist as a person. His working day is spent in a world rich in positions—foremen, engineers, managers—but poor in groups. Almost inevitably, people working together find themselves encountering differences of opinion and similar problems. In the medieval shop such difficulties were settled on a personal basis. The partners knew each other. Problems appear less serious and last more briefly when their roots are evident in the expected peculiarities of Hans Schmidt. In the modern factory, impeded communication between workers and their managers complicates the solution of difficulties. The worker believes that a gripe to the foreman will lose itself somewhere between the foreman and the big shots. Yet his needs remain unmet and so the worker's helplessness and frustration come to be expressed in the dread that packs his stomach each morning when it is time to go to work. He may contrive ways of exerting power, power becoming compensation for unheeded problems. Then we have the struggle for power and recognition embodied in demands for altered wages, working conditions, and union recognition. Nobody will deny that other grievances disturb the work relations of modern industry but we have long failed to see strikes as at least partly rooted in individuals who are overlooked as persons.

Cultural adjustments to problems of impersonality have already been devised and we may expect still further development of those islands of helpfulness that dot our community. Staffed by experts of varying professional hues, the marriage clinics in cities, personnel counselors in factories, probation officers, social workers, and similar agencies offer the guidance, advice, kindliness, and help that kin groups and friends provide in more intimately organized communities.

The lessons of impersonality and heterogeneity indicate that human personality is not the product of atomistic social relations added up one to another. Rather patterning is a function of the total social situation through which the individual moves in time. The quality attached to interpersonal interaction is as important for understanding patterning as the content of that interaction. For the student of personality *how* people talk must receive as much attention as what they say. We continue this lesson by examining the impact of demographic and associated social qualities on character structure and personality.

CHARACTER STRUCTURE AND POPULATION

Starting with the assumption that character structure is socially conditioned, David Riesman (1950:7–9) proceeds to look for relationships between "the population growth of a society and the historical sequence of character types." By examining the pattern of industrialization he secures evidence of an s-curve of population growth and distribution. Communities of "high growth potential" are to be found at an early point curve and are heavily weighted toward younger age groups. Birth and death rates both remain high in such communities and the generations succeed each other rapidly. A community at a later place on the curve, in the phase of "transitional growth," feels the weight of middle-aged groups and as a rule experiences low birth and death rates. Finally, we have communities that have passed through these earlier phases of development and are starting to experience a net decrease in population. Their phase is one of "incipient population decline." From the individual standpoint these demographic processes reflect variations in survival chances, availability of food, and reproduction of offspring. Riesman expects that these conditions are related to personality and demonstrates how each of the three phases of the population curve encourages a particular style of personality. Groups with high growth potential develop "tradition-directed people," transition groups develop "inner-directed people," and communities showing incipient population decline produce persons who are "other-directed." A summary of the author's thesis appears in Table 5.

The three phases of social organization may be compared by saying that the tradition-directed person has his culture mediated by a relatively small number of persons whom he knows intimately and who control his behavior with the aid of shame. The inner-directed person, however, imbued with family-learned principles, is fitted to receive signals from authorities who resemble his parents. He goes through life obeying an internal pilot which, whenever he gets off course, calls him back by initiating a feeling of guilt. The other-directed person responds to signals from a wide social area in which the distinction between the familiar and the strange has broken down. Says Riesman (*1950:25*), "As against guilt-and-shame controls, though of course these survive, one prime psychological lever of the other-directed person is a diffuse *anxiety*" that may correspond to what psychoanalysts refer to as fear of the loss of love. The reader will recall from previous sections that it is quite possible for a cross-section of a population to reveal simultaneously both earlier and later character types.

PERSONALITY AND CIVILIZATION

Rather than use the term *civilization* synonymously with *culture*, as is sometimes done, we propose to restrict the word to designate a very complex culture. If we can distinguish between relatively small- and large-scale societies, then a civilization is to be found at the latter end of a continuum (Wilson and Wilson, *1945:24–26*; Odum, *1953*).

A small-scale society comprises relatively few interdependent people, living in linked communities, participating for satisfaction in a relatively narrow circle of human relationships. The communities are themselves small in scale, containing few groups or associations. Mem-

TABLE 5. Characterological Correlates of Population Movements

Demographic Condition	Other Social Characteristics	Character Structure and Personality
Birth and death rates equally high. Any decline in mortality rates permits population growth heavily weighted on side of the young. This condition found in contemporary India, Egypt, and China.	These are stable communities marked by long enduring, slowly changing culture patterns and a stable social structure. Even deviants, like the shaman, are sometimes fitted into social roles.	People are tradition directed, with a tendency to follow traditional forms. Only to a limited degree are decisions regarding life goals felt to be open to choice. Attention is focused on securing external conformity and overt obedience.
Usually, due to sanitation, more food, or trade, a decline in mortality takes place without any drop in fertility. Population proceeds to increase rapidly, as in Europe between 1650 and 1900.	The rising population puts great pressure on the adaptive efficiency of the culture. There is an increase in personal mobility; rapid accumulation of capital, expansion of production, exploration, and colonization; and an increase in the functional division of labor.	Inner direction becomes the principal mode of securing conformity. Strict adherence to tradition ceases to be necessary: "... the source of direction ... is implanted early in life by the elders and directed toward generalized but nonetheless inescapably destined goals." In association with the many novel situations presented to the individual an internal system of channeling choice—"a psychological gyroscope"—is instituted. Tradition continues to limit choice but is "splintered" by the "increasing division of labor and stratification." This type of character persists today in the "'old' middle class—the bankers, the tradesman, the small entrepreneur."

Demographic Condition	Other Social Characteristics	Character Structure and Personality
In the period of incipient population decline the birth rate follows the death rate downward. The community moves toward a time when the birth rate will plunge below the lowered death rate, so that the total population will decline.	The decrease in progeny is accompanied by profound changes in values. Children cease to be an economic asset. With the growth of scientific thought rational thinking about reproduction is substituted for religious and magical views. Hours of work are short, people have material abundance and leisure. Industrialization, service industries, and bureaucratic organization distinguish the community, which is further marked by a high rate of literacy obtained through compulsory schooling.	Other direction supplies a psychological mechanism for securing conformity. The character type may be seen in the large cities of the United States, among the young and upper income groups, as well as in bureaucratic and salaried employees. Much of the culture comes to be experienced "through a screen of words." The peer groups become more important to the child whose goals are social popularity and approval. Known and impersonal contemporaries become the important sources of direction for the individual. The goals shift readily even though great sensitivity to the signals of others remains unaltered.

SOURCE: Adapted from Riesman, 1950:9–24.

bers enjoy limited control over the material environment and the amount of wealth is not great. A large-scale society includes many people who remain in interaction over a wide area through trade, war, or political administration. The communities in such a society tend to be more complex and contain a multitude of groups and associations. The members enjoy greater control over the material environment obtained through the development of scientific procedures. People possess considerable wealth. In short, civilizations are rich, powerful, and characterized by impersonality.

The Individual in Civilization

It is common to hear that the cultures of small-scale communities more than civilizations restrict individual variation. In the former it it said that "the individual is much more rigidly limited ('determined') regarding his thinking and behavior. Primitive human society, Mead[2] claims, 'offers much less scope for individuality—for original, unique or creative thinking and behavior on the part of the individual self within it or belonging to it—than does civilized human society . . .' He goes on to say that the evolution of civilized society 'has largely depended upon or resulted from a progressive social liberation of the individual self and his conduct . . .'" (Mullahy, 1950:436).

Since a large-scale community can borrow freely in a wide society it attracts immigrants and travelers with diverse ideas and behaviors, develops greater trade and specialization, and enjoys greater variety in art, dogma, and recreation. It follows that a civilization boasts a greater number of roles and patterns of behavior than occur in the culture of a small-scale group. Such diversity in culture, however, often is not associated with a proportionately greater opportunity for individual expression. The many diverse behavior patterns may not be available for anyone to choose and use. This is the case when the positions of a social structure are not equally accessible to all of the community's members. Birth, aptitude, skill, training, as well as

[2] The reference is to George Mead.

temperament or inclination may determine who will occupy what status. Inasmuch as civilized communities commonly contain castes and classes that constitute relatively segmented areas of living, each with its own limited number of alternative patterns of behavior, it follows that stratification further limits opportunities of cultural participation.

A large village in western Pakistan possesses far greater cultural variety than a trading post settlement in northern Ontario or in Yukon Territory. Potters spin their wheels, cultivators labor with trowels and plows, women milk buffaloes and churn butter, carpenters repair water wheels, the blacksmith hammers at his forge, and weavers make homespun to peddle in surrounding villages. Meanwhile shopkeepers sit and drowse, landlords lounge and gossip, and schoolchildren chant in both Urdu and English and sometimes also Arabic. Yet any one citizen of the village cannot participate in even half of these activities. A potter has no use for plows or cultivation, cannot afford to send his children to school even if free, and knows he is not welcome to lounge with the gentry even if his time permitted. His experience of variety, however, is definitely richer than the Kaska Indian's. Men tend to follow not only the occupations of fathers in rural Pakistan but are limited by convention, time, and financial means to patterns of behavior that have come to be regarded as proper to their social stations. A villager's freedom may be greater than the Eskimo's in terms of potential choice but actually many men never leave the village of their birth or the occupation of the lineage.

It seems safe to conclude that large-scale communities vary in terms of how freely they facilitate participation in cultural roles and patterns or in how tightly they restrict taking advantage of diversity. Examination would probably show a bimodal distribution between rigid civilizations allowing little choice for individuals and those allowing greater freedom. No culture, however, makes freely accessible all of its elements to every member of the community.

It may seriously be argued from another perspective whether the more diversified culture automatically allows for greater individual choice in all walks of life. Observers tend to agree that a high degree of conformity is an outstanding feature in American civilization. Conformity hardly suggests individuality and must be kept in mind when discussing the diversity of our overall culture. Conformity may rise and fall with respect to certain areas of life. Little conformity to religious practice is demanded in urban America but the strict punishment reserved for sexual deviation and the hounding of political nonconformists following World Wars I and II illustrate how rigidly we suppress free choice of sexual and political behavior.

The alleged suppression of individuality in small-scale communities is by no means universal. William Wallace (1947) points out that the Hupa Indians of California are tolerant of personality deviation "because they believe that a man acts differently or wrongly because one of his ancestors did likewise and he cannot really help himself." In association with such relative tolerance of nonconformism the range of individual variation may be quite broad.

Objective and Subjective Complexity

Ernest Beaglehole (1949:256) emphasizes the importance of distinguishing between the objective complexity of a culture and its subjective impact on the person. An objective definition of complexity allows the anthropologist to count various features of a culture and then numerically to assess the way of life as more or less simple in comparison to some other. Subjective complexity is *postulated* for the members of the community and is more difficult to demonstrate. Are civilizations subjectively more complex than their simpler, contemporary cultures? Mead (1949b) in her work on heterogeneity suggests an affirmative answer to this question.

Beaglehole is not convinced of the thesis that in objectively complex cultures the subjective complexity of the "carrier" is also great— that such people have a rich and varied experience by virtue of living in a highly varied sociocultural environment. Rather he suspects that an individual will always "give meaning to his cultural forms on the basis of a psychological awareness that is everywhere in every society limited by inertia, custom, and habit." In other words, by participating in relatively delimited segment of community life the person's inner awareness of culture comes to be approximately the same in small- and large-scale groups.

The same author recommends that when intercultural comparisons are necessary we compare to some small-scale community not that abstract thing which nobody wholly encompasses—"modern civilization"—but rather that we take a specific subculture in modern society and compare it to a particular exotic culture. Such a method will indicate, he believes, that the diversity of modern culture as subjectively experienced is far less than we ordinarily believe.

Civilization and Socialization

We have several times mentioned the greater problems of adjustment faced in large-scale communities despite their relative abundance of adaptive resources. This tenor of speaking has carried us well along to where we shall want to ask questions about the relationship of mental illness to specifiable features of group membership because the state of mental health is also an aspect of personality.

However, there is one final problem to consider. Do special difficulties attach to the socialization process in an objectively complex civilization that are not found in simpler communities? Nadel (1951:96) believes they do. He points out that the diversity of statuses in large-scale communities poses special problems of training and fitting persons to occupy those positions. The quality of intimacy in the small-scale community in association with the relatively limited number of available positions to be filled combine to assist in the firm modeling of nearly every individual for the positions he will occupy. In modern life statuses are "less well or less directly known." Heterogeneity means that the individual cannot predict many statuses of later life, therefore cannot adequately prepare or be fitted for them. Our high degree of diversity, therefore, causes us frequently to be unsuccessful or incomplete in preparing persons for their future social roles.

Nadel's conclusion makes no allowance for the effectiveness of an other-directed personality in satisfactorily learning proper roles on relatively short notice. Other people, however, have also pointed out the educational shortcoming which he describes. Apparently role training is an area of modern civilization in which our educational skills require elaborate development.

Suggestions for Further Reading

"Plural society" is a concept sometimes applied to heterogeneous communities in which contrasting behavior patterns clash with each other and in which persons reared by homogeneous values are confronted with valuational and other kinds of diversity. Barnes has written on a plural tribal society in "History in a Changing Society" (*1951*), and Irvin Child describes tertiary heterogeneity in *Italian or American?* (*1943*). Williams' paper, "A Psychological Study of Indian Soldiers in the Arakan" (*1950*), discusses administrative problems fostered by heterogeneous values in a nation like India. Mayo's work is of fundamental significance in the study of human factors in industrial situations. *The Social Problems of an Industrial Civilization* (*1945*) may be recommended for the general reader. In *Faces in the Crowd* (*1952*) Riesman has published a second book on inner- and outer-directed people in America; it consists primarily of interview material. Common fallacies in talking about personality and its development in large- and small-scale communities are examined in Seeman's "An Evaluation of Current Approaches to Personality Differences in Folk and Urban Societies" (*1946*). Questions concerning the range of cultural participation may lead some readers to Kluckhohn's study of "Participation in Ceremonies in a Navaho Community" (*1949c*). This is one of the very few studies of its kind. An interesting exercise in qualitatively measuring sociocultural change is promised by taking the Victorian Era as a base line and comparing it to the modern Euroamerican community. A useful reference work for this project would be *Ideas and Beliefs of the Victorians* (*1950*).

PART FIVE

PSYCHIATRIC PROBLEMS

Chapter 15

GROUP MEMBERSHIP AND
PERSONALITY DISORDER

The careful definition of terms is no less fundamental for maintaining logical order in scientific discourse than it is important in philosophy. A trained, courageous philosopher adheres to his definitions even when they force him to make distinctions between, or to class together, things in a way that common sense finds difficult to tolerate. This steadfastness, so admired in men like Spinoza, is too little shared by social scientists (Hampshire, *1951*). It may be argued that the development of social science is retarded by the fact that it relies too heavily on common sense, often following the opinion of laymen or nonscientists who are subtly governed by deeply rooted prejudices.

Much confusion and contradiction have attended attempts to use concepts like psychopathology or personality disorder cross culturally. An outstanding textbook in anthropology claims that "the very definition of what is normal or abnormal is relative to the cultural frame of reference" (Herskovits, *1948*:66). Possession among African or New World Negroes, we read, cannot be considered psychopathological because the behavior is socially patterned. Here it is legitimate to object that the forms of illness encountered in psychiatric clinics and the content of neuroses and delusions also receive social patterning. Are they then not psychopathological? Herskovits indicates that by psychopathological he understands *undesirability* for he says that "such descriptions as hysteria, autohypnosis, compulsion, have come to rest easily on the tongue. Employed solely as descriptive terms their use in technical analysis of the possession phenomenon may be of some utility. But the connotation they carry of psychic instability, emotional imbalance, departure from normality recommends the use of other words that do not invite such a distortion of cultural reality." There is no reason why the vocabulary of psychiatry cannot be used with the same objectivity and freedom from distortion as labels of social organization like "class," "cross-cousin marriage," or "endogamous."

An attempt to relate psychopathology or personality disorder to group membership initially requires agreement on the signs by which such disorder may be recognized. The accepted definition must then firmly be adhered to or else we invite ill logic and self-contradiction. With the possible exception of the term "mental illness" for a special form of psychopathology, discussion of psychopathology will remain non-evaluative. Paraphrasing William James's observation, we assume that to classify a phenomenon as deriving from mental derangement decides nothing about the value of that phenomenon in a particular community. Psychopathological behavior, as recognizable by the following definition, may be socially functional or dysfunctional. The social dynamics of the behavior must be explored by the social investigator.

A DEFINITION OF PSYCHOPATHOLOGY

For present purposes a definition of psychopathology with cross-cultural or universal applicability is essential. The definition like a yardstick must serve the same purpose in whatever community it is employed. We shall define as psychopathological any behavior that meets one or a combination of the following eight signs:[1]

---

[1] The definition here advanced is adopted from Jules Massermann, *1946*. See in the glossary of that book terms like "neuroses," "anxiety syndrome," and "psychoses." Note the broad nature of our definition. Later a distinction will be drawn between relatively voluntary and involuntary psychopathology. Terms like "mental illness," "mental dis-

1. *Anxiety.* In first place as an indicator of psychopathology stands anxiety together with its physiological manifestations. These manifestations include a racing or pounding heart (palpitation); rapid, shallow, or difficult breathing; the sensation of a lump in the throat (globus); trembling; abdominal "flutters"; a sweaty, flushed, or pale skin; incontinence in severe attacks; and finally, feelings of apprehensiveness which may mount to a terrifying sense of impending catastrophe and panic.[2]

Now is the time to raise the question whether everyone does not at some time or other experience anxiety in one or another of these forms. Such is no doubt the case. It must be pointed out that although such states frequently occur in a population, they need not therefore be regarded as psychiatrically normal. Furthermore, episodes of anxiety may be highly transitory or they may persist and require extensive therapy to bring them under control. In either case psychopathology is indicated. Clinicians are agreed that no clear line separates the psychiatrically normal from the abnormal. For practical purposes they make the distinction of health and ill health a matter of degree, but not of kind.

2. *Defenses Against Anxiety.* Continuing with indicators of psychopathology, Massermann (1946:286–287) draws attention to "various pervasive *defenses* and *fixations*" that, while relatively incapacitating or handicapping, more or less protect the individual against the full realization of anxiety. Take, for example, the phobia, a morbid dread of some object, situation, or act. The phobic object often unconsciously symbolizes a previous experience productive of anxiety. Phobias may hamper living seriously. The Attawapiskat Cree Indian who feared to venture into a canoe or into the forest by himself faced a serious predicament in a community that allowed few alternatives to hunting and trapping as means of livelihood. Obsessions—

---

orders," or "behavioral disorders" are used synonymously to refer to involuntary psychopathology. Psychopathology or psychiatric abnormality is thus the larger category and includes both voluntary and involuntary disturbances of activity, thought, and feeling.

[2] Compare to the description of "catastrophic breakdown" in Maslow and Mittelmann, 1941:59–60, 106, 174.

persistent conscious ideas or desires—likewise defend against anxiety. The victim generally recognizes his obsession to be irrational. Finally, compulsions guard against anxiety. Handwashing constitutes one of the most familiar compulsions, the washing perhaps being a means of undoing a preceding "dirtying" act, like masturbation (Fenichel, 1945:289).[3]

3. *Sensorimotor Dysfunctions.* Often anxiety comes to be associated with sensory, motor, or organ (i.e., psychosomatic) dysfunctions. The incapacity may then represent a crippling adaptation to the threatening emotion. That is to say, as long as the symptoms remain, conscious anxiety is minimized and obsessive or compulsive states are avoided (Massermann, 1946:287). Preceded pages have brought out how anxiety and guilt about sex relationships, for example, may express themselves through impotence or frigidity, dysfunctions that automatically preclude or discourage the performance of the sex act. Sensorimotor dysfunctions also include symptoms like muscular weakness and easy fatigability, inertia, aversion to effort, and general aches and pains to which some psychiatrists apply the name "neurasthenia." Soldiers in battle are sometimes the unwilling victims of these symptoms.

4. *Neuroses and Psychoses.* Anxiety, its manifestations, and those relatively incapacitating defenses against it like phobias and sensorimotor incapacities all constitute behaviors which psychiatrists group as neurotic. Massermann distinguishes the psychoses from neuroses by seeing the former as "a group of relatively grave disorders of behavior most of which satisfy the legal criteria of *insanity* in that the patient is unable to care for himself and/or constitutes a danger to others" (Massermann, 1946:293). Chronic attachment or severe attacks of the following behaviors identify a psychosis or a psychotic epsiode:

5. *Reality Distortion.* When the person loses contact with reality or experiences marked distortions of reality as that state is defined in

---

[3] Such compulsions have a wide distribution, having been found in Europe and America. The author encountered an instance of compulsive handwashing among the Attawapiskat Cree in northern Ontario.

the group to which he belongs, we encounter another indication of psychopathology. Reality distortion as used here may manifest itself in thought disorders, visionary hallucination, and auditory or other delusions. Clearly, hallucinatory and other distortions may deliberately be induced through the use of drugs and alcohol, an aspect of the matter to be examined more closely later.

Examples of reality distortion in a non-European milieu are contained in the following two cases reported from the Gold Coast, West Africa (Tooth, 1950:34–35, 46–47). One reason for selecting material from an exotic community is to make very clear that all peoples recognize delusional thinking. The first report illustrates a relationship between personality disturbance and what anthropologists call "culture contact," a topic about which more will be said in chapter 16.

A Ga schoolteacher, aged 40, came from a strictly religious family with a good record of intellectual achievement and, so far as could be ascertained, no history of mental illness. He was educated at one of the Mission schools in Accra, did unusually well and was eventually appointed to his old school as a teacher. At the age of 25 he became attracted to a girl whose moral standards were not approved of by his parents. He stated, and there is no reason to disbelieve him, that up to this time he had had no sexual experiences, in his own words "I thought I was an impotent man." Permission to marry this girl was refused and a more eligible fiancee was provided by his parents. But one night, when his father was away from home, she came to the house and seduced him; when it became obvious that she was pregnant, he married her to avoid a scandal. But this irregularity came to the ears of the Mission, he lost his job and was transferred to a small school in another district. He was happy in his home life but felt that he had disgraced his family and fallen out of favor with the Mission, his work suffered and more moves followed. He became worried about his future and started to read books on mysticism and to cultivate the society of a reputed mystic. In this setting his psychosis started; he felt that "the ego" of his wife was troubling him, and on one occasion, assaulted her at the command of the hallucinatory voices. He became convinced that his life was under control of "a guardian," that his thoughts were magnetised, and that he was "the centre of the world." Finally, he could no longer concentrate on his work and resigned his appointment. Shortly afterwards he became violent, was certified and sent to the Mental Hospital.

A Lobi woman from the Lawra district, aged about 40, was brought for examination by her brother who said that she had been in her normal good health until about three months before, when she was noticed to be whispering to herself and pointing to imaginary things. She talked nonsense and gave the impression that she was being persecuted by imaginary people.

Obviously it is no error for a shaman to see his familiars under conditions where his community expects that he will encounter them. On the island of Crete is Frangocastello where annually the villagers see a spectral army, the materialized souls of 385 soldiers who were killed in battle during the Greek War of Independence (Fielding, 1953). An Englishman was unable to verify this vision which has been credited to "mass auto-suggestion." Inasmuch as the community supports the hallucinator in this instance we cannot with full justification brand him as a distorter of reality. Similarly, it is not distortion for the Athapaskan Indian to believe in dangerous emanations coming from a corpse when his belief logically follows from the premises of the tribe. On the other hand, there is no doubt that the anxiety aroused by the Indian's belief is to some degree psychopathological. Here we see one way in which group membership conditions anxiety, often in order to protect the organization of the group itself.

6. *Distortions of Affect.* Persistent and severe disorders of affect such as are encountered in manias, depressions, extreme emotional blunting, or in "a lack of correspondence between affect and idea" (Massermann, 1946:293) comprise another category of symptoms indicative of psychiatric abnormality. The following case from West Africa illustrates mania (Tooth, 1950:34):

An Akwapem woman, aged about 36, had suffered for eight years from periodic attacks of mania, in which she would become restless, noisy and abusive, but only towards other women. In these attacks she would strip herself and try to pick quarrels with women in the street and the market. According to her mother, the illness started after she had been living with her husband, a prosperous business man in Cape Coast, for about five years. Both were Christians and they had been married "under the Ordinance," but the marriage was childless. Eight years ago, the husband had returned from a business trip bringing another woman with him; the patient refused to stay in the same house with her and came home to her family. For a while she was quiet and sad but later became excited and aggressive. Attacks of mania, alternating with mild depressive spells, have persisted up to the present time . . .

7. *Regression.* Behavior like extreme passivity in, or profound withdrawal from, social relationships; extreme aggressivity; and open masturbation or soiling constitute a category of acts which Massermann (1946:293) labels markedly regressive. The word *regression* indicates the author's belief that behaviors like these represent a falling back on "earlier and experientially more satisfactory modes of behavior" (296). Regression sometimes appears when a person ceases trying to cope with difficult problems in his life and lapses into helplessness or destructiveness.

8. *Personality Disintegration.* Psychopathology sometimes appears in erotic, hostile, or other impulses that exist severed from control. The individual becomes carried along in the tide of these urges, powerless to organize them or muster up control. Such severance may be transitory. Such is the case when some people come under the influence of alcohol. In some psychotics disintegration remains a chronic attribute of personality. The following incident drawn from the Kaska Indians illustrates a severe but temporary severance of control over behavior (Honigmann, 1949a:237):

7:22:45
An Indian woman had been drinking most of the night with white men. Early in the morning she rushed into the ethnographer's cabin, waking his family. Her hair was disheveled and emotionally she appeared to be in a state of intense agitation. She half fell, half threw herself on the floor alongside our bedding and began sobbing and moaning incoherently. Following attempts to comfort her, she finally quieted down and permitted herself to be led home. No sooner had a few clothes been taken off than she rushed out of the house in her petticoat

and stockinged feet. Sobbing anew she rushed into the home of a nearby white man and, climbing into his bed, began to kiss and lie on top of him. The man tried to urge her out of the building but she would not be persuaded. Instead she began to plead, saying: "You want full blooded Injun? You like full blood Injun? I like you." This began to annoy the white man who swore in anger and ordered her out of his home. At this point the woman reacted with even greater rage and began a stream of obscenity which provoked the man to try to push her out the open door . . .[4]

9. *Derangement of Intellectual Capacities.* Finally, the label "psychopathological" will be applied to any acute or chronic inability to perceive, interpret, or manipulate reality. Here is a form of dissociation again familiar in drunkenness and one that makes driving while intoxicated a hazardous performance. We are all familiar with the drunk who cannot judge distance, fails to remember what he has said, and cannot pick himself up when he stumbles. Chronic derangement of intellectual and other adaptive capacities occurs in organic cerebral diseases like cerebroarteriosclerosis (hardening of the arteries in the brain).

Psychiatry and Social Abnormality

These nine characteristics provide a relatively culture-free standard by which to recognize psychopathological behavior. They provide a definition of psychiatric abnormality in the same way that a dictionary provides the signs by which to recognize a cat, door, or house. Behavior will be classed as psychopathological when one or more of these criteria are manifested.

In an earlier chapter we spoke of deviants—individuals who noticeably overplay or underplay roles or who innovate socially approved and prohibited roles. Deviance can also be termed social abnormality but is theoretically distinct from psychopathology or psychiatric abnormality. The distinction between these concepts is important.

---

[4] This woman died from exposure on New Year's Day, 1950. She had apparently become intoxicated and frozen to death in subzero weather.

Social abnormality always exists relative to a group inasmuch as it designates behavior which conspicuously departs from the norms of a specific community. Our definition of psychiatric abnormality leaves such behavior largely independent of specific groups. Social and psychiatric abnormality are not *necessarily* the same thing, even though the two phenomena may overlap. The following propositions will clarify the distinction between the two types of abnormality:

1. Particular states of psychiatric abnormality may be regarded as quite appropriate in some particular community. If socially expected at periodic intervals such states—for example, trance or drunkenness—will simultaneously be normal socially as well as psychopathological.

2. Individuals prone to experience certain recurrent or even permanent psychopathological states may be rewarded or otherwise utilized in their community because of their idiosyncratic behavior. These persons, however, represent socially approved deviants who are also psychiatrically abnormal.

3. Social deviation may be expressive of, or it may encourage, psychopathology. For example, the disapproved nonconformist will be subject to fairly intense strain which can lead to anxiety feelings. Strong anxiety feelings may further be productive of compulsive behavior.

4. Of course, social deviance may exist without psychopathological counterparts. The unmarried concubines among the Nuer, women of strong character not desirous of matrimony, represent deviants yet are not noticeably psychiatrically abnormal. Incidentally, such women are recognized as temperamentally unfit for married life; their behavior is not stigmatized as immoral (Evans-Pritchard, *1951*:118).

The relationship between social and psychiatric abnormality deserves a good deal more exploration. How likely is it that abnormality in one sphere will more often than not be accompanied by abnormality in the other? Until the distinction between these two orders of phenomena is clearly understood it makes little sense to talk of a relationship between them. Once psychopathology is clearly defined, however, attention can be devoted to the social and cultural factors associated with that condition.

There is an impressive amount of evidence suggesting that membership in a particular community helps to determine the kind of psychiatric abnormality exhibited by a person. Such evidence will now be reviewed.

Specialized Psychopathologies

In this category belongs amok, a pattern of behavior first described for the Malays but also observed frequently among the Balinese, Fuegians, Melanesians, Siberians, and in India (Ackerknecht, *1943;* Van Loon, *1927*). Three stages are distinguishable in the disturbance as studied in Bali (Beaglehole, *1938*). The onset, marked by grief, may follow the thwarting of some desire. Depression in turn gives place to confusion, retirement from the world, and brooding; the individual appears to be nursing his grievances. Finally comes the stage where the person, worked up into a trancelike condition, mobilizes all of his energies and rushes to commit bloody violence. Beaglehole reasons that the Balinese, being an introverted people, in the second stage intensify their introversion as an attempt to cope with tension. The extreme withdrawal fails to produce relief and so extraversion, which in normal life remains limited to ceremonies and funerals, appears to facilitate the working off of tensions.

Lattah represents another relatively specialized pattern of psychopathology which has been reported not only for Malaya but also for the Philippines, Siberia, among the Ainu (where it ends in amoklike symptoms) and Eskimo, and perhaps also in Madagascar (Ackerknecht, *1943*:60–61). Among the Eskimo and Siberian natives *lattah,* or "Arctic hysteria," is usually limited to women. The disturbance is marked by echolalia and echopraxia, that is, the subject echoes everything said to him and mechanically repeats the gestures and actions of another person. In Europe and America similar compulsive imitation occurs in schizophrenia. Russian soldiers sometimes exploited the Chuckchi of northeastern Siberia by leading echopraxic victims toward a pond and at the last minute turning aside while the native tumbled into the water.

Resembling *lattah* is the behavior disorder in which Kaska Indians of the southern Yukon abruptly fled from their camps to sit in the snow (Honigmann, *1949a*:239–240). Such behavior is similar to Malayan women running into the jungle where they remain for some time and then return home with their clothes torn to shreds.

Pibloktoq, a disturbance affecting primarily women and never touching children, prevails among the Eskimo of western Greenland (Brill, *1913*:514–520). The form of the disorder markedly differs from subject to subject and varies from one seizure to the next. Generally the onset is marked by singing that increases in intensity until loss of consciousness ensues. Often patients will tear off their clothing, run out of the house, throw around objects, and imitate the calls of birds. Victims may show congestion of the head, bloodshot eyes, and foam from the mouth. Any opposition they encounter will generally be resisted violently. Brill believes the seizures stem from a want of love. He maintains that women who are ill treated by their husbands or who suffer from jealously show the greatest likelihood of being overcome by *pibloktoq.*

It is by no means certain that amok, *lattah,* and *pibloktoq* constitute fully specialized disorders. Symptoms from each syndrome are encountered in European and American psychiatric practice. Overlap between the syndromes is considerable, for example between *lattah* and *pibloktoq.* Hence it would seem that these patterns are less specialized than used to be thought. On the other hand the syndromes remain relatively distinct and incidence correlates with specific culture areas. Anthropology and psychiatry possess no adequate explanations to link these disorders to particular communities.

Cannibalistic Obsessions and Compulsions

Obsession with cannibalism or a compulsive craving for human flesh have been reported for certain Eskimo tribes and from the Marquesa Islands. The classical area of these symptoms, known as the *wiitiko* psychosis, lies between Lake Winnipeg and Labrador, that is, among the Cree and Ojibwa Indians of Canada's northland (Cooper, 1933:20–24). It is difficult to obtain clear accounts of the *wiitiko* psychosis. Anthropologists who have not seen a native affected by the disorder must rely on what they are told about the ailment by native informants. Such accounts generally indicate that the patient is seized by a craving for human flesh or an obsessive fear lest he be driven to eat such flesh. If the individual accedes to the compulsion and consumes this food there follows a belief that he has been transformed into a cannibalistic ogre with heart of ice—a *wiitiko*. Frequently stories of these terrifying beings are told among the Indians. Some anthropologists designate the belief of being transformed into a *wiitiko* to be a delusion. We cannot accept this designation because the belief is fully supported by the community. The belief in transformation itself is not diagnostic of psychopathology.

Ruth Landes's description (1938:24) differs slightly from the course of the *wiitiko* psychosis as outlined above. She sees the term *windigo* applying to "severe anxiety neuroses with special reference to food [that] manifest themselves in melancholia, violence, and obsessive cannibalism." The disturbance occupies two stages. In the initial phase a subject, generally someone who faces starvation in winter while he lives isolated in the bush, withdraws into melancholia. His misfortune may be ascribed to sorcery. The hungry man, Landes writes, "lies inert . . . brooding over the possibilities of cannibalism, wanting to eat men and yet afraid." He sees people in the guise of tempting animals. Sleep is poor. If care and nursing do not succeed in effecting relief then he enters the second stage, marked by the cannibalistic compulsion. Human flesh is eaten, ostensibly while the victim is possessed by a *wiitiko*. He believes that he has incorporated the ice-being's appetite. However, a victim with strong shamanistic power may direct violence against whoever sorcerized him. Such a man will not give in to cannibalism. Weaker persons, unable to resist cannibalistic compulsions, must be put to death to protect the community. It does not appear that Landes ever directly observed the progressive deterioration in behavior about which she writes.

While stories of forced cannibalism are common among the northeastern Indians the people themselves regard the act with abhorrence, even when carried out under necessity. The present writer during the course of field work in the James Bay area heard of people who had been forced by privation to eat human flesh but he did not hear every such individual described as a *wiitiko*. Saindon (1928:27–28; 1933:11), the missionary, speaks of having encountered a woman "suffering from 'Windigo.' She avoided any meeting with neighbors, would look at nobody, and transformed the persons around herself into animals. She refused to pray, spoke little, did not work, ate with reluctance, suffered, and despaired of being cured." Seeing the people around her in the guise of animals made her eager to kill the game. Yet she perceived that they were also human beings and so the idea of killing them was conflictfully repugnant.

Cooper (1933:21) emphasizes that the *wiitiko* disorder occurs among people who, while abhorring cannibalism, are sometimes driven to practice it when faced by starvation. He regards the craving for human flesh as "directly traceable to prevalent environmental and cultural conditions in the northeastern Canadian woodlands, where death by starvation has been relatively very common, perhaps more common than in any other part of the world, and where the native culture includes both a rigid taboo on and a profound horror of cannibalism."

Marquesans also speaks of people who become obsessed by fondness for human flesh. "Such a man would kidnap children of his own tribe or even kill and eat his own wife or children" (Kardiner, 1939: 142, 220–226). This behavior too has been related to food scarcity and attendant anxiety. In Marquesan communities people become anxious about being eaten by hungry neighbors and defend against such anxiety by developing their own cannibalistic tendencies.

Caution is necessary in considering the hypothesis that food scarcity is predictably linked with cannibalistic obsessions. The incidence of cannibalistic disorders among the Eskimo is much less than among the Cree. Are the Eskimo better provided with food than the Cree? The Athapaskan-speaking Indians of northwestern Canada, adjacent to the Ojibwa and Cree, share the latter's familiarity with starvation but cannibalistic disorders among Athapaskans are apparently rare in comparison to what occurs farther east (Cooper, 1946:296). It is indisputable that cannibalistic disorders appear more frequently in some communities than in others. That they have a root in group membership also seems beyond serious dispute. The conditions associated with this pattern of psychiatric abnormality need more investigation.

Thanatomania

While not limited to one or two regions of the globe, like the specialized psychopathologies, thanatomania illustrates well how group membership conditions sensorimotor dysfunctions. The term refers to illness or death resulting from belief in the efficacy of magic. A well verified and documented phenomenon, thanatomania demonstrates how deeply into organismic processes the influence of the group may reach.

Webster (1948:486) points out that "death madness" is quite common. "A man may die because he has violated some dread taboo or thinks that he has fallen into the clutch of malignant spirits. . . . A doctor may pronounce him doomed, perhaps because his soul has gone away and cannot be recovered. The patient accepts the inevitable and proceeds to die without delay." Thus in the community people's faith in sorcery may be periodically reinforced as sickness and death are repeatedly ascribed to sorcerers. The following case illustrates the speed with which a suggestion of black magic may take effect.

. . . Canon Roscoe, long a missionary in British East Africa, tells how three men were once brought to him to have their wounds dressed. Two of them had been badly clawed by a leopard, but the third bore only a scratch on the neck. "I attended to him last and after dressing his wound I said, 'There is not much the matter with you; you will soon be well.' To my surprise he said, 'I am dying.' Thinking he had got an exaggerated idea of his wound, I talked to him for a few moments and then dismissed them all, telling them to come again in the morning. Next morning two of the men came, but the third with the scratch on his neck was missing, and when I asked for him I was told that he was dead. He had gone home and, saying that he had been killed by magic, died in a short time. So far as it was possible to discover, no complications had arisen, but he was convinced that the animal had been caused by magic to attack him and the power of his imagination had done the rest."[5]

Cures from magical fright may be equally dramatic. Cannon (1942:170–171) gives the case of a converted native in North Queensland who was taken sick. A physician could find no fever or other symptoms of disease. It was explained, however, that the patient "had had a bone pointed at him by Nebo and was convinced that in consequence he must die." When the physician persuaded the alleged sorcerer to deny before the patient that he had pointed a bone "the relief . . . was almost instantaneous." That evening the patient was back to work, quite happy, and possessed of his strength.

Thanatomania is more than simply the consequence of knowledge that a sorcerer has been at work. A readiness to believe in sorcery must be present and is usually acquired in childhood. Only in the presence of deep-seated faith can sorcery achieve its dastardly effects.

How does thanatomania operate in the victim? The physiologist, Cannon, believes that the emotion of fear together with the profound physiological disturbances associated with intense fear can, if they endure, kill the organism. Inability to eat and drink while under the influence of strong fear, plus despair combine to induce tremendous emotional stress. Warner (1937), on the basis of field work among Australian natives, emphasizes the role played by interpersonal relations in thanatomania. The victim of sorcery sees his kinsmen withdraw all support from him. His neighbors alter their attitudes, regarding him as in a different category from ordinary mortals. The effect, of course, is to abandon the victim to his own depleted resources which are insufficient to sustain life. Even before death occurs the group begins to mourn. This symbolism of the victim cut off from the ordinary world and placed with the dead increases the suggestion of helplessness and finality.

---

[5] Quoted in Webster, 1948:488.

Communities which hold that magic can kill also believe that there are magical means of avoiding or throwing off the effects of sorcery.[6] Curative or countermagic operates by restoring confidence and often works with the same efficacy as sorcery (Mead, *1950b*:80).

Intoxication

A clear-cut relationship between group membership and psychopathology appears in the regular and socially patterned use of toxic agents like drugs and alcohol. Intoxication means the appearance of several of those signs of psychiatric abnormality listed above. Ritual and nonritual intoxication may be distinguished.

Ritual intoxication through drugs is exemplified by the peyote meetings that occur in several American Indian tribes (Brant, *1950*; LaBarre, *1938*; Malouf, *1942*). These all-night ceremonies include eating in prescribed fashion the green or dry buttons of a cactus plant imported from Mexico. Two stages of subsequent intoxication have been noted. In the first phase the peyote produces exhilaration, a sense of well-being, elation, and superiority, all accompained by talkativeness. Gradually incoherent speech and confusion of ideas become manifest. Disturbances of vision also follow and the "drunken" person experiences brilliant hues. The room or tent in which the rite takes place assumes the quality of a picture, indicating a disturbance in the perception of reality. The second phase of intoxication produces depression, a feeling of exhaustion, and lack of coördination of muscular processes (e.g., staggering). Apparently peyote does not interfere with rational thinking. The action of the drug, which has been demonstrated to be nonhabitforming, thus shows itself to be selective.

The Kiowa-Apache and other tribes too believe that peyote has curative properties. They explain that it relieves illness by bringing about God's intercession. Modern peyote meetings have taken the place of aboriginal shamanism. No trace of group disapproval attaches to peyote intoxication. While the use of the drug as well as the ac-

---

[6] See below, pp. 420–422.

companying ritual have long been under attack by Christian missionaries, the peyote users themselves have incorporated to form the Native American Church. In 1949 an Oklahoma radio station, which had allowed time for Baptist students to attack the peyotists, afforded the Indians an opportunity to reply to their detractors.

Some of the social functions of the peyote cult are indicated in the following passage (Brant, 1950:220):

> The peyote religion functions as an emotional outlet and partial integrating force in a situation which is generally characterized by extreme individualism, economic insecurity, and marked health anxieties. The absence of anything resembling an integrated tribal or intertribal community; the individualism, jealousies, and resentments engendered by the system of individual land allotments; the feelings of dependency fostered by paternalistic government control over social and economic matters—all these provide fertile ground for the growth of mutual suspicion and distrust between individuals and between groups. It is in this context that the peyote cult constitutes the religious symbol of what might be called a "Pan Indian" movement, asserting minority group solidarity within the larger cultural framework.

Our own community also induces intoxication on ceremonial occasions. The New Year's Eve celebration calls for ritual drunkenness. An United States Air Force bomb squadron studied by the author expected that officers would drink themselves into intoxication while celebrating the promotion of one of their number. Enlisted men sometimes also became intoxicated to celebrate a friend's birthday.

In Highland South America alcoholic intoxication forms an integral part of holiday behavior. E. C. Parsons (1945:122–123) reports that little or no stigma attaches to drunkenness and not the slightest feeling of guilt. People do not believe that immoderate drinking is regrettable and never condemn a person for any behavior while he is drunk. In the early stages of intoxication the drinker is talkative, lighthearted, and self-assured, speaking with self-confidence even to whites. Quite often "they go singing along the road, boasting of their merits or advantages." In the later stages of drunkenness some men go to sleep and others break into fighting, "springing about in the wildest way, challenging the other or shaking off the women who try to intervene."

Drunkenness may have magical consequences in the thinking of a community. Mild intoxication among the Papago represents a means of bringing " the longed-for rain that will make the fields green and bring food to the Desert People" (Joseph, Spicer, and Chesky, 1949:76). Wine "is a symbol of the renewal of life with the coming of rain and it is a purification of the mind and heart . . ."

Material collected by Ruth Bunzel (1940) in Central America suggests how a person's behavior under intoxication may be conditioned by cultural factors. She compares two towns, Chichicastenango in Guatemala and Chamula in Chiapas, Mexico. The former represents a wealthy market center whose standard of living ranks above the average for Central America. Land constitutes an important source of interpersonal stress. Family organization being patrilineal, the land belongs to the dead ancestors who permit descendants to use it. For this privilege the living must place candles and offerings at shrines and in churches. Bitter quarrels between brothers accompany the inheritance of land, each brother jealous lest he receive too little. The sons try to persuade the father to surrender the land before he dies but the head of the family resists. Ownership of the land gives the old man power and leaves him in a position to command his children's earnings as well as to dominate their lives. Another source of tension in Chichicastenango lies in the ancestors who punish sins by sending illness and death. The people further believe that every individual's life is linked to some animal that must not be killed by the linked individual lest the latter die. Yet nobody knows the animal to which his life is associated! People dread inadvertently killing the animal patron. From this short sketch we appreciate that Chichicastenango comprises an anxious group of people. The strains under which they live correlates with widespread suspicion of sorcery in interpersonal relations. Partial relief from the weight of all this tension occurs in drinking on market days and during festivals. People drink chicha, a fermented fruit juice, as well as aguardiente, distilled sugar water. Drinkers become very drunk and then sexual transgressions as well as quarreling become rampant. These acts will be punished by the ancestors, a consideration that scarcely serves to reduce frustration and strain. Small wonder that some men try to stay drunk, borrowing all they can to avoid the return of sobriety. Often they emerge from the spree battered, bloody, bruised, and suffering from terrific hangovers.

The Chamula people also have their anxieties but their way of life does not condition as much interpersonal frustration. Here there is nobody who, like the Chichicastenango father, seeks to cling to land and power, frustrating members of his immediate family. People place greater value on the sharing of wealth. They are not burdened by guilt. When these Indians get drunk they fall asleep. Although they also drink aguardiente they experience no hangovers. As a rule little quarreling marks intoxication except when fighting is initiated by deviant members of the community. Drinking and drunkenness are regarded as pleasant social experiences in Chamula.

Bunzel's work suggests the provocative hypothesis that aggression during intoxication, compulsive clinging to drunkenness, and hangover in a community are dependent on a high level of anxiety plus guilt that stems from drinking. Partial corroboration of this prediction is found in Horton's work (1943, 1945, 1953). He reports the strength of alcoholic aggression in a group to be connected with the importance of sorcery in that community. Sorcery constitutes a threat leading to the inhibition of normal aggressive impulses. The dissolution of cortical control under intoxication permits such impulses to escape despite the fear of sorcery. Horton finds that the presence of strong subsistence and acculturation anxieties, reflecting a low degree of cultural control over food production or over the actions of a dominant foreign group, also correlate positively with degree of insobriety. In general his study demonstrates a relationship between insobriety on the one hand and anxiety-inducing factors in the social environment on the other.

Alcoholic drinking may be relied upon in a community to promote interpersonal relations and coöperation toward important social goals. This is more or less the function of alcohol at a social party in the United States. Zingg (1942) points out that alcohol enables the

Tarahumara Indians of Mexico to escape from shyness and inhibition. Through intoxication the whole world is made kin. Drinking represents a basic condition for coöperative labor. Important for courtship and marriage it is also required for sociability, the curing of disease, and the performance of rites of passage or other ceremonies. Most of Tarahumara life pivots around drinking. Intoxication, however, gives the Indians an illusion of values that do not exist in reality and defeats the achievement of goals like surplus wealth or increased control over the material environment. Other dysfunctions also follow from heavy drinking, even in communities where it is approved.

Inebriation

Inebriety, a form of psychopathology marked by the compulsion to drink to intoxication, also relates to group membership. Glad (1947) points out that on the basis of available statistics American-Jewish and American-Irish males in the United States are at polar opposites as far as inebriety rates run. Low inebriety characterizes Jews in general while a high incidence of alcoholism marks Irish immigrants from rural Ireland as well as their lower-class descendants who "comprise the chief source of American-Irish population in the United States." The difference in degree of inebriety between these two ethnic groups is revealed in the fact that 3.0 percent of all Irish rejected for the Army on account of neuropsychiatric reasons were rejected for chronic alcoholism as compared with figures of 2.2 percent for Negroes, 1.2 percent for Italians, 0.6 percent for Portuguese, and 0.2 percent for Jews. Not a single Chinese rejected for neuropsychiatric reasons was rejected because of chronic alcoholism. To what can such differences be connected? Glad relates what appears to be a reliable difference in degree of inebriety between American-Jewish and American-Irish males to different experiences encountered by each category in the home. In each cultural tradition boys become exposed to different attitudes toward drinking. Jews tend to regard drinking as socially practical, as part of religion. The goals of drinking among Jews are thus removed from the effects of alcohol per se. The Irish, however, regard drinking more as a good way of promoting fun, pleasure, and conviviality. In other words, "the use of alcohol is directed toward states in which the physiological and psychological changes produced by alcohol are of prime importance." Enculturation of such attitudes toward the use of alcohol among the Irish appears to be favorable for the development of inebriation.

Group Membership and Psychosomatic Dysfunction

Sensorimotor impairments, it will be recalled, may be related to anxiety states that trouble the patient. Several workers have studied the relationship between group membership and psychosomatic dysfunction. Jurgen Ruesch (1953) finds membership in American social classes to be significantly related to form of disease and sees psychosomatic disorders particularly strong in the lower-middle class. Such dysfunctions are associated with the "excessive repressive tendencies" of that community. Illness enables lower-middle-class people to express their unsolved psychological conflicts. The lower classes, with their ability to discharge hostility freely and their exposure to machines, reveal a high incidence of fractures, accidents, and traumatic diseases. The author does not suggest that accidents in the lower class serve to solve psychological conflicts, as is the case with so-called accident-prone people (Dunbar, 1947, chap. 8). Upper-class people, burdened with an "overbearing superego and cultural traditions," according to Ruesch, manifest a relatively large incidence of neuroses and psychoses, especially of the manic-depressive type.

Clyde Kluckhohn (1949a:201) finds that "in the United States today schizophrenia is more frequent among the lower classes; manic-depressive psychosis is an upper-class ailment. The American middle class suffers from psychosomatic disturbances such as ulcers related to conformance and repressed aggression." In this connection it is of interest that Margaret Mead (1949c:534) predicts an increase in psychosomatic disturbances with increasing heterogeneity in a community. Such florescence of psychosomatic ailments, she says, represents a use of divergent idiosyncratic symptoms to express disorientation. Sometimes such divergence disappears in favor of standardization as when a hysterical movement sweeps the community and people adopt its forms of behavior.

A stimulating study shows how group membership and psychosomatic dysfunction are related in the coal mining community of England, whose way of life changed drastically in the last half century (Halliday, *1948*). Apart from tremor, anxiety, pallor, abdominal pain, and ulcers one of the dysfunctions rampant among the miners is nystagmus. This disease manifests itself in a continuous rolling of the eyeballs. Although no evidence exists to show that the ailment is transmitted by microörganisms, when sufferers joined a work group hitherto free of the affliction the disease began to spread to the unaffected members. Halliday sees these symptoms associated with the thwarted satisfactions that coal miners encounter in their work. The men have ceased to find tranquility on their jobs. Their frustrations are an outgrowth of the changes that have altered the mining community.

Previous to World War I the workers were "strong, hardy people" who dwelt in towns and villages located near the mines. They lived in relative isolation from the outside world. Their way of life possessed a high degree of homogeneity as well as personalism. People grew up, played, worked, and worshiped together. Sons followed their fathers into the mines. Friends remained together all their lives. A town presented a high degree of solidarity. Work in the mines was performed almost entirely by hand, the work groups setting their own pace. In the relatively quiet pits men could hear the cracking of strata that signalized a cave-in. Such a warning gave them an opportunity to escape from impending catastrophe. Miners were proud of their calling, feeling that what they produced constituted a social good. Through the years mechanization of the pits increased so that by 1930 almost 90 percent of English coal came to be removed by machinery. Quiet vanished from the pits and danger signs could no longer be heard for the noise of machines. Machinery stole the feeling of leisure and deprived men of the belief that they set their own pace. Miners came to feel that standards were being set by impersonal circumstances over which they lacked any control. Mechanization also broke down the traditional work groups at the same time that the towns lost their isolation from the outside world. In 1930 the depression came along and produced widespread unemployment which further threatened the security of the miners. Without jobs many felt confused. The mining community had become a sick society (Halliday, 1948:194):

> The social disintegration and the social ill-health of the "outer society" of the miner were reflected by corresponding happenings in his "inner society," in the form of emotional disintegration and psychological ill-health, manifested typically in neurotic and psychosomatic illness, poor working output, absenteeism, strikes, and even biological infertility. As the sickness of the community increased, the psychological ill-health of its members therefore also increased, as was shown by the rising prevalence of these disorders that was indicated by statistics.

Other Evidence of Group Influence on Psychopathology

Psychiatrists have long been aware that the content of delusions and the form of psychotic activity are patterned according to the culture of the patient's group. Delusions of grandeur in which the patients identified with Napoleon have been succeeded by identification with Hitler or Franklin D. Roosevelt. In the Northern Territories of the Gold Coast where culture contact has been slight the delusional system of psychotics is "almost invariably concerned with the ramifications of the fetish system. The fact of lunacy means that an offense has been committed either against the nature spirits, who then trouble the offender in the form of dwarfs or fairies, or against the ancestral hierarchy who appear and influence the sufferer in person." In the southern part of the Gold Coast the mentally sick more commonly identify with an anthropomorphic God. Here delusions of great wealth appear while radios and other similar instruments figure in psychotic thought (Tooth, 1950:52).

Possession can be termed psychopathological only if in that state the individual loses contact with his environment or if he feels himself possessed by forces not admitted to exist by the community.

Trance is closely identified with possession in that the subject may believe himself possessed while he is dissociated. It is clear that possession and trance do not appear with the same frequency in all communities, indicating again how group membership may influence psychopathology. Typical possession phenomena are encountered among the Khasas of the cis-Himalayan region where "persons suffering from abnormal or hypernormal mental conditions" respond during certain festivals "by shaking their limbs, particularly the head, and the speed of the movement increases with the speed of the drum beats, so that they soon lose control of their movements, foam at the mouth and start irrelevant talks" (Majumdar, *1944*:156–157). The possessed show remarkable strength, strip themselves naked, scarify their bodies, and eat or drink tremendous quantities before they finally faint or drop unconscious. Villagers regard the possessed with reverence because they shelter gods; the words they utter are the speech of gods. Note that it is the dissociated state that to us indicates psychiatric abnormality and not that the possessed believe they speak words of gods.

The acceptance of dissociation in a community plus the fact that trance or possession may be rewarded play a large part in determining the frequency of these behaviors. Among the Balinese, for example, trance may be turned on and off almost at will, even by children, and is widespread during ceremonies (Belo, *1949*). Stress experienced by the members of a group may also be associated with a high incidence of trance and possession. Belo (*1949*:12) says, "There can be no doubt that certain tensions and anxieties set up in the Balinese by the restraints, the fears, and the general inhibitory patterning of their emotional life are relieved by these outbursts." Ackerknecht (*1943*: 63–64) reviewing the literature notes that "periods and situations of heightened social tension like acculturation make for a tremendous increase in possession." Involuntary compulsions, like the "dancing mania" (choreomania) of the Middle Ages or of Thuringia in 1920 (L. Paul, *1952*) are sometimes referred to as possessions; their etiology is far from clear although we know that they spread across Europe like contagious diseases.

Tooth (1950:38) demonstrates how psychotic symptoms differ in frequency between West Africa and Europe and hence are apparently related to group membership. While depression in a European psychotic characteristically appears in company with self-reproach based on real or fancied shortcomings in West African psychotics self-reproach is very rare. In Europe self-accusation carries the risk of suicide which, as might be expected, is of negligible incidence in an African mental hospital: ". . . amongst 680 lunatics in the Accra mental hospital in 1947, there were only three cases of self-inflicted wounds and no successful suicide: this low figure is certainly not due to lack of opportunity." Even the psychoses associated with senescence and menopause are differently patterned between Europe and the Gold Coast. In Africa elation more likely than depression will appear in these illnesses. "The absence of depressed patients is most strikingly demonstrated by a casual visit to an African mental hospital where, under infinitely more depressing conditions, the atmosphere of tense unhappiness usually found in European mental hospitals is replaced by an unrestrained and misdirected exuberance of spirits."

Like Tooth, Carothers (1948) finds little evidence of depressive states among Africans in mental hospitals. He too reports absence of obsessional neuroses, arteriosclerosis, and ideas of guilt in involutional melancholia. "Frenzied anxiety" is common but he missed most of the types of anxiety witnessed in Europeans who become mentally sick. These differences from European patterns of disturbed behavior are ascribed to cultural factors although he does not dismiss the possibility of genetic endowment playing a role. Striking is the fact that in Kenya a large proportion of the cases of acute mania (at least 42 percent) had been holding responsible positions when they fell ill. Commenting on the absence of obsessional neuroses Carothers says that only when an individual is forced to stand alone in an individualistic social structure where he has to develop his own ethical code can such neuroses thrive. Concerning the absence of guilt in involutional melancholia he observes that ideas of guilt play small part in African personality which rather responds to the sense of shame. "There is thus no conception of universal truth or justice, or of right or wrong in any general sense, and in Raum's words, 'The child becomes conditioned to a morality whose demands become less stringent the remoter they are from the "initial situation" of the family.'" The preponderance of "frenzied anxiety" is explained by the inability of the African to sustain anxiety for long periods as well as by "ill-developed power of self-criticism with a constant tendency to look outside himself for the causes of misfortune."

India exhibits a very low frequency of schizophrenia, which European and American psychiatrists encounter two or three times as often as manic-depressive psychoses (Dhunjibhoy, *1930*). In India schizophrenia is rare compared to the latter disease.

Further insight into the relationship of group membership and psychopathology is furnished by impotence.[7] Mead (*1949f*:210–213) points out that community patterns may emphasize to men the difficulties of male techniques of mastery. Bali with its crystallinely impersonal social life illustrates such a case. Here the dramatic forms constantly remind the male of his uncertain potency. In Arapesh neither the fear that potency will fail nor the belief that much is to be expected of men are patterned. Rather the folklore perpetuates the myth of strongly sexed women who can seduce a man or steal part of his body for a sorcerer. The Manus people find little pleasure in sex and likewise do not phrase the man's role as filled with strain. "The civilized male," Mead says in summary, "always runs the risk that civilization may dictate to and so reduce his spontaneity."

CONCEPTS AND INTENSIVE RESEARCH

As already brought out earlier in this book, concepts are among the most important tools of science. With them the researcher isolates phenomena and relates them to other conceptualized events.

The evidence cited in this chapter strongly supports the hypothesis that psychopathology is a function of group membership. In certain voluntary forms of psychiatric abnormality, like drug and alcoholic intoxication, the connection is clear. In the more involuntary disturb-

---

[7] See above, pp. 273–274.

ances of personality, the psychoses, evidence indicates that cultural factors help determine the pattern of falling ill as well as the incidence of the illness itself.

Considerable more light needs to be thrown on the variables lying between culture on the one hand and involuntary psychopathology on the other. Personal stress is one such intervening variable to be examined in the succeeding chapter. Intensive research has only begun to be carried out in this interesting and significant area where psychiatry and social science adjoin. An explicit definition of what is connoted by "behavior disorder" or "psychiatric abnormality" should be of considerable utility in developing more knowledge in this neglected field.

Suggestions for Further Reading

Similar to the definition of psychopathology with which this chapter started is Honigmann's "Toward a Distinction Between Social and Psychiatric Abnormality" (*1953b*). A number of writers have recognized the need for a cross-cultural conception of what constitutes personality disorder. Especially pertinent are Wegrocki's "A Critique of Cultural and Statistical Concepts of Abnormality" (*1953*), Money-Kyrle's "Some Aspects of State and Character in Germany" (*1951*), and Berndt and Berndt's "The Concept of Abnormality in an Australian Aboriginal Society" (*1951*).

An extensive literature on the social factors related to intoxication and inebriation has appeared in recent years, partly resulting from the leadership of the Section of Studies on Alcohol, Yale University. Recommended are Williams and Straus' "Drinking Patterns of Italians in New Haven" (*1950*) and Bacon's *Sociology and the Problems of Alcohol* (*1946*). The social norms governing drinking are explored for the Kaska Indians in Honigmann and Honigmann's "Alcoholic Drinking in an Indian-White Community" (*1945*). Cooper (*1949*) has written a careful paper reviewing the place of stimulants and narcotics in South American culture.

Devereux brings out the relationship between mental illness and culture in his study of the psychotherapy of a Plains Indian, *Reality and Dream* (*1951*). For other case material see Keesing's "The Papuan

Orokaiva vs. Mt. Lamington: Cultural Shock and Its Aftermath" (*1952*); Joseph and Murray's *Chamorros and Carolinians of Saipan* (*1951*), especially pages 229–290; Spiro's "A Psychotic Personality in the South Seas" (*1950*), and Hallowell's "The Social Functions of Anxiety in a Primitive Society" (*1949*). Jewell touches on the problem of diagnosing mental illness across cultural boundaries in "A Case of a 'Psychotic' Navaho Indian Male" (*1952*). Behavior in an American Indian group illustrates the relationship between self-disturbance and supportive ritual movements. See Spindler's "Personality and Peyotism in Menomini Indian Acculturation" (*1952*).

Chapter 16

CULTURAL FACTORS IN MENTAL HEALTH

O f great significance for the mental hygiene movement is the increasing evidence that mental illness is not everywhere equally prevalent. Certainly voluntary forms of psychopathology, like drunkenness and trance, are easily encouraged. The incidence of involuntary psychopathology (i.e., mental illness) also varies between communities but the reasons for this are not yet clearly established. The problem in this chapter is to explore what we know of the relationship between sociocultural factors and mental disorder. Much more research on this question is needed to develop a mature, effective, and prophylactic mental hygiene movement (International Congress on Mental Hygiene, International Preparatory Commission, *1949*).

THE DIFFERENTIAL FREQUENCY OF MENTAL ILLNESS

The west coast of James Bay and the adjacent Cree-Ojibwa country constitute an area with relatively high rates of mental disturbance (Landes, *1938*). Speaking of the cases he personally encountered, Saindon (*1928*) describes Indians suffering from catalepsy, somnambulism, hypochondriasis, complete lethargy, hallucination, and anxiety so intense that it interferes with economic and social obligations.

In northern Ontario, near the muddy estuary of the Attawapiskat River, lives a community of Swampy Cree Indians. We find them to be a deeply anxious people. Their insecurity manifests itself in phobic fears, hallucinations, and in psychotic episodes which some-times result in hospitalization. The men are also frequent victims of accidents. Perhaps accidents, like phobic fears of forest and river, relieve men from the obligation of striving for fur and food in a nig-gardly environment. The Attawapiskat Indians believe in *otchipwéak*, or "white strangers," who wander around the country menacing the natives. Although widely accepted and constituting a part of reality as socially defined, the intense fear of these creatures helps to aug-ment the constant tension under which the Indian lives. No psy-chiatrist could label the native community of Attawapiskat as very healthy. Children grow up in an atmosphere of dread and economic uncertainty. Their parents are models for psychopathology.

Western Europe and America have been identified as other areas with high rates of mental illness. It is true, however, that Europe and America are countries in which psychiatry and mental hygiene have achieved their fullest development. Schools and clinics diligently search out signs of psychiatric abnormality. Trained personnel can readily recognize such signs. Also, many western European coun-tries, like the United States and Canada, keep relatively complete records of cases of mental illness. We have no comparable sources of data for the countries of Asia and Africa, hence comparison is diffi-cult. When, however, psychiatrists do visit non-European commu-nities and keep careful records of their experience their evidence reinforces the hypothesis that rates of mental illness in Europe and America are disproportionately high.

The following facts reveal the scope of mental hygiene problem in the United States (Rennie and Woodward, 1948:138–139; Wein-berg, 1952:362–367):

In 1944 more than 50 percent of the average daily census of hospital patients was suffering from mental disease, mental defect, or epilepsy.

Thirty to 75 percent of people who go to doctors are suffering primarily from psychoneurotic difficulties.

One person in five goes to a doctor yearly for some nervous ailment.

Twenty-seven of 100 consecutive patients admitted to the mental services of the outpatient clinics of the University of Chicago Hospital were found to be neurotics, 23 had questionable organic disease, and only 50 had clear-cut organic disease.

Of 450 admissions to the medical and surgical wards of New York Hospital 45 patients (10 percent) had severe or moderately severe personality disturbances and 90 patients (20 percent) had mixed personality disturbances.

Prewar figures indicate that one out of 20 people counted at the age of 15 will in the course of a lifetime enter a psychiatric hospital on account of mental illness. Another one out of twenty will be too ill to work for a longer or shorter time but will not go to the hospital. Thus one person out of ten will in the course of his life need treatment on account of mental illness.

Mental Disorder in Kenya

An investigation based on 558 Africans certified insane and admitted for the first time to the only mental hospital in Kenya colony revealed a rate of 3.4 cases of insanity per 100,000 population (Carothers, 1948). In 1938 the admission rate to mental hospitals in England and Scotland was 57 per 100,000 while in the period 1917–33 rates of first admissions of all races in Massachusetts varied between 72 and 86 per 100,000. Taking Negroes alone, in Massachusetts the figure comes to 161 per 100,000. The African admission rate is therefore vastly lower than anything found in Great Britain and America. The difference in rates is only partly related to "the rule for Africans to look after their insane relatives." For example, on three native reserves which Carothers checked, a census turned up 205 mentally disordered out of a total population of 616,000. The mental hospital already contained 23 people from these reserves, giving a rate of 0.37 mentally ill per 1,000 population. In 1938 in England and Wales 3.9 patients came under the care of mental hospitals for every 1,000 persons. "If the same proportion occurred here as in England and Wales there would be over 2,400 insane from these reserves." Of course, Europeans live longer than Africans so that cases of insanity occurring in later life should be subtracted from the figures. Nevertheless, there is an enormous gap between the figure of 228 and that of the 2,400 that would correspond to British incidence. Carothers concludes that "the incidence of insanity in Kenya Africans (at least those living at home in their reserves) is probably very much lower than in Europe or America." On the other hand, the sex incidence of mental disorder on the reserves does not differ markedly from what is found in other parts of the world.

Tabulating the available data for Africans in Kenya and for American Negroes, Carothers discovers systematic differences in the frequency with which common mental illnesses occur between the two populations. Each of the following types of disorder is more likely to incapacitate the Negro in America than the African in Kenya (Table 6).

TABLE 6. Comparative Frequencies of Mental Illness

Disease	Kenya Africans Rate per 100,000 per Annum	American Negro Rate per 100,000 per Annum
Organic psychoses	1.12	75.5
Epilepsy	0.12	4.9
Mental defect	0.40	6.0
Psychopathic personality	0.10	1.4
Schizophrenia	0.99	44.1
Paranoia	0.07	5.2
Manic-depressive psychoses	0.13	13.4
Involutional melancholia	0.05	0.6
Psychoneuroses	0.07	2.9
Unclassified psychoses	0.39	7.4

Carothers' work strongly suggests that the Africans of Kenya whom he saw are relatively a mentally healthy people.

Mental Health Among Hutterites

Examination of enclaves located within national communities of the Western world affords further evidence for the conclusion that rates of mental disorder vary between groups. The Hutterites constitute such an enclave in the United States. Social scientists selected them for intensive investigation because they enjoy a reputation of unusual mental health (Eaton, Weil, and Kaplan, *1951*). In the absence of quantitative data the qualitative evidence is summed up as follows: "Severe mental illness, requiring hospitalization, suicide, crime, juvenile delinquency and divorce—these and other indicators of personal tension so common in the American society at large, seem exceedingly rare among the more than 8,500 adherents of this religious kinship group." Neurotic and even more seriously disturbed persons are encountered among the Hutterites and are looked after within the colonies.

The Hutterite community is healthy, in the tentative opinion of the authors, partly because its slow-changing culture contains relatively few of the contradictions found in American life. The people are not like many Americans torn between such contradictory values as: "Honor your parents; they had experience in life. BUT the old generation is old fashioned. Youth must seek progress."

Hutterite mental health depends not only on the absence of stress resulting from rapid change and conflicting values. The Hutterite community also practices considerable coöperation. Members hold property in common and care for widows and other dependents left by death. Psychologically the community "provides social security from the womb to the tomb" and through its belief system "promises certain salvation" in the afterlife. Close identification between members of the family may also aid mental well-being. Children are wanted; their birth and rearing represent some of life's most important functions. The lack of intense concern with social mobility, that "rat race" or "treadmill" characterizing other American subcultures (Whyte, 1951:208), may also be significant. Hutterites all wear the same clothes, eat together, and live in homes furnished with standard and simple equipment. "Hutterites believe it to be sinful to enjoy what they define as 'worldly luxuries,' such as radios, pleasure cars, fashionable clothing, jewelry and other material goods." Although these people increasingly borrow more traits from general American culture they "are trying hard to assimilate selectively," using their basic values as guides for deciding how to change their way of life. Of carefully controlled assimilation the authors point out that "only a stable community which has considerable control over its members through their allegiance and loyalty to its way of life, can make such a planned adjustment to conflicting ideas with which the community comes into contact." It is well not to forget that the Hutterites also enjoy a high degree of genetic homogeneity. As one of America's most inbred groups they may have acquired some genetic immunity against mental disorder.

Mental Health in the Air Force

The Air Force may be regarded as another cultural enclave in our national community. Within the Army Air Corps of World War II two categories of personnel could be distinguished, flying and ground personnel (Grinker and Spiegel, 1943). Members of these categories differed in their resistance to anxiety. This difference in turn related to (1) the tasks which the men performed, (2) the cultural sentiments held toward those tasks, (3) the dangers to which men's jobs exposed them, and (4) what men could or could not do in the face of those dangers. The helplessness of ground crews turned out to be of crucial importance for understanding their greater susceptibility to mental disorder.

Both air and ground personnel in the North African war theater expressed a profound love of, and interest in, airplanes. Such feelings were universal patterns in Air Corps culture. However the ground force possessed "few of the identifications so important to the development of the kind of morale which has proved protective against the traumata of war." They were not trained to serve in combat and came under officers who conformed more to office administrators or technical experts than to leaders of men. The ground force carried out an essentially civilian type of work but the same remained subject to the traumata of war. When some of these men were exposed to the psychological traumata of war, their general resistance toward the development of anxiety was considerably lower than in the combat personnel of the Ground Forces. Mostly such shocks affected the men maintaining the airfields in the forward areas where the Air Corps found itself most helpless against surprise attacks. The planes on which the mechanics worked provided excellent targets for sudden enemy raids. Hiding proved difficult and any offensive impossible.

Among flying personnel a different situation obtained, "the emotional attitude toward planes is, of course, similar to that among the ground personnel, but immensely reinforced by the close connection with the actual function of aircraft flight. The identifications which so effectively increase the individual ego span, are multiple. The crews of heavy bombardment planes form strongly cohesive units within the squadron, itself a powerfully unifying and protective force" (107).

Air crew members enjoyed flying. The discipline of formation flying contributed toward group solidarity within a squadron. The morale of the fliers did not stay perfect. Lack of preparation for combat flying among men who had been attracted by the glamour attached to the Air Corps, poor living conditions and food, lack of recreational facilities, and loss of friends proved damaging factors. In spite of these strains the incidence of neuroses of war in flying personnel remained low. An absence of predisposing traits in these men cannot be overlooked as possibly related to the high degree of mental health that air crew men maintained. They had all been carefully selected and comprised a volunteer group. Also worth pointing out is the fact that both ground and flying personnel had a flight surgeon available in the squadron whose job it was to detect early signs of psychopathology. He would take preventative steps to keep the men healthy.

The data from Attawapiskat, Kenya, the Hutterites, and the Air Corps support the following conclusions:

1. Mental illness resembles other facets of personality in being related to group membership. Culture in part determines the pattern of mental illness found in a community.

2. Environmental and economic rigors, reflecting the technological efficiency of a culture, the presence of conflicting values, and helplessness in the face of danger are some specific factors producing stress. Like the presence of mentally sick adult models, these factors influence patterns of mental disorder in the community.

3. Social coöperation or solidarity, cultural homogeneity, slow and selective sociocultural change, and training and preparation for stress

are some factors favorable to mental health. Adequate means of pro-
phylaxis against breakdown cannot be overlooked in this connection.
Furthermore, genetic resistance and careful selection of personnel
may help to condition a low incidence of psychopathology in a particular community.

4. Comparative studies of community life are useful for revealing
differences in the incidence of mental disorder and also reveal factors
related to those differences.

The needs of preventative psychiatry require that sociologists and
anthropologists carry out with increasingly careful methods many
more comparative studies in the area of mental health and illness.

CULTURAL SOURCES OF STRESS

Contemporary psychiatric theory generally accepts stress or tension
as one of the foremost factors affecting mental health. The amount
of personal stress which an individual experiences depends partly on
his personal life history, that is, on the particular vicissitudes he encounters. The problem for us is how social and cultural conditions
determine the stress or vicissitudes encountered by people in communities.

Clearly not all communities engender or maintain equal stress. In
some groups prescribed paths to ends facilitate tension reduction for
members. In other communities tension reduction may be chronically
blocked. The first have "easy" cultures and the latter "tough" ways
of life (Arsenian and Arsenian, *1948*). A tough culture builds up
tenseness and is marked by a high rate of suicide not socially approved, considerable incidence of neurosis and psychosis, much crime,
a large discrepancy between the contemporary life and projections
of a future existence, and general malaise reflected in the use of drugs
or patterns of escape like hoboism and utopianism. Tschopik (*1951:*
172) cites the Aymara of Peru as living under tough cultural conditions. A pessimistic, dour people, their unresolved problems are not
even ended with death.

Culture may be a source of stress primarily in childhood or adulthood. Stress may also continue to be encountered with little variation

throughout life. Children's distress may be handled in such a way as to eliminate its signs soon or else the signs may be maintained into adulthood. Subsections of a community may be forced to bear a larger share of stress by virtue of a dominant group's culture patterns (Kardiner and Ovesey, *1951*). Tension may vary from one period to another, reflecting either change in culture or in the external problems which the culture is unable to solve.

Child-Rearing Routines and Stress

Much has been written concerning the distressful effects of particular child-rearing routines. Often such discussion is about the experiences of individuals who have come to the psychiatric clinic. There illness is related to traumatic but socially deviant patterns of child care. To what extent do the socially standardized experiences of early life induce stress and affect mental health?

The Kaska Indians form a relatively anxious group of people whose defenses against certain types of insecurity handicap them in satisfying their needs (Honigmann, *1949*a). The Kaska personality is chronically disturbed by an unfulfilled desire for emotional warmth —a drive to which he cannot respond. In defense he tries to suppress all feeling hoping thus to obliterate the anxiety produced by his ambivalent attitudes toward affection. The defense works in a wide variety of situations but it incapacitates the individual in relations with a spouse and interferes with sexual and other marital satisfactions. Thus, anxiety and relatively incapacitating defenses against it are two psychpathological signs in the Kaska community.

These two features of Kaska personality can be traced to customary patterns of rearing the Indian child. The early warm care and adequate satisfaction of needs received by the Kaska infant contrast with his later experiences. When the child is between two and three years old the formerly indulgent mother begins to deny emotional warmth and reduces her generous attention to the youngster. Affectionally the mother rejects the baby and withdraws into impersonal aloofness. Following upon an initial period of extreme gratification the new maternal attitudes severely traumatize the child. The self-confident expectations which had been encouraged toward the world suddenly encounter disappointment. The child's ability to secure comfort and attention fail. Affect-hunger and emotional constriction appear as consequences. A person grows up who regards all strong love relationships with fear while at the same time hankering back to the period of abundant affectional gratification. Such a personality organization is socially normal in the Kaska community. The isolated and emotionally constricted Indian is not the deviant he would be in our midst. Psychiatrically, however, he is disturbed.

We have already indicated how sex training of the child that identifies sex with sin may condition the sexual impulse to anxiety and engender behavioral conflicts. Similar disharmony in personality may follow when conflicting values are taught with respect to aggression, competition, or achievement (Weinberg, 1952:103–104).

Kardiner and Ovesey (1951) discuss how the Negro child's socialization traumatizes the developing person. They report parents neglecting gratification of children's affectional needs. Such emotional blunting in turn conditions dysfunctions of the sexual apparatus. A number of cultural factors determine the standardized patterns of child rearing which Kardiner and Ovesey report. First is the exclusion of Negroes from equal participation in American life. The economic deprivation that results reinforces emotional neglect, especially in the Negro lower classes. In this segment of the community broken homes and conflictful relations between parents further traumatize the child. Children then grow up to be suspicious and mistrustful of everyone. Their immense anxiety manifests itself in frigidity and impotence and frequently leads the individual to alcohol and narcotics, which become obsessive needs against recurrent fears.

Adult Life Expectations and Stress

In adult life stress or tension is culturally engendered when that emotional state is related to (1) adaptive or adjustive inadequacy of culture patterns, (2) unrealizable goals socially engendered, (3) socially patterned terrors, (4) social catastrophes following from standardized behavior patterns, (5) contradictory social demands and expectations, and (6) culture contact. These sources of stress deserve close attention because it is likely that they provide favorable circumstances for the genesis of mental disorder.

1. *Cultural Inadequacy.* Personal stress in community life is encouraged when socially standardized behavior patterns are inadequate for satisfying biological and psychological needs in a particular milieu.

Thus, culture patterns may be markedly inefficient for mediating between the individual's basic drives and the natural resources available for satisfying the organism's demands. "The patterns of the culture may be such that no matter how conscientiously people practice the available patterns they do not get full satisfaction—people still go hungry or cold or wet part of the time" (Gillin, 1951:2). We assume that the efficiency of one particular culture can be measured in relation to another way of life. Unfortunately, anthropology has scarcely begun to develop standards for the measurement of cultural efficiency. Indications point to a growing awareness of the problem.

The inadequacy of culture patterns for need fulfillment is illustrated by the Cree Indians of Attawapiskat. We have already described these Indians as often subject to mental disorder, including accident proneness. Partly, anxiety in their lives may be traced back to conditions in childhood which partly reflect the adaptive inadequacy of certain culture patterns. As children many persons who are now adult experienced hunger, sometimes while they still nursed and the mother's milk dwindled from starvation. Following infancy came further periods of acute starvation. Even in normal times, parents' apprehension about hunger must have communicated itself to children. Such chronic anxiety helped set the worrisome personality so widely found in this community. Apprehension over illness represented still another threat operating in the life of the growing individual. It remains a double-barreled threat because material survival plus social prestige depend upon trapping and fowling. These forms of endeavor demand unhampered self-exertion and physical health.

Both as regards food production and the maintenance of health, Attawapiskat Indian culture is inefficient compared, say, to that of

the urban United States. In part the inefficiency reflects how the region has been depleted of fur-bearing animals. The community, however, could not keep up with such environmental change. It neither
invented nor borrowed new economic activities capable of meeting
organismic needs. Note that there is no question of blaming the Indians for this low level of adaptive efficiency. Expecting people to be
able to direct cultural change in necessary directions is a little like
expecting somebody to lift himself by bootstraps. Game became very
scarce in Attawapiskat following the introduction of guns and the
start of intensive trapping for the Eurocanadian fur trade. The community could not respond to a depleted milieu as Indians did long
ago by moving someplace else. This traditional solution was rendered
inoperative by culture contact. Eurocanadians have only just begun
to utilize their wealth and knowledge of biological science to restock
the area with beaver. Meanwhile, the threat of starvation and illness
continues to be distressful to these people.

Attawapiskat illustrates how alterations in the geographical environment, following from the appearance of a foreign culture, may
reduce the efficiency of a native culture and affect the personalities
of individuals. Changes in social relations stemming from culture
contact may also promote distress as will be demonstrated below.

2. *Unrealizable Social Goals.* Personal tenseness in a community
stems partly from the degree to which the culture includes wants
without correspondingly patterning means through which these goals
may be achieved (Gillin, *1951*:2).

Communities frequently inculcate aspirations for which there exist
no ready paths to achievement. Sometimes the achievement of goals
that are held out as desirable to all segments of a community becomes
especially difficult for particular subgroups and categories. People in
Jonesville, as in all American towns, learn to strive to better their
station in life (Warner and associates, *1949*). Only in part can the
high achievement level held out to the citizens of Jonesville be realized by all. Through schooling, lower-class children may theoretically
prepare themselves for professional and commercial careers as well as
for mobility into the middle class. The schools are open to all social

classes. Nevertheless all pupils do not equally measure up to the teachers' expectations. Lower-class children lack advantages initially possessed by middle- and upper-class youngsters when it comes to doing well in school. For example, lower-class boys and girls are not as strongly motivated toward education. They lack that push toward and interest in school which is more frequently found in middle-class homes. Here there is sure to be a small collection of books and reading is a familiar experience. Lower-class children are not less able to learn but they remain only dimly aware of the middle-class values that their teachers expect. They care little for such things as manners, vocabulary, leadership qualities, community responsibility, and "proper" speech habits (Green, 1947–48; Warner, Havighurst, and Loeb, 1944:101–107). Middle-class children find school more congenial, they attend longer, and receive better grades: ". . . the higher an adolescent's class position the better his chances are to receive high grades. Conversely, the lower one's position in the prestige structure, the more likely the adolescent is to receive low grades" (Hollingshead, 1949:173).

Although certain common ideals are urged on all Americans— like achievement of financial and social success—our culture intensifies distress by not allowing all segments of the population equally to realize those ideals. "The social system does not provide all competitors with equal opportunities . . . the class system is maintained in part by the control of institutional offices by the upper classes. This control is achieved either by placement of persons who belong to the higher classes in key offices, or by allowing only upward mobile persons who have the 'right attitudes' to have access to them" (Hollingshead, 1949:452).

3. *Socially Patterned Terrors.* A culture's belief system may contribute to anxiety. As Gillin (1951:3) puts it, "Every culture has certain conventional means of dealing with such an unseen world. Is the balance between the belief system and the patterns for response to it sufficient to provide security?"

By no means do cultures automatically balance supernatural threats with rituals, like sacrifice or confession, through which the resultant anxiety can be reduced. The sense of sin culturally encouraged may be overpowering and may lead to acute stress even when confession or other rites exist or when God's love is assured. In another religion there may be no rituals capable of relieving the image of a stern, morally exacting Supreme Being who exists beyond all compromise.

Not only supernatural beliefs have this effect. The community may endorse other beliefs. Fear that these ideals may not be attained can then truly be terrifying. People who dare not relax from keeping up with neighbors live under nearly constant tension. Sometimes the ideal is chastity, popularity, bravery, modesty, or even aggressivity in some communities. Any fall from these virtues promotes much guilt, shame, or distress. Tooth (1950:5–36) reports that on the Gold Coast only rarely do unmarried mothers become mentally disturbed. These people also recognize no illegitimacy laws. Similarly Africans of the Gold Coast do not aspire to limit the size of the family. They don't fear pregnancy. As in many parts of Africa social status still depends mainly on hereditary privileges. The community owns the land and life can continue without money so that worry over financial matters also rarely occurs as a cause of breakdown. Invented terrors are less, or at least different, in cultures like that of the Gold Coast than they are in the modern, Western world.

4. *Catastrophic Social Events.* Widespread conditions like war, unemployment, and economic depression currently threaten many people in the modern world. Three factors are especially significant in counteracting the anxiety produced by these catastrophes: group solidarity, the belief that control over the threat is available, and a sufficient supply of tools, guns, or other material resources to counteract the shock. The lesson drawn from the Air Corps in North Africa illustrates how these factors operate. The ground technicians, it will be recalled, felt their danger more keenly than the fliers, partly because there was little they could do when attack came from the skies. Catastrophes may be less unbearable if they simultaneously affect a number of one's neighbors. On the other hand, stress is particularly hard to bear when the victim alone must shoulder the blow. (Maslow and Mittelmann, 1941:209).

Hiroshima and Nagasaki are akin to laboratory situations in which we can study the psychological effects of atomic disaster, a form of terror now threatening millions of people in the civilized world. In both cities the air raids caught the populace by surprise (Janis, *1951*). Survivors report a sudden, sharp awareness of threat to personal survival. Further shock came from seeing so many citizens burned, cut, and maimed. Fear reactions persisted for weeks among a sizable proportion of the populations. A diffuse apprehensiveness, as well as sustained reactions of depression, remained with many during the postdisaster period. However, psychoses, traumatic neuroses, and other severe disorders only rarely followed the A-bomb attacks. Morale did not drop in Hiroshima and Nagasaki further than it did in Japanese cities bombed with conventional weapons. The atomic raids developed relatively little sustained hostility toward the United States. Instead, as in Europe during the bombing of World War II, some citizens blamed their own leaders for the bombing. The fact that lasting psychiatric casualties rarely followed bombing attacks in Japan or in Europe (96) does not mean that strategic air war is not intensely disturbing to civilian populations. Anxiety runs high during air raids although the presence of other people caught in the same terror contributes toward some degree of emotional support.

In modern urban communities individuals in distress and cut off from families are often unable to find needed support. People in the impersonal environments of the modern world spend a large proportion of time working among strangers in whom they cannot confide and from whom they can expect little guidance. People in quandaries rarely secure support from casual acquaintances as they might from close kin or intimate friends. Professional psychiatric services, as the Air Force data indicate, are of great value in supporting mental health under impersonal social conditions.

5. *Contradictory Social Demands.* Contradictory demands and expectations readily lead to personal tension. Children, for example, may be expected to remain obedient through adolescence at the same time that parents and teachers urge self-reliance or responsibility. Americans from early age are trained to compete for success on the

one hand and to show brotherly love with befitting humility on the other. We hold freedom as a great value but are vague and inconsistent concerning areas where liberty must be limited for the common good.[1] As Americans we have all confronted these conflicts. In a few people they become extreme, incapacitating the individual for his customary duties (Slotkin, *1952*, chap. *12*).

Karen Horney (*1937*) points out that a neurosis is characterized not only by anxiety and rigidity of behavior. There may also be conflicting tendencies for which the neurotic tries to compromise in his behavior. These inconsistent aims, she suggests, reflect the life-ways of the community and will differ at various times and places. Furthermore, in every community some area of life presents special difficulty. In this area conflicts and anxieties are particularly likely to develop. In America sex, aggression, and competition furnish three danger zones. To develop healthily every American must learn non-handicapping defenses against anxiety from these sources. The neurotic stands out as someone who has failed to find useful defenses. He cannot handle sexual, aggressive, and competitive situations, with their conflicts, efficiently. He may compete by becoming hypercompetitive only to fear the consequences of his extraordinary ambition. Or he may block ambition out of consciousness but then suffers from frustration and social criticism. The neurotic may become hostilely competitive and then he strives always to hurt others. Thus he can feel superior. Such destructive tendencies, however, arouse anxiety because they conflict with other values in modern life.

Communities that do not expect competitive behavior to the same degree that we do have no problem of this type. Similarly where sex is a natural function not surrounded with danger it is unlikely that many people will develop anxieties and conflicts over sexual expression.

------

[1] Opposition over mutually inconsistent basic ideals, values, or dogmas is felt in social relationships as well as within the person. Social conflict of this kind is particularly disturbing because people often do not fully understand its nature. See Wilson and Wilson, *1945*:125–157.

6. *Culture Contact.* Where two or more ways of life come into contact a profusion of stress will very likely be encountered. Culture contact occurs whenever people who have been socialized in one tradition interact with representatives of a different way of life. Relations between representatives of different cultures are commonplace in the modern world. Machines have overcome space and time and in so brief a period that new patterns of social relations have not yet appeared to prepare us for successful living in a very heterogenous society.

Often what happens in culture contact is this: An invading group fails to understand the values and expectations of its hosts. Demands are made on the hosts for which the latter lack established patterns of response. The foreigner's behavior appears strange and nearly wholly incomprehensible. Tension piles up on both sides of the relationship. Perhaps the invader is the white European or American colonial administrator who comes endowed with tremendous prestige that instigates voluntary imitation of his customs by natives. Pursuing imitation at the expense of the standardized behavior patterns may engender social and personal conflict.

The strain of living under these conditions is well revealed in the statement by a native Solomon Islander: "You white men give us orders. . . . The white man has come and tells us to behave like *his* father. Our own fathers, we must forget them. . . . In the olden days we did this thing, we did that thing. We did not stop and say to ourselves first, 'This thing I want to do, is it right?' We always knew. Now we have to say, 'This thing I want to do, will the white man tell me it is wrong and punish me?'" (Hallowell, *1945b*:193).

An extreme development of tension occurs during detribalization, when the individual steps out of his circle of kin, friends, familiar environment, and traditional life-ways to work in some heterogeneous urban quarter or mining town. Here he finds himself surrounded by strangers who have been similarly transplanted. Of course, none of these migrants are trained to live under these conditions. Carothers (*1948*) discusses certain psychiatric consequences of detribalization in East Africa. Having found the incidence of insanity among Africans in Kenya to be much lower than in Europe or America, and discovering no difference in the sex incidence of mental illness, he encountered other facts demanding explanation. For example, between 1939 and 1943 a large excess of males were admitted to mental hospitals. Substantial differences in admission rates occur within racial groups. "For instance the Kikuyu (a Bantu Negro tribe numbering 634,000) showed a rate of 9.3 per 100,000, whereas the Kamba (another Bantu Negro tribe numbering 453,000) showed a rate of 2.1; the Nandi (a Half-Hamite tribe numbering 50,000) showed a rate of 5.2, whereas the Turkana (a Half-Hamite tribe numbering 62,000) showed a rate of *nil;* the Somali (a Hamite tribe numbering 40,000) showed a rate of 9.0, while the Borana (a Hamite tribe numbering 26,000) showed a rate of 1.5." The rate of admissions for immigrants, 33,000 persons who have entered Kenya in recent years from other parts of Africa, and living mainly in towns, is higher than in any Kenya tribe.

What do these facts mean?

Of 558 first admissions to the mental hospital, 337 came from their homes on the reserves, 200 were certified while working in townships, and 21 while living as squatters on European estates. The author calculates that among Africans living on reserves the certification rate is about 2.3 per 100,000 population, among squatters (who retain their cultural identity and kin ties) 2.5, but among Africans living amid strangers the rate rises to 13.3 per 100,000. Most of the Africans in towns are men. Not all tribes are equally represented in the detribalized population. The most detribalized tribes also show the highest certification rates. Immigrants are, of course, detribalized, a fact explaining their high first admissions figure. Limiting a further climb in insanity rates among detribalized Africans, Carothers believes, is the fact that the bulk of employed natives remain away from home a relatively short time. Detribalization thus remains superficial.

Geoffrey Tooth (1950), who worked in the Gold Coast, also sees rapid culture change reducing the African's capacity to adjust to his environment.[2] His analysis reveals some of the conflicts suffered by the "educated" African. Frustration affects those natives who have attended European schools in the belief that literacy would enable them to grasp the white man's power and equal his great wealth. To complete this schooling many Africans went in debt so that they must first overcome an economic hurdle when they go to work. The literate worker's earnings go largely to repay the loans made by relatives. This means a low standard of living for the ambitious person who attended school in the hope of getting ahead. "The young man has therefore to choose between cutting himself adrift from his family and living his own life, or sacrificing his personal comfort and happiness to fulfill his obligations." Christianity presents other conflicts. To become a convert is relatively expensive and leads to tension should the marriage result in childlessness. People in the Gold Coast value children but Christians cannot marry a second wife in order to produce offspring. To preserve one value, monogamy, the Christian has to sacrifice another cherished ideal—reproduction. Competition is not important in producing maladjustments in illiterate rural communities of the Gold Coast but among the educated it becomes more significant. In one case "An Ewe, aged 33, had done well in school in his home town and went to work in one of the large stores where, after 15 years, he was one of the three most promising senior clerks, one of whom was due for promotion to store-manager. There was great competition for this job for which the patient was finally selected and posted to Kumasi, within a month his illness had started. He was brought back to his home where it was generally believed that he had been 'poisoned' by his rivals" (Tooth, 1950:38). Not only

---

[2] Carother's findings in Kenya are not entirely borne out by Tooth's work on the west coast. While males outnumber females in the single mental hospital of the Gold Coast, Tooth does not find that figures for male incidence are lower in the north where detribalization is rare than in the south where that condition is common. "In fact, the reverse is the case." Also, compared to Carother's figure of a rate of 3.4 new admissions per 100,000 annually Tooth writes that "the incidence of lunacy in the sample areas of the Northern Territories is shown to be between 96 and 60 per 100,000, both these figures are probably underestimates."

did the man suspect fellow employees of hurting him but he attacked one of them. For this he received a month's prison sentence. He also complained of thoughts being put into his head by means of radio—a modern touch in a delusion.

Culture contact has altered the aboriginal culture patterns of the Wisconsin Ojibwa and so skewed their personality structure "in a nonintegrative direction" that the people are at a psychological impasse for which no relief is in sight (Hallowell, *1950b*). A primary reason for the depleted psychological resources of these Indians lies in the fact that culture change among them did not include the development of a value system to replace the one destroyed by the impact of Euroamerican culture. Christianity never entirely supplanted the aboriginal belief in helpers who both sanctioned behavior and bestowed good fortune. The person's inner life, says Hallowell, "has been emptied of the deep convictions, motivations and goals that were all integrated in terms of the older belief system and its concomitant stabilized values." In addition conflict and anxiety stem from the fact that the people have lost their traditional occupations while new vocational opportunities on the reservation remain limited. Men no longer fill their role as providers. They suffer from impaired self-esteem and loss of security as women fill the gap by taking factory jobs. Woman's employment, however, disturbs the children who in consequence run wild.

OPTIMA OF MENTAL HEALTH

Few persons can claim to have maintained perfect mental health throughout life. Obviously there are degrees of psychopathology. If everyone on occasion may manifest some signs of psychiatric abnormality how can a condition of mental health be recognized? Can psychological well-being be defined in positive terms rather than as freedom from psychopathological symptoms?

Most readers will read this section already convinced that mental health is desirable. Such a conviction is unimportant for present purposes. Our aim is to spell out a definition of mental health applicable under a variety of cultural conditions. The criteria supporting the definition are less objective than the criteria for ascertaining of psychopathology given above. This makes the definition more difficult to employ as a yardstick. In exotic communities particularly a sound knowledge of the way of life will be required before mental health can be ascertained by the criteria given below.

Three universal, positive indicators of optimal mental well-being are: adaptive adjustment, integration, and cognitive adequacy (Smith, 1950). No one of these by itself assures adequate mental health. Rather all three must be present.

Adaptive Adjustment

No individual can feel well unless his needs, biological and psychological, meet satisfaction. Satisfaction of needs and tensions result in a state of homeostasis or dynamic equilibrium. Adaptation, the satisfaction of needs related to the person's survival, and adjustment are related to the resolution of intrapersonal and interpersonal tensions.

This initial criterion of mental health says nothing concerning whether dynamic equilibrium is better achieved through active mastery of the environment, passive compliance with the environment's demands, or through renunciation of the world in favor of a spiritualized existence. In fact each path has attracted followers and renunciation has been seriously defended as the ideal solution for tension reduction by a number of Eastern philosophers (Humphreys, 1952). We must remember, however, that people sometimes deliberately induce tension—either for future release or for the pleasure that tension itself affords (Murray and Kluckhohn, 1953:35–37). The reading of a spine-chilling mystery story delightfully achieves this end.

Integration

Meeting the dilemma created by positing tension reduction as the first criterion of adequacy is a concept designating organismic integrity. Integration or self-realization refers to a state in which the person avoids being rent by conflicts. The individual feels free and able to channelize his energies along any path of adaptive adjustment—

whether it be active striving, passive mastery, or renunciation. In other words, tension or unsatisfied organismic demands are not indicative of mental illness unless the individual feels himself unable to realize the satisfaction of his needs. Integration also refers to the coördination of needs, means, and goals. The goals of the organism are compatible with the resources of his culture and environment. In solving his biological and psychological problems the integrated individual retains a sense of harmony or self-consistency.

It may be objected that the psychotic gains a measure of intrapersonal integration through his illness at the cost of cutting himself off from the real world. Severe encapsulation is not equivalent to mental health because it denies adequate perception of reality—the third criterion of well-being.

Cognitive Adequacy

In any community the individual's well-being demands that his cognition and perception of reality—his capacity to select and interpret stimuli—be adequate to insure both adaptive adjustment and integration (Abt and Bellak, 1950:60). Reality always exists as it has been defined by a particular culture. No community—and therefore no culture—can survive with a conception of reality that fails to afford any prediction or control over the environment. In other words, a completely unpredictable interpretation of the world promises the extinction of the group just as a psychotic's world-view may threaten his survival. Slavish conformity to cultural interpretations of reality in situations of social change is indicative of ill health when they reduce integrity or weaken feelings of self-realization.

Combination of the Criteria

Ideally, maximization of the three criteria constitutes mental health. In any particular community, however, an optimal degree of mental health may be achieved without maximization of all three indicators. The three factors may even be incompatible under some circumstances. Smith (*1950*) writes:

Consider, for example, the value conflicts such as those between "Christian" altruism and competitive individualism that Lynd [*1939*], Horney [*1937*], and other writers have found in present American culture. Adjustment to this cultural environment may often be achieved only at the cost of defective integration—through internalizing conflicting values—or of distorted perception of self or of the society to which one is adjusting. The point is certainly not a new one. Or take the lot of people caught in a nearly unsupportable situation, such as the inmates of the concentration camp described by Bettelheim [*1943*]. Here some of the open alternatives were passive adjustment with regressive disintegration, active resistance and consequent annihilation, or the pursuit of a tenuous encapsulated integration, made possible by translating the threatening experience to a level of unreality. What seems clear is that one or more features of ideal mental health had to be sacrificed for the sake of mere psychological existence, and that even in this extreme situation more than one pattern of adjustment, integration, and cognitive adequacy was possible.

People frequently maintain a measure of integration and adjustment through cognitive distortion. The notion that everybody enjoys equal opportunity to reach socially desirable goals, for example, may be manifestly false. Yet the dogma can contribute importantly to psychological and social stability. Compromises of this sort are not necessarily unworkable in terms of well-being. Rather they may maintain the individual over long periods. However, no compromise between fiction and reality can continue when it deprives the person of control over his environment and exposes him to chronic frustration or deprivation. Such maladjustment will soon damage feelings of integrity. Optimal mental health will then be lacking.

GROUP MEMBERSHIP AND PERSONALITY REINTEGRATION

Even the most isolated, small-scale community is familiar with some form of mental illness. Of course, classification of symptoms will vary between communities and still greater will be the difference between opinions of what produces mental disorder. Often the etiological interpretation will guide the steps taken to reorient the disturbed person. Although in small-scale communities the cure pre-scribed for mental illnesses includes much magic, nevertheless ele-ments of modern, scientific psychotherapy can often be discerned in such practices.

In all parts of Latin America people recognize an intense form of anxiety, "magical fright." Local shamans successfully treat this ail-ment (Gillin, *1951*:112–113). In San Carlos, fictitious name for a Guatamalan town, the symptoms of "the fear" include a jumpiness of the pulse plus loss of appetite, weight, and energy. Natives explain these disturbances saying that the patient has lost his soul. Curing in turn makes unconscious use of suggestion and also seeks to pro-vide insight that will restore integration of the personality. Gillin writes:

There are several standard features of the cure. First, the curer at-tempts to clear up immediate physical complaints, not hesitating to use pharmaceutical preparations obtained from the pharmacy as well as herbal remedies from the folkloristic pharmacopaeia. Second, the patient is drawn out of his psychic isolation by making him the center of a rather elaborate set of preparations and giving him some responsibility. He is made the center of attention and given tangible evidence that other persons "care" about his condition and fate. Third, an elaborate ritual explaining the procedure to God, the patron saint, and a great list of other saints involves the church, the home altar, a special ground altar, the assistance of a Principal, and numerous prayers throughout the cure. Fourth, an expedition is made to the site of the alleged fright and in ritualistic form, but more familiarly than with the saints, the evil spirits or renegade saints of the curers are called and asked to help in the return of the soul, while an offering of worldly goods is left for their benefit. Fifth, the patient is massaged with eggs which are supposed to draw the evil out of him, and the eggs at some stage in the total cure are broken into water and an augury read from the shapes seen therein. It is believed that the shapes depict the scene and circumstances of the soul loss in realistic form, that they are visible only to curers. . . . Sixth, the patient has a mixture of alcohol, herbs and essences blown over his body and imbibes some of the same mixture. Thereby the evil aires are blown out of the body and otherwise eliminated (through cathartic action of the drink). Seventh, the patient is "rubbed down"—given a good massage, wrapped in blankets and left to sweat in the smoke of sacred copal incense.

To understand why the curing practices of small-scale communities sometimes enjoy success, the reader should think about the nature of psychotherapy in modern psychiatric practice. Maslow and Mittelmann (1941:273) define psychotherapy as "a method of treatment which aims to help the impaired individual by influencing his emotional processes, his evaluation of himself and of others, his evaluation of and his manner of coping with the problems of life. It may also include, if need be, influencing and changing his environment and thus altering the problems he has to deal with and simultaneously increasing his potentialities of mastery and integration." A number of these processes stand out quite clearly in the San Carlos data. Of course, they are practiced unselfconsciously and nonscientifically.

The attention devoted to the patient serves to build up the depressed man's confidence and sense of self-esteem. Explaining the procedure to God brings a whole host of powerful reassuring symbols —saints, altars, and church—to bear on the patient. To these symbols the person has been conditioned to respond with both awe and confidence. They are "sacred"—extraordinary and powerful. The call upon evil spirits is to be understood similarly, they are the causes and if their support is assured then the problem is well under control. Calling up these ideas generates powerful emotions that help to effect a cure. An offering of "worldly goods" serves the same purpose as paying the psychiatrist his fee. Wealth makes the ritual valuable because it measures it in familiar terms. This further assures the patient that the procedure is by no means inconsequential. The payment also helps the sick person do something positive about his illness. The importance of doing something in order to gain control of stress and threat has already been indicated. The egg and massage rites furnish reassurance and provide a suggestion of cure. In the absence of any scientific theory of psychiatric abnormality, rubbing the patient with an egg affirms that illness once installed can also be withdrawn from the human body. The rubbing and sweating probably also condition agreeable physical sensations in the body that contribute to the cure. Naturally faith in the rites and in the ability of the curer play a large part in the reintegration of the San Carlos neurotic.

Curers in small-scale communities have been known to seek to change the patient's environment in order to help him stay well. Thus in one Spanish American village a medicine man handled a husband's supposed bewitchment by a woman who was not his wife, first by dissolving the love spell cast by her rival. Then he advised the man's wife to pay more attention to her personal attractiveness. In another case a practitioner offered a woman "sophisticated advice" concerning useful coquettish techniques by means of which she could hold her husband's attention (Senter, 1947:54).

Curing some kinds of psychiatric abnormality in small-scale communities is not radically different from the techniques of modern psychotherapy. Psychotherapy that is successful often continues the process of patterning begun early in life. It reëducates the personality in new ways of action, thought, and feeling (Dollard and Miller, 1950). By aid of the psychotherapist, anxiety and other undesirable covert and overt behaviors are unlearned and replaced by appropriate new patterns of response. Lest we give too optimistic a picture of the status of contemporary psychiatry, it is well to recall that many types of behavioral disorders are not readily cleared up by existing practices. The frontier of psychiatric research is a most challenging and important one. At the same time there is resistance within our society to fully utilizing the knowledge of psychiatry. Our attitudes, Weinberg (1952:516–517) suggests, lag behind scientific knowledge in this vitally important area of mental health.

Suggestions for Further Reading

The position of mental health in America and the extent of serious psychiatric disorder in this country are subjects admirably treated in Weinberg's *Society and Personality Disorders* (1952), chapters 15–19. Sociocultural factors in mental disturbance are explored in Maslow and Mittelmann's *Principles of Abnormal Psychology* (1941), pages 195–

270, but the reader should also see Cameron's *The Psychology of Behavior Disorders* (*1947*), pages 15–52, and Weinberg, chapters 5–9. Faris and Dunham (*1938*) have written the classic monograph on social correlates of psychoses in *Mental Disorders in Urban Areas*. Faris (*1944*) reviews the topic in "Ecological Factors in Human Behavior." A very critical inquiry into the hypothesis connecting an increase in mental illness with cultural complexity is found in Beaglehole's "Cultural Complexity and Psychological Problems" (*1949*).

There is little literature on the care and handling of psychiatrically abnormal people in exotic communities. The treatment of the mentally ill among the Bemba, an East African kingdom, is summed up by Davidson in "Psychiatric Work Among the Bemba" (*1949*), while Gillin's "The Fear" (*1950*) talks about neurosis and psychotherapy in a Latin American community. "Some Interpersonal Aspects of an Oriental Religion" is an instructive article in which Stunkard (*1951*) discusses how Zen Buddhism incorporates psychiatric techniques and principles.

PART SIX

CONCLUSION

Chapter 17

REVIEW AND ASSESSMENT

Long ago some men became convinced that people are not only everywhere the same but also different, but that people of the same community or nation tend to conform in behavioral tendencies. Somewhat later it became clear that the personality differences which mark off one community from another represent acquired patterns of response. Only very recently did anthropologists begin to apply scientific procedures in theory and method to study these phenomena. The tangible result of this application is a considerable collection of monographs and shorter studies descriptive of the personalities of the Samoans, Arapesh, Kaska, Balinese, Lesuans, Comanche, Plainvillers, Alorese, Kwoma, Navaho, Hopi, Chinese, Germans, Russians, Aymara, Maori, Kwakiutl, Eskimo, and other peoples.

THEORY AND METHOD

Several varieties of approach have been carried on by anthropologists interested in personality. Genetic studies seek to relate childhood experiences with adult behaviors. Descriptive studies concern themselves with painting a verbal picture of how people act, think, and feel, the social scientist emulating the sometimes more perspicacious novelists. Functional studies, like genetic investigations, also attend to correlation. Rather than remaining occupied only with childhood and adulthood functional studies make connections between two or more aspects of modal personality to each other or aspects of personality to other conditions in the sociocultural milieu. Of all these approaches genetic studies are, perhaps, currently the most popular and have also aroused the sharpest criticism of culture and personality research.

Culture and personality executes these approaches with a relatively slight technical vocabulary. Some workers in the field believe that our conceptual tools are inadequate because they remain too close to everyday notions and that here resides a danger of confusion. That is to say, it is difficult to speak precisely in familiar words because their very familiarity conveys unintended meanings. *Culture, personality, pattern,* and *character structure* are some of the terms we try to use precisely and a fairly adequate body of theory has evolved which specifies the relationship between these concepts. Agreement is increasing that *culture* and *personality* are not, as was once believed, mutually exclusive categories. Rather personality is now seen as the reflection of a segment of culture in the individual. In consequence, culture and personality may be defined as the branch of anthropology which studies culture in the individual or as concerned with the relationship of modal personality to membership in some enduring group.

Not only is the technical vocabulary of the field slight but in some respects the available methods also do not satisfy the needs of research workers. Particularly is this true with regard to the interest that has grown up in studying the character structures of modern, complex nations. In some respects the model which developed when anthropologists worked solely in small-scale exotic communities continues to serve in specifying certain basic operations to be performed on a national scale. Certain amendments to that model, however, have come to be increasingly desirable, yet are slow in appearing. The difficulty of adding controlled sampling to the traditional anthropological method, that depends on winning rapport with fluent and willing informants, is responsible for this delay and represents an as yet unsolved problem. The introduction of sampling procedures to anthropology appears to be one of the most likely methodological innovations in the next decade.

Anthropology in general and culture and personality in particular, by virtue of their diverse approaches to the subject matter of human behavior, invite the participation of humanists, scientists, and social engineers. Perhaps in no other field of knowledge does it become more readily apparent how much these fields overlap.

As humanists our legitimate interest may be in knowing man and his manifold forms of his behavior. The humanist often looks for a kind of truth that is immediate more than it is theoretical or deductive. The instance of a Cheyenne warrior's pride, his resolute abstinence from sexual intercourse until his child is grown—these things are allowed to move us. Such study promotes the same richness that sometimes comes from travel or from sheer living. It is actually a way of extending the orbit of customary life to embrace more unfamiliar experience.

Scientists inquire into the relationships between facts. They aim to understand as well as to uncover new knowledge. The scientist often feels little concern with the pragmatic advantages of learning more about human behavior. Knowledge for him has its own reward. Products of scientific work in culture and personality include the systematic descriptive accounts of comparative behavior as well as the theoretical papers which try to order the data in a universal frame of discourse and to establish predictable relationships between them.

A social engineer is primarily concerned with using knowledge. World War II gave a big spurt to applying knowledge of comparative personality and the interest in such application remains alive. Especially promising is the hope of some applied scientists to enlighten the area of intercultural relations.

PATTERNS AND PATTERNING

Culture and personality, like cultural anthropology, focuses on the patterned behavior of groups. The basic facts with which each discipline deals, however, remain the discrete, personal acts of individuals, the specific forms of tools, living rooms, thoughts, and fears. From these facts are abstracted the standardized modes of physical setting or behavior. A subjective element necessarily enters into the process of pattern derivation but especially does it operate when the patterns are highly generalized, that is, when they group together many subsidiary patterns in "superpatterns" like "deference," "Apollonian," and others. Relating patterns to one another in a particular community poses the question of how widely such associations can be traced through other communities. Once this question is raised the social scientist clearly moves from a historical or descriptive to a full-fledged scientific perspective. Very little consideration has as yet been given to the procedures involved in constructing particular hypotheses out of the patterns derived in single cultures, generalizing them for cross-cultural validation, and then proceeding to test these generalizations. Here, of course, we confront the relatively immaturity of culture and personality. Data collection up to now has occupied far more attention than has testing of hypotheses. Indications for the future, however, point to a more nearly equitable distribution of emphases.

Patterning provides a suitable term to designate the overall process by which individuals in groups develop modal behavioral tendencies. However, too often patterning is taken to mean learning in the narrowest sense and there has been little explicit realization "that the method of child rearing, the presence of a particular literary tradition, the nature of the domestic and public architecture, the religious beliefs, the political system, are all conditions within which a given kind of personality develops" (Mead, *1951d*:74). Broadly speaking, patterning refers to the relationship between personality development on the one hand and any other relevant factors of group membership —actions, ideas, things, physical arrangements—on the other. This is merely another way of rephrasing the statement that culture interacting with the biological endowment of the organism stimulates modifications in the organism which, becoming relatively fixed, constitute predictable patterns of personality. Learning theory, with the emphasis on reward and punishment, helps us to understand how many patterns of behavior become established but it is not adequate to explain all patterning. For example, if a certain illness—diabetes or schizophrenia—can be called behavior then, except in cases where secondary rewards are associated with being sick, learning theory does not help explain why members of one community regularly manifest that behavior.

Conventional learning theory also needs expansion to account for the unintended consequences that accompany certain types of learning situations. For the more adequate understanding of how such consequences develop attention must be devoted not only to *what* is transmitted in the learning process but also to *how* that transmission takes place. Absorptive learning is a concept that further modifies the psychologist's conventional approach to learning and has been found useful to account for the formation of preferences, tastes, and attitudes. In a similar way students of psychosomatic medicine have discovered in "emotional contagion" a useful concept for describing how symptoms of illness maintain themselves in particular groups.

The relative plasticity of the human organism, man's capacity for symbolic thought, and his primary drives are the basic raw materials with which patterning operates. For example, as the basic hunger drive comes to be satisfied through a particular routine of feeding, symbolic values attach to the agent responsible for nurturance as well as to the food. Preferences are acquired. A preference also represents a kind of drive, a secondary drive or motive. While motivation is often loosely referred to as a force, it is impossible to defend logically the notion of covert, postulated preferences, wishes, or other secondary needs "causing" motor behavior in the organism. Motivation theory strongly recommends frank acceptance of covariation or correlation to replace the common-sense notion of causality. Explicit attention to the significance of correlation thinking in culture and personality research is seriously needed in contemporary theory. The student of culture and personality looks not for causes but for predictable relationships between sociocultural variables—including personality patterns. Motivation theory has one further value, that is to bridge the gap between the earlier experiences of an individual and his subsequent behavior at a later time. The gap is closed by ascribing to him a persisting motive to act. The intervening variable, motivation, aids in explaining connections between earlier and later events in the life cycle and also in accounting for the systematic character of personality.

Personality largely becomes formed through group participation, which is to say that group membership standardizes individual behavior. Every individual participates in a number of subgroups that make up his largest effective group, the national or tribal community. In each of these subgroups some elements of activity, thought, and feeling receive patterning. The group effects patterning through the interpersonal nexuses in which the individual participates. Direct and indirect social interaction shapes behavior and so (in large, complex, modern nations) do the mediated social relations in which people participate when, for example, they hear an arousing radio political speech by a national figure. The influence of the group reaches deep into the nuclear area of the personality and also extends far along the length of the life cycle, from birth to death. For various reasons, however, the increment of new learning tends to decline with age.

Patterning does not mean that all members of the group come to possess precisely uniform systems of personality. The unique endowments individuals bring to social life, the various distinct groups to which each person may belong, idiosyncratic resistances to learning, and failure of intragroup communication limit the extent to which different individuals are affected by interpersonal pressures and preserve personal diversity. Deviance stands at a more extreme degree of diversity. By deviant behavior we mean conspicuous behaviorial diversity in a specific group. The deviant occurs in all groups and is not immune from patterning in other areas of his behavior. Even deviant behavior may be patterned, or at least socially limited, so that it can be said that the rapist never develops among the Arapesh nor the kind and gentle lover among the Manus. The alcoholic also appears in the Jewish family but is more frequent among the Irish.

By extending permission, approval, disapproval, and physical punishment groups discipline their members. Evidence suggests that those sanctions or disciplines which occur in childhood are particularly important and continue to exert a lasting influence throughout the life span of the person. Especially effective are disciplines imposed in the areas of sex, aggression, hunger, and dependency. Successful consummation of these activities in childhood has a tonic effect on the personality. Interference with drives and motives, however, tends to weaken the ego. All communities blend permissive with restrictive disciplines but the distribution of each component may not be equal between groups—a subject about which we do not have precise knowledge.

Standardization of overt and covert behavior takes place in all groups and contributes to survival by insuring the transmission from one generation to another of the skills and relationships that lead to successful living. In the transmission of these manifest patterns many more subtle value orientations are implicitly perpetuated from one generation to another. Socialization in the norms of one community imposes limits on the degree to which we can readily understand patterns constituting another way of life. Many people require that their sensitivity to unfamiliar or contrasting modes of behavior be deliberately cultivated. The study of culture and personality may help in acquiring the ability to perceive different frameworks for action or distinctive value orientations in exotic communities.

EARLY EXPERIENCE

The interpersonal relationships of early childhood are not sufficient in themselves to pattern all items of the personality manifested in later life. Yet they are important. Especially crucial, according to current theory, are those interpersonal sequences which become highly charged with emotion. Affect-laden situations may accompany the child's early feeding, weaning from the breast, sphincter training, and physical development. Considerable early training occurs prior to the acquisition of language but we find it useful to assume that unconscious mentation nevertheless occurs in early childhood as part of the first learning. Evidence suggests that consistency in the form of a few dominant emotional qualities links the separate sequences of parent-child relations. Discontinuity in such qualities also arises, however, following from social recognition of changes in the child's development. We need more evidence to be clear that consistency in early training is stronger in one community than another.

Efforts to find specific variables of early childhood correlating with personality characteristics of later childhood or adulthood have met with relatively little success. Length of breast feeding or age of bowel training are apt to be significant only when they reveal a particular emotional quality (for example, severity or indulgence, the parent's gentleness or the baby's strength) and are integrated into a consistent configuration of early experience that reveals these primary emotional patterns. Extreme permissiveness in early routines may contribute toward a flexible or uncompulsive personality. The hygienic routines of the American mother who feeds her baby with a bottle and is worried about his early physical development communicates in these situations a reminder of the importance of things and a distrust of spontaneous rhythms and tastes. Consistently in the succeeding years eating and growing up will be seen as a question of dutiful self-conscious direction. The style of interpersonal behavior in later life stems from parent child interaction. There are communities in which the child is treated symmetrically, like an incomplete adult; complementarily, as essentially different from the adults, or reciprocally, receiving things and owing other things (tears, achievement, of feces) to adults. From attitudes focused upon maturation derive values relative to achievement while from the degree of expressiveness in the early environment the child "catches" emotional spontaneity or emotional suppression. Human relationships may be held out as a pleasant experience or they may be discouraged and people cut asunder through a learned distrust of people or a value on standing alone. The playing field inculcates other values that are often consistent with the value orientations of the community as a whole.

As is well known, negative discipline or punishment may be imposed by cowing the child and undermining his self-esteem or by implicitly stressing the dignity and respect to which he is entitled. Especially interesting is discipline sloughed off on terrifying supernaturals that spares parents from children's hostility and conditions in the latter a relatively weak sense of guilt.

Attitudes patterned toward the self are inculcated all through early life in the disciplines which mold the child's behavior toward the external world. Parental domination or frustration at the hands of adults may sow seeds of uncertain self-esteem. Adults then achieve a sense of strength by once more frustrating those whom they subordinate in power relationships. Affiliation with a renowned family, possession or repudiation of wealth, subordination to superior classes, all pattern a feeling of greater or less self-esteem in particular communities. Attitudes toward wealth, its acquisition and distribution, are also learned in every community. So are attitudes toward genital behavior and toward the roles of one's own and the opposite sex. Every group must limit to some degree the expression of hostility, whose unleashed discharge would bring destruction. On the other hand, the arrangements of social life may promote interpersonal frustration and threat, thereby encouraging the development of hostility and aggression. Devious channels allowing for the approved release of aggression in community life frequently include some form of scapegoating or witch-belief. Hostility is thus projected on the scapegoat and aggression may be vented against the witch. Sometimes provision occurs for the release of aggression through sports and in other relatively nonlethal channels (Murdock, 1949:90).

The accumulated literature on culture and personality contains information on additional early experiences significant in patterning but often such information is scanty and unevenly distributed as far as a sample of world societies goes. Systematic attention to other types of early experience would be useful in order to achieve a sense of what culture and personality studies have encompassed and what lines of inquiry might productively be explored in future research.

Every individual is subjected to hundreds of agents who contribute to patterning his personality. The earliest of these and the most important in setting before the child the expectations of the community are the parents. The family, however, does not possess the same form universally so that the role of the parents in the early years varies. Evidence indicates that the independent nuclear family has different dynamics in developing personality than the large, extended family in which individual responsibility and initiative do not flourish. Whether punishment is administered by parents themselves or sloughed off on servants and bogeymen is a condition related to the development of a predominant sense of guilt or shame. Style of relationship with adults in the family also conditions style of interpersonal behavior in the larger community. Even the attitudes adopted toward political authorities may be modeled after the attitudes which the child is encouraged to adopt toward parents. Siblings and peers constitute further sources of interpersonal behavior patterns.

OTHER ELEMENTS IN PATTERNING

Once the individual leaves the family to participate in the larger society he finds himself playing established roles which prescribe the limits and directions of behavior that he follows. Some statuses may be more congenial than others and therefore people sometimes show reluctance to quit a status. Many communities utilize dramatic rituals to wean members from particular statuses and help them assume new role behavior.

Leadership is one status that has aroused particular interest among social psychologists and anthropologists. Indications are that while the leader always operates with reference to established culture patterns he does not simply remain the follower of tradition. Occupational position of the individual and the degree of occupational differentiation also make their impact upon personality. Especially fruitful have been the studies of leadership by social psychologists and anthropologists. Leaders vary from culture to culture in the roles they play but indications are that they constitute a relatively highly selected category of the community's members. Successful leaders always remain cognizant of established cultural values but are not simply followers of tradition (Erasmus, 1952:175–177).

The ever-increasing studies of social stratification indicate that personality patterns also vary between the social divisions of a community and the character structure may also differ between, say, social classes. On the other hand certain relatively peripheral patterns (like the endorsement of loyalty and responsibility as values) may cut across social divisions and unify the community. Because of the characterological differences between the members of different social strata each such social class or caste develops its own distinctive ethos. Relationship of subethoses to the national or community ethos is a problem around which there has been little systematic inquiry. Areal ethoses characterize regions and appear to bear some relationship to geographical factors although the lines of such a relationship are quite intricate.

Primary and secondary heterogeneity are social conditions that foster relearning and hence prove especially useful for understanding personality patterning. The previous skills of a "migrant" from one cultural setting to another are rendered partly useless or at least often fail to bring rewards in his new environment. The courtesies, proprieties, and niceties of a former way of life may become symbolic of boorishness and ignorance. Children, aided perhaps by an other-directed character structure, make adjustments to heterogeneity more readily than adults but actually little information is on hand concerning the impact of the heterogeneous cultural stimuli on the individual's adjustive apparatus. A heterogeneous community is a special kind of plural society and as such provides a model in which intercultural relations can be studied more conveniently than in the wider world. Students of intercultural relations would be well repaid to develop the use of these models to discover principles of intercultural relations and intercultural strategy.

Whether there is a direct relationship between objective cultural complexity (such as might be found in a heterogeneous community) and the subjective or psychological experiencing of that complexity is another matter about which there remains considerable doubt. The entire area of the subjective experiences of individuals in small- as contrasted with large-scale communities has received only speculation. Such comparative data as are available provide few clues for solid hypothecation.

GROUP MEMBERSHIP AND PSYCHOPATHOLOGY

Not only the normal modal personality represents the influence of group membership but also the personality which manifests psychiatrically abnormal or psychopathological trends. Accumulating evidence demonstrates quite forcefully that group life contributes toward the patterning of psychopathological behavior.

Psychopathology in its broadest meaning denotes a condition of personality marked by any degree of anxiety, incapacitating defenses against anxiety, sensorimotor dysfunctions related to anxiety, reality distortion, distortions of affect, regressive behavior, personality disintegration, and derangement of intellectual capacities. These are behaviors which, by definition, constitute evidence of psychiatric abnormality. The evidence for the statement that psychopathology, defined by these criteria, is responsive to group membership comes from data on so-called "specialized" psychopathologies, by our knowledge of how certain voluntary behavior disorders (like trance, drunkenness) are unequally represented in the world, and by evidence that culture influences the content of psychotic thought as well as psychotic activities. The patterns of group and community living may also occasion stress in individuals which in turn conditions personality dysfunction. Studies of detribalized communities and other groups undergoing social change indicate not only a preponderance of stress in such cases but also an apparently high incidence of mental illness.

Suggestions for Further Reading

The unfinished problems of method and content that urge themselves on the student of culture and personality resemble those which Doob has summed up as remaining for social psychologists. Topics like sampling, correlation, and hypothesis construction are taken up in chapter 19 of Doob's *Social Psychology* (1952). For a somewhat more positive approach, a neat appraisal of the current position of culture and personality studies grew out of an interdisciplinary conference sponsored by the Viking Fund. The proceedings have been published in *Culture and Personality*, edited by S. Stansfeld Sargent and Marian W. Smith

(*1949*). Murray's statement on "Research Planning: A Few Proposals" in these proceedings represents especially appropriate reading at this point.

A model for future students of field problems and one which might mark the opening of a new era in anthropological research is Spindler and Goldschmidt's "Experimental Design in the Study of Culture Change" (*1952*). It is reasonable to expect that future research will lead to predictive statements concerning what behavioral limits or potentialities may be associated with groups possessing certain patterns of modal character structure. Such research depends on carefully formulating hypotheses against an awareness of historical events. The method is well illustrated by Wallace in "Some Psychological Determinants of Culture Change in an Iroquoian Community" (*1951*) and in the classic "The Change from Dry to Wet Rice Culture in Tanala–Betsileo" by Linton and Kardiner (*1947*), as well as in the studies of British and American personality by Margaret Mead.

BIBLIOGRAPHY

ABEGG, LILY

1952. *The Mind of East Asia* (London, Thames and Hudson).

ABEL, T. M., and HSU, F. L. K.

1949. Some Aspects of Personality of Chinese as Revealed by the Rorschach Test (*Rorschach Research Exchange and Journal of Projective Techniques*, 13:285–301).

ABERLE, DAVID F.

1951. The Psychological Analysis of a Hopi Life-History (*Comparative Psychological Monographs*, 21, no. 1).

ABT, LAWRENCE E., and BELLAK, LEOPOLD (eds.)

1950. *Projective Psychology* (New York, Alfred A. Knopf).

ACKERKNECHT, ERWIN H.

1943. Psychopathology, Primitive Medicine and Primitive Culture (*Bulletin of the History of Medicine*, 14:30–67).

1945. On the Collection of Data Concerning Primitive Medicine (*American Anthropologist*, 47:427–432).

ALLEN, FREDERICK L.

1931. *Only Yesterday* (New York, Harper & Brothers).

ALLPORT, GORDON W.

1950. Basic Principles in Improving Human Relations. In Bigelow, K. W., *Cultural Groups and Human Relations* (Boston, Beacon Press).

AMES, L. B., LEARNED, RUTH JANET, METRAUX, W., and WALKER, R. N.

1952. *Child Rorschach Responses* (New York, Paul B. Hoeber).

ARGYLE, M.

1952. Methods of Studying Small Social Groups (*British Journal of Psychology, General Section*, 43:269–279).

ARSENIAN, JOHN, and ARSENIAN, JEAN M.

1948. Tough and Easy Cultures (*Psychiatry*, 11:377–385).

Asch, Solomon E.
  1952. *Social Psychology* (New York, Prentice-Hall).
Bacon, Selden D.
  1946. *Sociology and the Problems of Alcohol* (Memoirs of the Section of Studies on Alcohol, Yale University, no. 1).
Baldwin, Hanson W.
  1952. West Point Lapse is Linked to Trend (*New York Times*, Jan. 15).
Barnes, John A.
  1951. History in a Changing Society (*Human Problems in British Central Africa*, no. 11, 1–9).
Barnouw, Victor
  1950. *Acculturation and Personality Among the Wisconsin Chippewa* (Memoirs of the American Anthropological Association, no. 72).
Barrett, E., and Post, G.
  1950. Introduction to Some Principles of Applied Cybernetics (*Journal of Psychology*, 30:3–10).
Bateson, Gregory
  1936. *Naven* (Cambridge, Cambridge University Press).
  1943. Human Dignity and the Varieties of Civilization. In *Science, Philosophy and Religion: Third Symposium* (New York, Conference on Science, Philosophy and Religion in Their Relation to the Democratic Way of Life).
  1947. Social Planning and the Concept of Deutero-Learning. In Newcomb, T. M., and Hartley, E. L., *Readings in Social Psychology* (New York, Henry Holt & Co.).
  1949a. Bali: The Value System of a Steady State. In Fortes, M. (ed.), *Social Structure: Studies Presented to A. R. Radcliffe-Brown* (London, Oxford University Press).
  1949b. Cultural and Thematic Analysis of Fictional Films. In Haring, D. G. (ed.), *Personal Character and Cultural Milieu* (Syracuse, Syracuse University Press).
  1949c. Some Systematic Approaches to the Study of Culture and Personality. In Haring, D. G. (ed.), *Personal Character and Cultural Milieu* (Syracuse, Syracuse University Press).
Bateson, Gregory, and Mead, Margaret
  1942. *Balinese Character: A Photographic Analysis* (New York, Academy of Sciences).

BAVELAS, A.

1942. A Method for Investigating Individual and Group Ideologies (*Sociometry*, 5:371–377).

BEAGLEHOLE, ERNEST

1938. A Note on Cultural Compensation (*Journal of Abnormal and Social Psychology*, 33:121–123).

1944. Character Structure, Its Role in the Analysis of Interpersonal Relations (*Psychiatry*, 7:145–162).

1949. Cultural Complexity and Psychological Problems. In Mullahy, Patrick (ed.), *A Study of Interpersonal Relations* (New York, Hermitage House).

BEAGLEHOLE, ERNEST, and BEAGLEHOLE, PEARL

1941. Personality Development in Pukapukan Children. In Spier, L., Hallowell, A. I., and Newman, S. (eds.), *Language, Culture and Personality* (Menasha, Sapir Memorial Fund).

1946. *Some Modern Maoris* (Auckland, Whitcombe and Tombs).

BEALS, L.

1951. On Bierstedt's Review of Powdermaker's *Hollywood—The Dream Factory* (*American Sociological Review*, 16:549–550).

BECK, SAMUEL J.

1944. *Rorschach's Test: I. Basic Processes* (New York, Grune & Stratton).

1945. *Rorschach's Test: II. A Variety of Personality Pictures* (New York, Grune & Stratton).

BELL, BERNARD IDDINGS

1952. *Crowd Culture, An Examination of the American Way of Life* (New York, Harper & Brothers).

BELO, JANE

1949. *Bali: Rangda and Barong* (New York, J. J. Augustin).

BENDIX, REINHARD

1951. The Image of Man in the Social Sciences (*Commentary*, 11: 187–192).

BENEDICT, RUTH

1943a. *Rumanian Culture and Behavior* (Mimeographed. Distributed by Institute for Intercultural Studies, Inc.).

1943b. *Thai Culture and Behavior* (Mimeographed. Distributed by Institute for Intercultural Studies, Inc.).

1946a. *The Chrysanthemum and the Sword* (Boston, Houghton Mifflin Company).

1946b. *Patterns of Culture* (New York, Penguin Books).

1949. Child Rearing in Certain European Countries (*American Journal of Orthopsychiatry*, 19:342–350).

1953. Continuities and Discontinuities in Cultural Conditioning. In Kluckhohn, C., and Murray, H. A. (eds.), *Personality in Nature, Society, and Culture* (New York, Alfred A. Knopf).

BENNETT, JOHN W.

1946. The Interpretation of Pueblo Culture: A Question of Values (*Southwestern Journal of Anthropology*, 2:361–374).

1948. The Study of Cultures: A Survey of Techniques and Methodology in Field Work (*American Sociological Review*, 13:672–687).

BENNETT, JOHN W., and TUMIN, MELVIN

1948. *Social Life* (New York, Alfred A. Knopf).

BERELSON, B.

1952. *Content Analysis in Communication Research* (Glencoe, Free Press).

BERNDT, RONALD M. and BERNDT, CATHERINE H.

1951. The Concept of Abnormality in an Australian Aboriginal Society. In Wilbur, George B., and Muensterberger, Warner (eds.), *Psychoanalysis and Culture* (New York, International Universities Press).

BETTELHEIM, B.

1943. Individual and Mass Behavior in Extreme Situations (*Journal of Abnormal and Social Psychology*, 38:417–452).

BIDNEY, DAVID

1947. Human Nature and the Cultural Process (*American Anthropologist*, 49:375–399).

BILLIG, OTTO, GILLIN, JOHN, and DAVIDSON, WILLIAM

1947–48. Aspects of Personality and Culture in a Guatamalan Community: Ethnological and Rorschach Approaches (*Journal of Personality*, 16:153–187, 326–368).

BRANT, CHARLES

1950. Peyotism Among the Kiowa-Apache and Neighboring Tribes (*Southwestern Journal of Anthropology*, 6:212–222).

BRENMAN, MARGARET

1940. The Relationship Between Minority Group Memberships and Group Identification in a Group of Urban Middle Class Negro Girls (*Journal of Social Psychology*, 11:171–197).

BRILL, A. A.

1913. Piblokto or Hysteria Among Peary's Eskimos (*Journal of Nervous and Mental Diseases*, 40:514–520).

BROWN, G. GORDON

1947. *Law Administration and Negro-White Relations in Philadelphia* (Philadelphia, Bureau of Municipal Research of Philadelphia).

1951. Culture, Society and Personality: A Restatement (*American Journal of Psychiatry*, 108:173–175).

BUNZEL, RUTH

1940. The Role of Alcoholism in Two Central American Cultures (*Psychiatry*, 3:361–387).

BURROWS, EDWIN G.

1952. From Value to Ethos on Ifaluk Atoll (*Southwestern Journal of Anthropology*, 8:13–35).

BUSIA, K. A.

1950. *Report on a Social Survey of Sekondi-Takoradi* (London, Crown Agents for the Colonies).

CAMERON, NORMAN

1947. *The Psychology of Behavior Disorders* (Boston, Houghton Mifflin Company).

CANNON, W. B.

1942. Voodoo Death (*American Anthropologist*, 44:169–180).

CAROTHERS, J. E.

1948. A Study of Mental Derangement in Africans, and an Attempt to Explain Its Peculiarities; More Especially in Relation to the African Attitude to Life (*Psychiatry*, 11:47–86).

CAUDILL, WILLIAM

1949. Psychological Characteristics of Acculturated Wisconsin Ojibwa Children (*American Anthropologist*, 51:409–427).

1952. *Japanese-American Personality and Acculturation* (General Psychology Monographs, 45:3–102).

CHAPPLE, ELIOT D., and COON, CARLETON S.

1942. *Principles of Anthropology* (New York, Henry Holt & Co.).

CHASE, STUART

1948. *The Proper Study of Mankind* (New York, Harper & Brothers).

1951. *Roads to Agreement* (New York, Harper & Brothers).

CHILD, IRVIN L.

1943. *Italian or American?* (New Haven, Yale University Press).

CHILDS, G. M.

1949. *Umbundu Kinship and Character* (London, Oxford University Press).

CHURCHMAN, C. WEST, and ACKOFF, RUSSELL L.

1950. *Methods of Inquiry* (St. Louis, Educational Publishers).

CLINE, W.

1936. *Notes on the People of Siwah and El Garah in the Libyan Desert* (Menasha, General Series in Anthropology, no. 4).

Code of Ethics of the Society for Applied Anthropology

1951. (*Human Organization,* 10, no. 2, 32).

COMMAGER, HENRY STEELE

1949. Portrait of the American. In Chase, J. W. (ed.), *Years of the Modern* (New York, Longmans, Green & Co.).

CONANT, JAMES B.

1951. *On Understanding Science* (New York, New American Library of World Literature).

1952. *Modern Science and Modern Man* (New York, Columbia University Press).

COOPER, JOHN M.

1933. The Cree Witiko Psychosis (*Primitive Man,* 6:20–24).

1946. The Culture of the Northeastern Indian Hunters: A Reconstructive Interpretation. In Johnson, F. (ed.), *Man in Northeastern North America* (Papers of the Robert S. Peabody Foundation for Archaeology, 3).

1949. Stimulants and Narcotics. In Steward, J. H. (ed.), *Handbook of the South American Indians* (Washington, Government Printing Office).

COTTRELL, LEONARD S., JR.

1951. Basic Research Objectives as a Strategic Factor in the Advancement of the Social Sciences (*Items,* 5, no. 2, 15–17).

CRISSMAN, P.

1943. Criteria of the Empirical Method (*Scientific Monthly,* 56:433–439).

CUSSLER, MARGARET, and DEGIVE, MARY L.
1952. *'Twixt the Cup and the Lip* (New York, Twayne Publishers).

DAI, BINGHAM
1944. Divided Loyalty in War (*Psychiatry*, 7:327–340).

DALTON, M.
1948. The Rate Buster (*Applied Anthropology*, 7, no. 1, 5–18).

DAVIDSON, S.
1949. Psychiatric Work Among the Bemba (*Human Problems in British Central Africa*, no. 7, 75–86).

DAVIS, ALLISON
1943. Child Training and Social Class. In Barker, R. G., Kounin, J. S., Wright, H. F. (eds.), *Child Behavior and Development* (New York, McGraw-Hill Book Co.).

1947. Socialization and Adolescent Personality. In Newcomb, T. M., and Hartley, E. L. (eds.), *Readings in Social Psychology* (New York, Henry Holt & Co.).

1948. *Social Class Influences on Learning* (Cambridge, Mass., Harvard University Press).

1953. American Status Systems and the Socialization of the Child. In Kluckhohn, C., and Murray H. A. (eds.), *Personality in Nature, Society, and Culture* (New York, Alfred A. Knopf).

DAVIS, ALLISON, and DOLLARD, JOHN
1940. *Children of Bondage* (Washington, American Council on Education).

DAVIS, ALLISON, GARDNER, BURLEIGH, and GARDNER, R.
1941. *Deep South* (Chicago, University of Chicago Press).

DAVIS, ALLISON, and HAVIGHURST, R. J.
1947. *Father of the Man* (Boston, Houghton Mifflin Company).

1953. Social Class and Color Differences in Child Rearing. In Kluckhohn, C., and Murray, H. A. (eds.), *Personality in Nature, Society, and Culture* (New York, Alfred A. Knopf).

DENNIS, WAYNE
1940a. Does Culture Appreciably Affect Patterns of Infant Behavior? (*Journal of Social Psychology*, 12:305–317).

1940b. *The Hopi Child* (New York, Appleton-Century-Crofts).

1941. The Socialization of the Hopi Child. In Spier, L., Hallowell, A. I., and Newton, S. (eds.), *Language, Culture and Personality* (Menasha, Sapir Memorial Fund).

DEVEREUX, GEORGE

1950. Status, Socialization, and Interpersonal Relations of Mohave Children (*Psychiatry*, 13:489–502).

1951. *Reality and Dream* (New York, International Universities Press).

DEXTER, LEWIS A.

1949. A Dialogue on the Social Psychology of Colonialism (*Human Relations*, 2:49–64).

DHUNJIBHOY, J. E.

1930. A Brief *Resumé* of the Types of Insanity Commonly Met With in India (*Journal of Mental Science*, 76:254–264).

DODD, STUART CARTER

1947. *Systematic Social Science* (Beirut, American University).

DOLLARD, JOHN, and MILLER, NEAL E.

1950. *Personality and Psychotherapy* (New York, McGraw-Hill Book Co.).

DOOB, LEONARD W.

1952. *Social Psychology* (New York, Henry Holt & Co.).

DuBOIS, CORA

1944. *The People of Alor* (Minneapolis, University of Minnesota Press).

1949. Attitudes Toward Food and Hunger in Alor. In Haring, D. G. (ed.), *Personal Character and Cultural Milieu* (Syracuse, Syracuse University Press).

DUNBAR, H. FLANDERS

1947. *Mind and Body* (New York, Random House).

DURKHEIM, ÉMILE

1938. *The Rules of Sociological Method* (Glencoe, Free Press).

EATON, JOSEPH W., WEIL, R. J., and KAPLAN, B.

1951. The Hutterite Mental Health Study (*Mennonite Quarterly Review*, 25:3–21).

EDMAN, I.

1951. Philosophy and the Age of Anxiety (*Listener*, 46:252–253).

EFRON, D.

1941. *Gesturing and Environment* (New York, Kings Crown Press).

EGGAN, DOROTHY

1952. The Manifest Content of Dreams: A Challenge to Social Science (*American Anthropologist*, 54:469–485).

1953. The General Problem of Hopi Adjustment. In Kluckhohn, C., and Murray, H. A. (eds.), *Personality in Nature, Society, and Culture* (New York, Alfred A. Knopf).

ELKIN, FREDERICK

1946. The Soldier's Language (*American Journal of Sociology*, 51: 415–422).

1950. The Psychological Appeal of the Hollywood Western (*Journal of Educational Sociology*, 24:72–85).

ELKIN, H.

1940. The Northern Arapaho of Wyoming. In Linton, R. (ed.), *Acculturation in Seven American Indian Tribes* (New York, Appleton-Century-Crofts).

ELWIN, VERRIER

1947. *The Muria and Their Ghotul* (Bombay, Oxford University Press).

EMBREE, JOHN F.

1949. American Military Government. In Fortes, Meyer (ed.), *Social Structure* (Oxford, Clarendon Press).

ENDELMAN, ROBERT

1949. The New Anthropology and Its Ambitions (*Commentary*, 8: 284–291).

ERASMUS, CHARLES JOHN

1952. The Leader vs. Tradition: A Case Study (*American Anthropologist*, 54:168–178).

ERICSON, M.

1947. Social Status and Child-Rearing Practice. In Newcomb, T. M., and Hartley, E. L., *Readings in Social Psychology* (New York, Henry Holt & Co.).

ERIKSON, ERIK HOMBURGER

1939. Observations on Sioux Education (*Journal of Psychology*, 7: 101–156).

1943. *Observations on the Yurok: Childhood and World Image* (University of California Publications in American Archaeology and Ethnology, 35, no. 10).

1948a. Childhood and Tradition. In Kluckhohn, C., and Murray, H. A. (eds.), *Personality in Nature, Society, and Culture* (New York, Alfred A. Knopf).

1948b. Hitler's Imagery and German Youth. In Kluckhohn, C., and

Murray, H. A. (eds.), *Personality in Nature, Society, and Culture* (New York, Alfred A. Knopf).

1950. *Childhood and Society* (New York, W. W. Norton & Company).

EVANS-PRITCHARD, E. E.

1951. *Kinship and Marriage Among the Nuer* (Oxford, Clarendon Press).

FARBER, MAURICE L.

1950. The Problem of National Character: A Methodological Analysis (*Journal of Psychology*, 30:307–316).

FARIS, ROBERT E. L.

1944. Ecological Factors in Human Behavior. In Hunt, J. McV. (ed.), *Personality and the Behavior Disorders* (New York, The Ronald Press Company).

FARIS, R. E. L., and DUNHAM, H. W.

1938. *Mental Disorders in Urban Areas* (New York, Rinehart and Company).

FARNSWORTH, DANIEL

1951. The 18-Year Old: An Indistinct Portrait (*New York Times Magazine*, Mar. 4, pp. 11, 36–38).

FENICHEL, OTTO

1945. *The Psychoanalytic Theory of Neurosis* (New York, W. W. Norton & Company).

FIELD, LIONEL

1950. The Mind That Still Eludes Our Grasp (*New York Times Magazine*, Nov. 19, pp. 9, 54–59).

FIELDING, XAN

1953. The Ghosts of Frangocastello (*Listener*, 49:187–188).

FORD, CLELLAN S.

1941. *Smoke From Their Fires. The Life of a Kwakiutl Chief* (New Haven, Yale University Press).

FORDE, C. DARYLL

1949. *Habitat, Economy and Society* (New York, E. P. Dutton & Co.).

FRANK, LAWRENCE K.

1939. Projective Methods for the Study of Personality (*Journal of Psychology*, 8:389–413).

1948. Forward. In Frank, L. K., Hutchinson, G. E., and Livingston, W. K., McCulloch, W. S., and Wiener, N. (eds.), *Teleological*

Mechanisms (New York, Annals of the New York Academy of Sciences, 50).

FRANKFORT, H.
1948. *Kingship and the Gods* (Chicago, University of Chicago Press).

FREEDMAN, P.
1950. *The Principles of Scientific Research* (Washington, Public Affairs Press).

FREEDMAN, RONALD, HAWLEY, AMOS H., LANDECKER, WERNER S., and MINER, HORACE M.
1952. *Principles of Sociology* (New York, Henry Holt & Co.).

FREUD, SIGMUND
1938. The Interpretation of Dreams. In Brill, A. A. (ed.), *The Basic Writings of Sigmund Freud* (New York, Modern Library).

FRISCH, O. R.
1953. Causality in Modern Physics (*Listener*, 49:138–139, 142).

FROMM, ERICH
1941. *Escape from Freedom* (New York, Farrar, Straus & Young).
1943. Sex and Character (*Psychiatry*, 6:21–31).
1949. Psychoanalytic Characterology and Its Application to the Understanding of Culture. In Sargent, S. S., and Smith, M. W. (eds.), *Culture and Personality* (New York, Viking Fund).
1953. Individual and Social Origins of Neurosis. In Kluckhohn, C., and Murray, H. A. (eds.), *Personality in Nature, Society, and Culture* (New York, Alfred A. Knopf).

FROMM-REICHMANN, FRIEDA
1950. *Principles of Intensive Psychotherapy* (Chicago, University of Chicago Press).

FURFEY, PAUL H.
1953. *The Scope and Method of Sociology* (New York, Harper & Brothers).

GESELL, ARNOLD and ILG, E. L.
1946. *The Child from Five to Ten* (New York, Harper & Brothers).

GILLIN, JOHN
1948a. Personality Formation from the Comparative Cultural Point of View. In Kluckhohn, C., and Murray, H. A. (eds.), *Personality in Nature, Society, and Culture* (New York, Alfred A. Knopf).
1948b. *The Ways of Men* (New York, Appleton-Century-Crofts).

1950. The Fear (*Atlantic, 186,* no. 2, 68–72).

1951. *The Culture of Security in San Carlos* (New Orleans, Middle America Research Institute, The Tulane University of Louisiana, Publication no. 16).

1952. Ethos and Cultural Aspects of Personality. In Tax, Sol (ed.), *Heritage of Conquest* (Glencoe, Free Press).

GITTELSON, Y.

1950. Sacred Cows in Collision (*American Scientist,* 38:603–609).

GLAD, DONALD DAVISON

1947. Attitudes and Experiences of American-Jewish and American-Irish Male Youths as Related to Differences in Adult Rates of Inebriety (*Quarterly Journal of Studies on Alcohol,* 8:406–472).

GOLDFRANK, ESTHER

1949. Socialization, Personality, and the Structure of Pueblo Society. In Haring, D. G. (ed.), *Personal Character and Cultural Milieu* (Syracuse, Syracuse University Press).

1951. "Old Man" and the Father Image in Blood (Blackfoot) Society. In Wilbur, G. B., and Muensterberger, Warner (eds.), *Psychoanalysis and Culture* (New York, International Universities Press).

GOLDMAN, I.

1950. Psychiatric Interpretation of Russian History: A Reply to Geoffrey Gorer (*The American Slavic and East European Review,* 9:151–161).

GOLDMAN-EISLER, FRIEDA

1953. Breast Feeding and Character Formation. In Kluckhohn, C., and Murray, H. A. (eds.), *Personality in Nature, Society, and Culture* (New York, Alfred A. Knopf).

GOLDSCHMIDT, WALTER

1950. Social Class in America—A Critical Survey (*American Anthropologist,* 52:483–498).

GOODE, WILLIAM J. and HATT, PAUL K.

1952. *Methods in Social Research* (New York, McGraw-Hill Book Co.).

GOODENOUGH, WARD

1949. Premarital Freedom on Truk: Theory and Practice (*American Anthropologist,* 51:615–620).

GOODFRIEND, ARTHUR

1950. *If You Were Born in Russia* (New York, Farrar, Straus & Young).

GORER, GEOFFREY

1948a. The American Character (*Life*, Aug. 18, pp. 23, 94–96).

1948b. *The American People* (New York, W. W. Norton & Company).

1949a. Some Aspects of the Psychology of the People of Great Russia (*The American Slavic and East European Review*, 7:155–166).

1949b. Themes in Japanese Culture. In Haring, D. G. (ed.), *Personal Character and Cultural Milieu* (Syracuse, Syracuse University Press).

1950. The Concept of National Character (*Science News*, 18:104–122).

GORER, GEOFFREY, and RICKMAN, J.

1950. *The People of Great Russia* (New York, Chanticleer Press).

GREEN, A. W.

1947–48. A Re-Examination of the Marginal Man Concept (*Social Forces*, 26:167–171).

GREENACRE, PHYLLIS

1953. Infants' Reaction to Restraint. Problems in the Fate of Infantile Aggression. In Kluckhohn, C., and Murray, H. A. (eds.), *Personality in Nature, Society, and Culture* (New York, Alfred A. Knopf).

GREENBERG, P. J.

1932. Competition in Children: An Experimental Study (*American Journal of Psychology*, 44:221–248).

GREGORY, R.

1949. *Discovery, or The Spirit and Service of Science* (Harmondsworth, Penguin Books).

GRINKER, ROY R., and SPIEGEL, JOHN P.

1943. *War Neurosis in North Africa* (Prepared and Distributed for the Air Surgeon, Army Air Forces, by the Josiah Macy, Jr., Foundation, New York).

GRUENBAUM, ADOLF

1952. Causality and the Science of Human Behavior (*American Scientist*, 40:665–676).

HADLEY, C. V. D.

1949. Personality Patterns, Social Class, and Aggression in the British West Indies (*Human Relations*, 2:349–362).

HALLIDAY, JAMES L.

1948. *Psychosocial Medicine: A Study of the Sick Society* (New York, W. W. Norton & Company).

HALLOWELL, A. IRVING

1945a. The Rorschach Technique in the Study of Personality and Culture (*American Anthropologist*, 47:195–210).

1945b. The Sociopsychological Aspects of Acculturation. In Linton, R. (ed.), *The Study of Man in the World Crisis* (New York, Columbia University Press).

1946. Some Psychological Characteristics of the Northeastern Indians. In Johnson, F. (ed.), *Man in Northeastern North America* (Papers of the Robert S. Peabody Foundation for Archaeology, 3).

1949. The Social Functions of Anxiety in a Primitive Society. In Haring, D. G. (ed.), *Personal Character and Cultural Milieu* (Syracuse, Syracuse University Press).

1950a. Personality Structure and the Evolution of Man (*American Anthropologist*, 52:159–173).

1950b. Values, Acculturation and Mental Health (*American Journal of Orthopsychiatry*, 20:732–743).

1953. Culture, Personality, and Society. In Kroeber, A. L. (ed.), *Anthropology Today* (Chicago, University of Chicago Press).

HAMPSHIRE, S.

1951. *Spinoza* (Harmondsworth, Penguin Books).

HARING, DOUGLAS G. (ed.)

1949. *Personal Character and Cultural Milieu* (Syracuse, Syracuse University Press).

1950. The Social Sciences and Biology. In *Beitraege zur Gesellungs- und Voelker-wissenschaft* (Berlin, Verlag Gebr. Mann).

HARSH, C. M., and SCHRICKEL, H. G.

1950. *Personality Development and Assessment* (New York, The Ronald Press Company).

HARTMAN, HEINZ, KRIS, ERNST, and LOEWENSTEIN, RUDOLPH M.

1951. Some Psychoanalytic Comments on "Culture and Personality." In Wilbur, G. W., and Muensterberger, Warner (eds.), *Psychoanalysis and Culture* (New York, International Universities Press).

HARTMAN, ROBERT S.
1951. Anthropology and Scientific Method (*American Anthropologist,* 53:591–593).

HAVIGHURST, R. J., and NEUBAUER, D.
1949. Community Factors in Relation to Character Formation. In Havighurst, R. J., and Taba, Hilda, *Adolescent Character and Personality* (New York, John Wiley & Sons).

HAWLEY, CAMERON
1953. *Executive Suite* (New York, Ballantine Books).

HENRY, JULES
1940. Some Cultural Determinants of Hostility in Pilagá Indian Children (*American Journal of Orthopsychiatry,* 10:111–120).

1948. Anthropology and Orthopsychiatry. In *Orthopsychiatry 1923–1948: Retrospect and Prospect* (New York, American Orthopsychiatric Association).

1949. The Social Function of Child Sexuality in Pilagá Indian Culture. In *Psychosexual Development in Health and Disease* (New York, Grune & Stratton).

HENRY, JULES, and HENRY, ZUNIA
1953. Doll Play of Pilagá Indian Children. In Kluckhohn, C., and Murray, H. A. (eds.), *Personality in Nature, Society, and Culture* (New York, Alfred A. Knopf).

HENRY, JULES, and SPIRO, MELFORD E.
1953. Psychological Techniques: Projective Tests in Field Work. In Kroeber, A. L. (ed.), *Anthropology Today* (Chicago, Chicago University Press).

HENRY, WILLIAM E.
1947. The Thematic Apperception Technique in the Study of Culture-Personality Relations (*Genetic Psychology Monographs,* 35).

1949. The Business Executive: The Psychodynamics of Social Role (*American Journal of Sociology,* 54:286–291).

HERLING, GUSTAV
1952. *A World Apart* (New York, Mentor Books).

HERMANNS, MATTHIAS
1949. *Die Nomaden von Tibet* (Vienna, Verlag Herold).

HERSKOVITS, M. J.
1948. *Man and His Works* (New York, Alfred A. Knopf).

1950. The Hypothetical Situation: A Technique of Field Research (*Southwestern Journal of Anthropology*, 6:32–40).

HIERONYMUS, A. N.

1951. A Study of Social Class Motivation: Relationship Between Anxiety for Education and Certain Socio-Economic and Intellectual Variables (*Journal of Educational Psychology*, 42:193–205).

HOLLINGSHEAD, AUGUST B.

1949. *Elmtown's Youth* (New York, John Wiley & Sons).

1950. Class Differences in Family Instability (*Annals of the American Academy of Political and Social Science*, 272:39–46).

HOLTON, G.

1953. On the Duality and Growth of Physical Science (*American Scientist*, 41:89–99).

HOMANS, G. C.

1950. *The Human Group* (New York, Harcourt, Brace & Co.).

HONIGMANN, IRMA

1951. *The Role of the Ethnographer in Determining Pattern* (Mimeographed).

HONIGMANN, JOHN J.

1946. *Ethnography and Acculturation of the Fort Nelson Slave* (Yale University Publications in Anthropology, no. 33).

1947. Cultural Dynamics of Sex (*Psychiatry*, 10:37–48).

1949a. *Culture and Ethos of Kaska Society* (Yale University Publications in Anthropology, no. 40).

1949b. Incentives to Work in a Canadian Indian Community (*Applied Anthropology*, 8, no. 4, 23–28).

1949c. There Isn't a Person (*Antioch Review*, 9:388–395). Reprinted by permission of the *Antioch Review*.

1950. Culture Patterns and Human Stress (*Psychiatry*, 13:25–34).

1952a. Community Relations in Great Whale River (*American Anthropologist*, 54:510–522).

1952b. The Testing of Hypotheses in Anthropology (*American Anthropologist*, 54:429–432).

1953a. *Theory of Ritual* (Chapel Hill, University of North Carolina Bookstore, mimeographed).

1953b. Toward a Distinction Between Social and Psychiatric Abnormality (*Social Forces*, 31:274–277).

HONIGMANN, JOHN J., and HONIGMANN, IRMA.

1945. Alcoholic Drinking in an Indian-White Community (*Quarterly Journal for Studies on Alcohol*, 5:575–619).

1953. Some Patterns of Child Rearing Among the Great Whale River Eskimo (*Anthropological Papers of the University of Alaska*. In press).

HORNEY, KAREN

1937. *The Neurotic Personality of Our Time* (New York, W. W. Norton & Company).

1939. *New Ways in Psychoanalysis* (New York, W. W. Norton & Company).

1945. *Our Inner Conflicts* (New York, W. W. Norton & Company).

HORTON, DONALD

1943. The Functions of Alcohol in Primitive Societies: A Cross-Cultural Study (*Quarterly Journal of Studies on Alcohol*, 4:199–320).

1945. The Functions of Alcohol in Primitive Societies. In *Alcohol, Science and Society* (New Haven, Quarterly Journal of Studies on Alcohol).

1953. The Functions of Alcohol in Primitive Societies: A Cross-Cultural Study. In Kluckhohn, C., and Murray, H. A. (eds.), *Personality in Nature, Society, and Culture* (New York, Alfred A. Knopf).

HSU, FRANCIS L. K.

1948. *Under the Ancestors' Shadow* (New York, Columbia University Press).

1949. Suppression Versus Repression (*Psychiatry*, 12:223–242).

1952. Anthropology or Psychiatry: A Definition of Objectives and Their Implications (*Southwest Journal of Anthropology*, 8:227–250).

HUMPHREYS, CHRISTMAS

1952. *Buddhism* (Harmondsworth, Penguin Books).

HUTTON, GRAHAM

1946. *Midwest at Noon* (Chicago, University of Chicago Press).

Ideas and Beliefs of the Victorians

1950. (London, Sylvan Press).

INKELES, ALEX

1953. Some Sociological Observations on Culture and Personality

Studies. In Kluckhohn, C., and Murray, H. A. (eds.), *Personality in Nature, Society, and Culture* (New York, Alfred A. Knopf).

INTERNATIONAL CONGRESS ON MENTAL HYGIENE, INTERNATIONAL PREPARATORY COMMISSION

1949. Statement (*Human Relations*, 2:65–98).

JACOBS, MELVILLE, and STERN, BERNHARD

1947. *Outline of Anthropology* (New York, Barnes & Noble).

JAHODA, MARIE, DEUTSCH, MORTON, and COOK, STUART W.

1951. *Research Methods in Social Relations. Part 1: Basic Processes* (New York, The Dryden Press).

1951. *Research Methods in Social Relations. Part 2: Selected Techniques* (New York, The Dryden Press).

JANIS, IRVING L.

1951. *Air War and Emotional Stress* (New York, McGraw-Hill Book Co.).

JENKINS, R. L., and HEWITT, L.

1946. Types of Personality Structure Encountered in Child Guidance Clinics (American Journal of Orthopsychiatry, 16:84–94).

JEWELL, DONALD P.

1952. A Case of a "Psychotic" Navaho Indian Male (*Human Organization*, 11, no. 1, 32–36).

JOHNS-HEINE, PATRICK, and GERTH, HANS H.

1949. Values in Mass Periodical Fiction, 1921–1940 (*Public Opinion Quarterly*, 13:105–113).

JOSEPH, ALICE and MURRAY, N.

1951. *Chamorros and Carolinians of Saipan* (Cambridge, Harvard University Press).

JOSEPH, ALICE, SPICER, ROSAMOND B., and CHESKY, JANE

1949. *The Desert People* (Chicago, University of Chicago Press).

KARDINER, ABRAM

1939. *The Individual and His Society* (New York, Columbia University Press).

1945. *The Psychological Frontiers of Society* (New York, Columbia University Press).

1949a. The Concept of Basic Personality Structure as an Operational Tool in the Social Sciences. In Haring, D. G. (ed.), *Personal Character and Cultural Milieu* (Syracuse, Syracuse University Press).

1949b. Psychodynamics and the Social Sciences. In Sargent, S. S., and Smith, M. W. (eds.), *Culture and Personality* (New York, Viking Fund).

KARDINER, ABRAM, and OVESEY, LIONEL

1951. *The Mark of Oppression* (New York, W. W. Norton & Company).

KARPMAN, B., LURIE, L. A., LIPPMAN, H. S., RABINOVITCH, R. D., LOURIE, R. S., LOWREY, L. G., and LEVY, D. M.

1951. Psychopathic Behavior in Infants and Children: A Critical Survey of the Existing Concepts. Round Table, 1950 (*American Journal of Orthopsychiatry*, 21:223–272).

KEESING, F. M.

1952. The Papuan Orokaiva vs. Mt. Lamington: Cultural Shock and Its Aftermath (*Human Organization*, 11, no. 1, 16–22).

KINSEY, ALFRED C., POMEROY, WARDELL B., MARTIN, CLYDE E.

1948. *Sexual Behavior in the Human Male* (Philadelphia, W. B. Saunders Co.).

KIPLING, RUDYARD

1949. *Kim* (London, The Macmillan Company).

KLINEBERG, OTTO

1944. A Science of National Character (*Journal of Social Psychology, S.P.S.S.I. Bulletin*, 19:147–162).

1949. Recent Studies of National Character. In Sargent, S. S., and Smith, M. W. (eds.), *Culture and Personality* (New York, Viking Fund).

1950. *Tensions Affecting International Understanding* (Bulletin 62, Social Science Research Council).

KLOPFER, BRUNO, and KELLEY, DOUGLAS M.

1942. *The Rorschach Technique* (Yonkers, World Book Co.).

KLUCKHOHN, CLYDE

1941. Patterning as Exemplified in Navaho Culture. In Spier, L., Hallowell, A. I., and Newman, S. (eds.), *Language, Culture and Personality* (Menasha, Sapir Memorial Fund).

1943. Covert Culture and Administrative Problems (*American Anthropologist*, 45:213–229).

1944a. The Influence of Psychiatry on Anthropology in America During the Past One Hundred Years. In Hall, J. K., Zilboorg, G., and Bunker, H. A. (eds.), *One Hundred Years of American Psychiatry* (New York, Columbia University Press).

1944b. *Navaho Witchcraft* (Papers of the Peabody Museum of American Archaeology and Ethnology, Harvard University, 22, no. 2).

1949a. *Mirror for Man* (New York, Whittlesey House).

1949b. Needed Refinements in the Biographical Approach. In Sargent, S. S., and Smith, M. W. (eds.), *Culture and Personality* (New York, Viking Fund).

1949c. Participation in Ceremonies in a Navaho Community. In Haring, D. G. (ed.), *Personal Character and Cultural Milieu* (Syracuse, Syracuse University Press).

KLUCKHOHN, CLYDE, GOTTSCHALK, L., and ANGELL, R.

1945. *The Use of the Personal Document in History, Anthropology, and Sociology* (Bulletin 53, Social Science Research Council).

KLUCKHOHN, CLYDE, and MORGAN, W.

1951. Some Notes on Navaho Dreams. In Wilbur, G. B., and Muensterberger, W. (eds.), *Psychoanalysis and Culture* (New York, International Universities Press).

KLUCKHOHN, CLYDE, and MURRAY, HENRY A. (eds.)

1953. *Personality in Nature, Society, and Culture* (New York, Alfred A. Knopf).

KLUCKHOHN, FLORENCE

1940. The Participant-Observer Technique in Small Communities (*American Journal of Sociology*, 46:331–342).

1950. Dominant and Substitute Profiles of Cultural Orientation: Their Significance for the Analysis of Social Stratification (*Social Forces*, 28:376–393).

KNIGHT, E. F.

1896. *Where Three Empires Meet* (London, Longmans, Green & Co.).

KOMAROVSKY, MIRRA, and SARGENT, S. STANSFELD

1949. Research into Subcultural Influences upon Personality. In Sargent, S. S., and Smith, M. W. (eds.), *Culture and Personality* (New York, Viking Fund).

KORNER, ANNELIESE F.

1950. Theoretical Considerations Concerning the Scope and Limitations of Projective Techniques (*Journal of Abnormal and Social Psychology*, 45:619–627).

KRACAUER, SIEGFRIED

1947. *From Caligari to Hitler* (Princeton, Princeton University Press).

KRIGE, J. D.

1948. *The Anthropological Approach to the Study of Society* (Durban, Natal University College).

KROEBER, A. L.

1935. History and Science in Anthropology (*American Anthropologist*, 37:539–569).

1939. *Cultural and Natural Areas of North America* (University of California Publications in American Archaeology and Ethnology, 38:1–242).

1948. *Anthropology* (New York, Harcourt, Brace & Co.).

1949. *World Renewal: A Cult System of Native Northwest California* (Anthropological Records, 13, no. 1).

1953. *Anthropology Today* (Chicago, University of Chicago Press).

LABARRE, WESTON

1938. *The Peyote Cult* (Yale University Publications in Anthropology, no. 19).

1945. Some Observations on Character Structure in the Orient: The Japanese (*Psychiatry*, 8:319–342).

1948. Folklore and Psychology (*Journal of American Folklore*, 61:382–390).

1949a. Child Care and World Peace (*The Child*, 13:156–157).

1949b. A Pattern for Modern Man (*Mental Hygiene*, 33:209–221).

1950. Aymara Folktales (*International Journal of American Linguistics*, 16:40–45).

LANDES, RUTH

1938. The Abnormal among the Ojibwa Indians (*Journal of Abnormal and Social Psychology*, 33:14–33).

LEE, DOROTHY

1953. Are Basic Needs Ultimate? In Kluckhohn, C., and Murray, H. A. (eds.), *Personality in Nature, Society, and Culture* (New York, Alfred A. Knopf).

LEIGHTON, ALEXANDER H.

1949. *Human Relations in a Changing World* (New York, E. P. Dutton & Co.).

LEIGHTON, DOROTHEA, and KLUCKHOHN, CLYDE
  1947. *Children of the People* (Cambridge, Mass., Harvard University Press).
LEITES, NATHAN
  1948. Psycho-Cultural Hypotheses About Political Acts (*World Politics,* 1:102–119).
  1953. Trends in Affectlessness. In Kluckhohn, C., and Murray, H. A. (eds.), *Personality in Nature, Society, and Culture* (New York, Alfred A. Knopf).
LERNER, D.
  1949. *Sykewar: Psychological Warfare* (New York, George W. Stewart, Publisher).
LERNER, E.
  1937. *Constraint Areas and the Moral Judgment of Children* (Menasha, Banta Publishing Co.).
LESSER, ALEXANDER
  1939. Problems Versus Subject Matter as Directives of Research (*American Anthropologist,* 41:574–582).
LEVY, DAVID M.
  1937. Primary Affect Hunger (*American Journal of Psychiatry,* 94: 643–652).
  1948. Anti-Nazis: Criteria of Differentiation (*Psychiatry,* 11:125–167).
LEVY, MARION
  1952. *The Structure of Society* (Princeton, Princeton University Press).
LEWIN, KURT
  1943. Forces Behind Food Habits and Methods of Change. In *The Problem of Changing Food Habits* (Bulletin of the National Research Council, no. 108).
  1951. *Field Theory in Social Science* (New York, Harper & Brothers).
LEWIN, KURT, LIPPITT, R., and WHITE, R. K.
  1939. Patterns of Aggressive Behavior in Experimentally Created "Social Climates" (*Journal of Psychology,* 10:271–299).
LEWIS, C.
  1946. *Children of the Cumberland* (New York, Columbia University Press).

LEWIS, OSCAR

    1951. *Life in a Mexican Valley* (Urbana, University of Illinois).

LINCOLN, JACKSON S.

    1939. *The Dream in Primitive Cultures* (Baltimore, The Williams & Wilkins Company).

LINDESMITH, A. R., and STRAUSS, A. L.

    1950. Critique of Culture-Personality Writings (*American Sociological Review*, 15:587–600).

LINEBARGER, P. M. A.

    1948. *Psychological Warfare* (Washington, Infantry Journal Press).

LINTON, RALPH

    1936. *The Study of Man* (New York, Appleton-Century-Crofts).

    1945. *The Cultural Background of Personality* (New York, Appleton-Century-Crofts).

LINTON, RALPH, and KARDINER, ABRAM

    1947. The Change from Dry to Wet Rice Culture in Tanala-Betsileo. In Newcomb, T. M., and Hartley, E. L. (eds.), *Readings in Social Psychology* (New York, Henry Holt & Co.).

LIPPITT, R.

    1940. An Experimental Study of the Effects of Democratic and Authoritarian Group Atmospheres (*University of Iowa Studies in Child Welfare*, 16:45–195).

LYND, R.

    1939. *Knowledge for What?* (Princeton, Princeton University Press).

MAAS, H. S.

    1951. Some Social Class Differences in the Family System and Group Relations of Pre- and Early Adolescents (*Child Development*, 22:145–152).

McDOUGALL, WILLIAM

    1920. *The Group Mind* (New York, G. P. Putnam's Sons).

McGRANAHAN, D. V., and WAYNE, I.

    1948. German and American Traits Reflected in Popular Drama (*Human Relations*, 1:429–455).

MACGREGOR, GORDON

    1946. *Warriors without Weapons* (Chicago, University of Chicago Press).

MAJUMDAR, D. N.

1944. *The Fortunes of Primitive Tribes* (Lucknow, Universal Publishers).

MALINOWSKI, BRONISLAW

1944. *A Scientific Theory of Culture and Other Essays* (Chapel Hill, University of North Carolina Press).

MALOUF, CARLING

1942. Gosiute Peyotism (*American Anthropologist*, 44:93–103).

MANDELBAUM, DAVID G.

1953. On the Study of National Character (*American Anthropologist*, 55:174–186).

MARGENAU, H.

1943. Theory and Scientific Development (*Scientific Monthly*, 57: 63–72).

MARTIN, JOHN B.

1953. *Why Did They Kill?* (New York, Ballantine Books).

MARWICK, M. G.

1952. The Social Context of Cewa Witch Beliefs (*Africa*, 22:120–135, 215–233).

MASLOW, ABRAHAM H.

1942. The Dynamics of Psychological Security-Insecurity (*Character and Personality*, 10:331–344).

1943a. Dynamics of Personality Organization (*Psychological Review*, 50:514–539, 541–558).

1943b. Preface to Motivation Theory (*Psychosomatic Medicine*, 5:85–92).

1946. Problem-Centering vs. Means-Centering in Science (*Philosophy of Science*, 13:326–331).

1949. The Expressive Component of Behavior (*Psychological Review*, 56:261–272).

1950. *Self-Actualizing People: A Study of Psychological Health* (*Personality Symposium*, no. 1, 11–34).

MASLOW, ABRAHAM H., and MITTELMANN, BELA

1941. *Principles of Abnormal Psychology* (New York, Harper & Brothers).

MASSERMAN, JULES

1946. *Principles of Dynamic Psychiatry* (Philadelphia, W. B. Saunders Co.).

MAYO, ELTON

1945. *The Social Problems of an Industrial Civilization* (Boston, Harvard Business School).

MAZER, M.

1951. An Experimental Study of the Hypnotic Dream (*Psychiatry,* 14:265–277).

MEAD, MARGARET

1930. *Growing Up in New Guinea* (New York, William Morrow & Co.).

1942a. *And Keep Your Powder Dry* (New York, William Morrow & Co.).

1942b. The Family in the Future. In Anshen, R. N. (ed.), *Beyond Victory* (New York, Harper & Brothers).

1946. Trends in Personal Life (*New Republic, 115,* no. 12, no. 1660, pp. 346–348).

1947a. The Application of Anthropological Techniques to Cross-National Communication (*Transactions of the New York Academy of Sciences, 9,* ser. II, 133–152).

1947b. Educative Effects of Social Environment as Disclosed by Studies of Primitive Societies. In Newcomb, T. M., and Hartley, E. L. (eds.), *Readings in Social Psychology* (New York, Henry Holt & Co.).

1947c. *The Mountain Arapesh V* (Anthropological Papers of the American Museum of Natural History, *41*).

1948a. A Case History in Cross-National Communication. In Bryson, L. (ed.), *The Communication of Ideas* (New York, Harper & Brothers).

1948b. The Contemporary American Family as an Anthropologist Sees It (*American Journal of Sociology, 53:453–459*).

1949a. Age Patterning in Personality Development. In Haring, D. G. (ed.), *Personal Character and Cultural Milieu* (Syracuse, Syracuse University Press).

1949b. Character Formation and Diachronic Theory. In Fortes, M. (ed.), *Social Structure* (Oxford, Clarendon Press).

1949c. The Concept of Culture and the Psychosomatic Approach. In Haring, D. G. (ed.), *Personal Character and Cultural Milieu* (Syracuse, Syracuse University Press).

1949d. The Implications of Culture Change for Personality Development. In Haring, D. G. (ed.), *Personal Character and Cultural Milieu* (Syracuse, Syracuse University Press).

1949e. On the Implications for Anthropology of the Gesell-Ilg Approach to Maturation. In Haring, D. G. (ed.), *Personal Character and Cultural Milieu* (Syracuse, Syracuse University Press).

1949f. *Male and Female* (New York, William Morrow & Co.).

1950a. *Coming of Age in Samoa* (New York, Mentor Books).

1950b. *Sex and Temperament* (New York, Mentor Books).

1951a. A Rejoinder to Jules Henry's Review of "Male and Female" (*American Journal of Orthopsychiatry*, 21:427–428).

1951b. Research in Contemporary Cultures. In Guetzkow, H. (ed.), *Groups, Leadership and Men* (Pittsburgh, Carnegie Press).

1951c. *Soviet Attitudes Toward Authority* (New York, McGraw-Hill Book Co.).

1951d. The Study of National Character. In Lerner, D., and Lasswell, H. D. (eds.), *The Policy Sciences: Recent Developments in Scope and Method* (Stanford, Stanford University Press).

1952a. Some Relationships Between Social Anthropology and Psychiatry. In Alexander, F., and Ross, H., *Dynamic Psychiatry* (Chicago, University of Chicago Press).

1952b. The Training of the Cultural Anthropologist (*American Anthropologist*, 54:343–346).

1953a. National Character. In Kroeber, A. L. (ed.), *Anthropology Today* (Chicago, University of Chicago Press).

1953b. Social Change and Cultural Surrogates. In Kluckhohn, Clyde, and Murray, H. A. (eds.), *Personality in Nature, Society, and Culture* (New York, Alfred A. Knopf).

MERTON, R. K.

1949. *Social Theory and Social Structure* (Glencoe, Free Press).

MERZBACH, A.

1949. Home Punishment of Young Children in a Jewish Community of Palestine: A Survey of Two Thousand Five Hundred Jewish Children (*Human Relations*, 2:305–317).

METRAUX, RHODA

1952. Some Aspects of Hierarchical Structure in Haiti. In Tax, S. (ed.), *Acculturation in the Americas: Proceedings and Selected Papers of the XXIXth International Congress of Americanists*.

MEYER, R. M.

1892–93. German Character as Reflected in National Life and Literature (*International Journal of Ethics*, 3:203–242).

MILLER, N. E., and DOLLARD, JOHN

1941. *Social Learning and Imitation* (New Haven, Yale University Press).

MILLS, C. WRIGHT

1951. *White Collar* (New York, Oxford University Press).

MOLONEY, J. C.

1945. Psychiatric Observations in Okinawa Shima: The Psychology of the Okinawan (*Psychiatry*, 8:391–399).

MONEY-KYRLE, ROGER

1939. *Superstition and Society* (London, Hogarth Press).

1951. Some Aspects of State and Character in Germany. In Wilbur, G., and Muensterberger, W. (eds.), *Psychoanalysis and Culture* (New York, International Universities Press).

MORGAN, WILLIAM

1932. Navaho Dreams (*American Anthropologist*, 34:390–405).

MOSTELLER, F. (ed.)

1949. *The Pre-Election Polls of 1948: Report of the Committee on Analysis of Pre-Election Polls and Forecasts* (Bulletin 60, Social Science Research Council).

MULLAHY, A.

1950. A Philosophy of Personality (*Psychiatry*, 13:417–437).

MURDOCK, GEORGE PETER

1934. *Our Primitive Contemporaries* (New York, The Macmillan Company).

1945. The Common Denominator of Cultures. In Linton, R. (ed.), *The Science of Man in the World Crisis* (New York, Columbia University Press).

1949. *Social Structure* (New York, The Macmillan Company).

1950. Family Stability in Non-European Cultures (*Annals of the American Academy of Political and Social Science*, 272:195–201).

MURDOCK, GEORGE PETER, FORD, CLELLAN S., HUDSON, ALFRED E., KENNEDY, RAYMOND, SIMMONS, LEO W., and WHITING, JOHN W. M.

1950. *Outline of Cultural Materials*, Third Revised Edition (New Haven, Human Relations Area Files).

MURPHY, GARDNER

1947. *Personality* (New York, Harper & Brothers).

1949. The Relationship of Culture and Personality. In Sargent, S. S., and Smith, M. W. (eds.), *Culture and Personality* (New York, Viking Fund).

MURRAY, HENRY A.

1949. Research Planning: A Few Proposals. In Sargent, S. S., and Smith, M. W. (eds.), *Culture and Personality* (New York, Viking Fund).

MURRAY, HENRY A., and KLUCKHOHN, CLYDE

1953. Outline of a Conception of Personality. In Kluckhohn, C., and Murray, H. A. (eds.), *Personality in Nature, Society, and Culture* (New York, Alfred A. Knopf).

MYRDAL, G.

1944. *An American Dilemma* (New York, Harper & Brothers).

NADEL, S. F.

1951. *The Foundations of Social Anthropology* (London, Cohen and West).

NEWCOMB, THEODORE M.

1950. *Social Psychology* (New York, The Dryden Press).

NEWTON, N. R.

1951. The Relationship Between Infant Feeding Experience and Later Behavior (*Journal of Pediatrics*, 38:28–40).

NORTHROP, F. S. C.

1946. *The Meeting of East and West* (New York, The Macmillan Company).

1949. *Logic of the Sciences and the Humanities* (New York, The Macmillan Company).

1953. *The Taming of the Nations* (New York, The Macmillan Company).

OBERHOLZER, E.

1944. Rorschach's Experiment and the Alorese. In DuBois, C., *The People of Alor* (Minneapolis, University of Minnesota Press).

ODUM, HOWARD M.

1953. Folk Sociology as a Subject Field for the Historical Study of Total Human Society and the Empirical Study of Group Behavior (*Social Forces*, 31:193–223).

OFFICE OF STRATEGIC SERVICES, ASSESSMENT STAFF

1948. *The Assessment of Men* (New York, Rinehart & Company).

ORLANSKY, HAROLD

1946. Jewish Personality Traits (*Commentary,* 2:377–383).

1948. Destiny in the Nursery (*Commentary,* 5:563–569).

1949. Infant Care and Personality (*Psychological Bulletin,* 46:1–48).

OSGOOD, CORNELIUS

1951. *The Koreans and Their Culture* (New York, The Ronald Press Company).

PARSONS, ELSIE CLEWS

1945. *Peguche* (Chicago, University of Chicago Press).

PARSONS, TALCOTT

1947. Certain Primary Sources and Patterns of Aggression in the Social Structure of the Western World (*Psychiatry,* 10:167–182).

PARTEN, M.

1950. *Surveys, Polls, and Samples* (New York, Harper & Brothers).

PAUL, BENJAMIN D.

1953. Interview Techniques and Field Relationships. In Kroeber, A. L. (ed.), *Anthropology Today* (Chicago, University of Chicago Press).

PAUL, LESLIE

1952. Rebellion of the Young (*The Listener,* 47:219–231).

PIAGET, JEAN

1929. *The Moral Judgment of the Child* (New York, Harcourt, Brace & Co.).

1952. *The Language and Thought of the Child* (New York, Humanities Press).

PIDDINGTON, RALPH

1950. *An Introduction to Social Anthropology* (Edinburgh, Oliver and Boyd).

PIERIS, RALPH

1952. Character Formation in the Evolution of the Acquisitive Society (*Psychiatry,* 15:53–60).

PLUMB, J. H.

1950. *England in the Eighteenth Century* (Harmondsworth, Penguin Books).

POLANSKY, N., LIPPITT, R., and REDL, FRITZ

1950. An Investigation of Behavioral Contagion in Groups (*Human Relations,* 3:319–348).

RAUM, O. F.

1940. *Chaga Childhood* (London, Oxford University Press).

RENNIE, THOMAS A. C., and WOODWARD, L. E.

1948. *Mental Hygiene in Modern Society* (New York, Commonwealth Fund).

RIBBLE, MARGARET

1944. Infantile Experience in Relation to Personality Development. In Hunt, J. McV. (ed.), *Personality and Behavioral Disorders* (New York, The Ronald Press Company).

RICHARDSON, F. L. W.

1950. Field Methods and Techniques (*Human Organization, 9,* no. 2, 31–32).

RIESMAN, D.

1950. *The Lonely Crowd* (New Haven, Yale University Press).

1951. Some Problems of a Course in "Culture and Personality" (*Journal of General Education,* 5:122–136).

1952. *Faces in the Crowd* (New Haven, Yale University Press).

RILEY, MATILDA WHITE, and FLOWERMAN, SAMUEL H.

1951. Group Relations as a Variable in Communications Research (*American Sociological Review,* 16:174–180).

ROBERTS, JOHN M.

1951. *Three Navaho Households: A Comparative Study of Small Group Culture* (Papers of the Peabody Museum of American Archaeology and Ethnology, Harvard University, 40, no. 3).

RODNICK, DAVID

1948. *Postwar Germans: An Anthropologist's Account* (New Haven, Yale University Press).

ROE, ANNE

1953. What Makes the Scientific Mind Scientific? (*New York Times Magazine,* Feb. 1, pp. 10, 22).

RÓHEIM, GÉZA

1947. Dream Analysis and Field Work in Anthropology. In Róheim, G. (ed.), *Psychoanalysis and the Social Sciences, 1* (New York, International Universities Press).

1949. The Technique of Dream Analysis and Field Work in Anthropology (*Psychoanalytic Quarterly,* 18:471–479).

1950. *Psychoanalysis and Anthropology* (New York, International Universities Press).

1952. The Anthropological Evidence and the Oedipus Complex (*Psychoanalytic Quarterly,* 21:537–542).

ROWE, JOHN HOWLAND

1953. Technical Aids in Anthropology: A Historical Survey. In Kroeber, A. L. (ed.), *Anthropology Today* (Chicago, University of Chicago Press).

RUBIN, MORTON

1951. *Plantation County* (Chapel Hill, University of North Carolina Press).

RUESCH, JURGEN

1953. Social Technique, Social Status, and Social Change in Illness. In Kluckhohn, C., and Murray, H. A. (eds.), *Personality in Nature, Society, and Culture* (New York, Alfred A. Knopf).

RUESCH, JURGEN, and BATESON GREGORY

1951. *Communication: The Social Matrix of Psychiatry* (New York, W. W. Norton & Company).

SAINDON, ÉMILE

1928. *En Missionant, Essai sur les Missions des Pères Oblats de Marie Immaculée* (Ottawa, Imprimerie du Droit).

1933. Mental Disorders Among the James Bay Cree (*Primitive Man,* 6:1–12).

SAPIR, EDWARD

1922. Culture, Genuine and Spurious (*American Journal of Sociology,* 29:401–430).

1927. The Unconscious Patterning of Behavior in Society. In Dummer, E. S. (ed.), *The Unconscious: A Symposium* (New York, Alfred A. Knopf).

SARGENT, S. STANSFELD

1950. *Social Psychology: An Integrative Discipline* (New York, The Ronald Press Company).

SARGENT, S. STANSFELD, and SMITH, MARIAN W. (eds.)

1949. *Culture and Personality* (New York, Viking Fund).

SARHAN, EL-DEMERDASH ABDEL-MEGUID

1950. *Interests and Culture* (New York, Columbia University Press).

SASLOW, G., and CHAPPLE, E. D.

1945. A New Life-History Form, with Instructions for Its Use (*Applied Anthropology,* 4:1–18).

SCHAFFNER, BERTRAM

1948. *Father Land* (New York, Columbia University Press).

SCHILDER, P.

  1942. *Goals and Desires of Men* (New York, Columbia University Press).

SCHULTZ, G. D.

  1950. Why Can't Our Mothers Breast Feed? (*Ladies Home Journal*, 67, no. 12, 43, 191–193).

SEEMAN, M.

  1946. An Evaluation of Current Approaches to Personality Differences in Folk and Urban Societies (*Social Forces*, 25:160–165).

SENTER, DONOVAN

  1947. Witches and Psychiatrists (*Psychiatry*, 10:49–56).

SERENO, RENZO

  1950. Psychological Warfare, Intelligence, and Insight (*Psychiatry*, 13:266–273).

SEWELL, W. H.

  1952. Infant Training and the Personality of the Child (*American Journal of Sociology*, 58:150–159).

SHAW, C., and McKAY, H. D.

  1942. *Juvenile Delinquency and Urban Areas* (Chicago, University of Chicago Press).

SHOUBY, E.

  1951. The Influence of the Arabic Language on the Psychology of the Arabs (*Middle East Journal*, 5:284–303).

SIKKEMA, MILDRED

  1949. Observations on Japanese Early Child Training. In Haring, D. G. (ed.), *Personal Character and Cultural Milieu* (Syracuse, Syracuse University Press).

SIMMEL, GEORG

  1950. *The Sociology of Georg Simmel* (Glencoe, Free Press).

SIMMONS, LEO (ed.)

  1942. *Sun Chief, The Autobiography of a Hopi Indian* (New Haven, Yale University Press).

  1945. A Prospectus for Field Research in the Position and Treatment of the Aged in Primitive and Other Societies (*American Anthropologist*, 47:433–438).

SLOTKIN, J. S.

  1950. *Social Anthropology* (New York, The Macmillan Company).

1952. *Personality Development* (New York, Harper & Brothers).

1953. Social Psychiatry of a Menomini Community (*Journal of Abnormal and Social Psychiatry,* 48:10–17).

SMITH, M. BREWSTER

1950. Optima of Mental Health: A General Frame of Reference (*Psychiatry,* 13:503–510).

SOROKIN, P. A.

1950. *Explorations in Altruistic Love and Behavior* (Boston, Beacon Press).

SPINDLER, GEORGE D.

1952. Personality and Peyotism in Menomini Indian Acculturation (*Psychiatry,* 15:151–159).

SPINDLER, GEORGE D., and GOLDSCHMIDT, WALTER

1952. Experimental Design in the Study of Culture Change (*Southwestern Journal of Anthropology,* 8:68–83).

SPIRO, MELFORD E.

1950. A Psychotic Personality in the South Seas (*Psychiatry,* 13:189–204).

1951. Culture and Personality (*Psychiatry,* 14:19–46).

SPITZ, RENÉ A.

1945. Hospitalism: An Inquiry into the Genesis of Psychiatric Conditions in Early Childhood. In *The Psychoanalytic Study of the Child, 1* (New York, International Universities Press).

SPITZ, RENÉ A., and WOLF, KATHERINE M.

1946. Anaclitic Depression. In *The Psychoanalytic Study of the Child, 2* (New York, International Universities Press).

STAGNER, ROSS

1937. *Psychology of Personality.* First Edition (New York, McGraw-Hill Book Co.).

1948. *Psychology of Personality.* Second Edition (New York, McGraw-Hill Book Co.).

STOUFFER, SAMUEL A., SUCHMAN, EDWARD A., DE VINNEY, LELAND C., STAR, SHIRLEY A., and WILLIAMS, ROBIN M., JR.

1949. *The American Soldier, 1* (Princeton, Princeton University Press).

STRECKER, A.

1946. *Their Mother's Sons* (Philadelphia, J. B. Lippincott Co.).

STREIB, GORDON F.

1952. The Use of Survey Methods Among the Navaho (*American Anthropologist*, 54:30–40).

STUNKARD, ALBERT

1951. Some Interpersonal Aspects of an Oriental Religion (*Psychiatry*, 14:419–432).

TANNENBAUM, FRANK

1951. The American Tradition in Foreign Relations (*Foreign Affairs*, 30:31–50).

THOMPSON, LAURA

1948. Attitudes and Acculturation (*American Anthropologist*, 50: 200–215).

1950. *Culture in Crisis* (New York, Harper & Brothers).

1951a. Perception Patterns in Three Indian Tribes (*Psychiatry*, 14: 255–263).

1951b. *Personality and Government* (Mexico, D. F., Ediciones del Instituto Indigenista Interamericano).

THOMPSON, LAURA, and JOSEPH, ALICE

1944. *The Hopi Way* (Chicago, University of Chicago Press).

TOMASIC, DINKO

1948. *Personality and Culture in East European Politics* (New York, George W. Stewart, Publisher).

TOOTH, GEOFFREY

1950. *Studies in Mental Illness in the Gold Coast* (H. M. Stationery Office, Colonial Research Publication no. 6). Reprinted by permission of the Controller of Her Britannic Majesty's Stationery Office.

TSCHOPIK, HARRY, JR.

1951. *The Aymara of Chucuito, Peru. I. Magic* (Anthropological Papers of the American Museum of Natural History, 44, part 2).

TUMIN, MELVIN M.

1950. The Hero and the Scapegoat in a Peasant Community (*Journal of Personality*, 10:197–211).

1952. *Caste in a Peasant Society* (Princeton, Princeton University Press).

UNDERWOOD, FRANCES W., and HONIGMANN, IRMA

1949. A Comparison of Socialization and Personality in Two Simple

Cultures. In Haring, D. G. (ed.), *Personal Character and Cultural Milieu* (Syracuse, Syracuse University Press).

VAN LOON, F. H. G.
1927. Amok and Lattah (*Journal of Abnormal and Social Psychology*, 21:434–444).

VOGT, EVON Z.
1951. *Navaho Veterans: A Study of Changing Values* (Papers of the Peabody Museum of American Archaeology and Ethnology, Harvard University, *41*, no. 1).

WALLACE, ANTHONY F. C.
1951. Some Psychological Determinants of Culture Change in an Iroquoian Community. In Fenton, W. N. (ed.), *Symposium on Local Diversity in Iroquois Culture* (Bulletin 149, Smithsonian Institution, Bureau of American Ethnology).

WALLACE, WILLIAM J.
1947. Personality Variation in a Primitive Society (*Journal of Personality*, 15:321–328).

WANG, KUNG-HSING
1946. *The Chinese Mind* (New York, The John Day Company).

WARNER, W. L.
1937. The Society, the Individual, and His Mental Disorders (*American Journal of Psychiatry*, 94:275–284).

WARNER, W. L., and associates
1949. *Democracy in Jonesville* (New York, Harper & Brothers).

WARNER, W. L., HAVIGHURST, R. J., and LOEB, M. B.
1944. *Who Shall Be Educated?* (New York, Harper & Brothers).

WARNER, W. L., and LUNT, PAUL S.
1941. *The Social Life of a Modern Community* (New Haven, Yale University Press).

WARNER, W. L., MEEKER, MARCHIA, and EELLS, KENNETH
1949. *Social Class in America* (Chicago, Science Research Associates).

WEAKLAND, JOHN H.
1950. The Organization of Action in Chinese Culture (*Psychiatry*, 13:361–371).
1951. Method in Cultural Anthropology (*Philosophy of Science*, 18:55–69).

WEBSTER, HUTTON

1948. *Magic: A Sociological Study* (Stanford, Stanford University Press).

WECKLER, L.

1949. Social Class and School Adjustment in Relation to Character Formation. In Havighurst, R. J., and Taba, Hilda (eds.), *Adolescent Character and Personality* (New York, John Wiley & Sons).

WEGROCKI, H. J.

1953. A Critique of Cultural and Statistical Concepts of Abnormality. In Kluckhohn, C., and Murray, H. A. (eds.), *Personality in Nature, Society, and Culture* (New York, Alfred A. Knopf).

WEINBERG, S. KIRSON

1952. *Society and Personality Disorders* (New York, Prentice-Hall).

WERNER, H.

1951. Symposium on Genetic Psychology. I. Introduction: The Conception of Genetic Psychology (*American Journal of Orthopsychiatry*, 21:472–475).

WEST, JAMES

1945. *Plainville, U.S.A.* (New York, Columbia University Press).

WHITE, LESLIE A.

1949. *The Science of Culture* (New York, Farrar, Straus & Young).

WHITING, BEATRICE B.

1950. *Paiute Sorcery* (Viking Fund Publications in Anthropology, no. 15).

WHITING, JOHN W. M.

1941. *Becoming a Kwoma* (New Haven, Yale University Press).

WHITING, JOHN W. M., and associates

1953. *Field Manual for the Cross Cultural Study of Child Rearing* (New York, Social Science Research Council, mimeographed).

WHITING, JOHN W. M., and CHILD, IRVIN L.

1953. *Child Training and Personality* (New Haven, Yale University Press).

WHYTE, WILLIAM H.

1951. The Wives of Management (*Fortune*, October, 86–88, 204, 206–208, 210, 213).

WILLIAMS, A. N.

1950. A Psychological Study of Indian Soldiers in the Arakan (*British Journal of Medical Psychology*, 23:130–181).

WILLIAMS, P. H., and STRAUS, R.

1950. Drinking Patterns of Italians in New Haven (*Quarterly Journal for Studies on Alcohol,* 11:51–91, 250–308, 452–483, 586–629).

WILSON, GODFREY, and WILSON, MONICA

1945. *The Analysis of Social Change* (Cambridge, Cambridge University Press).

WILSON, MONICA

1951a. *Good Company* (London, Oxford University Press).

1951b. Witch Beliefs and Social Structure (*American Journal of Sociology,* 56:307–313).

WISDOM, JOHN O.

1952. *The Foundations of Inference in Natural Science* (London, Methuen).

WISSLER, CLARK

1922. *The American Indian* (New York, Thomas Y. Crowell Co.).

WOLFENSTEIN, MARTHA

1949. Some Variants in Moral Training of Children. In *Psychoanalytic Study of the Child,* 5 (New York, International Universities Press).

WOLFENSTEIN, MARTHA, and LEITES, NATHAN

1947. An Analysis of Themes and Plots (*Annals of the American Academy of Political and Social Science,* 254:41–48).

1950. *Movies: A Psychological Study* (Glencoe, Free Press).

WOLFF, K. H.

1945. A Methodological Note on the Empirical Establishment of Culture Patterns (*American Sociological Review,* 10:176–184).

YOUNG, FRANCES BRETT

1941. *Portrait of a Village* (London, British Publishers Guild).

ZBOROWSKI, MARK and HERZOG, ELIZABETH

1952. *Life is with People* (New York, International Universities Press).

ZINGG, ROBERT M.

1942. The Genuine and Spurious Values in Tarahumara Culture (*American Anthropologist,* 44:78–92).

ZNANIECKI, FLORIAN

1952. *Cultural Sciences: Their Origin and Development* (Urbana, University of Illinois).

INDEXES

Author Index

481

Subject Index

Abnormal, 369
  See also Mental illness; Psychopathology
Accident proneness, 398
Accra, 373
Acculturation, 201
  See also Intercultural relations
Adaptation, 27–28, 417; difficulties of, promoted through early indulgence, 238; failure of culture to provide, 407–408
Adjustment, 27–28, 417
Adolescents, American, 181
Adult-child relations, 249–251, 260, 288–301, 436; complementary, 250; reciprocal, 251; relationship to class, 324–325; symmetrical, 249–250, 262
Affect hunger, 254, 406
Affectivity, 252–255; among Negroes, 327; distortion of, 374–375
Africans, *see* Akwapem; Bemba; Ga; Gold Coast; Kenya; Lobi; Mental illness, Africa; Nandi; Nuer; Nyakyusa; Pondo; Somali; Turkana; Umbundu; West Africa
Age, effect of discipline and, 235; old, 278–279; relationship to learning, 206; patterning and, 303
Age patterning, 259–261
Aggression, 60, 279–286, 375, 389, 412; class and, 324, 325; economy and, 282; intoxication and, 386–387; socio-cultural sources of, 280; synergy and, 282; witchcraft and, 285–286

Aggression training, 219–220, 282–285, 435; Negroes, 118–119, 327
Ainu, 378
Air Force, 24, 36, 174, 197–198, 201–202, 305, 385, 402, 410
Air raids, 411
Akwapem, 374
Alcohol, functions of drinking, 386
Alorese, 182; child training among, 237–238
Ambition, 412
American Indians, 200, 262, 269, 276, 321
  See also Plains Indians and tribal names
American-Irish, 388
American-Jews, 388
Americans, 19, 43, 59, 62–63, 75, 79–80, 81–82, 130–132, 136, 144, 152, 175–176, 178–179, 180, 180–181, 186, 188–189, 190, 198–199, 204–205, 210, 216, 235–236, 244–245, 246, 251, 254, 256, 265, 266, 268, 272–274, 275, 278, 288, 289, 291, 293, 294, 299, 300, 301–302, 303–304, 339–340, 341, 348, 355, 364, 387, 388, 389, 395, 408–409, 411–412; class differences among, in child training and personality, 316–320; mental health among, 422; mental illness among, 398–403; urban, 338
  See also, Jonesville, Plainville, Prairie City
Amok, 378
Anaclitic depression, 237

about, 103; frustration and pain in, 239, 286; in heterogeneous communities, 352–355; later, 435–436; mental illness and, 405–406; rapid culture change and, 347–355; significance of, 53–56, 148–149, 173; social organization and, 308
   See also Adult-child relations, Consistency
Chinese, 59, 99–100, 102, 123–124, 134, 160, 193, 267, 276, 282, 297, 298, 310, 340, 388
Chinese-Americans, 123–124
Chippewa Indians, 161
   See also Ojibwa Indians
Choreomania, 392
Christianity, and native life, 415
Chuckchi, 379
Civilization, 437; definition, 359; personality patterning and, 362–365
Class, 110, 117–119, 152, 210, 267–268, 293, 363, 436–437; anxiety and, 322–325; child training and, 315–320; mental illness and, 389; patterning and, 314–315, 315–326, 330–332, 343–344; sex behavior and, 315, 332; social, 315, 343–344; stress and, 409; world and self views and, 321, 327, 330
   See also Lower class, Middle class, Professional class, Upper class, Working class
Class conflict, 323, 330–332
   See also Intercultural relations, between classes
Colonial administration, 349
Coming of Age in Samoa, 72
Communication, intercultural, 82–83
Community, atomistic, 152–153; definition, 26, 27; enclave, 349; heterogeneous, 58, 228–229, 345–355, 362–365; homogeneous, 58, 345–347; large and small scale, 359–360
Comparative method, 19
Competition, 3–6, 190–191, 256, 308, 310, 401, 410, 412, 415

Compromise, British readiness to, 79
Compulsions, 372, 392
Concentration camps, 225
Concepts, in culture and personality, 21–46, 428; by postulation, 141–145, 293–294
   See also Conceptualization; Pattern, covert
Conceptualization, 88, 141–145; in science, 369–370
Configuration, 98
Conflict, 417–418; in social organization, 307
   See also Values, conflict between
Conscience, 291–294
   See also Guilt
Consistency, in child training, 228–236, 242, 292, 304
   See also Discontinuity
Content analysis, _see_ Thematic analysis
Continuity, in child training, _see_ Consistency, Discontinuity
Correlation, 153–154, 196, 431
   See also Causality
Coup counting, 353
Cradle board, 50
Cree Indians, 380–381, 397–398
   See also Attawapiskat Indians, Great Whale River Indians
Crime, and class, 332
Crisis orientation, 105, 107
Crow Indians, 213
Cultural relativity, 78, 81
Culture, adaptation and, 407–408; change of, 222, 307, 343, 344–345, 350–351, 414–416; change of, and mental illness, 401, 403, 414–415; change of, and psychosomatic illness, 389–391; complexity of, 362, 437; conflicts in, 411–412; covert, 22; definition of, 22–23, 47, 142, 169; easy and tough, 404; efficiency of, 407–408; functions of, 27–28; goals in, 408–409; heterogeneous, 345–355, 437; historical development of, distinguished from personality de-

velopment, 52; homogeneous, 345–347; homogeneous, and mental health, 403; ideal, 115–116; mental illness and, 403, 404–416; overt, 22; patterning and, 201; as source of stress, 404–416; symbolic elaboration in, 260; technological change, effects on family of, 290–291; uneven change in, 178; variety in, 342, 347–351, 358, 362–365
  See also Group Membership, Learning, Patterning
Culture and personality, aims of a course in, 84; as clinical science, 90; criticism of, 68; definition, 3, 18, 29, 345–346; descriptive approach in, 57–61, 427; distinction between the concepts of, 17–18, 21, 28, 428; field work techniques in, 108–138; functional approach in, 61–64, 68, 427–428; genetic approach in, 48–57, 68, 148–149, 427; interdisciplinary nature of, 196, 429; method in, 54–55, 57, 58, 63–64, 67, 68, 428; method, criticism of, 32–33; nature of, 171; phylogenetic approach in, 64–68; phylogenetic approach in, criticism of, 65–68; psychology and, 3, 29, 34; purposes in study of, 69–84; qualitative nature of research in, 108; scientific status of, 52–53, 54, 88
  See also Genetic approach
Culture contact, *see* Intercultural relations
Cumberland County, 337
Czechs, 215, 230

Dakota Indians, 35, 41, 127, 207
  See also Sioux Indians
Dancing mania, 392
Dating pattern, 278, 338
Death madness, *see* Thanatomania
Defenses, 371–372
Degenerative circle, 41–42
Deity, attitudes toward, deriving from relations to parents, 295
Delinquency, 196–197

Delusions, 369, 373; patterning of, 391
Demagogues, 304
Democracy, 183
Demography, patterning and, 300, 334, 358–359
Depression, 393
Derangement, 376
Descent, 276
Descriptive approach in culture and personality, 57–61, 427
Detribalization, 413–414, 438
Deutero learning, 177, 183
Deviance, 211–214, 339, 432; approved and disapproved, 211–212, 364; in homogeneous communities, 346; psychopathology and, 370, 376–378
Die Strasse, 163
Differentiation, of groups, 222; sexual, as related to emphasis on suckling, 246, 275
Diffusion, 129
Dinarics, 63
Disasters, 410, 411
Discipline, 214–220, 432–433; age and, 235; effects of, 217–220; permissive and restrictive, 214–215, 215–217, 262
Discontinuity, 286; in child training, 6, 180–181, 229, 232–234
Discrimination, 405, 406
Disease, 430–431; cultural heterogeneity and, 355; patterning of, 192–193, 194
  See also Psychosomatic illness
Disequilibrium, 343
  See also Opposition, social
Diversity, complementary and uncomplementary, 220–221
Divorce, 289
Dobuans, 23
Doll play, 255, 281
Drama, *see* Plays
Dream interpretation, 119–120, 137; verification in, 157–159
Drinking, alcoholic, 387, 388, 395
  See also Intoxication
Drives, 185–187
  See also Motivation
Drugs, *see* Intoxication